Approaches to Teaching the Works of Carmen Martín Gaite

Approaches to Teaching World Literature

For a complete listing of titles,
see the last pages of this book.

Approaches to Teaching the Works of Carmen Martín Gaite

Edited by

Joan L. Brown

The Modern Language Association of America
New York 2013

Library of Congress Cataloging in Publication Data
Approaches to teaching the works of Carmen Martín Gaite / edited by Joan L. Brown.
pages cm. — (Approaches to Teaching World Literature ; 128)
Includes bibliographical references and index.
ISBN 978-1-60329-131-6 (cloth : alk. paper) — ISBN 978-1-60329-132-3 (pbk. : alk. paper)
ISBN 978-1-60329-169-9 (EPUB) — ISBN 978-1-60329-170-5 (Kindle)
1. Martín Gaite, Carmen—Study and teaching. 2. Martín Gaite, Carmen—
Criticism and interpretation. I. Brown, Joan Lipman, – editor of compilation.
PR6623.A7657Z55 2013
828'.64—dc23 2013012286

Approaches to Teaching World Literature 128
ISSN 1059-1133

Cover illustration of the paperback and electronic editions: photograph of Carmen Martín Gaite,
by Joan L. Brown, New York City, October 1980

Second printing 2016
Printed on recycled paper

Published by The Modern Language Association of America
85 Broad Street, suite 500, New York, New York 10004-2434
www.mla.org

CONTENTS

The Canonical Novel *El cuarto de atrás* / *The Back Room*

ACKNOWLEDGMENTS

My heartfelt thanks go to the contributors to this volume. Their essays honor the author so many of us knew. I am grateful to survey respondents who shared their teaching experiences, bibliographies, and hopes for this book. I thank Mark J. Brown, Ana María Martín Gaite, Rosemary G. Feal, and Richard A. Zipser for their encouragement and support along the path to publication. Zelda B. Lipman contributed to my new translation of Carmen Martín Gaite's autobiographical sketch. This volume has benefited from the advice and editing of Margit Longbrake and Michael Kandel of the MLA.

PREFACE TO THE VOLUME

Carmen Martín Gaite is the most-studied contemporary woman writer of Spain, according to *MLA Bibliographies* of the past three decades. Her literary career spanned the most riveting years in Spain's modern history. The future king of Spain, among others, presented Martín Gaite with her country's major literary awards and prizes. She was the first woman to win Spain's National Prize for Literature and the only person ever to win it twice. In 1985 she was chosen to be an honorary fellow of the MLA, joining this elite roster of the world's best authors.

This is a writer whose avowed goal was to bring reading (and viewing) pleasure to others, returning the favor for the pleasure that she herself took in writing. Her status as a preeminent subject of scholarship is, in large measure, a result of scholars' enjoyment of her works, and this fascination is not limited to professors. Nearly all of Martín Gaite's books have remained in print from the time they first appeared, luring successive generations with their eloquent prose, inventive forms, and acute social observations. She made contributions in virtually every literary genre, including screenplays, poetry, drama, children's stories, television series, and the novels for which she is best known. In addition to her fiction, she held a doctorate and published acclaimed volumes of literary and cultural analysis of Spain in the eighteenth and twentieth centuries. She also kept detailed journals, delivered erudite lectures, and created artistic collages, all of which were published posthumously. It can be argued that among her creations, her own life was one of the most remarkable. With intense curiosity, intellectual rigor, and love of adventure, Martín Gaite invented her life story. She was the brilliant, beautiful Spanish girl from the provinces who rose to become a writer honored throughout the world.

The present volume is a guide to teaching the works of Carmen Martín Gaite, including both pedagogical tools and critical foundations. Its goals are to introduce and contextualize the works of this important author and to stimulate and support their teaching at many levels of instruction. While her literature can be the subject of a single course, it is likely that one or more of her works will enrich courses on broader subjects. From a high school advanced placement literature course to undergraduate Spanish courses to graduate seminars on literature or theory to literature courses in translation, Martín Gaite's works make for vivid classroom experiences. Her writings offer cultural insight, social and historical analysis, enactments of theory, pitch-perfect language, and a wise view of human nature. These and other aspects of Martín Gaite's oeuvre are explored from different critical perspectives and linked to successful teaching methods in part 2 of this volume.

This unique compendium appears not long after the writer's lifetime. Many of the authors of these essays knew Martín Gaite. She had friends across generations and nationalities, and this collection reflects the same range. Volume contributors come not only from the United States but also from Spain, Puerto Rico, England, and Ireland. A few of the younger generation of scholars represented here were introduced to Martín Gaite by their professors, who are themselves contributors. Others knew her in Spain or when she came to this country as a visiting professor. This collection is a labor of love—a tribute from scholars and teachers to the author who brought her magic to everything she created.

Part One

MATERIALS

Introduction

Carmen Martín Gaite's life spanned three-quarters of the twentieth century. Although her experiences are inseparable from her literature, Martín Gaite wrote only one explicitly autobiographical piece during her lifetime, the 1980 sketch that appears in this volume, both in Spanish and in a new English translation. It was written for my *Secrets from the Back Room* ("Un bosquejo autobiográfico"). The sole critical biography of her that currently exists is the comprehensive essay by José Teruel that opens the first volume of her complete works, in which he characterizes her life as being "en 'obras'" ("Nombres" 9; "in the 'works'"). He traces the influences that shaped her development as a writer and helped her become the woman who reached the pinnacle of contemporary Spanish literature.

Growing Up in Salamanca, 1925–48

Martín Gaite was, as she enjoyed saying, a girl from the provinces.[1] Her provincial upbringing shaped her sensibility, with the paradoxical result that she was far from provincial. On 8 December 1925, María del Carmen de la Concepción was born in the traditional city of Salamanca, in the province of Castilla y León, Spain. She grew up there, on a placid town square, and spent long summers in the Galician countryside. Her loving and cultured parents raised her to think independently. Both her father, a brilliant attorney, and her mother, a wise and beautiful daughter of a professor, valued education, including education for women ("Bosquejo"). Their extensive library was a testament to their love of literature—a love that was transmitted to Carmen and her older sister, Ana María. Martín Gaite's liberal parents insisted on a secular education for their two daughters, something that was uncommon at that time.

Her early childhood was spent in a less harried era, before television or traffic jams. Provincial serenity fostered her imagination and her observational skills. Life in the provinces also may be seen as contributing to her lifelong quest for adventure. The strict confines of Salamanca, under the watchful "ojo gigantesco" ("gigantic eye") of the cathedral clock overlooking the main square, described in her first novel, *Entre visillos* (*Behind the Curtains*), were too stifling ([2007] 24 [ch. 1]; 18). Although the famous café on the main square in Salamanca was, and still is, called the Novelty, its name is as ironic as it is iconic. Novelty, excitement, and adventure were scarce in the Salamanca of her youth, so she sought them elsewhere.

For Martín Gaite's generation of Spaniards, history contravened many of their personal choices. Born under the dictatorship of Primo de Rivera (1923–30), Martín Gaite lived through the Second Republic (inaugurated in 1931) and was eleven years old when the Civil War began in July of 1936. She was one of the *niños de la guerra* ("children of the war"), the generation whose first memory of the war was that it interrupted their summer vacations. The war ended her plans to follow her sister (known as Anita) to Madrid to the Instituto-Escuela, an elite liberal secondary school. Instead, she spent the Civil War (1936–39) in Salamanca, where Franco had his headquarters. Although Martín Gaite's immediate family survived the war, her uncle was assassinated by the Franco forces, and she learned not to discuss her family's political views outside the home.

In Salamanca, Martín Gaite completed high school at a girls' school that would appear in her first novel. In 1943 she enrolled in the University of Salamanca in a five-year program leading to a degree in Romance philology. She graduated in 1948. In 1949 she left for Madrid to pursue a doctorate in philology, and her family joined her the following year. Her parents lived in an imposing apartment at number 35 Alcalá Street for the rest of their lives. Martín Gaite also lived there until she married.

National Recognition in Franco's Spain, 1949–75

When she first moved to Madrid, Martín Gaite stayed with two retired family maids in a small apartment that her father had bought for them. A classmate from Salamanca, Ignacio Aldecoa, was a student at the University of Madrid at that time, and he introduced her to his friends, all writers. This group—including Martín Gaite; her future husband, Rafael Sánchez Ferlosio; Jesús Fernández Santos; Medardo Fraile; Alfonso Sastre; and Aldecoa's future wife, Josefina Rodríguez—would become known to literary historians as the *generación del medio siglo* ("generation of mid-century"). This generation came of age during the strict censorship of the immediate postwar era. They turned to social realism as a tool for communicating realities of everyday life to a reading public that was denied a free press.[2]

Although Martín Gaite wrote fiction that fit well within the realistic mainstream of the postwar era, she also had divergent, parallel interests. Influenced by Franz Kafka, Italo Svevo, William Faulkner, and others, she was fascinated by innovative forms and modes, especially those of fantastic literature. As she astutely noted in a journal entry years later, all her literature involves one of two things: either the extraordinary from a realistic perspective or the realistic from an extraordinary perspective ("Toda mi literatura oscila entre lo excepcional soñado desde lo cotidiano y al revés" [*Cuadernos* 572]).

In the company of her friends, none of whom was a committed student, Martín Gaite began writing short stories and publishing them in literary magazines. In 1949 she became seriously ill with typhus, and was taken by ambulance back to Salamanca to recuperate. When she recovered, she wrote a disjointed novella entitled *El libro de la fiebre* ("The Book of Fever"), in which she tried to capture the fantastic images of her febrile state. She decided to publish only a few fragments of the book during her lifetime; the novella was published posthumously in 2007.

In 1950 she became engaged to Sánchez Ferlosio, and in 1953—after he fulfilled his military service—they were married in Madrid. They moved into a penthouse apartment at 43 Doctor Esquerdo Street, which her father gave them as a wedding present. That apartment with a large terrace, later immortalized in her most famous novel, *El cuarto de atrás* (*The Back Room*), would always be her Madrid home.

Martín Gaite's next short novel also evoked elements of the fantastic. *El balneario* (1955; "The Spa") involves nightmarish happenings at a spa in the countryside, with a surprise ending. It won the Café Gijón Prize of 1954. (Prizes were commonly bestowed at the end of the year a work was written, and its publication followed early the next year.) The Gijón Prize was awarded by an elite circle of critics that regularly met at the Café Gijón, a famous Madrid literary café. This was Martín Gaite's first critical recognition. She and her husband suffered a personal tragedy in the same year: six months after their son, Miguel, was born, he died suddenly of meningitis.

In 1956 Martín Gaite gave birth to a daughter, Marta Sánchez Martín. When Marta learned to talk, she mispronounced the name Carmen in a way that delighted her mother, calling her Calila. This nickname was used by Martín Gaite's closest friends. Martín Gaite called herself Calila in conversation and correspondence and referred to herself this way in her journals. Those who knew her as a child, including members of her family, called her Carmiña, the Galician diminutive of Carmen.

The novel that launched her career was *Entre visillos*, written in the social-realist mode that predominated in the years after the Civil War. It is a closely observed, multifaceted coming-of-age story set in a provincial town that is unnamed but clearly Salamanca. *Entre visillos* won the prestigious Nadal Prize of 1957 and appeared in 1958. Her novella "Las ataduras" ("Binding Ties"), about a gifted young woman from Galicia and the rural life she leaves behind, was published in 1960. (Each of these two novellas appeared in books that also featured selected short stories, beginning with the second edition of *El balneario* and the first edition of *Las ataduras*.)

For her birthday in 1961, the author's five-and-a-half-year-old daughter gave her the first of what would become many all-purpose journal notebooks; selections from them were published posthumously as *Cuadernos de todo* (2002; "Notebooks about Everything"). In 1963 *Ritmo lento* ("A Slower Rhythm") appeared; the novel explores the psychological development of a supremely lucid young man who cannot adapt to the hypocritical world around him. It was runner-up for the 1962 Biblioteca Breve Prize, though it was the winner from Spain. That year, for the first time, the prize went to a Latin American novel (Vargas Llosa's *La ciudad y los perros* [*The Time of the Heroes*]).

In the ensuing decade, Martín Gaite rediscovered her passion for scholarly research. She received a grant to investigate don Melchor de Macanaz, a fascinating eighteenth-century figure who was pursued by the Inquisition. Her book on his life and tribulations, *El proceso de Macanaz* ("Macanaz's Trial"), was published in 1970. In this same year she and her husband separated, unable to repair their marriage; their divorce was finalized years later because divorce was illegal during the Franco era. They remained on friendly terms and parented their daughter jointly. When Martín Gaite died, Sánchez Ferlosio was a pallbearer at her funeral.

While investigating the life of Macanaz, whom Martín Gaite fondly called "mi muerto" ("my dead man"), she became fascinated by courtship customs of the eighteenth century, especially one whereby a married woman could enjoy the attentions of a male escort. Her research led to a dissertation that earned her a 1972 PhD with honors. It was revised and published as *Usos amorosos del dieciocho en España* (*Love Customs in Eighteenth-Century Spain*). In 1973 she published her collection of essays *La búsqueda de interlocutor* ("The Search for a Conversational Partner"), which probed issues such as the influence of advertising on women and the characteristics of an ideal conversational partner.

Her reentry into the world of novel writing came with her 1974 *Retahílas* ("Yarns"). It is a night-long conversation between an aunt in her forties and her nephew in his twenties. Set in a family mansion in Galicia to which they have returned, the dialogue explores the passions and conflicts of both generations.

While working on her own projects (and she always had several in development at the same time), Martín Gaite also translated the works of others for publication. For Spanish readers she translated literature written in Portuguese, Italian, French, and English. Translation was an avocation that she continued throughout her life. Among the authors whose works she rendered into Spanish were Italo Svevo, Primo Levi, Natalia Ginzburg, Charles Perrault, Antoine Saint-Exupéry, Rainer Maria Rilke, William Carlos Williams, George MacDonald, and Emily Brontë.

Madrid and the United States, 1975–2000: International Fame in the Democratic Era

Franco's death in 1975 meant the end of censorship and the beginning of the task of recovering distant memories. Although Martín Gaite began taking notes for her unique novelistic memoir *El cuarto de atrás* on the day Franco died, her first novel after the dictatorship was a more spontaneous response to freedom: *Fragmentos de interior* (1976; "Inner Fragments"), a fast-paced story involving the household of a fractured, modern Madrid family. In 1976 she also published the first iteration of her poetry collection *A rachas* ("In a Gust of Wind"), which would be updated and reissued in 1993 and 2000, and the commissioned biography *El conde de Guadalhorce* ("The Count of Guadalhorce"). In 1976 she began a job as weekly book critic for the newly created newspaper *Diario 16*, a position she held until 1980.

Martín Gaite's next novel secured her place in world literature. In 1978 *El cuarto de atrás* appeared to rapturous reviews, winning Spain's National Prize for Literature. The novel evoked multilayered critical commentary that continues unabated. The story involves a nocturnal conversation between a woman who unequivocally represents the author and a mysterious man in black who may or may not exist. The author's visitor, a sharp literary critic, elicits long-suppressed memories of the Civil War and its aftermath; as they speak, pages mount next to her typewriter. This unusual hybrid introduced what would become the major strands of the contemporary Spanish novel: history, memory, metafiction, and the fantastic. The same year, her novellas and short stories were reprinted in a single volume, *Cuentos completos* ("The Complete Stories"). At the end of the year, Martín Gaite experienced a harsh blow: her father died in October and her mother in December.

In April 1979 Martín Gaite made her first of what would be many visits to the United States, to attend a conference on the contemporary Spanish novel at Yale University. During this eye-opening trip, she discovered New York City. In the fall of 1980, she spent a semester in New York as visiting professor at Barnard College. Because she felt that the city was too fast-paced to capture in words, she began creating collages to record her experiences. The collages were published posthumously in 2005 as *Visión de Nueva York* ("Vision of New York"). Her first novella for younger readers was published in 1981, entitled *El castillo de las tres murallas* ("The Three-Walled Castle"). She returned to the United States in the fall of 1982, as a visiting professor at the University of Virginia.

Martín Gaite's book of literary theory *El cuento de nunca acabar* ("The Never-Ending Story"), subtitled "Apuntes sobre la narración, el amor y la mentira" ("Notes on Narrative, Love, and Lies"), was published in 1983, marking the culmination of a long-standing project. She appeared in a television program about Salamanca for the series *Esta es mi tierra* ("This Is My Land"), speaking her own dialogue while leading viewers through landmark sites ("Salamanca"). She wrote the screenplays for a television series on Santa Teresa de Jesús. In the fall of 1984 she again came to the United States, as visiting professor at the University of Illinois, Chicago.

When Martín Gaite returned to Spain, she suffered her most painful loss. Her daughter died of pneumonia on 8 April 1985. Anxious to get away from the Madrid apartment they had shared, she moved to an even lonelier one in upstate New York, where she spent the semester as a visiting professor at Vassar College. Her posthumously published piece "El otoño de Poughkeepsie" ("Poughkeepsie Fall") is a moving account of her experiences during this time (*Cuadernos* 611–30).

Personal tragedy coincided with public acclaim. In this same year, the MLA chose Martín Gaite as an honorary fellow, based on nomination letters from scholars from around the world. Her second novella for young readers, *El pastel del diablo* ("The Devil's Cake"), was published in 1985. This and its predecessor *El castillo de las tres murallas*—both stories of young girls and their quests for truth and freedom—were combined in one volume, *Dos relatos fantásticos* ("Two Fantastic Tales"), in 1986, and republished together as *Dos cuentos maravillosos* ("Two Marvelous Tales") in 1992.

Usos amorosos de la postguerra española (*Courtship Customs in Postwar Spain*), a nonfiction study of the postwar relations between the sexes in their cultural context, appeared in 1987. A huge popular and critical success, it won the Anagrama Prize for Nonfiction. Historians credit the book with inaugurating the field of material culture in Spain. Her collection of essays on literature by women, *Desde la ventana* ("From the Window"), appeared that same year. Her play *A palo seco* ("On Its Own") was performed in Madrid; it was published in 1994.

Martín Gaite became a celebrity in the 1980s. Improbably, *El cuento de nunca acabar* became a best seller, and it was the first of many. She was a main attraction of the annual spring Feria del Libro de Madrid (Madrid Book Fair), where she greeted hundreds of fans as she signed copies of her books. Like a movie star, she walked through the fairgrounds in Retiro Park surrounded by film crews; after her death, the book fair established the Carmen Martín Gaite Pavilion in her honor. Her photograph was the centerpiece of bookstore displays. She appeared on television, though she turned down many more opportunities than she accepted. She once remarked that a writer in Spain could make a career of television appearances, to the point where he or she would never write. She refused to court this danger.

In 1988 Martín Gaite was awarded the Prince of Asturias Prize, shared with the poet Ángel Valente. Presented in Oviedo by the future king of Spain (Felipe, prince of Asturias), it recognized her lifetime of work. Her most-translated novel (though unfortunately still not into English) was published in 1990. *Caperucita en Manhattan* ("Little Red Riding Hood in Manhattan"), about a triumphant American girl in New York City, rewrote the Perrault fairy tale for contemporary audiences. (The novel's heroine, Sara Allen, was named after a newly born American girl, my daughter Sarah Brown.)

Another award came in 1992: the Castilla y León Prize for Literature. *Nubosidad variable* (*Variable Cloud*) appeared the same year. The story of two middle-aged women who rekindle their childhood friendship through letters, the novel charts the social changes of Madrid in the nineties. The following year, Martín Gaite devoted her energies to a television project, adapting popular novels by Elena Fortún into the series *Celia*. In 1993 she published a collection of reprinted essays, *Agua pasada* ("Water under the Bridge"); another collection of reprinted articles was published posthumously in 2006 (*Tirando del hilo* ["Unraveling the Skein"]).

In 1994 Martín Gaite received the National Prize for Literature (Premio Nacional de las Letras) in recognition of a lifetime of achievement; she was the only person to win this prize twice. Two other works were published that year.

The novel *La Reina de las Nieves* (*The Farewell Angel*) is a loose reworking of the Hans Christian Andersen fairy tale "The Snow Queen," which had been her daughter's favorite. *Esperando el porvenir* ("Waiting for the Future") is a memoir, illustrated with photographs, about Ignacio Aldecoa and their generation of Spanish authors. Her novel *Lo raro es vivir* (*Living's the Strange Thing*) appeared in 1996. It traces the story of a struggling woman in her thirties whose very accomplished mother has just died; the woman comes to terms with her loss and with her own future as a mother. Martín Gaite came to the United States in 1996 to deliver lectures at Cornell University and the University of Delaware. These would be her last talks in this country. Her lecture notes were among those collected posthumously in the 2002 volume *Pido la palabra* ("May I Have the Floor?").

Her last finished novel appeared in 1998. *Irse de casa* ("Leaving Home") tells the story of a sophisticated clothing designer who achieves great success in the United States but returns to Spain to find that her roots—and her heart—remain in the provincial city where she was born. In 1999 her play *La hermana pequeña* ("The Little Sister"), composed and set back in the Franco era, was staged and published.

The Writer's Legacy

Martín Gaite died 23 July 2000, after a brief illness. She is buried on a hill in the family cemetery at El Boalo, near their country home in the mountains outside Madrid. Her daughter, mother, and father rest next to her. Her last, unfinished novel *Los parentescos* ("Family Ties") appeared in 2001, with an introduction by one of the many women writers whom she mentored. In this novel a young male protagonist tries to decipher the complex secrets and bonds of a modern-day blended family, assembling clues from intriguing sources.

Since Martín Gaite's death, an already extensive legacy has been expanded at the behest of Anita Martín Gaite, who has had published many of the works that her sister left behind. With the exception of forthcoming volumes of her complete works (a total of seven are planned), the corpus of literature by Martín Gaite now is closed. Her manuscripts and papers are housed in the Biblioteca de Castilla y León in Valladolid. They are currently being cataloged and digitized for use by scholars around the world.

Her works resist classification, as is true for any trailblazer. She not only lived through many literary and historical periods but also defined them. Her novels trace huge transformations in Spain over the course of the twentieth century. In the immediate postwar era she contributed to documentary realism and, at the same time, to the surrealist exploration of dreams. In the late postwar period and the transition to democracy, she explored psychological and formal aspects of the novel; *El cuarto de atrás* pioneered the hybrid novel, combining fiction with nonfiction, which still defines contemporary Spanish literature. Her novels written in the democratic era reflect rapid changes in Spanish society, through the experiences of characters whose lives are revealed in interesting ways. Alongside the novels, for which she is best known, she made important contributions to other genres: nonfiction (eighteenth-century studies, cultural studies, and literary theory), poetry, theater, and visual media.

A work by Carmen Martín Gaite is recognizable by certain constants: a welcoming intelligence that shines through, a deceptive simplicity of structure, graceful language with colloquial dialogue, and a deep understanding of human nature. Her work across media has overarching themes. Among them are the need for and difficulty in achieving meaningful communication, the relation between dreams and reality, the complexity of affective bonds, and the quest for individual freedom, especially for women.

Although it is difficult to quantify, the single unifying aspect of her works is located outside the text, in the pleasure they afford to students and teachers alike. She was always conscious of her audience. As she wrote in a guest essay in *PMLA*, "The miracle of the readers' actual materialization will not occur unless the text extended to them is a firm, well-made bridge" ("Virtues" 351). The bridges that Carmen Martín Gaite extended were sound. They have already transported many, and they will continue to transport new generations of readers into her worlds, for years to come.

NOTES

[1] Much of the information in this introduction comes from conversations and correspondence that I had with the author over many years. Other sources are her autobiographical sketch, her reminiscences in *Esperando el porvenir*, her interviews (esp. those with Cantavella [Martín Gaite, "Carmen Martín Gaite"] and with Soler Serrano), her notebooks (*Cuadernos*), and her essays.

[2] This group, also called the *generación de los cincuenta* ("generation of the fifties"), is defined by their birth dates in the mid-1920s, which led them to experience the Civil War as children. They used social-realist modes to obliquely critique postwar society—obliquely because of Franco's censors. A heterogeneous group, they shared a desire to document reality. Literary critics argue for different waves and tendencies within this generation. Martín Gaite's group of friends in Madrid was the first wave (Martínez Cachero 172).

Resources for Teaching

Texts and Editions

When citing a work by Martín Gaite, volume contributors use the most recent print edition available, but reference may be made to an earlier edition as needed—usually a teaching edition or an edition in which the text differs from the most recent one. The authoritative *Obras completas* ("Complete Works") is more for reference than for the classroom, because of the number of works contained in each volume. But one or more volumes of the *Obras* (vol. 1 is *Novelas I, 1955–1978*; vol. 2 is *Novelas II, 1979–2000*; vol. 3 is *Narrativa breve, poesía y teatro*) would be excellent for an advanced seminar devoted to the author.

Although numerous editions of Martín Gaite's texts currently exist, the future will bring consolidation. The Madrid publisher Siruela now holds the rights to many of Martín Gaite's works, producing beautiful print editions at reasonable cost as well as electronic versions of several novels. Siruela will acquire more titles as contracts with other publishers expire. Anagrama of Barcelona, having long-term contracts to publish some of Martín Gaite's books, is exploring the possibility of offering electronic as well as print versions.

For a listing of first editions, notable subsequent editions, teaching editions, recent editions, and English translations of Martín Gaite's works, see appendix B.

Background Resources

For background on Spanish history and culture, Raymond Carr's *Spain: A History* provides an overview from prehistoric times to the end of the twentieth century. "Spain from 1931 to the Present" (Balfour), the final chapter in Carr's book, is an especially useful companion piece to works by Martín Gaite. It covers the complex historical period in which the author lived, ending with the observation that "in the new Spain, reconciliation with the past remains unfinished business" (282). Unresolved issues are dealt with more fully in Paul Preston's *Spanish Civil War* (esp. the prologue, ch. 10 ["Franco's Peace"], and epilogue). Preston's book is available in a Spanish translation that American students find readable.

The author herself supplies the most relevant and also the most popular cultural reader to accompany her fiction: *Usos amorosos de la postguerra española* (*Courtship Customs in Postwar Spain*). In the book's nine chapters she analyzes the governmental imperatives and the prevailing social mores that shaped her generation of Spaniards, and especially women, as they came of age during the Franco years. Survey respondents find it quite teachable because of its accessible style. More general in scope are David T. Gies's anthology *The Cambridge*

Companion to Modern Spanish Culture and John Hooper's *The New Spaniards*, which endeavor to transmit a comprehensive view of contemporary Spanish society.

Literary context for Martín Gaite's fiction is found in critical histories that span the twentieth century. Among the more recent are Jordi Gracia and Domingo Ródenas's *Derrota y restitución de la modernidad, 1939–2010* ("Defeat and Restoration of Modernity"), Gies's *The Cambridge History of Spanish Literature*, Domingo Ynduráin and Francisco Rico's *Historia y crítica de la literatura española: Época contemporánea, 1939–1980* ("History and Criticism of Spanish Literature: The Contemporary Era"), Jordi Gracia and Francisco Rico's *Historia y crítica de la literatura española: Los nuevos nombres, 1975–2000* ("History and Criticism of Spanish Literature: New Authors"), and Harriet Turner and Adelaida López de Martínez's *The Cambridge Companion to the Spanish Novel: From 1600 to the Present*. These edited volumes convey a panoramic survey of twentieth-century Spanish literature.

Critical Resources

The most comprehensive volume on Martín Gaite's fiction is Catherine O'Leary and Alison Ribeiro de Menezes's *A Companion to Carmen Martín Gaite*, which offers a critical survey of the author's novels, short stories, children's novels, essays, historical writings, plays, and poetry. The book is particularly strong in its synthesis of existing criticism in English and Spanish, weaving secondary sources into its discussion of each work. A review of prose fiction that Martín Gaite published during her lifetime is contained in José Jurado Morales's *La trayectoria narrativa de Carmen Martín Gaite, 1925–2000* ("The Narrative Trajectory of Carmen Martín Gaite").

Survey respondents for this Approaches volume reported that the most widely used guide to the author's fiction is my *Secrets from the Back Room: The Fiction of Carmen Martín Gaite*, which covers Martín Gaite's first four novels as well as her novellas, short stories, first volume of poetry, and first children's novel. Mercedes Jiménez's *Carmen Martín Gaite y la narración: Teoría y práctica* ("Carmen Martín Gaite and Narrative: Theory and Practice") analyzes narrative technique in this same group of works. Picking up where the preceding volumes left off, *El laberinto intertextual de Carmen Martín Gaite: Un estudio de sus novelas de las noventa* ("The Intertextual Labyrinth of Carmen Martín Gaite: A Study of Her Novels from the Nineties"), by Nuria Cruz-Cámara, analyzes the author's novels written in the last decade of her life.

Comprehensive studies of Martín Gaite's short fiction include Jurado Morales's *Del testimonio al intimismo: Los cuentos de Carmen Martín Gaite* ("From Testimony to Interiority: Stories of Carmen Martín Gaite"), which classifies short stories and novellas according to themes, and Pilar de la Puente Samaniego's *La narrativa breve de Carmen Martín Gaite* ("Carmen Martín Gaite's Short

Fiction"), which situates them in three historical periods. For introductions to each of Martín Gaite's works, including all posthumous publications, the *Obras completas*, edited by José Teruel, is an authoritative resource; the first three volumes contain her novels, short fiction, poetry, and theater.

Two edited collections, published by the Society of Spanish and Spanish-American Studies nearly twenty years apart, feature stimulating criticism of Martín Gaite's fiction. The first is a seminal anthology produced by Mirella d'Ambrosio Servodidio and Marcia L. Welles: *From Fiction to Metafiction: Essays in Honor of Carmen Martín Gaite*. This volume contains now-classic analyses of the author's narratives of the 1950s, 1960s, and 1970s, with special emphasis on *El cuarto de atrás* (*The Back Room*). More recently, Kathleen M. Glenn and Lissette Rolón Collazo's edited volume *Carmen Martín Gaite: Cuento de nunca acabar / Never-Ending Story* offers thoughtful analyses of the author's fiction and nonfiction. Although this collection extends its reach into the 1990s, its best-represented work is also *El cuarto de atrás*.

Another valuable collection of critical analyses of Martín Gaite's works is contained in the extensive section "Cartapacio: Carmen Martín Gaite" in the Spanish journal *Turia*. Its essays span the author's fiction, nonfiction, and poetry and include some of her posthumous publications; they also feature reminiscences by her sister and others. A useful scholarly Internet resource is the special Martín Gaite section of the online journal *Espéculo*, edited by Emma Martinell. It features links to wide-ranging critical essays, an interview, and bibliographies. Additional bibliographical resources can be found in Jurado Morales's "La mirada ajena: Medio siglo de bibliograpfía sobre la obra de Carmen Martín Gaite" ("A View from Outside: Half a Century of Bibliography on Carmen Martín Gaite"), covering secondary literature up to several years after the author's death, and Martinell's *Al encuentro de Carmen Martín Gaite: Homenajes y bibliografía* ("Introducing Carmen Martín Gaite: Tributes and Bibliography").

Last, the special double issue of the journal *Ínsula,* dedicated to the legacy of Martín Gaite and edited by Teruel (*Legado*), is a landmark collection of new scholarship and new reflections by her peers. Its essays explore Martín Gaite's relationships with other writers and analyze her historical, theoretical, filmed, and posthumously published works.

Interviews

Martín Gaite gave many interviews over her lifetime, a task that she took seriously.

Journal interviews of enduring interest are by Celia Fernández (Martín Gaite, "Entrevista" [1979]), by Alicia Ramos ("Conversación" [1980]), and by Héctor Medina ("Conversación" [1983]), in all of which the author discusses her literary convictions and analyzes her novels through *El cuarto de atrás*. A landmark interview is by Marie-Lise Gazarian Gautier ("Conversación . . . en

Nueva York"); in it Martín Gaite discusses the prerequisites for good conversation, the pleasure of writing, the evolution of *El cuarto de atrás*, and the intense rhythm of New York City. An interview by Martinell in the online journal *Espéculo* features Martín Gaite's mature reflections on a variety of subjects, including translation, criticism, and her readers (Martín Gaite, "Entrevista" [1998]). The longest and perhaps the most poignant exchange is contained in Juan Cantavella's book of interviews. His eighty-page interaction with Martín Gaite is aptly entitled "Carmen Martín Gaite: Contemplar la vida con una pluma en la mano" ("Contemplating Life, Pen in Hand"). Taking stock near the end of a long career, she answers questions about inspiration, critics, the writer in society, and her own relation to literature.

Filmed interviews include a fascinating conversation with Joaquín Soler Serrano, first broadcast by Radiotelevisión Española; it is now available for download, and excerpts are posted on *YouTube*. Subjects discussed include language, literature, and childhood memories. The DVD *Carmen Martín Gaite: In Search of Conversation*, issued posthumously by Films for the Humanities and Sciences, includes footage from this interview. The brief trailer for the DVD provides an inviting introduction for students, with a clip of Martín Gaite explaining her convictions about conversation and writing in the modern world.

Literary-Historical Time Line for Carmen Martín Gaite

1923–30	Dictatorship of General Miguel Primo de Rivera
8 December 1925	Carmen Martín Gaite is born in Salamanca.
1931	The Second Spanish Republic is proclaimed. King Alfonso XIII goes into exile.
1933	José Antonio Primo de Rivera, son of the former dictator, forms the Falange Española ("the Falange").
July 1936–1 April 1939	Spanish Civil War
1939–45	World War II
1939–75	Francisco Franco rules Spain as dictator. From 1939 to 1943 his retaliation against Republicans includes mass executions, imprisonment, and forced labor. In the 1940s, the press is strictly controlled and censored. Those who fought on the Republican side in the Civil War are excluded from public life.
1943–48	Martín Gaite attends the University of Salamanca and earns a *licenciatura* (five-year degree) in Romance philology.

1948	She moves to Madrid and enrolls as a doctoral student at the University of Madrid. She begins writing and publishing short stories.
1949	She becomes seriously ill with typhus but makes a complete recovery. She writes *El libro de la fiebre* ("The Book of Fever") about her illness and publishes fragments of it; the novella will be published posthumously (2007).
14 October 1953	She marries Rafael Sánchez Ferlosio, a writer.
1953	Spain and the United States sign an agreement under which American military bases are established in Spain.
1954	Martín Gaite wins the Café Gijón Prize for her novella *El balneario* (1955). Her son, Miguel, is born; he dies of meningitis six months later.
1955	Spain becomes a member of the United Nations.
22 May 1956	Martín Gaite's daughter, Marta Sánchez Martín, is born.
1957	Martín Gaite's first novel, *Entre visillos* (1958; *Behind the Curtains* [1990]), wins the Nadal Prize.
1960	She publishes the novella *Las ataduras* ("Binding Ties").
1961	Her daughter gives her a catch-all notebook as a birthday present. Excerpts from Martín Gaite's journal notebooks over decades will be published posthumously in *Cuadernos de todo* (2002; "Notebooks about Everything").
1963	Martín Gaite publishes *Ritmo lento* ("A Slower Rhythm"), a novel completed in 1962, and it is runner-up for the Biblioteca Breve Prize. She turns her attention to scholarly research.
1966	Manuel Fraga's Press Law of 1966 grants more freedom to the press.
1970	Martín Gaite publishes the nonfiction study *El proceso de Macanaz* ("Macanaz's Trial"). She and Sánchez Ferlosio separate and will divorce once divorce is legalized (after the dictatorship ends).
1972	She defends her doctoral dissertation and earns a PhD with honors. She publishes her revised dissertation, *Usos amorosos del dieciocho en España* (*Love Customs in Eighteenth-Century Spain* [1991]).

1973	She publishes the volume of essays *La búsqueda de interlocutor* ("The Search for a Conversational Partner").
1974	She publishes the novel *Retahílas* ("Yarns").
20 November 1975	Franco dies. Two days later, Juan Carlos I, grandson of Alfonso XIII, succeeds him as king. The transition to democracy begins.
1976	Martín Gaite publishes the novel *Fragmentos de interior* ("Inner Fragments") and *A rachas* ("In a Gust of Wind"), a poetry collection that will be updated and reissued in 1993 and 2000. She also publishes the biography *El conde de Guadalhorce* ("The Count of Guadalhorce"). She begins working as a book critic for the new Spanish newspaper *Diario 16*, a job she continues until 1980. Adolfo Suárez, transition leader of the UCD (Center-Democratic Union) and former Francoist official, is appointed president by King Juan Carlos.
15 June 1977	The first democratic elections since 1936 are held. Suárez is elected president.
1978	Martín Gaite publishes *El cuarto de atrás* (*The Back Room* [1983]). The novel wins the National Prize for Literature. Her stories and novellas are united in *Cuentos completos* ("The Complete Stories"). The government passes the Constitution of 1978, which allows the separation of church and state and lays the groundwork for Spain's seventeen autonomous regional communities.
October–December 1978	Martín Gaite's father and mother die within months of each other.
April 1979	Martín Gaite visits the United States for the first time to participate in a conference at Yale University.
Fall 1980	She is visiting professor at Barnard College. She begins a series of collages that will be published posthumously as *Visión de Nueva York* (2005; "Vision of New York").
1981	She publishes the novella for children *El castillo de las tres murallas* ("The Three-Walled Castle"). She films a television program about her native Salamanca, which airs in 1983. Suárez resigns.
23 February 1981	In an attempted military coup, Lieutenant Colonel Antonio Tejero fires gunshots that interrupt the in-

	auguration of Leopoldo Calvo Sotelo, the new president. King Juan Carlos appears on Spanish television and calms the nation.
Fall 1982	Martín Gaite is visiting professor at the University of Virginia.
October 1982	The socialist Felipe González (of PSOE, the Socialist Workers' party, which was outlawed under Franco) is elected president, and his party comes into power. The transition to democracy is completed, and many vestiges of Francoism are eliminated.
1983	Martín Gaite publishes the book of literary theory *El cuento de nunca acabar* ("The Never-Ending Story"). She writes the screenplays for a television series about Santa Teresa de Jesús.
Fall 1984	She is visiting professor at the University of Illinois, Chicago.
8 April 1985	Her daughter dies of pneumonia.
Fall 1985	Martín Gaite is visiting professor at Vassar College.
1985	She publishes the children's novella *El pastel del diablo* ("The Devil's Cake"). She is named an honorary fellow of the MLA.
1 January 1986	Spain is admitted into the European Economic Community, which will become the European Union.
1986	Martín Gaite publishes *Dos relatos fantásticos* ("Two Fantastic Tales"); its novellas, *Castillo* and *Pastel*, will be reissued in 1992 as *Dos cuentos maravillosos* ("Two Marvelous Tales").
1987	Martín Gaite publishes *Usos amorosos de la postguerra española* (*Courtship Customs in Postwar Spain* [2004]), which wins the Anagrama Prize for Nonfiction. She publishes *Desde la ventana* ("From the Window"), on literature by women. Her play *A palo seco* ("On Its Own") is performed and will be published in 1994.
1988	She is awarded the Prince of Asturias Prize, presented by the future king of Spain.
1990	She publishes *Caperucita en Manhattan* ("Little Red Riding Hood in Manhattan"), a novel for children and adults.

1992	She is awarded the Castilla y León Prize for Literature. She publishes the novel *Nubosidad variable* (*Variable Cloud* [1995]). The Olympic Games are held in Barcelona, and Seville hosts the World's Fair.
1993	Martín Gaite writes the screenplays for the television series *Celia*. She collects previously published essays in *Agua pasada* ("Water under the Bridge"). More reprinted articles will be published posthumously in *Tirando del hilo* (2006; "Unraveling the Skein").
1994	She is awarded the National Prize for Literature. She publishes the novel *La Reina de las Nieves* (*The Farewell Angel* [1999]) and the generational memoir *Esperando el porvenir* ("Waiting for the Future").
1996	She publishes the novel *Lo raro es vivir* (*Living's the Strange Thing* [2004]). She gives her last lectures in the United States, which are among those published posthumously in *Pido la palabra* (2002; "May I Have the Floor?"). Conservative José María Aznar (of the PP or Popular Party) is elected president.
1998	Martín Gaite publishes the novel *Irse de casa* ("Leaving Home").
1999	Her 1959 play, *La hermana pequeña* ("The Little Sister"), is staged and published.
23 July 2000	Martín Gaite dies in Madrid after a brief illness. Her unfinished novel *Los parentescos* ("Family Ties") will be published in 2001. She is buried in the family cemetery near their country home in El Boalo, outside Madrid.

Part Two

APPROACHES

Introduction

This volume is devoted to teaching the works of Carmen Martín Gaite, Spain's most acclaimed twentieth-century woman writer. Its contents reflect the findings of an MLA survey sent to instructors around the world. The essays in part 2 support diverse pedagogical goals in many institutional settings, from secondary school through graduate school. Although most of the courses described in these essays are taught in Spanish, contributors chart ways in which the same methodologies can be used in English.

Contexts and Contents

The framework for presenting the essays in part 2 features division by historical period and literary genre. For a twentieth-century Spanish writer who is best known for her novels but whose output was diverse, the logic for this organization is clear. Students will approach any Spanish author from the twentieth century in the context of the country's changing political situation. This is especially true for Martín Gaite, who chronicled social changes in Spain for over fifty years.

Students will need to contextualize her works with regard to four periods. These are the Civil War of 1936–39, the Franco dictatorship of 1939–75 (including the first postwar and later postwar eras), the post-Franco transition to democracy (from 1975 to 1982, when the Socialists were elected) and the democratic era (1977 to the present). This historical frame situates Martín Gaite's works within the political, sociocultural, and literary currents of her times.With regard to genre, these essays present nine novels, a novella, a poetry anthology, a play, a television series, and five collections of nonfiction prose. Some valued writings not discussed in the volume are the author's poignant short stories of the 1950s and her celebrated first novella *El balneario* (1954; "The Spa"). Also absent are the novels *Lo raro es vivir* (1996; *Living's the Strange Thing* [2004]) and *Irse de casa* (1998; "Leaving Home"), both of which contain fascinating depictions of contemporary women's lives. All of these have been taught by survey respondents. It is my hope that instructors will consider teaching these works, using the methodologies applied to the texts that are presented here. Other works that have not yet been taught are also worthy of consideration. These include Martín Gaite's posthumously published journals and essays, her collage art, and her other screenplays for television and film.

Even though suggested teaching levels range widely, instructors will find a surprising degree of transferability of the methods described in these essays. Current pedagogical best practices are evident throughout, notably in the area of problem-based, or active, learning. All contributors endorse at least a portion of the traditional model of the classroom lecture, usually to give students needed information. At the same time, they show a contemporary concern for student autonomy. These instructors not only solicit student queries and opinions but also foster student interaction and boost achievement through inventive techniques. Student writing is emphasized in many essays, and the goals of that writing are often ambitious. Formats range from guided journaling to automatic writing to meditative writing to rewriting fairy tales and finishing a novel.

Those who are interested in teaching in translation will find that the English translations of Martín Gaite's fiction and nonfiction are excellent. They convey both the sense and spirit of the originals, and her translators have earned praise for their efforts. An accomplished translator herself, Martín Gaite helped her translators while she was alive, answering every query. None of her works presently exists in more than one published English translation, so there is no possibility of evaluating competing versions. Instructors in North America will encounter some minor lexical issues relating to British English in translations of her novels. For example, the title *Variable Cloud* (for *Nubosidad variable*) would be "Variably Cloudy" in American English. *The Farewell Angel* (*La Reina de las Nieves*) and *Living's the Strange Thing* are also in British English. Nevertheless, American students have no trouble understanding these translations.

The essays in this volume can be read in any order, since each stands on its own. It is also possible to read them in the order in which they appear, to trace the author's development. Contributors approach Martín Gaite's works from multiple vantage points, using paradigms associated with sociology, anthropology, narratology, literary history, structuralism, historiography, anthropology, psychology, feminism, translation studies, and media studies. Tensions among competing approaches involve privileging one lens over another, but the critical constructs are not mutually exclusive. For the reader who is approaching the literature of Martín Gaite for the first time, the essays by Frieda H. Blackwell, Joan L. Brown, Randolph D. Pope, and Roberta Johnson will serve as an introduction to her best-known works. For someone who is familiar with the Martín Gaite canon and looking for something new, the essays by José Teruel, Carlos Feal, Lissette Rolón Collazo, and Jessamy Harvey will be of interest. Essays that are particularly relevant for teaching Martín Gaite in a women's literature course include those by Soledad Fox, Ofelia Ferrán, Janet Pérez, and Johnson. For the instructor who would like to incorporate Martín Gaite's works into a world literature course, the essays by David K. Herzberger, Pope, and Johnson are useful points of departure.

Novels of the Spanish Post–Civil War Era

The first section focuses on teaching Martín Gaite's fiction from the years following the Civil War, when censorship was especially strict. Blackwell presents techniques (including a chart of the novel's narrators) that help advanced undergraduates understand the world of *Entre visillos* (1958; *Behind the Cur-*

tains [1991]). Students learn to read between the lines to explore social realities for women, symbolic spaces, language use, structure, and personally relevant themes. Patricia O'Byrne enters *Entre visillos* through the door of narratology. Her approach builds critical skills while clarifying subtle narrative features used to communicate themes. The course she describes is taught in English to second-year college students, who read the novel in Spanish but also in English to ensure comprehension.

Martín Gaite's award-winning nonfiction study of this era, *Usos amorosos de la postguerra española* (1987; *Courtship Customs in Postwar Spain* [2004]) is combined with *Entre visillos* in Fox's course for upper-level undergraduates. This pairing allows students to delve into the predicaments of middle-class Spanish women under Franco and facilitates comparison with other contemporary Spanish women writers. For novice readers in high school or college, Jacqueline Gowen-Tolcott and Brown share methods for teaching "Las ataduras." They demonstrate that by supplying sociocultural, literary-critical, and linguistic support, instructors can equip students for independent critical analysis.

Novels of the Late Postwar Era and the Transition to Democracy

More advanced undergraduates in United States study-abroad programs in Madrid are the designated cohort for Teruel's essay on *Ritmo lento* (1963; "A Slower Rhythm"). In a course on Spanish literature of the second half of the twentieth century, students keep detailed reading journals that address specific questions; the journals lead them to engage in formal, historical, and autobiographical analysis as they situate the novel in Spanish literary history. Martín Gaite's 1974 novel *Retahílas* ("Yarns") is united with *Entre visillos* in María Luisa Guardiola's upper-level undergraduate courses, one of which is a seminar on Martín Gaite. Using diverse secondary sources, students discern the development of the author's writing style, including her emphasis on spoken language, in the context of continually evolving themes.

The final essay in this section addresses Martín Gaite's first work to be exempt from censorship. Feal demonstrates how *Fragmentos de interior* (1976; "Inner Fragments") can productively be taught to advanced undergraduates or graduate students as the culmination of a contemporary Spanish literature course that begins with Carmen Laforet's *Nada* (1945), using formalist, psychological, and sociological approaches.

The Canonical Novel El cuarto de atrás / The Back Room

The essays on the author's most acclaimed novel, *El cuarto de atrás* (1978; *The Back Room* [1983]), are sequenced according to teaching level, from beginner to advanced. The first essay, by Brown, presents methods for teaching the novel in English in an undergraduate literature-in-translation course. Pedagogical goals include empowering students to read as translators and as knowledgeable critics; a sociocultural approach is informed by translation studies. Dale J. Pratt explains how the novel can serve as a culminating text in a survey of Spanish literature course organized around the theme of the fantastic and how to equip students to explore sophisticated theoretical, sociocultural, and historical aspects of Martín Gaite's novel.

History and fiction are the prime subjects of Herzberger's essay. In a course geared to advanced undergraduate and graduate students, *El cuarto de atrás* is contextualized and then analyzed as a transgressive narration of the past that rebuts the official historiography of the Franco era while exploring fiction, history, memory, gender roles, and dissent. From reading the author's words to emulating the process of their creation, Emily C. Francomano approaches the novel as a book about reading and writing that can develop students' abilities in both areas. In a writing-intensive, discussion-based upper-level course on women writers, *El cuarto de atrás* (which is read after *Entre visillos*) is used as a springboard for write-to-learn activities derived from research on college writing programs. At the graduate level, María Fernández Babineaux Lamarque shows how Martín Gaite's nonfiction can be used to elucidate this novel and those of other canonical writers. A course on stylistics and theory pairs novels with readings from *El cuento de nunca acabar: Apuntes sobre la narración, el amor y la mentira* ("The Never-Ending Story: Notes on Narrative, Love, and Lies"), and a course on modern Peninsular literature does the same with *Usos amorosos de la postguerra española*.

Novels of the Post-Franco Democratic Era

Along with reading and writing, Martín Gaite had a passion for rewriting classics of so-called children's literature. In her essay on *Caperucita en Manhattan* (1990; "Little Red Riding Hood in Manhattan"), Rolón Collazo demonstrates how this fascination can be transmitted to students at advanced high school through upper-level undergraduate levels. Bolstered by a foundation in narratology and a compendium of classic folktale motifs, students are motivated to analyze the novel and to creatively rewrite fairy tales of their choosing.

Reading and writing are also treated in the two essays on the novel *Nubosidad variable* (1992; *Variable Cloud* [1995]). Pope describes an advanced undergraduate course that features analysis and imitation of Martín Gaite's use of writing. Imitation is achieved first through letter writing and then through weekly exercises in meditative writing that encourage students to devote time to nurturing the self. The female self is intensively explored in Ferrán's essay on teaching this novel. In a graduate course on contemporary Spanish women writers, theoretical readings by French feminists and others supply a foundation for meaningful exploration of the concept of *écriture féminine*, or uniquely female writing, as it applies to *Nubosidad variable*.

Vilma Navarro-Daniels describes teaching Martín Gaite's *La Reina de las Nieves* (1994; *The Farewell Angel* [1999]) in a writing-in-the-major course. The novel's metafictional, intertextual, and ekphrastic elements, as well as its depictions of democratic Spain, are elucidated through student research projects and intensive writing.

Martín Gaite's posthumous novel *Los parentescos* (2001; "Family Ties") is the subject of Isabel Estrada's essay. What could be considered a drawback—that the author died before finishing the novel—becomes an opportunity for students in an advanced undergraduate Spanish literature course, who work in groups to create their own written endings.

Poetry, Theater, and Television

This section features essays about three of the author's other genres. Martín Gaite's poetry is introduced by Josefa Álvarez in her essay on teaching the collection *A rachas* (1976, 1993, and 2000; "In a Gust of Wind") to intermediate and advanced undergraduates. An arsenal of learning strategies, supported by a guide to the poems' form and content, enables students to analyze poetic structures and interpret themes that are largely autobiographical. Pérez addresses theater in her essay on teaching a play written and set in the Franco era, *La hermana pequeña* (1999; "The Little Sister"). In two graduate courses on twentieth-century Spanish literature, gender theory is the lens through which the author's world is brought into focus, contextualizing both the play and other works that reflect changes in Spain during Martín Gaite's lifetime.

The medium of television is presented by Jessamy Harvey. In a university course for continuing education students, the six-episode television series *Celia* is taught in tandem with one of the Elena Fortún novels on which the series was based. In this course, childhood is used as an organizing paradigm (much like race, class, or gender) that enables scrutiny of cultural assumptions.

Selected Essays

Johnson's culminating essay on teaching Martín Gaite's nonfiction constitutes the last section. It covers *La búsqueda de interlocutor* (1973; "The Search for a Conversational Partner"), *Usos amorosos del dieciocho en España* (1972; *Love Customs in Eighteenth-Century Spain* [1991]), *Usos amorosos de la postguerra española*, and *Desde la ventana* (1987; "From the Window"). Establishing connections between her fiction and her nonfiction, Johnson discusses how the two evince Martín Gaite's own brand of quiet feminism—even though the author rejected the label "feminist" because of its strident connotations. In language, literature, culture, history, and theory courses at many levels, Martín Gaite's essays are shown to be valuable enrichments that students will find both enlightening and engaging.

Teaching *Entre visillos* in Its Sociohistorical Context

Frieda H. Blackwell

Carmen Martín Gaite's novel *Entre visillos* (translated by Frances M. López-Morillas as *Behind the Curtains*), winner of the 1957 Nadal Prize and published in 1958, stands as a prime example of the neorealist or social realist novel that was popular in Spain in the 1950s.[1] Because of its critical acclaim and the stature of its author, the novel merits inclusion in undergraduate senior-level twentieth-century Spanish literature courses, which are traditionally organized chronologically and feature works that exemplify major literary periods. Its objectivist style, shifting like a camera among individuals and groups, portrays young people growing up in a provincial capital—which Martín Gaite acknowledged to be Salamanca (Brown, "Nonconformist Character" 166)—during the repressive 1950s. Although her text offers particular challenges to students at this level because of its colloquial language and multiple narrators, it can, with proper study aids, allow students to develop their ability to read not only the lines but also between the lines, as they become more aware of narrative voice, characterization, settings, vocabulary, and connections with other genres, all in its sociohistorical context.

My own introduction to the objectivist novel was Rafael Sánchez Ferlosio's *El Jarama* (1955; *The River*), generally recognized as the prototype of this genre, which I read as a college junior in a study-abroad program in Seville, Spain. I felt overwhelmed reading an authentic text and not a student edition, never quite sure I had comprehended the novel's main points. Additionally, *El Jarama*'s lengthy dialogues seemed tedious, and I wondered why nothing happened in more than 350 pages, except the character Luci's drowning, recounted in only a few paragraphs. I remember telling fellow students it was the most boring book I had ever read. Years later, I realized that much of what Sánchez Ferlosio communicates lies in the spaces of the unsaid and the insinuated. The strict censorship of the Franco regime, which even in the spring of 1975 prevented my professors at the University of Seville from answering questions about "Grises" (Fascist riot troops) at the university or about the jailing of a newspaper editor, forced writers to communicate their criticism indirectly. Once I understood the context, the text, with its implied social criticism, became more interesting.

Using Reading Guides to Enhance Comprehension

My undergraduate reading experience, as well as subsequent teaching experiences, gave me insight into the kinds of guidance that students, even at the advanced level, need in reading novels. Although they may have taken an introduction to Hispanic literature course or a literary survey, many students are uncomfortable facing an authentic text not specifically designed for them. They first need help comprehending the literal level, so they have a solid foundation for further interpretations. To that end, I developed a series of focused study questions for *Entre visillos* about basic plot elements and narrative voice, beginning with chapter 1: ¿Cómo empieza la novela, y quién es la voz narrativa en las primeras dos páginas? A continuación, ¿qué tipo de narración hay en este capítulo? ("How does the novel begin, and who is the narrative voice in the first two pages? In the following pages, what type of narration is contained in this chapter?"). Students bring written answers, in complete sentences, on the chapters assigned for each class period, and we review those answers orally to start class discussion. This supported or guided reading method gives students the security that they have comprehended and can begin discussing the main points of a sophisticated, complex narrative. I cover chapters 1–5 in week 1, chapters 6–11 in week 2, and chapters 12–18 in the final week. Other full-length texts discussed in the course are Miguel de Unamuno's *Niebla* (*Mist*), Federico García Lorca's *Bodas de sangre* (*Blood Wedding*), Carlos Sastre's *Escuadra hacia la muerte* (*The Condemned Squad*), and Miguel Delibes's *Los santos inocentes* ("The Innocent Saints").

Identifying the narrative voice in *Entre visillos* is crucial to understanding the work. Chapters shift between a third-person omniscient narrator and the first-person narrative of Pablo Klein. The third-person narrator usually focuses on sixteen-year-old Natalia's experiences with classes at the Instituto Femenino; social activities with friends; and time spent with family in their upper-middle-class residence, presided over by her aunt Concha since the death of her mother. To present Natalia's thoughts, which contrast with her public communications, the narrator includes lengthy sections of her diary. Occasionally the third-person narrator shifts attention to Natalia's sisters, her friend Gertru, or Elvira, daughter of the recently deceased director of the Instituto. To help students identify these shifts, I created a chart that identifies the narrative voice and key events or topics of each chapter. (The chart that I distribute to students is in Spanish; an English version appears as the appendix to this essay.) The chart aids students in keeping track of who narrates, since the narrator's perspective shapes the story and occasionally the same event appears in several chapters, recounted in each by a different character. The inclusion of extensive dialogues reproduced verbatim also allows the author to weave other perspectives into the fabric of the novel. As John Kronik summarizes, "Now within, now without, the deft reader quickly learns the rules of the game and lets the duplicating perspectives corroborate a reality any one of whose units may be suspect for its partiality or incompleteness" (54). As students realize that the male speaks in first person but the third-person narrator generally mediates female communication (except in private diaries and letters), they see how these narrative patterns reflect a patriarchal society that values male speech but not that of females, even as the novel's mosaic of perspectives undercuts a monolithic authorial voice.

Exploring the Novelistic World of Entre visillos

Sociohistorical Realities

The world of *Entre visillos* is a provincial town in the early 1950s. From 1939 to 1975, Spain suffered under a Fascist dictatorship that abolished basic human rights, including those that women had gained under the Second Republic (1931–36). The Franco regime propagated the ideal of womanhood as the self-sacrificing Catholic wife and mother. Helen Graham notes that, under the dictatorship, the lives of upper-class women differed markedly from those of the lower class. Poor women struggled to survive, having low-paying and marginalized jobs, since frequently the male breadwinner of the family had died in the war or been imprisoned in a Republican labor camp. The 1938 Fuero del Trabajo ("Work Decree") forbade women to work outside the home and granted men a supplemental family bonus. "The regime promoted an 'ideal' image of womanhood as 'eternal,' passive, pious, pure, submissive woman-as-mother for whom self-denial was the only road to real fulfillment" (184). The Church supported the regime's propaganda, holding up the Virgin Mary as the ultimate role model for women. Legal and social limitations on women continued until Franco's death.

Entre visillos, through its objectivist style, reflects these societal expectations in a variety of ways, even as it subtly criticizes them. The detailed descriptions of Natalia's house and the conversations among her aunt, her sisters, and her all point to women's limited status. Natalia complains about wearing uncomfortable women's clothes for a party at the Casino (a social club with a large dance floor) and relishes her education at the Instituto. She is what Martín Gaite later called a "chica rara," or "odd girl," a nonconformist who struggles against social strictures, defined as "Este paradigma de mujer, que de una manera o de otra pone en cuestión la 'normalidad' de la conducta amorosa y doméstica que la sociedad mandaba acatar" (*Desde la ventana* 99; "This model of a woman who in one way or another questions the 'normality' of the amorous and domestic conduct that society demanded"). Nuria Cruz-Cámara argues that the *chica rara* emerges from the monochromatic atmosphere created by Francoist rhetoric ("'Chicas'" 107). Natalia's rebellion, culminating in her conversation with her father about a college career, although not completely realized, offers an alternative to the life of domesticity awaiting her friend Gertru. "Martín Gaite presents Natalia as a symbol of hope in the struggle against the discrimination and repressiveness of traditional society" (Brown, "Nonconformist Character" 169).

Other female characters offer variants of female conduct in this closed society. Tía Concha constantly voices traditional values. Natalia's three older sisters represent women's limited possibilities in the prevailing social paradigm. Mercedes embodies the spinster, still single at twenty-six. Josefina married a man of whom the family disapproved and lives in a poorer section of town. Julia struggles in her relationship with her domineering boyfriend, Miguel, an experimental filmmaker who pressures her to join him in Madrid against their father's expressed wishes. Elvira tries to rebel against social mores by dabbling in modern art and quoting contemporary poetry. Yet she finally agrees to marry the conventional Emilio. Lower-class women had even fewer options than well-to-do women. Rosa the *animadora*, or mistress of ceremonies, at the Casino represents the single working girl, whom upper-class women treat as a social pariah, stating, "Gente de ésa no queremos" (104; "We don't want people like her" [109]). Although, as Janet Pérez notes, she may dream of marriage and a family, she is trapped because "none of the men who attempt to seduce her would think of marrying her" ("Carmen Martín Gaite" 176). Only Pablo Klein, who lives in the same boardinghouse, befriends her. Because he is male and beyond provincial social mores, he can interact with the Casino crowd, Rosa, and the pseudo-bohemians at Yoni's studio, crossing social classes, whereas she cannot. Natalia's school friend Alicia highlights other problems facing young lower-class women. She is indelibly marked by shabby clothes: "esa chaqueta de traje sastre que trae encima del vestido azulina" (219; "that suit-jacket that she wears on top of her blue dress" [238]). Natalia's aunt barely condescends to speak to Alicia when Alicia visits Natalia to study Greek. Natalia rebelliously tells Alicia, "Y a mí qué me importa si le gustas o no, eres mi amiga" (218; "What do I care if she likes you or not, you're my friend" [237]). When Natalia stops at Alicia's small house one day, she encounters Alicia's stepmother, a harried working woman trying to manage a beauty shop and simultaneously caring for several children (188; 203). Natalia notes the stark difference between this existence and that of her aunt, who worries about proper etiquette, not survival. She also compares her educational opportunities with those of Alicia, who cannot afford further schooling and will probably be a village schoolteacher (219; 238), one of the few "decent" occupations open to poor single women.

Symbolic Spaces

Looking at the spaces the characters occupy also helps students understand the work's social and historical context as well as its implied social criticism. Joan Brown observes that Martín Gaite "effectively functions as an anthropologist to her own culture, reporting her findings to an esteemed reader" ("Carmen Martín Gaite" 74). Upper-class women typically move among home, school, church, and the Casino. These venues seem to offer females variety, but each venue ultimately constitutes another circumscribed routine. As Marsha Collins observes, the novel's spaces create a "sense of claustrophobia for females" (69–70). Catherine Bellver details Martín Gaite's use of "gendered spaces," arguing that although females invade the spaces of men, such as Yoni's studio, their incursions are short-lived ("Gendered Spaces" 41). Even the world of nature, especially the riverbank, that seems to represent freedom to females like Natalia and Elvira, offers only temporary respite from the confinement of the city's labyrinthine streets and closed houses (45).

The vocabulary associated with these spaces, which Tiffany Gagliardi calls the "rhetoric of enclosure," underscores the sense of suffocating entrapment. The cathedral tower visible at every angle in the city and the casino balcony where adults keep vigil over the young people interacting on the main floor represent the power of the Church and a rigid social hierarchy to regulate all social interactions (433). As students begin to formulate their own text-based interpretation, they must move from the literal level to understanding how certain novelistic elements assume symbolic importance. Thus the comparison of the cathedral tower's clock face to a giant eye (24; 18) points symbolically to the Church's intrusive gaze into all aspects of parishioners' lives. The clock and the hollow giant figures in the fiesta parade of chapter 1 (13; 5) function as metaphors for the hollow, hypocritical lives described in the novel.

Martín Gaite's use of spatial elements to effect social criticism connects closely to the work's title and message. *Visillos* are "curtains," especially "sheers" that often frame a window, letting in light but blocking a clear view of the panorama beyond. Women occupy interior spaces in contrast to exterior spaces, the streets that men occupy, and windows provide connections as well as barriers between these two worlds. In her 1987 collection of essays, significantly entitled *Desde la ventana* ("From the Window"), Martín Gaite writes, "[L]a ventana condiciona un tipo de mirada: mirar sin ser visto. Consiste en mirar lo de fuera desde un reducto interior, perspectiva determinada, en última instancia, por esa condición ventanera tan arraigada en la mujer española y que los hombres no suelen tener" (36; "The window preconditions a type of looking: looking without being seen. This consists of viewing what is outside from an interior stronghold, a perspective that is determined, ultimately, by that condition of 'windowgazing' so prevalent among Spanish women but not men"). Females look at life "entre visillos," or "between the curtains," from inside their rooms. In contrast, Pablo Klein wanders the city's streets gazing between the window curtains of the houses he passes, imagining "la vida estancada y caliente que se cocía en los interiors" (215; "the warm, stagnant life that was fermenting inside them" [234]). Even the verb *cocía* ("was cooking or simmering") links closed domestic interior space to females. Males can move freely and speak for themselves; women view life passively from "between the curtains" and have others speak for them.

Autobiographical Connections

Autobiographical aspects of *Entre visillos* also connect the work to its social and historical context, with the caveat that a work of fiction never simply retells the author's life. Martín Gaite confesses that she utilized her youth in Salamanca to create elements of her fictional world. (I show students photos of Salamanca to help them better visualize the novelistic spaces.) Brown identifies four areas in which the world of *Entre visillos* overlaps with Martín Gaite's personal experience: "the oppressive conformity of provincial life," "the circumscribed role allotted women," "education under Franco," and the "political realities of postwar Spain" ("One Autobiography" 40–44). Pointing out examples of this overlap—the separation of the sexes in school (*Entre visillos* 96 [*Behind the Curtains* 99], 206 [224]) is one—helps students understand not only the political and social reality in which Martín Gaite produced her work but also how she transformed the stuff of life into the stuff of fiction.

Many students, especially males, complain that the female characters in *Entre visillos* discuss only clothes, parties, boyfriends, and girlfriends. I agree but observe that when a repressive government systematically censors free expression, what is not discussed becomes significant. As the novelist Juan Goytisolo explains in his essay "Los escritores españoles frente al toro de la censura" ("Spanish Writers Bullfighting with the Censor"), the novel of the postwar years in Spain came to assume the function of disseminating facts about everyday life, since the newspapers faced even stricter censorship than the novel (*Furgón* 60–61). *Entre visillos*'s one mention of Franco is his photo hanging in the Instituto (96; 100). Characters make only passing references to the "guerra" (201; "war" [219]). That Natalia's father, a "negociante adinerado," according to Pablo (209; "wealthy business man" [227]), made a fortune in wolfram or tungsten mining (214; 232) subtly links him to the Franco regime, because Franco shipped this ore, used for strengthening steel and required in armaments, to Hitler during World War II (Preston, *Franco* 453). The Civil War and its ongoing repercussions seem like the elephant in the living room, affecting everyone but not openly discussed by anyone. The characters' banal conversations highlight the grim reality that Spaniards could discuss only trivialities publicly, given the danger they faced for expressing divergent views on serious topics. By extension, the novel raises issues of human rights and freedoms.

Genre Models and Innovations

Comparing the text with genres such as the bildungsroman and the *novela rosa*, or romance novel, both popular during this era, underscores both the work's uniqueness and its connection with literary tradition. The bildungsroman chronicles the passage from adolescence to adulthood as the protagonist develops ethical values and integrates into prevailing social structures, "the reconciliation of the individual with the bourgeois social order" (Lowe 97). *Entre visillos* tells how Natalia tries to make this transition. Her teacher encourages her to consider a college career, even as her father rejects that idea. This novel, unlike the traditional bildungsroman, leaves her choices open instead of following her progress to adulthood. Natalia's search for personal identity in the face of enormous social pressure to conform to female roles designated by a patriarchal society resonates with students, both male and female, who likewise feel pressure to adopt popular ideals of dress, social standing, and careers that lead to economic success.

The regime used the *novela rosa* to advance Francoist ideals of womanhood. As Mercedes Jiménez says, the stories of exuberant females gave women a way to satisfy longings for erotic adventures and luxury sadly missing in their lives (14). Unlike the *novela rosa*, *Entre visillos* never offers traditional marriage as a panacea for the female search for identity and fulfillment, nor does it offer escapist adventures or sentimentalism. Rather, it presents photographs of life not airbrushed. Natalia has no interest in marriage, and even characters like Gertru, Elvira, and Julia who have *novios* ("boyfriends or fiancés") seem frustrated in these relationships, because they are often treated like powerless children. Discussing *Entre visillos* as a bildungsroman or a *novela rosa* can show how writers under censorship used established fictional forms to effect social criticism by subverting reader expectations. Showing students how fictional works can engage in a literary dialogue enriches their reading of a given text.

Enduring Sociocultural Themes

Although every novel reflects the singular social and cultural experiences of its creator, great literature like *Entre visillos* builds bridges from the particular to the universal. Santos Sanz Villanueva points out that Martín Gaite often treats the theme of singleness and provincial life but eventually moves to consider what he describes as "el anhelo doloroso e inalcanzable de lograr la autenticidad" (367; "the painful and unattainable longing to achieve authenticity"). Individuals, especially during college, work to create an authentic self as well as sort out how they fit (or do not fit) into the dominant social structure. Natalia reveals her struggles with such questions through the pages of her diary. Her mind-set differs radically from that of her friend Gertru, who "has no chance for an individual identity" (Talbot 88). Pablo Klein finds life in the provincial city so boring that he leaves after one semester with no repercussions, an option not open to most females. All the characters, in one way or another, must deal with the social roles assigned them and determine if they will accept or rebel against them. I would like students to understand *Entre visillos* first as a text on its own terms, then as a reflection of a particular historical and cultural milieu, and finally as an expression of our common humanity—of the struggles we all face to develop, learn, and find our place in society even when we feel different, as an outsider like Pablo or an insider like Natalia struggling against stultifying domestic roles, looking at life "through the curtains."

NOTE

[1] References in this essay to *Entre visillos* are to the 2008 Destino edition. Translation page numbers refer to López-Morillas's *Behind the Curtains*; all other translations are my own.

APPENDIX: *ENTRE VISILLOS*: NARRATIVE VOICE AND KEY EVENTS OR TOPICS, BY CHAPTER

PART 1: VACATIONS, SUMMER HOLIDAYS, AUGUST TO SEPTEMBER

Chapter	**Narrative Voice**	**Key Events, Featured Characters or Topics**
1	3rd person	Natalia writes in her diary.
2	1st (Pablo)	Pablo arrives by train.
3	3rd	Goyita and memories of summer
4	1st (Pablo)	Pablo visits family of don Rafael
5	3rd	Gertu and Natalia at bullfight. Go to Casino
6	1st (Pablo)	Pablo's experience at boardinghouse
7	3rd	Julia fights with her fiancé, Miguel.
8	1st (Pablo)	Pablo receives letter from Elvira.
9	3rd	Julia—her letter to Miguel
10	3rd	Elvira receives visit from Emilio.
11	1st (Pablo)	Pablo. Rosa has left town. He meets Elvira.

Total of six chapters in the third person, five in the first (Pablo).

PART 2: FALL SEMESTER, OCTOBER TO DECEMBER

Chapter	**Narrative Voice**	**Key Events, Featured Characters or Topics**
12	3rd person	Fight between Gertru and Ángel. Party at Yoni's house—Julia, Mercedes, Pablo
13	1st (Natalia)	Natalia at school. Takes a walk with Pablo but turns down invitation for coffee.
14	3rd	Elvira, Teo. Natalia receives school advice from Pablo.
15	1st (Pablo)	Pablo at school. Invites Natalia for coffee, and she accepts.
16	1st (Natalia)	Natalia and Alicia study at Natalia's house. Petrita visits.
17	3rd	Gertru. Bridal shower
18	1st (Pablo)	Pablo. At train station. He leaves. Julia leaves. Natalia thinks about leaving.

Total of three chapters in the third person, four in the first (2 by Pablo, 2 by Natalia).

Altogether there are nine chapters in the third person, nine in the first (7 by Pablo, 2 by Natalia).

A Narratological Approach to the Teaching of *Entre visillos*

Patricia O'Byrne

Although many novels by postwar women writers are worthy of study and less challenging to undergraduate students, *Entre visillos* (1958) not only provides an engaging insight into contemporary women's lives, it also proves an excellent text for developing an awareness of narrative features. These two disparate aspects are interrelated in the novel: we can safely assume that the repressive climate that *Entre visillos* reproduces was a key factor in informing the text's subtle, covert narrative techniques. While exploring the experiences of sixteen-year-old Natalia Ruiz Guilarte and those around her, including her teacher Pablo Klein, *Entre visillos* conveys a multilayered depiction of provincial life during the 1950s in the unnamed but instantly recognizable Spanish city of Salamanca.

I teach the novel in Ireland as part of a required undergraduate literature course designed for students in their fourth semester. The group consists of students who have taken intensive beginner's Spanish in college and students who have had five years of high school Spanish. Some are majoring in humanities; others are from joint degree programs. I have also taught the novel in translation to graduate students and have used the same approach described here, adjusted to the level of the group. The maximum number of students in an undergraduate group is twenty-five; at the graduate level, smaller numbers permit more individual participation.

Teaching in English While Reading the Novel in English and Spanish

Although no college lecturer in a Hispanic studies department would espouse this option, I allow my students to read Martín Gaite's novel in English translation so that they can fully comprehend it, while expressing the expectation that they will also read it in the original Spanish. To this end, I ordered several copies of Frances López-Morillas's translation of *Entre visillos*, entitled *Behind the Curtains* (1990), for the college library; but students must purchase the novel in Spanish, as we use the original text in class. Sometimes they read the novel first in English and then in Spanish; sometimes they read both versions at the same time. Lectures are delivered in English, and class discussion is also in English.

Since I believe that this dual-language approach is necessary for students who may only have had three semesters of Spanish, I take responsibility for ensuring that students understand that any translation is always an interpretation of the original text. I consider López-Morillas's translation reliable, although, like any reader of the novel in the original, I would have translated some phrases differently. Also the translation's American English is not without problems for readers whose English was acquired in Europe—as in Dublin, where I teach. A particular issue is the register of speech for characters in the novel, notably when terms of affection or familiarity are used. One example is: "—Por favor, mujer, qué bobada, yo qué le voy a decir" (21; "Goodness, sweetie, what a foolish thing to ask, I wouldn't say anything to her" [14]).[1] Perhaps because in the British Isles our exposure to American English of that era is mostly limited to film, such expressions—and there are several of them in the novel—conjure up for us images more appropriately situated in an American diner than in the sitting room of a bourgeois Spanish family. This can result in a transposition of the reader's imagined fictive setting.

A further difficulty with any English version of the novel concerns the colloquial dialogue of young people, because no translation can suggest all the nuances of the original Spanish. For example, Martín Gaite captures perfectly the sense of moral superiority that the young women in the Casino feel toward Rosa, the dance hall singer, when Pablo's dance partner says of her, "–No sé cómo se llama ni me interesa tampoco" (103; "I don't know what her name is and I don't care to know" [107]). The arrogant dismissal of Rosa is contained not only in the words; the venom in the speaker's voice is conveyed by the snappy, angry rhythm of the Spanish utterance, especially when "interesa" is hissed. Similarly, intonation is important in one young man's (Luis Colina's) immature expression of admiration for another (Ángel), when he says, "–Es un león, desde luego, para las mujeres" (151; "Of course, he's a tiger for the women" [162]). Like so many of the novel's short dialogue lines, this one has to be read aloud, with the emphasis on "león," or at least silently with the intonation of speech to capture the testosterone-fueled force behind this expression of admiration. The novel's dialogue is so vivid that it almost directs our facial gestures and hand movements.

Much of the humor and tone of the novel is attributable to the cadences that significantly expand the semantic range of the characters' comments. This dimension of Martín Gaite could be described as Joycean (e.g., the popular example from *Ulysses* "—Eh, mister! Your fly is open, mister!" [327]), insofar as the utterances come alive only as we read them aloud and savor the rhythm of the speech of the Dubliner or the Salmantino (native of Salamanca).[2] To supply what is lost in translation, it helps to read passages from the original aloud in class. When reading aloud, students engage in a very different way with the dialogue, and the setting of the novel takes on a life that is not easily accessed by the reader of the English translation. Discussion of differences between the English and Spanish also provides an incentive for students to read the text in the original.

Background: Social and Cultural Context

It is important that students be made aware of the social and cultural context of *Entre visillos*—namely, the stifling social and moral codes that shaped the lives and informed the thinking of young women during the first twenty-five years of the Franco dictatorship. Otherwise, characters' behavior will not be comprehensible. For example, the letter from Julia, Natalia's twenty-seven-year-old sister, to her fiancé, in which she refers to her apology for what took place between them once when they were alone by the river and concludes with the line "Rezo por ti. Te quiero. Adiós, Julia" (110; "I'm praying for you. I love you. Goodbye, Julia" [114]), could be interpreted as the words of a neurotic, unbalanced person instead of the expression of an average, conforming, middle-class young woman. The tragic irony is lost when we cannot appreciate the moral turmoil of Julia, who is a victim of the period's patriarchal and moral repression.

Awareness of the literary milieu in which Martín Gaite wrote her novel is also enlightening and enriches the reading experience. In her essay "La chica rara" ("The Odd Girl"), she recognizes that Carmen Laforet's Andrea in *Nada* (1945) was the "audaz pionera" (112; "audacious pioneer") of the female character she labels the "chica rara":

> Este paradigma de mujer, que de una manera o de otra pone en cuestión la "normalidad" de la conducta amorosa y doméstica que la sociedad mandaba acatar, va a verse repetido con algunas variantes en otros textos de mujeres como Ana María Matute, Dolores Medio y yo misma. (111)
>
> This model of woman, who in one way or another questions the "normality" of the amorous conduct and domestication that society demanded of women, will be repeated in various guises in other texts by women such as Ana María Matute, Dolores Medio, and me.

These protagonists do not normally have girlfriends, preferring the friendship of men; they reject all types of confinement and yearn for an ill-defined freedom that they find in open spaces outside the family home. The essential characteristic of their behavior is their "inconformismo" (113; "nonconformity"). Martín Gaite places her characters Natalia and Elvira from *Entre visillos* in this category.

Readers should be aware that the novel belongs to a tradition of women's writing of the postwar period, when women confronted and questioned their oppressive existence through their writing. Any criticism of the limitations of their role in life had to be veiled or implied, because the censorship process—to which all novels were submitted before publication—would not have permitted criticism of the regime, the Church, or the society they extolled. During the Franco years (1939–75) the press and other media were so tightly controlled that the novel, in the words of Juan Goytisolo, "cumple en España una función testimonial que en Francia y los demás países de Europa corresponde a la prensa" (*Furgón* 61; "[the novel] in Spain fulfills the same testimonial function as the press does in France and other democratic European countries"). The neorealist novel of the first two postwar decades, a type of testimonial to negative aspects of contemporary society, was not as politically inspired as many of the more radical novels of social realism. But at very least it represents, in the words Martín Gaite uses to describe Eulalia Galvarriato's 1947 novel *Cinco sombras* ("Five Shadows"), "[un] espejo negativo de conducta" ("a negative mirror of conduct") and "un grito de protesta" ("a shout of protest") ("Chica rara" 115).

In order to voice discontent and protest, narrative was adapted to circumvent censorship—thus the popularity of the objective technique, whereby the author refrained from commenting and merely depicted events that prompted readers to question the values of a society that allowed such injustice or in which people led vacuous, meaningless lives. Rafael Sánchez Ferlosio's novel *El Jarama* (1956; *The River*) is usually cited as the supreme example of an objective literary technique used to indict contemporary society, but many women novelists employed subversive narrative techniques to the same end, although they were not often acknowledged. Akiko Tsuchiya states that women writers express their oppression "through techniques of literary camouflage" (214), and *Entre visillos* is an excellent illustration of such camouflaging narrative devices. That it was described by the censor of the day as "Una historia provinciana de un grupo de chicas, sus estudios y sus amores" ("A provincial story about a group of girls, their studies and their love lives" [Censor 27]) shows how successful the novelist was in concealing her appraisal of the repressed lives of young women in this provincial town.

Narratology and the Novel

The narrative techniques used by Martín Gaite in *Entre visillos*, such as the range of narrators or the use of multiple focalizations or points of view, challenge passive readers to make the links between characters, because the narrator offers no assistance, and to evaluate their conflicting interpretations and attitudes. While this detective-like role may delight an experienced reader, the response of the linguistically challenged and inexperienced student of literature tends to be frustration. In order to convey an understanding of the narrative devices at work in the novel—an understanding that assists students in their reading of the text, in particular of the opening chapters—I introduce some core concepts of narratology.

After I provide students with introductory lectures on the social and literary context of the novel, they are required to read three chapters of the text in Spanish (at this point in the course the availability of the translated text in the library has not been announced). Class discussion centered on who is telling the story elicits a confusion of responses: some students think it is Martín Gaite, some Natalia, some Pablo Klein. Using the knowledge we already have of terms such as first-person, third-person, and omniscient narrator, we identify the different narrators and separate them from the author. We identify characters and their relationship to one another and question whether the blurring of characters and speakers is intended by the author. Students who need to can now take advantage of brief chapter outlines available on the *Moodle* e-learning platform, which assists those with language difficulties.

For each session, students must read a certain number of chapters and focus on what they tell us about life during the period and how it is communicated. A group of three to four students make a twenty-minute presentation on the assigned chapters at the start of a class, and this presentation is followed by commentary from the other students; the final thirty minutes of the hour-and-forty-minute session is devoted to a lecture that incorporates students' contributions and considers narrative aspects. The objective is for students to identify most of the narratological concepts before terminology is introduced. When they have read about a third of the novel and are becoming aware of shifting perspectives and narrators, I present the basic concepts and terminology of narratology.

I explain that narratology is the study of narrative and of the narrative dimensions of any text and that its application is not confined to literature. It has been described etymologically as the "science of narrative" (Onega and García Landa 1), though opinions may vary whether or not it is desirable to consider any study of a literary work scientific. The approach of the original structuralist narratologists, such as Tzvetan Todorov, Roland Barthes, and Gérard Genette, involving a more formal analysis of narrative, has expanded significantly because of the influence of the theories of Wayne Booth, Mieke Bal, and many others. More recently German narratologists, such as Tom Kindt, Monika Fludernik, and Manfred Jahn, have come to the fore in the field of narrative studies.

Narratology is now used to refer to a variety of approaches to the study of narrative. Students in their reading will encounter references to narratology according to different approaches: structuralist, poststructuralist, contextualist, classical, postclassical, applied, or feminist. For the purposes of my course, I am selective and therefore adopt what is best described as a contextual narratological approach. It concentrates on Genette's classification of narrators and scheme of focalization and on Booth's concept of the implied author, as these are among the most useful tools for an enhanced reading of *Entre visillos.* Additional concepts are introduced, if time permits and where appropriate: Jahn's concept of camera-eye narration, the real reader, the implied reader, and the narratee.

Narratological Aspects of Entre visillos

After a lecture sketching the history and introducing the basic concepts of narratology and its principal theorists, we consider the characteristics of autodiegetic, homodiegetic, heterodiegetic, extradiegetic, and intradiegetic narratives and classify each of the text's narrators. (The definitions are provided for the students online through *Moodle*.)[3] Natalia as narrator gives rise to discussion since she is not only an autodiegetic narrator involved in the story world but also a diarist. What does her dual role add to the novel? This question leads to a discussion of the character and highlights how the diary format draws attention to her need to communicate and to her sense of isolation. The diary also affords Martín Gaite's "odd girl" a safe haven in which to raise taboo issues, such as the steering of young girls into marriage, attitudes toward women's education, and the restrictive clothing of women—all topics that are mentioned in the opening pages. The diary, moreover, raises the issue of the reliability of the narrator and also the question of the intended or implied reader.

Focalization, the perspective from which events are narrated, is a key narrative feature in *Entre visillos* and arises in the students' early discussion of narrator type. An understanding of focalization provides the discerning reader with in-depth information on the focalizing character's outlook and priorities. Unlike most other girls, who consider the eligible males or the female competition, when Natalia visits the Casino, her perspective allows readers to contemplate how small and insignificant everything seems from the balcony (69; 68). When the focalizing agent in the Casino is Goyita, Natalia's contemporary, the reader's attention is drawn to the people present: "Se sentaron en la mesa de Mercedes, Isabel y chicas mayores. . . . Cantaba la animadora, una rubia muy llamativa, y hacía calor" (42–43; "They sat at a table with Mercedes, Isabel, and some older girls. . . . The mistress of ceremonies, a very flashy blonde, was singing, and it was hot" [39]). It is Goyita who classifies the women a few years her senior as "older" and the mistress of ceremonies as a "flashy blonde."

In addition to the many instances of variable focalization, the novel provides examples of multiple focalization, whereby the same episode is presented through the eyes of different characters. Natalia describes in almost four and a half pages the first time Pablo accompanied her and Alicia on their way home from school (181–85; 196–200), whereas his recollection is of an encounter without any particular significance: "Con aquella Natalia Ruiz Guilarte había hablado un día, al principio de curso, una vez que la acompañé hasta su casa, y algo me había contado de que quería estudiar carrera y no la dejaba su padre" (210; "I had spoken to Natalia Ruiz Guilarte one day at the start of the school year, once when I had walked her home, and she had told me something about wanting to go to the university and that her father wouldn't let her" [228]). Readers must then question her interpretation of the encounter in relation to his and, indeed, the reliability of her narration of events involving Pablo.

Although the narrative of Pablo Klein is also autodiegetic, he has qualities that we usually associate with a heterodiegetic narrator (i.e., one external to the story): at one level he is part of the diegesis or fictional world, yet he is often outside it, commenting critically. In one example he is climbing the stairs to Elvira's house, behind a group of young women: "Sus tacones se movían de un peldaño a otro y hacían variar la postura de sus cuerpos esforzadamente, como en los saltos de la cámara lenta. Llegaron al rellano y se detuvieron, una de ellas llamó en la primera puerta" (52; "Their high heels moved from one stairstep to another and forced the posture of their bodies to change, as in the jerks of a slow-motion camera. They reached the landing and stopped; one of them knocked on the first door" [50]). His role as an external focalizer is equally as important as his role as autodiegetic narrator. (This quotation also serves to introduce the concept of camera-eye narration, which is so prominent in the novel.)

Heterodiegetic narrative can be an effaced narrative—referred to by Genette as an "absent narrator account" (*Narrative Discourse* 244)—and there are many examples in the text of the heterodiegetic narrator in this capacity: "Salieron a la calle. Había dejado de lloviznar, pero hacía un poco de viento, . . ." (118; "They went out on the street. It had stopped drizzling but there was a little wind, . . ." [124]). More frequently the heterodiegetic narrator is selective yet quite subtle in what he tells the reader: "Federico, mientras se servía la séptima copa de coñac de la tarde, le estaba diciendo a Mercedes . . ." (161; "Federico was saying to Mercedes as he served himself the seventh glass of cognac of the afternoon . . ." [173]). In a deceptively functional, casual manner, readers are being directed how to evaluate the character of Federico. The finesse of this narrative act is similar to that used in Natalia's diary, where we also find important information presented in an understated way:

> Dice [Gertru] que ella este curso por fin no se matricula, porque a Ángel no le gusta el ambiente del Instituto. Yo le pregunté que por qué, y es que ella por lo visto le ha contado lo de Fonsi, aquella chica de quinto que tuvo un hijo el año pasado. En nuestras casas no lo habíamos dicho; no sé por qué se lo ha tenido que contar a él. (11)

> She [Gertru] says that this year she's not even going to register, because Angel doesn't like the atmosphere at the High School. I asked her why not, and apparently it was because she told him about Fonsi, that girl in the fifth-year class who had a baby last year. We hadn't said anything to our families about it; I don't know why she had to tell him. (3)

This entry from Natalia's diary informs readers about the attitudes of boyfriends and parents, about the fear of parents, and about how the young women deal with this situation.

The Role of the Implied Author

The concept of the implied author is controversial but at the same time recognized even by its critics as "one of the most successful concepts in the academic study of literature in the twentieth century" (Kindt and Müller, *Implied Author: Concept* 2). I believe it is particularly relevant in the study of postwar Spanish fiction and a central part of what Hans-Jörg Neuschäfer refers to as the "discurso de la censura" (10; "discourse of censorship").[4] Booth, reaffirming the place of the author in the literary text, used the term "implied author" to refer to the real author's "second self":

> However impersonal he may try to be, his reader will inevitably construct a picture of the official scribe who writes in this manner—and of course that official scribe will never be neutral towards all values. Our reactions to his various commitments, secret or overt, will help determine our response to the work. (71)

Entre visillos is an excellent text for an analysis of the role of the implied author. Without any knowledge of the concept, students refer to it in their discussion of narrators, for the most part confusing the implied author with the real author. I have found it useful to introduce the term early in the study of the novel, because it clarifies the role of the author in a text that in many ways mirrors her personal experience, thus deterring students drawn to a simplistic biographical approach. If the implied author can be understood to represent "the nexus of values and norms in the textual world" (Kindt and Müller, *Implied Author: Explication* 4), how is this representation communicated in the novel?[5] When analyzing passages, students become aware of how imperceptibly these values are absorbed by the reader. An analysis of the implied author in *Entre visillos* inevitably leads to a consideration of the implied reader, but the time constraints of the course rarely allow its full development.[6]

To illustrate the key narratological aspects of the novel, I have found it more beneficial to examine in detail specific sections of text rather than present many different examples. It is to be expected that students will be confused initially with the new terminology, and it helps them to have their definition sheet in hand during the early stages. Of the seven class sessions (of one hour and forty minutes' duration), two are devoted to the social and literary context, five to the narrative dimension.

An advantage of developing an awareness in students of narrative features is that it is a transferable skill, and for this reason I ask them to provide examples of features from texts, films, and television programs with which they are familiar. As a culminating assignment in the study of *Entre visillos* through narratology, students choose and submit for approval their own essay title on a narratological aspect of the text. This term paper reinforces and expands their understanding of both the novel and the theoretical concepts used to explore its complexities.

NOTES

[1]When a translation has no page reference, it is mine. Spanish page references are to the 2008 Destino edition of *Entre visillos*.

[2]In a lecture Martín Gaite gave in University College Cork (Ireland) in 1983, she emphasized the influence of Joyce and other censored authors on her and her contemporaries. She recalled how they stayed up nights to read a copy of *Ulysses* that was in circulation and then spent nights discussing it.

[3]Posted definitions include those of reader and implied reader, narratee (a textual construct denoting the person to whom the narrator is telling the story), author and implied author, reliable and unreliable narrators, camera-eye and simultaneous narration, and narrators according to diegetic (fictional-text) level. Among these narrators are the omniscient narrator (who knows, as Gerald Prince says, "practically everything" about the story [68]); the homodiegetic narrator, whose text contains some first-person pronouns indicating that the narrator was "at least a witness to the action" (Jahn N1.11); the autodiegetic narrator, the protagonist or hero speaking in the first person; the heterodiegetic narrator, who is not a character in the story; the intradiegetic narrator, a character in the fictional world who invokes another, embedded fictional world; and the extradiegetic narrator, who is not part of the fictional world and is only involved in framing the text. Focalization (a term introduced by Genette [*Figuras III*]) or point of view is also covered in these definitions, with emphasis on the key question: "Who sees?" Among focalizations are zero focalization, when events are narrated from an omniscient point of view, also referred to as nonfocalized narration; fixed focalization, when events are presented from the point of view of a single character or focalizer; variable focalization, when events in the story are presented through the eyes of a number of focalizers; multiple focalization, when the same event is presented from the perspective of different focalizers; internal focalization, when the information given is from the character's point of view; and external focalization, when the information given by someone in the fictional world refers to characters' actions and speech, without access to their thoughts or feelings. Further references for students to use in exploring these concepts are Abbott; Herman, Jahn, and Marie-Laure; Jahn; and Prince.

[4]Neuschäfer uses the term to refer to "formas de hablar indirectas y encubiertas, ya que la enunciación directa del pensamiento podía ser peligrosa" (10; "indirect and covert forms of expression, as direct communication of thoughts could be dangerous").

[5]This is how Kindt and Müller summarize the views of many narratologists, including Shlomith Rimmon-Kenan and Seymour Chatman.

[6]Prince defines the implied reader as "a real reader's second self (shaped in accordance with the implied author's values and cultural norms)" (10).

Cellophane Girls: Feminine Models in *Entre visillos* and *Usos amorosos de la postguerra española*

Soledad Fox

> He viajado bastante, conozco toda América . . . y creo sinceramente que donde la mujer se conserva más mujer es aquí. No en vano pertenece a un pueblo donde todo es tradición.
>
> —María Teresa Casanova, in an interview cited in *Usos amorosos de la postguerra española*
>
> I have traveled a lot; I know North and South America quite thoroughly . . . and I sincerely believe that here in Spain women are still the most womanly. It is because they belong to a country where tradition means everything.

The first time I taught *Usos amorosos de la postguerra española* to an undergraduate class, the result was disappointing. The context was a seminar called The Cultures of Spain, the sort of impossible survey course that is supposed to cover Spanish literature and civilization from the origins of the Iberian Peninsula to the present day. *Usos amorosos*, which to me was (and still is) an accessible, amusing, and fascinating portrait of the mores of the life of young women in the high Franco period, seemed impenetrable to all but a few of my students. In the first class discussion, I realized that students were jarred by the nonfiction genre of the text (no plot or characters to follow) and that the cultural references in the book were far too specific. Most important, students had insufficient cultural or historical context to understand why the postwar generations of Spain lived under such fierce repression or why the intensely retrograde (and to the modern reader somewhat ridiculous) consequences of this way of life were amusing to the author—and to their professor.

My syllabus for this class was planned in such a way that I did not have time to provide the necessary context. As a general rule, and this became clear in my first year of teaching different facets of modern Spanish literature, students know little about Spain beyond what they learn in classes taught by Peninsular specialists in Spanish departments. Because Spanish literature—twentieth-century literature especially—is inextricably linked to socioeconomic and political contexts, my classes have come to include much more history than I ever imagined they would. *Usos amorosos* now works very well in my seminars, specifically in two advanced courses: Contemporary Spanish Literature and Women in Twentieth-Century Spain. In both we read *Usos amorosos* in conjunction with *Entre visillos*, which allows students to see the nonfiction as well as fiction of Carmen Martín Gaite and how in both genres she portrays the severe norms according to which girls and women lived in postwar Spain. These two works focus on the lifestyle of middle-class women and describe how these women were especially targeted and affected by the national Catholic project of the Franco regime. Though my classes are taught in Spanish, both books are available in English translation, as are many of the secondary sources that enrich comprehension.

It is important to include material—whether literary or historical—that shows how other sectors of Spanish women lived under conditions of real hardship and poverty. The life of the ideal Spanish middle-class girl in Martín Gaite's works was that of a privileged minority and had little to do with the general reality of Spain after the war. The vast disenfranchised portion of the female population represented in other works (the poor, prostitutes, political prisoners, intellectuals) contrasts with the churchgoing, lemon-biscuit-baking models of chastity and the new femininity. Martín Gaite's portraits of women should be compared with those in novels before and after hers that portray women who were excluded from the new status quo and that questioned it, such as Carmen Laforet's *Nada*, Mercè Rodoreda's *La Plaza del Diamante* (translated as *The Time of the Doves*) and *La Calle de las Camelias* (*Camellia Street*), or Dulce Chacón's *La voz dormida* ("The Sleeping Voice").

Students should also be familiarized with the institutions that created such norms for women (especially the Church and the Sección Femenina, the women's branch of the fascist Falange). The Franco regime put a great deal of pressure on women. As Helen Graham observes:

> Women were envisioned as the source not only of physical reproduction (i.e., babies for the *patria* [homeland]) but also correct ideological reproduction via the socialization of children in the home—the goal here being the imposition of a social hierarchy. But, to ensure this outcome, the state could not really afford to let the private sphere remain entirely "private." Control, especially of women, had to be enforced. Women thus became the target both of a cult of morality and of the educational and low-level welfare ministrations of state agencies. Although the Church should be included in this category, predominant here was the Sección Femenina de Falange. (187)

Without this sociological background, students may assume that mid-twentieth-century Spain was simply old-fashioned. They may see some similarities with the conservative culture in the United States in the 1950s. This comparison is worth noting, but the particularities of the situation in Spain must be established.

Entre visillos

As both *Entre visillos* and *Usos amorosos de la postguerra española* focus on young women and gender relations, they are complementary. I suggest reading the novel first and then looking at *Usos amorosos* to tease out the sociological structures that affect how the novel's characters behave. *Entre visillos* was written thirty years before *Usos amorosos*, so the author's 1957 and 1987 perspectives on the lives of young Spaniards can be compared. Because the characters are mainly in their twenties or late teens, students can more readily identify with them. The characters and students have issues in common: social cliquishness, conflict with authority figures, first romances, and career ambitions. That *Entre visillos* is set in a provincial town like Salamanca, the author's hometown, gives the work an autobiographical dimension. This backwater—as opposed to Madrid or the glamorous summer resorts such as San Sebastián—can also be seen as a metaphor for Spain as a whole.

The title, translated by Frances López-Morillas as *Behind the Curtains*, is a good starting point for discussion. What does it mean? What relevance does it have to the characters' experiences? *Visillos* are those sheer, usually synthetic panels, ubiquitous in Spanish homes, that like blinds let some light through but maintain the family's privacy. They represent the separation of the female domestic sphere from the public world of the street. *Visillos* are among the many material objects that circumscribe the middle-class female in Franco's Spain. There is the *mesa camilla* ("brazier"), the round table with overhanging tablecloth skirts and a coal heater—electric in today's models—at its center, which is the domestic social gathering place. There are the *galletas de limón* ("lemon biscuits"), the baking of which is a refined and acceptable leisure activity. There are Dop-brand shampoo (significantly still a luxury two decades after the war) and the bracelets, compacts, and stiff, uncomfortable party dresses that embodied women's aspirations. Signifying more than materialism in the consumer sense, these objects represent the order, boundaries, and control to which females were subjected. Their world was hermetic and completely homogeneous, and the only dissonance came from outside.

Any kind of foreignness was denigrated during the Franco years. From 1939 on, Spain was akin to a self-colonized possession ruled by the military and the Church. Individualism, intellectualism, cosmopolitanism, and more generally impurity (whether national, political, religious, or racial) were feared as threats that reeked of the vanquished Republicans and had to be suppressed at all costs. Throughout Spain, even local cafés named Cosmopolita or anything else with a worldly touch were renamed Nacional. As students read, they should be able to pick up many counterpoints and tensions between the domestic and the outside world. In *Entre visillos*, the alien is seen in its most moderate form in the character of Marisol, the girl from Madrid. She is roughly of the same social class as the local girls but too sophisticated with her fast talk, chic short hair, and heavy makeup. She is, in fact, the worst thing a female under Franco could be, an *exagerada* who pays no heed to the strict rules of modesty and discretion.

Two characters who are more explicitly outsiders are Pablo Klein, one of the main narrators, and Rosa, both in town temporarily. Pablo, who spent part of his childhood there but was never part of the social fabric, is as out of place as his foreign surname suggests. In town to teach German at the local secondary school, he stays at a dreary boardinghouse, where he meets Rosa, a fellow guest there for the season to entertain at the Casino. Her job is to amuse the locals when she is performing, but when the show is over, she is a pariah, thought of as little better than a prostitute by everyone except Pablo, who is not ruled by nationalist, chauvinist prejudices. Through his eyes the reader feels an instant sympathy for Rosa, while the rest of the socially acceptable characters—alternately righteous, pretentious, and puerile—seem pathetic and ridiculous.

Natalia, the one indigenous outsider and an intermittent narrator, instinctively rejects the norms imposed on her, her sisters, and her friends. This young woman yearns for independence, and her diary offers the only intimate point of view aside from Pablo's. Why can't she conform, as the other girls do with apparent enthusiasm? What exactly does she resist and reject? The world of her sisters and their friends is governed by the fear of being different. In an early scene, a group is chatting on the street. When one of the girls can't decide whether to follow the group upstairs to a *mesa camilla* breakfast, she is immediately chastised by Julia, Natalia's sister. Dawdling in the street is unacceptable because people are looking at them, and drawing attention to oneself is forbidden: "Anda, no hagáis el ganso. . . . Os mira la gente" (15; "Come on, don't be stupid. . . . People are looking at you" [8]).

How does the imperative to conform dehumanize the characters and prevent them from relating to one another? This dehumanization is particularly evident in relations between the sexes. Almost all the young women are obsessed with catching a boy with a secure future, yet their doll-like demeanor makes it difficult for boys to relate to them. One young man at the Casino complains about the lack of appeal of these "niñas de celofán" (100; "cellophane girls" [103]), and indeed the young women seem as artificial and fragile as the *visillos* that shield their daily existence. Only Natalia is interested more in going to a university and pursuing a career than in getting married. Education is another topic for class discussion. What role does it play in the lives of these characters? How is it related to gender and class? To what end are women discouraged from pursuing a career or having any involvement in a traditionally masculine world? To what extent can anybody in *Entre visillos* entertain an outlook on life that is not in keeping with the ideological and social strictures of the dictatorship? A few characters—Elvira and Emilio, in particular—initially seem sophisticated, engaged with art, literature, and ideas, but in the end it is quite clear that their sophistication is just a thin veneer. The society portrayed in the novel is hermetic, uniform, and stagnant. In *Usos amorosos* students will become more aware of the political and cultural strings that control the characters in *Entre visillos* as if they were marionettes. This second text shows students that the world of the novel is not simply old-fashioned or conservative but the product of a specific political program of propaganda and social engineering.

Usos amorosos de la postguerra española

The retrograde nature of social life under Franco was not an accidental by-product but the main ideal of the regime. In the first chapter of *Usos amorosos*, Martín Gaite quotes an article, published in *La hora* in 1948:

> Que sea español nuestro amigo y nuestro criado y nuestra novia, que sean españoles nuestros hijos. Que no haya sobre la bendita tierra de España otras costumbres que las nuestras. Y si esto es un feroz nacionalismo, pues mejor. . . . No queremos el progreso, el romántico y liberal, capitalista y burgués, judío, protestante, ateo y masón progreso yanqui. Preferimos el atraso de España. (29)

> Our friend, our servant, our sweetheart must be Spanish; our children must be Spanish. Nowhere in our blessed Spanish land should there be any customs but our own. And if this is fanatical nationalism, so be it. . . . We don't want progress—romantic, liberal, bourgeois, Jewish, Protestant, atheistic, Masonic, Yankee progress. We prefer Spain's backwardness. (30)

How did this vision of the country affect people's day-to-day lives, and especially those of young women? Women had two options in life: marriage or the convent. The former was as serious a commitment as the latter, because under Franco there was no divorce. The young women's obsession with landing a good husband in *Entre visillos* can be better understood in this practical context. To make things worse, women in the postwar period far outnumbered men, so a large sector of the female population faced spinsterhood. Remaining unmarried did not go against the values of the time, but few young women wanted to end up spinsters. They were not supposed to be independent, not supposed to work, yet much of the female population had been orphaned or widowed during the war and was in dire straits financially. Many women did in fact work in agriculture, in factories, and many were maids or prostitutes, but middle-class women needed a certificate from the government Servicio Social ("social service") in order to do just about anything. Without that certificate they could not belong to an association or group, have a driver's license, or get a passport. The ideological apparatus that governed this social service determinant of women's fate was the Sección Femenina, run by Pilar Primo de Rivera. In a graduate seminar or undergraduate course that examines in greater depth the subject of women in twentieth-century Spain, students may want to read more about this organization than what Martín Gaite offers. Following the work of Jo Labanyi, they might also consider to what extent the Sección Femenina, despite its goals, was feminist or provided an opportunity for emancipation for some women.[1]

Membership in the Sección Femenina was not for everyone, but time in its Servicio Social program was required: service or classes, ranging from exercise to the performance of domestic duties, of five hundred hours spread out over six months. All single or widowed women between the ages of seventeen and thirty-five who wanted to pursue advanced studies or find employment were required to participate. From 1945 on, women were legally required to complete the program, which was aimed at morally purifying them and ensuring their futures as ideal Spanish mothers. Martín Gaite describes this service as a sort of "vacuna obligatoria contra el tifus" (64; "a mandatory vaccination against typhus" [61]). The idea of the Sección Femenina as a vaccination shows how much of a threat the impure woman was considered to be in this society. Though many women found an identity, entertainment, or pleasure in the Servicio Social, the process undeniably had a brainwashing aspect, closely tied to the education women already received at home and in Catholic all-girls schools. Pilar Primo de Rivera declared that women had no creative talent and that all they could do was try to interpret men's ideas.

In the bourgeoisie, one of the few exceptions to the Sección Femenina norm was the *niña topolino*.[2] Martín Gaite exemplifies this type of frivolous, stylish, rich girl through the character of Marisol in *Entre visillos*. The *topolino* girl defied Sección Femenina values by celebrating a more Continental lifestyle, one that included smoking and hanging out at sidewalk cafés in affluent neighborhoods. But only a privileged minority could afford to pay attention to fashion at the time; most women strove merely to be *arregladas* ("put together") and firmly encased in the curve-hiding girdle, a sort of suit of armor for modesty. It is crucial that students take into account the factor of class in these categories of women. To look put together was both a moral and a class issue. Poverty and immorality were seen as two sides of a coin and were implicitly linked to the mayhem associated with the Second Republic. Despite prevailing notions of Christian charity, poor urban areas were considered nests of disease and sexual depravity. From these areas, from the makeshift suburbs, and from the provinces came the maids and prostitutes. The former were stereotyped as greedy and shifty, the latter—with their tight dresses and heavy makeup—as the antithesis of the pure, ideal woman. The fallen woman, personified by Rosa in *Entre visillos*, was a necessary evil: men needed fallen women in order to wear themselves out a bit before settling into marriage.

Spanish women were trained to keep their homes spotless and run them with military order. What perfumes were to the *Parisienne*, bleach was to the Spanish housewife. Martín Gaite points to the irony of trying to keep a man through cleanliness: "No estoy segura de que los hombres se alejaran siempre del 'mal ambiente' doméstico repelidos por la enfermedad del desorden, sino muchas veces por el exagerado olor a desinfectante con que se trataba de prevenir"

(119; "I am not sure men always escaped from the 'unpleasant' home environment because they were repelled by the disease of disorder, but rather by the pervasive smell of preventive disinfectant" [108]).

It was hard to be a seductress when one was expected to be on the same team as Franco and the pope. The goal was clear for women: they had to be, along with their husbands, the pillars of the family, and they had to transmit the same repressive education that they had received:

> El padre junto a la madre como un bloque indestructible ante el cual se estrellaba cualquier actitud que no fuera la del respeto.
>
> De la misma manera había que mirar a Franco y al Papa. Encadenados uno a otro, apoyándose mutuamente en aquella cruzada del espíritu contra la materia. . . . [S]us retratos aparecían con frecuencia uno cerca del otro en aulas, sacristías y despachos, en el *ABC*, en el cuarto de estar de muchas casas. Crecimos bajo la vigilancia de aquellos dos rostros. . . .
>
> Y el niño lo percibía, ya lo creo. Percibía en casa, en la calle y en la escuela una atmósfera tensa . . . que coartaba la espontaneidad. . . ."
> (21–22)

> Together the father and mother were an indestructible rock on which any attitude other than respect would shatter.
>
> You had to look at Franco and the Pope in the same way; chained to one another, supporting each other in the crusade of spirit versus matter. . . . [T]hey were often found together in photos: in lecture rooms, sacristies and offices, in the pages of the *ABC*, in the living room of many houses. We grew up under the watch of those two faces. . . .
>
> And children certainly did understand that. At home, in the street and at school, they could feel tension in the air, an atmosphere of inhibition that restricted spontaneity. (23)

But how were these pure, doll-like beacons of Catholic nationalism to accomplish their goal of acquiring a husband? The enterprise was ridden with impossibility and confusion. Young women had to be active but pretend to be passive. They were encouraged to project enthusiastic silence—in other words, to not speak until spoken to (and even then very little), and to wear a feminine smile at all times. They often tried to imitate haughty film characters with disastrous results.

> Eran aquellas muchachas que, al exagerar su intento de imitar a las mujeres "difíciles" del cine, no discernían bien las ocasiones en que venía a cuento exhibir esa altivez, y en cuanto se les acercaba un hombre arrugaban la nariz con gesto de desdén, mirando al vacío. Así pensaban estar inflamando unos ardores que muchas veces no existían más que en su imaginación. (169)

> These were the girls who overdid their attempts to imitate the "difficult" women in the movies, and did not choose opportune times to show their haughtiness. The minute a man approached, they wrinkled up their noses disdainfully and looked away. They believed that this attitude would inflame an ardor that often existed only in their imagination. (151)

In the light of this ideology, designed to infantilize and paralyze a woman's personal development, the ridiculous behavior of some of the characters in *Entre visillos* makes more sense and is more sympathetic. If the young women seem stuck up, phony, and inflexible, it is because these are the values that have been deeply ingrained in them.

Teaching *Entre visillos* and *Usos amorosos de la postguerra española* in sequence is rewarding because of their shared historical and sociocultural base. Both works show the bizarre, strict, and—at least in retrospect—often amusing program to which Spanish women were subjected throughout the 1940s, 1950s, and much of the 1960s. They offer an in-depth portrait of the middle-class woman in the Spain of the period. When students reflect on the repression—individual, sexual, and psychological—of the characters in *Entre visillos* and of the examples in *Usos amorosos*, they must be made aware that these women were the lucky ones. The gulf between them and the disenfranchised, including prostitutes and those in the teeming prisons for women all over Spain, is important. Disenfranchised women can be seen in several other works, such as Rodoreda's *La Calle de las Camelias* and Chacón's *La voz dormida*.

NOTES

In this essay, the English translation of *Usos amorosos* is by Margaret E. W. Jones (*Courtship Customs*), and that of *Entre visillos* is by López-Morillas (*Behind the Curtains*). All other translations are mine. Quotations in Spanish are from the 2007 Destino edition.

[1] Time allowing, Labanyi's "Resemanticizing Feminine Surrender" could be assigned.

[2] The use of the term in Spain was inspired by the tiny, jaunty Fiat 500 Topolino. In Italian, *topolino* means "little mouse" or "scamp."

Teaching "Las ataduras" in the Advanced Placement Spanish Course or Introductory College Literature Course

Jacqueline Gowen-Tolcott and Joan L. Brown

Of all Carmen Martín Gaite's works, the one that United States students are likely to encounter first is her 1960 novella "Las ataduras" ("Binding Ties").[1] Thanks to its inclusion (since 2003) in the advanced placement Spanish literature curriculum, thousands of secondary school students read the work each year.[2] It also has a place in one of the college courses that the AP program attempts to duplicate, specifically a survey of Spanish literature from the eighteenth century to the present. In such a course, the novella is a logical candidate for the unabridged work of literature that caps a semester of anthologized excerpts. It also can be a valuable part of advanced undergraduate or graduate courses on contemporary Spanish literature. Advanced students can benefit from some of the more sophisticated pedagogical tools deployed at lower levels.

Despite its ubiquity, "Las ataduras" is in some ways an unlikely choice for novice students of Spanish literature, since it presents significant challenges. A series of scenes whose chronology loops back on itself; settings that jump unannounced between Spain and France; and subtle themes, such as parental jealousy and conflicted female ambition—these are just a few of the complexities that must be confronted. When these literary elements are combined with the cultural and linguistic unknowns encountered by a twenty-first-century student in the United States, the wall blocking the way to comprehension can look formidably high.

The multifaceted rewards of "Las ataduras" justify all efforts to reach the summit of understanding. Successful readers will gain a nuanced portrait of a little-known region of Spain, Galicia, in the early Franco years. This cultural knowledge becomes an invitation for comparisons between Spain, France, and the Americas; it also affords exploration of still-topical issues, such as gender roles and definitions of success. Linguistic benefits come with exposure to Martín Gaite's masterful use of language, including her rich vocabulary and authentic dialogues. And literary-critical skills will be honed through analysis of the novella's subtle structure and themes. Once the barriers to comprehension are surmounted, "Las ataduras" offers a wealth of opportunities for students at all levels to learn about Spanish language, literature, and culture.

Supported Reading as the Key to Comprehension

In this essay we describe the supported reading approach that we have used successfully to teach "Las ataduras" to student populations whose knowledge of Hispanic literature was largely confined to what we previously taught them in the same course. The initial goal of this approach is to remove sociocultural, literary-critical and linguistic obstacles to comprehension. Once such barriers are cleared, more ambitious creative techniques maximize student engagement with the text. These culminate in expansion activities that elicit original critical analysis. By providing the foundational elements that these learners require, this approach gives them the platform—and the confidence—to reach levels of attainment that can be surprisingly high.

A brief synopsis of the novella reveals why supportive intervention is needed. "Las ataduras" is divided into five sections of unequal length, and the breaks are easy to miss, marked by asterisks in the *Cuentos* version and by blank space in the AP anthology ("Las ataduras" [*Abriendo puertas*]). The story is told by an omniscient narrator; dialogues and a letter introduce characters' voices. Simultaneous conversations constitute the first two sections: one between the schoolteacher Benjamín and his wife, Herminia, in Galicia, and the other between their daughter Alina (Adelaida) and her French husband, Philippe, in Paris. The third section is an extended flashback to Alina's youth in the village of San Lorenzo de Piñor, near Orense in Galicia. After her grandfather dies and her friend Eloy departs for (South) America, the previously indomitable Alina withdraws, finding her father's attentiveness claustrophobic. A superior student, she graduates from secondary school and enrolls at the University of Santiago. Almost immediately, she falls in love with Philippe, becomes pregnant, and leaves school to marry. The fourth section returns to Paris and the present. Alina writes an optimistic card to her parents, though she cries as she finishes it. The short fifth section closes with the two parents in Spain. They do not know, though the reader does, that a letter from their daughter is on its way.

Sociocultural Background

Because this story has direct autobiographical connections and since it is routine to present the author when introducing any work of literature, students will appreciate a glimpse of Martín Gaite as they begin to read. Part 4 of the DVD *Carmen Martín Gaite: In Search of Conversation*, entitled "Las ataduras," offers excerpts from a 1987 television interview in which she discussed the work and her ties to Galicia. "Yo mi infancia la recuerdo más bien como gallega que salmantina" ("I remember my childhood as more Galician than Salamancan") she observed earlier (Personal interview). The village of San Lorenzo de Piñor is where she spent her summers, at a family home described in her 1974 novel *Retahílas* ("Yarns"). As an expansion activity, students can find images of Galicia and Santiago de Compostela on the Internet and share them with their classmates.

Secondary school students can research and give oral reports on the author's life, work, and times, using Internet sources (e.g., Martinell, *Espéculo*; online encyclopedia entries); the instructor must check these reports (usually *PowerPoint* presentations) before they are delivered. At the college level, the professor can transmit biographical information—possibly reading the paragraph of "Un bosquejo autobiográfico" ("An Autobiographical Sketch") that begins, "En verano íbamos puntualmente a veranear durante dos o tres meses al pueblo de San Lorenzo de Piñor . . ." ("We always went to spend the summer. . ."). If time allows, the entire sketch may be assigned as supplementary reading.

Students should also learn about the location and language of Galicia, one of Spain's seventeen autonomous regions. The Galician language is glimpsed in a brief refrain sung by Benjamín to his daughter, and in the DVD interview the author mentions the stereotypical Galician traits of nostalgia and longing (*saudade*) as possible factors in Alina's sadness. Though it is likely to have been covered by this point in the course, the sociohistorical setting of the novella—including the impact of the Civil War on Martín Gaite's generation of Spanish children and the repressive social policies of the Franco era, especially for women—also must be conveyed.

Critical Basics: The Elements of Fiction

Conveying the fundamentals of literary criticism involves isolating and examining the key elements of a work of fiction. It is effective to present the basic categories of setting, characterization, plot, style, and themes. At this level, style (use of language, point of view, and all other techniques) is the most difficult element. A useful ongoing assignment is to have a student begin each class by giving a five-minute summary of the portion of the work read for that day. These brief reports, which should cover setting, characterization, plot, style, and themes, serve to orient the class; the assignment also hones each presenter's ability to synthesize what is important. To make the reports more challenging (though also more time-consuming), the instructor can add a discussion topic as a requirement, so that after the analysis the student leads the class in a discussion.

Content Synthesis, Vocabulary, and Cultural Information

Once students have mastered the framework needed to understand the novella, pedagogical emphasis can move to content synthesis, vocabulary expansion, and enriched cultural information. Before the first reading assignment, transmission of a global prereading summary is suggested, noting the five sections of the work, their chronology, and the regions in which they are set. It is advisable to distribute a specific summary of a section immediately after a student has given a synopsis of that section, though students can also read along as the report is delivered.

Comprehension questions will ensure that students focus on main points as they read, and the questions are best given as prereading aids. They should be concrete and specific: ¿Quién habla al principio del cuento? ¿Cuál es su profesión? ¿Quién es Herminia? ¿En qué estado de ánimo está el hombre? ¿Por qué? ("Who is speaking at the beginning of the story? What is his profession? Who is Herminia? What is the man's emotional state and why?"). Students can prepare these questions for the class in which that portion of the novella will be discussed, with the expectation that the answers may be solicited by an unannounced quiz or in-class questioning. For more accomplished readers, the questions might be introduced not before but in class, as oral or written comprehension checks. Still another option is to have students divide into pairs to devise questions for each day's reading—ten a day—which, after being vetted by the instructor, are delivered to the class.

Like reading comprehension questions, vocabulary lists are most helpful when distributed before discussion of a reading segment, so that students can prepare by looking up definitions, in English or Spanish. Instructors may generate the lists by reading through the novella and underlining words and structures that they expect to cause problems (e.g., *pulpero*, which here is "a preparer and seller of octopus"). Because anthologized pedagogical versions of "Las ataduras" offer glosses, some words and expressions may already be defined. Examples of lexical items to be mastered by novice readers, in order of appearance in the text, are *los muelles* (*cama*) ("bedsprings"), *darse la vuelta hacia* ("to turn toward"), *atragantado/a* ("impossible to swallow"), and *rebullir* ("to stir"). Organization of section-by-section vocabulary lists according to parts of speech, making idioms a separate category, is another option.

In an intermediate literature course, where vocabulary lists may be viewed as too basic, or in a class with a number of heritage speakers (a likelihood in AP Spanish literature classes),[3] a two-part alternative can replace instructor-generated lists. First, each student takes responsibility for looking up words that impede his or her understanding. Second, each student prepares a vocabulary assignment of ten to twenty items (at the instructor's discretion), identifying new (unknown) words or expressions. For each item, the student will supply a dictionary definition in English or Spanish, including part of speech and, if a noun, gender; copy the entire sentence in which the item appears in "Las ataduras"; and use the word or expression in an original sentence that demonstrates mastery of its meaning in context. For students who object to copying whole sentences, it is helpful to explain that this exercise improves one's command of the language. They may be interested to know that Martín Gaite herself used to copy out portions of *Don Quijote* from time to time, to combat writer's block.

Cultural enrichment is the most open-ended aspect of a supported methodology, and students can assume as much responsibility for research in this area as their instructor wishes. Regardless of who gleans the information, certain cultural references will need to be explained. Among these are the Galician *pazo*, or country mansion, mentioned when the son of the owners, the *señorito del pazo*, shows an interest in Alina; the figurine of San Roque or Saint Roch, described by Alina in the local church, with his thigh sore and dog offering bread; the concept of the climactic *romería* honoring the town's patron saint, which for San Lorenzo would be 10 August; the myth of Oedipus, who loved his mother and unknowingly killed his father, here inverted, in an accusation by Philippe, with the father seemingly obsessed with his daughter; the concept of *oposiciones*, competitive exams that must be taken by applicants for an academic or professional position; the idea that liberals in Spain considered themselves anticlerical—like Benjamín, who also believes in women's education—because the Catholic Church was a conservative social force and an ally of Franco, even though the village priest was often a fondly regarded community stalwart, personified here by don Félix.

Though it is a luxury rather than a necessity, culinary information can be a memorable cultural unit for "Las ataduras." Of course, the most lavishly described item—octopus steamed all day at the fair (*Cuentos* 129–31; "Ataduras" [*Abriendo puertas*] 122–24)—is not likely to be available. But the characteristic spice that goes on it, *pimentón* ("smoked paprika"), is equally delicious with olive oil on boiled potatoes, a dish that can be transported easily and even assembled in class. (Authentic *pimentón de la Vera* is sold in Williams-Sonoma stores, and tienda.com is also a source.) *Rosquillas* are another food mentioned in the text; recipes for these anise-flavored doughnuts can be found online, or American sugar doughnuts can serve as a stand-in.

Techniques for Eliciting Critical Interpretation

When most of the questions about the novella have been answered—notably those concerning chronology, lexicon, and cultural referents—students are ready to move to more sophisticated interpretation. Encouragement and guidance are needed to help them build their critical skills in Spanish, even though these may be well developed in English. Recommended activities include directed discussion, open-ended discussion, scene enactment in groups, and character role-playing.

For directed discussion, a nonhierarchical, full-class approach is particularly effective. The instructor first writes a word or phrase—a character's name, for instance, or a place-name or theme—on the board and circles it. Students are asked for their ideas about it. When they speak, the instructor records their contributions around the circled word or phrase and links them to it with connecting lines. Students feel empowered by this nonjudgmental recognition of ideas, and even those who are usually reticent are likely to become involved.

Open-ended discussion can begin by focusing on the family. Alina's affective ties raise two overarching issues: the question of personal freedom and the question of women's roles in the family and society. It can be difficult for today's students to imagine the restrictive environment of Spain in the 1940s and 1950s. One way to give them an idea of what it was like is to have them interview their grandmothers or great-grandmothers, asking if they experienced limitations based on gender and sharing their stories with the class. The prophetic observation by Alina's grandfather is undoubtedly the work's best cue for discussion of family ties: "Las verdaderas ataduras son las que uno escoge, las que se busca y se pone uno solo, pudiendo no tenerlas" ("Ataduras" [*Abriendo puertas*] 110; *Cuentos* 119; "True ties are those that you choose, the ones you search for and you alone impose, being free *not* to have them" [Brown, *Secrets* 75).[4] After analyzing this quotation, students can divide into pairs to find other thematically interesting passages that they would like to discuss with the class.

Role-playing allows students to appreciate the main characters' motivations and conflicts. Student volunteers are recruited to play characters—for this novella, the most obvious ones are Benjamín, Herminia, Alina, and Philippe. The instructor can move four desks to the front, turn them around to face the class, and give each character a name tag. Each member of the class, including the four who are role-playing, is asked to devise two questions for each character. Going around the room, students ask their questions, and the student playing the character questioned must answer in character. Though students know to base their answers on the story and decline questions that they feel cannot be answered, their perceptive renditions of characters' feelings can sometimes amaze both their classmates and their teacher. Scene enactment is yet another way to bring the work to life. Students can select a scene and dramatize it for the class, or they can invent a missing scene and present it.

Take-home essays and in-class examinations will crystallize the main ideas in "Las ataduras." Students who are new to literary analysis in Spanish will benefit from a listing of themes and questions about them. Especially at the secondary level, this technique obviates misunderstanding while still encouraging creative engagement with the text. A compendium of themes that works well is the following, which includes some from the author herself (*Cuentos* 8):

> la oposición entre lo que se sueña y lo que se hace, la importancia de los lazos afectivos (las ataduras afectivas), la falta de comunicación entre personas, el ansia de libertad, el temor a la libertad, la oposición entre pueblo y ciudad, los efectos en los hijos de las expectativas para ellos que tienen los padres, las dificultades que enfrenta la mujer en una sociedad tradicional, y otros temas que encuentre
>
> the conflict between what one dreams of doing and what one does, the importance of affective ties, the lack of communication between individuals, the desire for freedom, the fear of freedom, the opposition between urban and rural ways of life, the effects of parental expectations on their children, the difficulties facing women in a traditional society, and other themes that you may find

Students can be asked to describe the relationship between Alina and her father and whether or not it can be considered normal, to explain which character could be a spokesperson for the author, to define emotional ties in the story and in the student's own life, to discuss whether or not Alina has achieved success, to analyze whether Eloy or another male character would have made a better husband for Alina than Philippe, and to assess the importance of familial expectations for Alina and in contemporary American life. Other essay questions can probe not themes but the work's style and structure, including its divisions, its temporal jumps (turning points, shifts in verb tense), its emphasis on nature (including the symbolic use of rivers), its language, and its multiple narrative perspectives.

"Las ataduras" as the Foundation for Literary Connections

The final phase of supported reading encourages students to connect "Las ataduras" to other works. In the AP course, the most logical comparison is with the short story "Las medias rojas" ("The Red Stockings"), by Emilia Pardo Bazán, which precedes this novella in the curriculum. Since both stories have female protagonists from Galicia who wish to change their circumstances, students should compare the two outcomes. At the college level, comparisons with other stories in *Cuentos completos* are both relevant and—since students have already bought the book in which they appear—convenient. For a culminating paper, students can read additional short stories from the volume and compare them with "Las ataduras." A stimulating subset of stories is "La chica de abajo" ("The Girl from Downstairs"), "Los informes" ("References"), and "La conciencia tranquila" ("A Clear Conscience").

Martín Gaite's "Las ataduras" may seem difficult for novice readers, but its rewards justify its challenges. The novella resonates with students because of its relevance to their own experience. Students identify with characters close to their age who are dealing with issues of attachment, separation, and fulfillment of aspirations. Comprehension can be achieved by supporting students in the areas of sociocultural, literary, and linguistic content. Through methodologies that are transferable to other texts, students can be equipped to engage with a fascinating and timely work of literature.

NOTES

[1] Since the work meets the classic tripartite definition of a novella or *novela corta*—an issue is presented, examined, and reexamined (Brown, *Secrets* 76; Jurado Morales, *Testimonio* 157)—we refer to it that way. The AP textbook used at Friends' Central School, *Abriendo puertas*, does not classify the work ("Ataduras" [2003]); another anthology of AP works calls it simply a *novela* (Rodríguez 786). Although Martín Gaite does not spe-

cifically mention "Las ataduras" in her prologue to *Cuentos completos*, the collection used by college students that is cited here, she did give her opinion about its genre to an interviewer, which is included on the DVD *In Search of Conversation* (*Carmen Martín Gaite*). According to her, the work's classification could go either way: "novela corta o cuento largo, como se quiera llamar" ("short novel or long story, whichever you want to call it").

[2]The statistics published by the College Board, from 2008, report that 13,028 students took the AP Spanish literature examination that year (*Fourth Annual AP Report*). Since some students who enroll in the course do not take the exam, the number of students who are exposed to the works on the Spanish AP reading list is believed to be even higher.

[3]According to the College Board statistics, 81.7% of those who took the AP Spanish literature exam in 2008 defined their ethnicity as Hispanic or Latino (*Fourth Annual AP Report*).

[4]English translations come from Brown, *Secrets*, where indicated; all others are by the authors of this essay. To date, the novella has not been published in English, though there are Web sites by and for United States students that contain full and partial translations (or attempted translations) of the work. In our pedagogy, translation is used only for definitions of new vocabulary items.

NOVELS OF THE LATE POSTWAR ERA AND THE TRANSITION TO DEMOCRACY

Ritmo lento and Carmen Martín Gaite's Role in the Renewal of the Spanish Novel of the 1960s

José Teruel

A Complex Yet Rewarding Novel for Advanced Undergraduates

Carmen Martín Gaite's groundbreaking 1963 novel *Ritmo lento* ("A Slower Rhythm") is a demanding work to read and a challenging novel to teach. This multilayered, discursive text is mostly composed of flashbacks by the protagonist-narrator, a young man who reflects on his life from the confines of a well-appointed mental institution. Eleven chapters of synchronic first-person recollections and self-analysis are framed by a prologue and an epilogue in the third person, supplying information for the reader to use in assembling the story. In addition to its innovative form, the novel has a strong historical dimension, linked to the changes in Spanish life and literature in the 1960s, and a direct autobiographical connection to the experiences and views of its author.

My method for teaching this extraordinary novel is to model an in-depth analysis of the text in a way that fosters student engagement. Through guided journal writing at home and intensive participation in class, students are able to understand the novel's context, grasp its contents, and formulate their own critical responses. The approaches I use when teaching *Ritmo lento* are formal, historical, and autobiographical. I conceive of these three not as separate compartments but rather as intertwined elements that continuously interact. I have always supported the merging of methodologies so that students, whose interests are of course varied, can place more emphasis on topics that appeal to them. A close reading meets the inevitable need to reinforce the importance of the text in literary analysis, an endeavor that assumes added dimensions when students are not natives of Spain. Study of the structure of the novel should not become a mere formal dissection; it should be a launching pad from which to interpret the content of *Ritmo lento* and to demonstrate that Luis Martín-Santos's *Tiempo de silencio* (*Time of Silence*) was not an isolated landmark, around 1962, in the revision of Spanish neorealist narrative.

Ritmo lento *as a Milestone Novel of the 1960s*

This essay is based on my experience teaching *Ritmo lento* in a course on contemporary Peninsular narrative for upper-level undergraduates in the Boston University Study Abroad program in Madrid. Conducted in Spanish, the course analyzes milestones in Spanish narrative of the second half of the twentieth century. The reading list is Rafael Sánchez Ferlosio's *El Jarama* (*The River*); Martín-Santos's novel; *Ritmo lento*; Juan Goytisolo's *Señas de identidad* (*Marks of Identity*); Esther Tusquets's *El mismo mar de todos los veranos* (*The Same Sea as Every Summer*); and the short stories "Te entrego, amor, la mar, como una ofrenda" ("I Leave You, My Love, the Sea as a Token"), by Carmen Riera, and "Mi hermana Elba" ("My Sister Elba"), by Cristina Fernández Cubas.

As is evident from the works selected, I pay close attention to the 1960s. It is a crucial decade: by then the ties to the European vanguard, which had been lost during the years of the Spanish Civil War and its aftermath, were recovered. This recovery permitted the representation of the historical impact of the conflict not only in the consciousness but also in the unconscious of fictional characters. Whereas the novel of the 1950s was centered on political alignments in society, the novel of the 1960s focused on the analysis of contradictions within individuals. This change of direction is fundamental for understanding both the necessary settling of accounts with the past in the narrative of the transition to democracy and the return to sentimentality that has occurred in Spanish literature in general since 1980. Martín Gaite herself made the following observation in a note to the third edition of her novel. *Tiempo de silencio* and *Ritmo lento*

> supusieron las primeras reacciones contra el "realismo" imperante en la narrativa española de postguerra, dos intentos aislados por volver a centrar el relato en el análisis psicológico de un personaje, yo influida por Svevo, él por Joyce. (61)

> constituted the first reactions against the predominant "realism" in postwar Spanish narrative, two isolated attempts to go back to focusing the story on the psychological analysis of a character; I was influenced by Svevo, [Martín-Santos] by Joyce.

The general renewal of Spain's literature in the 1960s and its writers' reflections on the discrepancy between what politics and what literature could accomplish were a consequence of developments in the country. The consolidation of the Franco regime after its gradual acceptance abroad and the steady changes in the dynamic of Spain's economy would alter substantially the way Spaniards lived together and how they adapted both psychologically and aesthetically. To help students understand this adaptive period in Spain's literature, I recommend the reading and use in class of short essays and poems by José María Castellet ("Tiempo de destrucción" ["Time of Destruction"]), Jaime Gil de Biedma ("Carta de España" ["Letter from Spain"]), Ángel González ("Preámbulo a un silencio" ["Preamble to a Silence"]), Goytisolo ("Literatura y eutanasia" ["Literature and Euthanasia"]), Martín-Santos ("Noticia del coloquio sobre realismo y realidad" ["News of the Colloquium on Realism and Reality"]), and José Ángel Valente ("Tendencia y estilo" ["Tendency and Style"] and "Ramblas de julio, 1964" ["Boulevards of July, 1964"]).

In contrast with a society that is becoming acquainted with haste and urgency, in *Ritmo lento* Martín Gaite presents a fictional character who is a victim of a slower rhythm, stuck in his decadent chalet in Ciudad Lineal, and despite the pragmatism of the new times, she suggests that a critical intellect is not a vital attribute. In this sense, the protagonists of the novels by Martín-Santos and Martín Gaite are related, as both demonstrate that intelligence, when used in the wrong way, can foster irresponsibility, maladjustment, and uprooting in daily life and personal relationships.[1] *Ritmo lento* is not only the story of a character who remains on the margins of reality but also evidence that the literary realism of the 1950s was no longer pertinent to the new Spanish reality.

Studies of Martín Gaite's work confirm that the cognitive frame of reference in her literary universe always emerges from lived experience.[2] *Ritmo lento* may be her most vigorous attempt to exorcise personal demons. Its publication and disappointing reception were followed by an eleven-year hiatus—which I would term a crisis—in her fiction, with a shift to the essay genre. Mindful of the boundaries between life and literature and cautious not to fall into the trap of making closed, unequivocal equations, one can usefully explore the autobiographical universe of the novel. It is here that we find the ultimate sense of the text, since Martín Gaite's work is an invitation to discover the double essence from which fictional beings emerge: "por una parte, inventan la realidad, pero, por otra (como creados que han sido por personas de carne y hueso), la reflejan" (*Cuento* 66; "on the one hand, they invent reality, but, on the other [having themselves been created by persons of flesh and blood], they reflect it"). The personal relationships of control and dependence (which, through the notion of bonds and kinship, are a recognizable constant in her narrative) and the configuration of her own experience as a *chica rara* ("odd girl," a type of nonconformist described in *Desde la ventana* ["From the Window"]) are the axes of her personal revelations in this novel.

My approach to *Ritmo lento* is designed to enable students to study the structure of the novel, to allow them to analyze through the text the psychological implications of historical and economic change, and to help them appraise the confessional dimension of the novel in both the author's biographical universe and her literary trajectory.

Guided Student Journals: Fostering Engagement with the Text

Before beginning any explanation of *Ritmo lento* in class, I have students conduct their own exploration of the novel through journals, asking them to jot down their observations and identify significant fragments as they read. This technique enhances student engagement with the text and elevates class discussion. I provide an outline covering essential topics: space, time, point of view, episodic structure, creation of character, and autobiographical connections. Three questions on each topic offer students both specific and open-ended possibilities for analysis.

Besides the classic format of professorial lecture and questions (some questions formulated by the professor, some by students), there are other valuable class participation techniques: paired discussion of a journal topic, its conclusions subsequently shared with the class; small-group discussion of a topic followed by a report to the entire class made by a designated member of the group; and leadership of class discussions by individuals. Each student's journal notebook is turned in to the professor after the final class devoted to the novel; it is later returned with pertinent comments. The journal is also one of the criteria for the final course grade.

Analyzing Space, Time, Point of View, Characterization, and Autobiography in the Novel

An Emblematic Space: The Old Chalet in Ciudad Lineal

In "El taller del escritor" ("The Writer's Workshop") and "Tiempo y lugar" ("Time and Place"), two lectures published posthumously in *Pido la palabra* ("May I Have the Floor?"), the author states that the first thing she imagines when she is going to write a novel is the setting. The origins of *Ritmo lento* can be traced back to her encounter in the fall of 1959 with an old chalet threatened with expropriation in Madrid's Ciudad Lineal: "La casa vista desde fuera es lo que llamó mi atención y provocó el deseo de amueblarla por dentro con recuerdos y vivencias que respondieran a las sugerencias emitidas por su exterior" (393; "The house seen from the outside is what captured my attention and sparked the desire to furnish it inside with recollections and personal experiences that would respond to the suggestions emanating from its exterior"). In the same vein, the protagonist of *Ritmo lento* comments, "Siempre me han atraído los interiores de las casas vistas desde fuera" (127; "I have always been attracted by the interiors of houses as seen from the outside").

The space offered by a real facade determined the novel's contents in a double sense, both social and personal. The relation of the two David Fuentes, father and son, with this crumbling chalet demonstrates the resistance to change of a certain social group. It embodies their desire to remain in a neighborhood designed by Arturo Soria at the end of the nineteenth century, while in the now materialistic city of Madrid lighted advertising was appearing, and a beltway called the M-30 as well as the reconstruction of the Paseo de la Castellana (then known as the Avenida del Generalísimo) were being planned. This neighborhood, threatened by the modern impatience to repair, may have served as a refuge for that "burguesía liberal y perdedora que creyó escapar de la vulgaridad de 1939" (Mainer, "Prólogo" 72; "liberal and defeated bourgeoisie that thought it had escaped the vulgarity of 1939"). But this house, about to be demolished, also may have served the author as an objective correlative for an intimate reality similarly threatened by destruction: her own marital situation with her husband, Sánchez Ferlosio, whom one could consider a *chico raro* of the same stock as her protagonist David Fuente (see Sánchez Ferlosio's autobiographical essay "La forja de un plumífero" ["The Writer's Forge"]):

> Fue aquella sensación de tiempo detenido la espoleta de la novela, aunque pudieron incidir detalles que ya no recuerdo de mi vida personal, podría estar cansada o triste aquella tarde o tener alguna preocupación de tipo doméstico, no me acuerdo, cualquiera sabe. (Martín Gaite, *Pido* 274)
>
> That sensation of time at a standstill was the springboard to the novel, although details that I no longer recall from my personal life could have had some bearing; I could have been tired or sad that afternoon or worried about some domestic matter, I don't remember, who knows?

For Martín Gaite the academic lecturer careful not to reveal inappropriate intimacies or lose the intellectual thread of her exposition, "I don't remember" could be the equivalent of "I don't care to remember." In addition to the springboard chalet, other spatial foci that are of special interest and that students should consider are the clinic (the narrative begins there), Valdelaire's farm in Salamanca (for a firsthand account of the Civil War), and the shantytown on the outskirts of the city (another generational experience evoked by other novelists of the period, including García Hortelano in *Nuevas amistades* ["New Friendships"] and Martín-Santos in *Tiempo de silencio*).[3]

Time for Recollection

Between the visit (in the prologue) to David's father by Lucía, David's former girlfriend, and the admission of David to the asylum (in the final part of the epilogue), the chronology of the novel unfolds imprecisely. Most significant is the time evoked in the recollections of the protagonist, framed by two letters: the one David receives from Lucía announcing her forthcoming marriage and the one from his father informing him of the expropriation of the chalet in Ciudad Lineal. David, confined to the asylum, turns inward, and through the fragmentary and discontinuous thread of his memory visits the decisive relationships in his life, seeking keys to help him understand his present state. It is as if, incapable of examining himself, he locates the secret of his identity in others. The narration is filled with long pauses. The *then* of events becomes mixed with the narration's *now*, in which the protagonist is disengaged from the traditional role models of his father and his friend Bernardo.

The story unfolds in a dialogue in which David recollects the few times he managed to engage in a satisfactory conversation. The dialogue interrupts his monologue in the same way that his past interrupts his present, but he is always aware of the falsifying power of memory and the falsifying rhythm of events. Because of this back-and-forth between monologue and dialogue, between memory and oblivion, between succession and simultaneity, David realizes that the only possible order for his story is a discontinuous, fortuitous one. Indeed, the chapters are not numbered. The disorder and the time shifting produce constant prolepsis and analepsis and facilitate the use of digression—rhetorical tools employed to underscore the capacity for discovery characteristic of recollection as well as the therapeutic effect of the word. We become aware of almost everything fragmentarily.

The slow rhythm affects the structure of the narration, in which reiterations and metaliterary reflections about narrative development abound (Mainer, "Prólogo" 70). Identifying the self-reflective passages in the novel is one of my teaching strategies and a fundamental task for students, who will then understand how all modern novels, at least since *Don Quijote*, reflect on their own structure and provide suggestions for how they should be read. *Ritmo lento* is related both to oral narrative (the true Martín Gaite narrative ideal), in which there is no "programa previo ni están prohibidos los vericuetos" (*Cuento* 51; "prior script nor prohibition of unevenness"), and to the treatment of time that is characteristic of poetry. These associations are achieved by banishing the image of a continuum, since David's memory concentrates on the turning points of his existence (as indicated by the chapter titles) and its light obscures or denies other areas. There are times in his life that are not narrated and that probably correspond to the periods of his greatest lack of control. Thus the selection and treatment of time is closely linked to his subjective point of view. The reader must "recomponer la otra cara de la escena" (Mainer, Introduction 45; "re-create the other side of the scene"), which contributes to the ambiguity of the novel.[4]

Point of View and Episodic Structure

The novel's prologue has a presentational function: from a point in time close to the conclusion, it introduces the reader to the novel's central conflicts: David's illness, his relationship with Lucía and Magdalena, and the scene at the bank that results in his confinement to an asylum. Students will resolve this foreshadowing later, since the novel reveals gradually and in nonchronological episodes how his personality has been shaped. The past and the network of his relationships are given episodically. The guiding thread is his wish to understand three issues: his abnormality (a term that goes back to his childhood conversations with Miguel Terán), the role of others in the formation of his character, and his inability to find a balance between reason and emotion.

The novel's epilogue is a perfect example of three narrative modes in the third person: the omniscient narrator, the narrator as witness, and the absent narrator who delegates his voice to a newspaper report. With these changes in point of view the author softens the sinister ending of the novel. The recovery of the epilogue, which was eliminated in the second edition, is in my opinion fundamental—and my students agree—since the epilogue shows how the novel wishes to examine a case of bad education. David is "la consecuencia de una educación solipsista y arbitraria de un padre que siempre quiso vivir al margen de la realidad" (Mainer, *Escritura* 268–69; "the consequence of a solipsistic and arbitrary education by a father who always tried to live on the margins of reality"). Above all, the drama and violence of the last sterile rebellion by David confirm a stance taken by the author against those drifters who had critical intelligence but ultimately lost their sense of reality.[5]

The Creation of a Character

Martín Gaite and Martín-Santos both addressed a series of questions that began to concern their generation around 1960: the real value of intelligence if it lacks practical application, the gulf between ideology and daily behavior, the weight of inheritance and upbringing, the exercise of responsibility in the changing times in which they lived, and people's involvement in their own failure. *Ritmo lento* stands out in its analysis of an aspect closely linked to these generational concerns: relationships of domination and the construction of the persona. The desire to escape family ties leads David to search for other ties, but he finds that reciprocity is impossible—as his relationships with Gabriela, Lucía, Magda, and Bernardo demonstrate. The more he separates himself from the models he used to imitate, the more he resembles them. For example, he futilely distances himself from his father in order to resemble Bernardo, a self-made man. The message of the novel concerning ties that bind is a constant in the author's narrative trajectory, even though in *Ritmo lento*, as in her posthumous novel *Los parentescos* ("Relationships"), there is emphasis on the power of bonds not chosen but imposed.

Students should examine the relationships between David and his family (his father, his mother, Aurora), his antagonist (Bernardo Ponce), his girlfriends (Gabriela, Lucía, Magdalena), his mentors (Terán, the shepherd Gumersindo, don Isaías), and his psychiatrist (Jaime Ferrer). Also to be taken into account are the ties among these other characters, which tangle the interpersonal web even further (note the ties that the father maintains with Aurora, Bernardo, and don Jaime). These relationships are variable, being subjective and temporal, and our acquaintance with them is limited to the perspective of David, who informs us gradually as his own maladjustment progresses. Through them, readers perceive the character of David, whose favorite activities are sharpening his mind and numbing his emotions. Nevertheless, aspects of his immaturity arouse sympathy: his abhorrence of the notion of modern haste; the episode of childhood rebellion against Uncle Alejandro; the clarity with which he analyzes his reluctance to adopt a clear direction in life; his solidarity in Villa Julia with don Mauro, the logic teacher who thought the world was full of erroneous signs. When comparing this novel with *Tiempo de silencio*, students always emphasize *Ritmo lento*'s prodigious capacity for scrutinizing behavior.

In my experience, the characterization of David is the topic that engages students the most. The instructor should not let this character study become a final objective but, rather, encourage students to move beyond a descriptive analysis of the text. It is also necessary to consider the historical implication of the novel's emphasis on mental structures and internal contradictions in contrast with the simplified psychologies of the Spanish novel of the 1950s. Studying characterization leads us to the autobiographical approach and a search for implicit revelations by the author that lie behind the devastating critique of her protagonist.[6]

Autobiographical Connections

There is autobiographical resonance in many facts, situations, and attitudes in the novel. I point to some resonances after students read "An Autobiographical Sketch": the home of the paternal grandfather near the Plaza Mayor, the small apartment near Manuel Becerra that Aurora's in-laws purchased for the newlyweds, David's version of the Civil War as a child in the episode with Gumersindo, the *tertulias* ("salons") in the bar of the Facultad de Letras, the Teatro Universitario, the visit to the shantytown (portrayed later in her reminiscence about Ignacio Aldecoa, *Esperando el porvenir* ["Waiting for the Future"]). There are autobiographical references in several digressions—for example, about the unpredictable results of the education of children who do not attend school or about David Fuente's resistance to showing his paintings, reminiscent of the obstinate literary silence of Sánchez Ferlosio. What I stress most in the novel from a confessional standpoint is the disillusionment with love. Love is no longer a panacea, no longer a lasting experience of happiness. *Ritmo lento* presents a revised version of the antiquated and naive concepts accepted by Martín Gaite in her early vignette *El libro de la fiebre* ("The Book of Fever") or by the young character Natalia in *Entre visillos* (*Behind the Curtains*). After *Ritmo lento*, sentimental relationships in her novels turn into struggles, resolved only by humor or irony.

Martín Gaite puts her personal stamp on the problem of communication. The relationships between her protagonist and the other characters, especially Bernardo and Lucía, are ones of domination between the strong and the vulnerable or between one who is incapable of sympathizing, admiring, or loving and one who needs to be the object of these emotions. The subtlety lies in the presentation of strong figures and vulnerable figures not as absolutes but in relative terms, conditioned by their interaction with another—note how David behaves with Lucía, with Bernardo. With Lucía, he is cold, distant, repelled by sentiments:

> Espectador de la realidad, su aproximación al mundo se resuelve en una valoración exagerada de su propia individualidad y de su incapacidad para encontrar un equilibrio entre razón y sentimiento. Su lucidez crítica, en relación con los defectos ajenos y con el orden convencional que acepta la mayor parte de las personas, le lleva a encerrarse en sí mismo, incapaz de proponer un modelo de comunicación afectiva que sea lo suficientemente válido, y en eso consiste su fracaso.
>
> (*Pido* 252 ["Reflexiones sobre mi obra"])

> His approach to the world, that of a spectator of reality, is characterized by an inflated appraisal of his own individuality and by his inability to find a balance between reason and emotion. His critical lucidity, with regard to the defects of others and to the conventional order of things accepted by most people, leads him to shut himself off, incapable of proposing a model of sentimental communication that could be valid, and in this incapacity lies his failure.

After we read these strongly worded remarks about her protagonist's social inability, it is natural for us to speculate on the cathartic effect the novel had for its creator. Once smitten with the facade of the old chalet that gave birth to the novel, Martín Gaite had to invent, in the etymological sense, what was occurring inside; and she likely drew on the interior of her own dwelling or consciousness. But despite the author's clear statement of her protagonist's failure, David Fuente does share certain values with her: the tendency to be skeptical of certainty; the rejection of convention at a time when in Spanish society, even in literary society, pragmatism was the norm; the search for clarity; and the disdain for haste, blind faith in the future, and false solutions. Martín Gaite shared these values also with Sánchez Ferlosio (Teruel, "Nombres" 38–45), from whom she separated in 1970.

Ritmo lento may be read as a confession of her ambivalence toward overrationality. If readers at times have a problem with David Fuente, it is because the author also had one. It is here that we see the ultimate meaning of the novel. *Ritmo lento* is above all a revelation of the dangerous extremes to which certain generational values, which were shared by Martín Gaite, could lead. Her message is that one should not confuse the desire to question an established ethic with its outright denial, which insists on blurring all issues and seeing danger in the innocuous. Her cautionary views are also evident in articles published in *Medicamenta* during the years in question, as the following titles reveal: "Recetas contra la prisa" ("Prescriptions to Remedy Haste"), "Personalidad y libertad" ("Personality and Freedom"), "La enfermedad del orden" ("The Illness of Order"), and "Quejosos y Quejicosos" ("Whiners and Complainers") (*Búsqueda* [2000] 80–88, 113–28).[7]

Ritmo lento *and the Role of the Reader*

When teaching this novel in an advanced undergraduate course, I value student participation highly, not only because of the nature of Martín Gaite's narrative design but also because of the ambiguity of *Ritmo lento* and the renewal of the pact of reading that the novel, along with *Tiempo de silencio*, represents. A major innovation of the Spanish novel of the 1960s, which has not been adequately studied, is the new relation established between text and reader, since an openly ambiguous text requires a reader who interprets as an accomplice, becoming an interlocutor rather than a mere bystander. This active role is rooted in the empathy established between reader and character. Of all the works of Martín Gaite, *Ritmo lento* demands of the reader the greatest degree of participation, and therefore I recommend its use in class. The author, always a very careful reader, wrote of *Tiempo de silencio* in a 1963 note:

> De *Tiempo de silencio* me llamó la atención la música, porque era y es lo nuevo, la forma de tirar la piedra que tuvo Luis. La letra de la canción se canta con la música. Se me dirá: "Aquella música sin letra no habría sido nada"; pero yo sostengo que sin letra aquella música no se habría inventado, y mucho menos sin la invención de una relación nueva entre lo contado y los que iban a escucharlo. (*Cuadernos* 99)
>
> In *Tiempo de silencio* what struck me was its music, which was and is an innovation, the way Luis hit the target. The words to the song are sung along with the music. You may say, "The music without the words would have been nothing"; but I maintain that without the words that music would not have been invented, and much less so without the invention of a new relation between what was sung and those who were going to listen to it.

Two fundamental issues emerge: inventing music and words is one enterprise, finding a new way to listen to them is quite another. The invention of a new listener is central in Martín Gaite's 1963 novel.

NOTES

This essay and all the quotations in it were translated by James Ray Green. I recommend as a text for *Ritmo lento* the latest edition published by Destino (2007). I have subsequently edited this novel for the first volume of the *Obras completas* (2008) and was able to correct errors and questionable editorial revisions. However, my edition is perhaps more appropriate for teachers than for students.

[1] For a comparative study of *Tiempo de silencio* and *Ritmo lento,* Brown's "*Tiempo de silencio* and *Ritmo lento*" and Mainer's "La novela de un chico raro" are essential.

[2] Examples of scholarship on the autobiographical connections in Martín Gaite's work are Calvi; Pittarello.

[3] For their journal writing on the topic of space in *Ritmo lento*, students are asked to point out the principal spatial foci of the novel, pay special attention to the relation of David Fuente (both father and son) to the old chalet in Ciudad Lineal, and describe the image of Madrid from the end of the 1950s through the early 1960s presented in the novel.

[4] On the topic of time in the novel, students use their journals to locate the most significant examples of prolepsis, analepsis, and digression; specify the principal characteristics of the treatment of time and underscore passages in the text in which the narrator reflects on the criteria for ordering events in the story (see esp. 182, 195, 281, and 369 of the 2007 edition); and consider the relation between the treatment of time and the title of the novel.

[5] To explore, in their journals, point of view and episodic structure, students are asked to define the different points of view in the three main sections of the novel: the prologue, the eleven central chapters, and the epilogue; analyze the purpose of the changes in point of view; and evaluate the role of the prologue and the epilogue in their own interpretation of the novel.

[6] In their journals, students analyze characters and note the differences in David's relationships, indicate traits of David's character that elicit feelings of sympathy and antipathy, and point out key moments in the development of his mental illness.

[7] The novel's autobiographical connections are explored in students' journals through the following prompts: Comment on the sentimental relationships in the novel and the notion of love that they project, paying special attention to the relationship between David and Lucía. After reading other autobiographical texts by the author ("Un bosquejo autobiográfico" [Brown, *Secrets* 193–206] and "Melodías de arrabal" [Martín Gaite, *Esperando* 81–114]), note similarities between these texts and *Ritmo lento.* What personal truths do you think Martín Gaite is revealing to the reader through her character David Fuente Vázquez?

Teaching *Entre visillos* and *Retahílas* as Representative of Martín Gaite's Oeuvre

María Luisa Guardiola

Teaching the Works of Carmen Martín Gaite in Advanced Literature Courses

I teach several courses on the literature of Spain of the second half of the twentieth century. The contents of these courses are organized around a major theme, such as the Spanish Civil War, the city, or memory and identity. No matter what the theme, a work by Carmen Martín Gaite is always well received by students. Her writing connects directly with the reader in an intimate way. Her style is spoken, colloquial, personal. My students enjoy being the interlocutor, the one who listens to and interacts with the narrator. Martín Gaite's writing offers new connections and new perspectives: she challenges the feelings of isolation so prevalent in our postmodern world and helps with self-understanding and knowledge. Her writings are ideal vehicles for nudging undergraduates out of their comfort zone. Her stance on human existence as a never-ending creative process in a world full of representations and simulacra challenges readers to be creative, to communicate with others, and to look within themselves for answers. The author tells us the importance of taking the risk to invent oneself, free from prior interpretations, a risk that sometimes occurs when we speak with a stranger.[1]

El cuarto de atrás (1978; *The Back Room* [1983]), probably her best-known novel, is the work I have used most frequently in advanced literature courses on Civil War and postwar literature and film and on memory and identity. Taught in Spanish, these courses are geared to majors, minors, and other students who are linguistically advanced. *El cuarto de atrás* is an individual and collective memoir of the postconflict years as seen by a woman who did not fit the mold imposed by the Francoist code under the auspices of the Sección Femenina.[2] The fantastic narrative element fascinates my students, who come to class wondering who the man dressed in black is. As in many works by Martín Gaite, beginning with *Retahílas* ("Yarns"), the conversation between the man dressed in black and the narrator is the catalyst for telling the story.

Given the excellent reception of Martín Gaite's works by my students and in response to the author's death in 2000, I decided to teach a course in her honor in 2002. I teach at Swarthmore College, and most of the students have solid literary and linguistic backgrounds. The course was offered to seniors who had already taken Spanish literature courses. There were a few Spanish majors, and other students took the course to become more familiar with Spanish culture before studying abroad or in order to improve their Spanish. The course covered a broad spectrum of Martín Gaite's works in chronological order, six novels and one play: *Entre visillos* (1958; *Behind the Curtains* [1990]), *Retahílas* (1974), *El cuarto de atrás*, *Nubosidad variable* (1992; *Variable Cloud* [1995]), *Caperucita en Manhattan* (1990; "Little Red Riding Hood in Manhattan"), *Lo raro es vivir* (1996; *Living's the Strange Thing* [2004]), *La hermana pequeña* (1999; "The Little Sister"). A few of the author's essays were assigned to help students understand the reading: selections from *Desde la ventana* ("From the Window"), *La búsqueda de interlocutor* ("The Search for a Conversational Partner"), *Agua pasada* ("Water under the Bridge"), *Usos amorosos de la postguerra española* (*Courtship Customs in Postwar Spain*), and other texts were distributed to students to complement the fiction.

Other works by Martín Gaite are included in an advanced-level Spanish women writers course. We usually read *Nubosidad variable* to examine the subversive theme of friendship among women. Sometimes I offer students a selection of short stories, in order to concentrate on the importance of personal relationships, the spoken word, and memory's legacy. I assign several nonfiction works as theoretical background for this course also, such as selections from *Desde la ventana* and *La búsqueda*. Students read seven or eight novels, and one to three weeks are allotted to each, depending on length.

Entre visillos *and* Retahílas *as Representative Works*

The theme of communication links most of the works by Martín Gaite, with specific concerns associated with the time at which they were written. Related ideas are writing and literature as a refuge, the interlocutor as a vital resource for eliciting conversation, the distinct voice of women, communication as the basis for understanding, and writing as a means to break silence and isolation. Notwithstanding the common themes that unite Martín Gaite's works, there are idiosyncratic elements in her earlier works that help us study the development of her writing technique. When we focus on the earlier novels, especially *Entre visillos* and *Retahílas*, this theme and its variations according to changes in the author's circumstances become apparent.

Entre visillos and *Retahílas* both show the development of Martín Gaite's spoken style and her immersion in the narrow, seemingly insignificant world of a small provincial Spanish city in the 1950s. In *Entre visillos*, she describes the repressed and tedious life of Spanish postwar youth. The consequences of the fifties generation's shortcomings are revealed in *Retahílas*, when the hopes and values of a new generation confront those of the previous one. No matter what the temporal setting, dialogue is offered as a medicine against the silence imposed by the repression and taboos of the long postwar period.

Entre visillos

I give the historical facts of the Spanish Civil War (1936–39) and the early postwar period (1939–53),[3] then Martín Gaite's biography using the author's

"Bosquejo autobiográfico" ("Autobiographical Sketch"). Students are asked to read the introduction to *Entre visillos* by Marina Mayoral from the 1997 Destino edition of the Clásicos Contemporáneos Comentados collection (reprinted in the 2007 Espasa Calpe edition). The novel is studied according to the categories of narrative technique, time and space, and characters and social divisions.

Narrative Technique

Martín Gaite breaks with traditional literary modes to create her own voice, a feminine language that appears spontaneous in that it includes many colloquial expressions, refrains, and other devices associated with the spoken word. Her chapters alternate between the first person and third, as follows:

Natalia's diary The diary is a written form women have traditionally used for self-expression and self-knowledge. In the early postwar years in Spain, it served as a refuge. Natalia's diary entries refer to recent events. Her colloquial expressions reproduce the rhythm of the spoken word and chronicle what other characters have said. In her diary, readers can therefore witness the creation and performance of different speech patterns.

Pablo Klein's narrative This narrative is written in the third person and relates to the past. His position as a main narrator is ambiguous, since he can be a direct witness or an incidental one. He tells what he sees and sometimes shares Natalia's perspective.

Julia's letter (ch. 9) Julia, Natalia's older sister, speaks naturally to her absent boyfriend, expressing her frustration with her surroundings in the provincial town. She wants to get married soon to escape to the capital, to gain at least some freedom.

The author replicates the dialogues, setting, and people of an unnamed town (Salamanca) in Spain in the 1950s. Characters develop through their speech and actions as they play their roles. The realism is enhanced by the multiple perspectives of the characters. This technique acquires an existential level because, although grounded in reality, it transcends the narrow settings of the provincial town.

Time and Space

The novel's unity depends on a few selected locations that convey the repressed atmosphere of the provincial town. The title itself refers to the viewing of the world from an essentially feminine, domestic, private space. *Mujeres ventaneras* ("women who look out the window") are a constant in Martín Gaite's work. The female characters of *Entre visillos* can only watch the outside world. The *mirador* ("enclosed balcony") is the best spot in the house because it allows the female characters to gather there and observe what is happening outside. A few will rebel, ineffectively, against their imposed passivity, but most will submit.

The time is provincial Spain of the 1950s. The prevailing patriarchal family model of that era enforces social rules and mores. Natalia feels and tries to defy the repression of this model. Her diary is the form that her defiance takes. She supports Julia's decision to leave town for the capital city.

Characters and Social Divisions

Natalia, Pablo, Julia, and Elvira are the main characters, and their defiance unites them. Natalia and Pablo are at the center of the plot; the other two characters orbit them and express a collectivity that responds in various ways to the restrictions endured by all. The minor characters are types, examples of the roles available that fall within the norm imposed by a tedious world that offers scant opportunity outside marriage. Class divisions are forgotten only at the nonexclusive Instituto Femenino ("high school for girls"). Natalia befriends her classmate Alicia Sampedro, who comes from the working class. Both Natalia's and Alicia's families resent this friendship, and the young women know that their relationship will not last after high school.

Entre visillos belongs to the bildungsroman genre. Natalia feels the isolation of a free-spirited woman in her teens who is shunned by the older women. Her sense of loss and loneliness is put into words in her diary, which is her refuge. The contradictions of postwar life are expressed in the form of oppositions: rebellion/conformity, alienation/communication.

Students watch the film *Calle Mayor* after reading and discussing *Entre visillos*. The visual representation of provincial life in Spain of the 1950s helps them better understand the authoritarian rule that oppressed women during the postwar years. The film and *Entre visillos* share a focus on women longing to find a man to marry. The idea of the modern Penelope waiting for her man appears in many literary works of the time. The film's thirty-five-year-old protagonist, Isabel Castro, is too old to have any hope of marrying. This bitter realization is something that she has in common with Mercedes, Natalia's sister in *Entre visillos*. It is useful to compare Martín Gaite's female characters, who have a small measure of independence, with the more constricted roles of women in *Calle Mayor*.

Retahílas

While *Entre visillos* presents a collage of society in order to explore the idea of written literature as a haven from provincial postwar Spain, the main device of *Retahílas* is dialogue. In the prologue and epilogue, the novel realistically introduces the rest of society. The eleven chapters are a series of interconnected *retahílas*, threads that tie together the intimate conversation between forty-five-year-old Eulalia and her twenty-four-year-old nephew Germán. The role of the interlocutor is central to their conversation.

Before we read the novel, I give students a historical outline from the 1950s until Franco's death in 1975. I explain the transition from social realism to the new literary forms of the 1960s and the experimental style in narratives of the 1970s. *Retahílas* (the novel the author declared her best, in a televised interview with Joaquín Soler Serrano in 1981) delves into the relationship of two characters who seek to know themselves and overcome their isolation. Isolation is a recurring theme in the author's work, so I give the students a list of relevant essays and quotations. The list includes *La búsqueda de interlocutor* ("The Search for a Conversational Partner"), which articulates the theory of communication that underlies *Retahílas*, and *El cuento de nunca acabar* ("The Never-Ending Story"), which explains the idea of a sought-after imaginary listener.

In *Retahílas*, the main character, Eulalia, confronts her past by talking with Germán, who acts as a mirror that reveals her problems to her—among them her failed marriage, loneliness, and the forfeited chance to be a mother. Germán, meanwhile, is eager to hear stories about his mother, who died when he was very young. Aunt and nephew open up to each other in a mutually sincere acknowledgment of their past. By naming the old taboos and family secrets, each unravels his or her own identity, which has been concealed by society's gender and age expectations. Confession becomes a healing act: *Retahílas* is a love story with words. (In *Cuadernos de todo*, the author reminds us that listening to a story is a loving deed: "sólo a alguien que te escuche con pasión le puedes hablar bien" ("A good conversation can only happen with somebody who listens passionately" [170]).

Eulalia and German's dialogue evokes the past, a recurrent motif in this author's works. Martín Gaite mentions that writing requires going back to origins. The power of the word is summarized in this statement: "Cuando vivimos, las cosas nos pasan; pero cuando contamos, las hacemos pasar" (*Búsqueda* [1973] 18; "When we live, things happen to us; but when we tell a story, we make them happen"). The importance of naming things to narrate memory is emphasized: "[L]as cosas sólo toman cuerpo al nombrarlas, y nadie, por ignorante que sea, deja de intuir el poder de las palabras para dar a la luz lo que, antes de ser designado o mentado, yacía sin rostro en el vientre del caos" (*Cuento* 257–58; "Things take shape only when they are named, and nobody, no matter how ignorant, stops believing in the power of words to give birth to whatever lay faceless in the womb of chaos, before it was ever designated or mentioned"). As I explain to my students, the title of the novel introduces the idea of "unraveling" words that will be sewn together by the written text. The double theme of ruin and the search for an interlocutor is woven within and throughout. The three things needed for there to be an intimate, transformative conversation are: a suitable location (Eulalia talks in the old living room of the family's Pazo de Louredo, a space that holds both personal and communal memories for nephew and aunt), unlimited time (the conversation takes place at night, when all is still and there is no rush), and a willingness to listen. The dialogue between Eulalia and Germán is not possible without a listener who draws out the thoughts and feelings of the speaker, and the conversation that results has the power to heal wounds from conflicts of the past.

Martín Gaite refers in several of her essays in *La búsqueda de interlocutor* and *El cuento de nunca acabar*, and in an epigraph to *Retahílas*, to a quotation from Padre Sarmiento emphasizing that eloquence resides in the listener: "La elocuencia no está en el que habla sino en el que oye" ([2009] 17; "eloquence does not reside in the speaker but in the listener").

Narrative Technique

When I taught the Martín Gaite course in 2002, the excellent 2003 edition of *Retahílas* by Montserrat Escartín Gual was not yet available. This is a meticulously edited critical edition with much about the works of Martín Gaite in general and *Retahílas* in particular. Escartín Gual presents the structure of the novel on three levels: the situational (here and now), the framed story where the past is revised, and the articulation of a theory of dialogue and the spoken word.

The novel's eleven chapters are linked: an idea that ends one chapter begins the next, and the motif of memory shapes the narrative with recurring sewing metaphors. The prologue presents information about the characters and their family in a nineteenth-century *costumbrista* style, emphasizing local customs. The epilogue returns to reality with the metaphor of the closing trunk. The impersonal narrator is used to frame and balance the different points of view. The characters do not act uniformly and have sometimes contradictory opinions. The point is made that a person, being not one entity but many, has more than one perspective. By narrating his or her own story, each character takes a hand in shaping his or her own life.

Time and Space

The nightlong conversation in *Retahílas* lasts about six hours. Psychological time is as important as real time. Because things are quiet and unhurried, it is possible to go back to certain memories. The almost-in-ruins Galician family house is a perfect setting to elicit the conversation between Eulalia and Germán because it brings them back to their childhood years, a necessary factor in any self-identifying narrative.

Characters and Social Divisions

Social commentary in *Retahílas* centers on gender roles rather than on class divisions. Martín Gaite criticizes the feminism of the 1970s for pursuing equality without taking into account gender differences and for being too rigid. Liberation is not possible for women who are caught up in the neurosis of an internal double discourse about familial and societal expectations. These expectations also affect Germán, who was banished from his sister's room (and from his only conversational companion) for playing with dolls. *Retahílas* offers Eulalia, a woman of Martín Gaite's age at the time Martín Gaite wrote the novel, the opportunity to invent her own voice. Communication, and therefore language, becomes the only salvation for each character. Eulalia, especially, will realize her potential as an individual after the long conversation with Germán. Language and identity are inextricably intertwined.

Teaching Resources and Methodologies

In my courses, a historical and sociological background session introduces each book. I use an insight approach when teaching the works of Carmen Martín Gaite. I give the students a "Guía de lectura" ("reading guide") and ask them to share their thoughts and feelings about the day's material before providing them with my own critical approach. A sample question from the guide for *Entre visillos* is, ¿Por qué es tan importante el diario de Natalia dentro del ambiente que rodea a este personaje femenino en una ciudad de provincias de la España de la época? ("Why is Natalia's diary so important within the context that surrounds this female character in a provincial town of postwar Spain?"). For *Retahílas* a typical question is, La lengua y la identidad están interconectadas en las obras de Carmen Martín Gaite. Explica la función del interlocutor para iluminar los espacios más recónditos de la mente de Eulalia. ¿Cómo se utiliza el diálogo como procedimiento de autoconocimiento en *Retahílas*? ("Language and identity are intertwined in Carmen Martín Gaites's works. Explain the role of the interlocutor to enlighten the most hidden spaces of Eulalia's mind. How is dialogue used as a self-knowledge technique in *Retahílas*?")

I also assign at least one essay on the material for each day. Essays that I have found particularly valuable to teach *Entre visillos* are Marsha Collins's "Inscribing the Space of Female Identity" and John Kronik's "A Splice of Life"; to teach *Retahílas*, Cecilia Burke Lawless's "*Retahílas* and the Loose Threads of Home, Sweet Home" and Gonzalo Navajas's "El diálogo y el yo en *Retahílas* de Carmen Martín Gaite" ("Dialogue and the Self in Carmen Martín Gaite's *Retahilas*"). I provide a bibliography on both novels along with a general bibliography and make available several additional essays on the e-platform *Blackboard*, such as Joan Brown's "One Autobiography, Twice Told: Martín Gaite's *Entre visillos* and *El cuarto de atrás*," Roxanne Marcus's "Ritual and Repression in Carmen Martín Gaite's *Entre visillos*," and Lynn Talbot's "Female Archetypes in Carmen Martín Gaite's *Entre visillos*." Films are used as resources to convey sociocultural information about Spain. In addition to *Calle Mayor*, the feature films *Tristana* and *La prima Angélica* are valuable. Print and video interviews with the author, particularly the interview by Soler Serrano after she returned from a five-month stay in the United States, are both informative and fascinating.

Specific activities for teaching *Entre visillos* and *Retahílas* are designed to enhance student engagement and comprehension. Students have two weeks to read each novel. Assignments include twenty-minute oral presentations on a theme related to the author's world or an aspect of a novel, character representation in class, and the writing of original dialogues based on a novel. Students may also create a collage suggested by a text. The collage assignment came from students in my Martín Gaite homage course after they read *El cuarto de atrás*, and I have since continued it and shared it with colleagues. Students write a twelve-to-fifteen-page term paper either on one novel or on a thematic approach to both; this paper may be and often is an extension of the oral presentation. For *Entre visillos*, students are often interested in the difficulty encountered by women seeking access to higher education and in the lack of freedom for men and women in a strictly traditional society; for *Retahílas*, they are often interested in gender and gender relations. Submission of an outline for the paper well in advance of the due date motivates students to do research as the course progresses, which adds to their understanding of the works and the period.

Entre visillos and *Retahílas* have many of the motifs and themes that characterize Martín Gaite's work. At the same time, their contrasting structural elements and time frames point to the breadth of her range. Studying these two novels in tandem shows her development and leads to a better understanding of her earlier works and a better perspective on the progression of her writing over time.

NOTES

[1] "Y solamente aquellos ojos que se aventuraran a mirarnos partiendo de cero, sin leernos por el resumen de nuestro anecdotario personal, nos podrían inventar y recompensar a cada instante, nos librarían de la cadena de la representación habitual, nos otorgarían esa posibilidad de ser por la que suspiramos" (*Búsqueda* [1973] 20; "And only those eyes that venture a fresh look at us, not reading us through the sum of our personal anecdotes, can invent us and reward us at every turn. They can free us from the chains of habitual performance, they can offer the possibility of being that we long for").

[2] The Sección Femenina was the female branch of the Falange, the fascist organization founded by José Antonio Primo de Rivera, in which all young women had to enroll and participate.

[3] In 1953, Spain's relations with her European allies and the United States improved. The United States supported Franco's anti-Communist position during the Cold War, and a military assistance agreement in 1953 established United States military bases in Spain (Cantarino 402).

Teaching *Fragmentos de interior* as Metafiction and Psychosocial History

Carlos Feal

A Comparative Analysis of Fragmentos de interior *and* Nada

I have taught *Fragmentos de interior* ("Inner Fragments") in courses on contemporary Spanish literature for advanced undergraduate students and on the twentieth-century Spanish novel for graduate students. Generally limiting the scope of these courses to the Franco years, I typically begin with Carmen Laforet's *Nada* (1945; the translation uses the original title) and finish with *Fragmentos* (1976). I have found it especially worthwhile to compare these two works. Although the narrative techniques differ—Laforet's neorealism, Martín Gaite's metafiction—the thematic parallels are striking. The action in both novels takes place close to the time period in which each was written: *Nada* is set in the early years after the Spanish Civil War, and the events narrated in *Fragmentos* occur at the end of September 1975, immediately before the dictator's death. That the sociological context manifests itself and that the psychological analysis is subtle undoubtedly add to the appeal of both novels. Students receive them enthusiastically and have little difficulty comprehending the plot or style of either.

Teaching Methodologies at an Advanced Level

My teaching methodologies for advanced undergraduates and graduate students emphasize contextualization; close reading of significant passages; critical writing, which includes short papers, essay exams, and a final course paper; and extensive discussion. The goal is to both enable and model critical literary analysis. Students are encouraged to hone their analytic abilities; at the same time, they learn what—and how—I think about the texts that we explore, using formalist, psychological, and sociological approaches. The ideas presented in this essay are communicated in class during the two weeks devoted to *Fragmentos*. Like the scholarly writings I assign (such as excerpts from Sobejano's *Novela española* for undergraduates and from Servodidio and Welles's *From Fiction to Metafiction* for graduate students), my lectures are intended to deepen students' understanding of the work and its aesthetic and historical contexts. For this novel, among the relevant contexts are metafiction and psychosocial history.

Although my analysis appears here in uninterrupted form, that is not the way it is delivered in the classroom: students are always welcome to interrupt me with a question or an observation, and I pause frequently with questions for them. In my experience, students are especially eager to discuss narrative technique and conflicts between parents and children.

Metafiction and Interior Monologues

In contrast to the realism of a work like *Nada*, *Fragmentos* uses the narrative devices of metafiction—that is, the author represents not just the real world but also the process of mirroring it through literature. In this way the novel becomes, at least partially, a reflection of itself; it is reality to the second degree.[1]

In *Fragmentos*, the characters are not merely men and women with specific occupations or physical and psychological characteristics; they are also narrators in their own right. One character, Diego, even attempts to write a novel that doesn't seem very different from the one we are reading. The crucial relationship between author and reader is rendered explicit when certain characters appear as real or potential receptors of the stories told by others.

The preferred vehicle for telling the multiple stories in the novel is the interior monologue, which the work's title announces: *Fragmentos de interior*. Gloria, Diego's lover, has the first monologue, in which she evokes a morning scene: "'Pareces un marido de comedia de Benavente,' le había dicho a Diego . . . tras sorprenderle hurgando en los papeles de su cajoncito. . . . '¿No comprendes que los amantes de ahora ya no escriben cartas?'" (11; "'You look like one of those husbands in a Benavente play,' I had said to Diego . . . when I surprised him going through the papers in his little drawer. . . . 'Don't you know that lovers today no longer write letters?'"). If, according to Gloria, the jealous Diego seems like "one of those husbands in a Benavente play," she is in the same boat. Her remark, formulated "con el suficiente aplomo" ("with sufficient aplomb") and "el suficiente desgarro" ("sufficient brazenness"), is eminently theatrical and precipitates his exit from the stage. Although she is proud of the line she delivered, "le amargaba la idea de haber estrangulado, al decirla, las palabras que sin duda estaba a punto de dirigirle él y que fueron sustituidas por aquel mutis brusco y silencioso" (11; "she was troubled by the idea that her sentence choked off the words that he was undoubtedly about to say to her and that were substituted instead by his abrupt and silent exit"). The tension between the lovers dissipates after Gloria's witty retort, but so too does the possibility of their understanding each other and exchanging true words. In this scene one of the work's basic themes emerges: the lack of communication leads the characters to enclose themselves in their own world (their interior monologue) or to adopt roles in which intimacy has been disguised.

The extent to which Gloria and Diego are incapable of giving their lives the rhythm they desire is evident from the start of their relationship. Something akin to a force or a role seizes them and makes of them actors who recite a text that is not their own. We therefore see them assume the very attitudes they criticize. They search for free love, exempt from ties, yet both end up—especially

Diego—in the role of traditional spouse, each with the same faults and anxieties. "Los amantes de ahora" ("the lovers of today"), as Gloria says, may not write letters to each other, but in their feelings they resemble the lovers, husbands, and wives of yesterday.

The Difficulty of Narration

Diego's most profound words may be found in an old letter he wrote to Agustina, his estranged wife, which shows his fear of becoming paralyzed by her absorbing passion; she is a woman "de un solo tema" (36; "with just one theme"), as Jaime, their son, describes her. In addition to reading the letter over and over, Agustina takes pleasure in the telling of the story of her first encounter with Diego, which she tirelessly repeats. She is a character "de narración única" ("with only one story"), as Agustina's daughter, Isabel, describes her. Unlike her mother, Isabel "conseguía hablar de los problemas familiares en un tono lúcido y desgarrado que nunca caía en la confidencia" (54; "managed to speak about family problems in a lucid and dispassionate tone that never descended into confidentiality").

Somewhat like Gloria, Isabel is dispassionate, whereas Jaime cannot separate from his mother. Brother and sister travel in opposite worlds; the physical distance between Agustina and Isabel, who lives with her father, reflects this affective distance, which Jaime, who lives with his mother, cannot attain. He is willing to hear his mother's story "como si jamás la hubiera oído" (55; "as if he had never heard it"). What's more, he weaves his own fantasy into its fabric: it is he, not his father, who walks toward that first encounter: "echó a andar . . . hacia O Penedo da Saudade, donde estaba esperándole, con un libro en la mano, Agustina Sousa, la que posteriormente había de ser su madre" (55; "he started to walk . . . toward O Penedo da Saudade, where, waiting for him with a book in her hand, was Agustina Sousa, the woman who later would become his mother"). The encounter takes place between the teller and the receptor-hearer of the tale. The "narración única" ("one story") has undergone a substantial change: although the father is a basic character in Agustina's tale, he has been excluded from the narrative by the very person who is destined to hear it. Diego therefore never finds a permanent place as either object or subject of the story.

Speaking to his friend Víctor, a painter, Diego criticizes those people "que emiten continuamente noticias pero que ya no son capaces de contarse ninguna historia" (58; "who continually transmit news but who are no longer able to tell any stories themselves"). He lucidly observes what goes on around him but is incapable of aligning his behavior with his ideas. Víctor sees it this way: "Pero me temo que sigues saliendo todos los sábados por la noche y no te puedes pasar sin esa gente a la que tanto criticas" (59; "But I'm afraid you keep going out every Saturday night and you can't get along without those people whom you criticize so much"). This conversation is the subject of Diego's interior monologue on the Saturday night that marks the beginning of the novel. Appropriately, Diego is alone; he has returned home and finds himself without Gloria—that is, without an interlocutor. Just as Víctor thought, Diego once again goes out. These nocturnal outings reaffirm his inability to reach inside himself and communicate his discoveries, his story. Víctor encourages him to write a novel: "Podrías . . . escribir eso que me has dicho de los sábados, si le metes nombres propios, sería un buen comienzo de novela" (59; "You could . . . write what you've told me about your Saturday nights, and if you put in names, it would be a good start to a novel").[2]

Unable to write his own story, Diego takes refuge in lines he has learned, which confirms his role as an actor. But even as an actor he falters when faced with his daughter's skill. Like her father, Isabel rejects the world of confidences, even though she possesses a vitality and strength that he lacks: "En las últimas conversaciones con ella se le había evidenciado dolorosamente el contraste de sus opiniones, aceradas y firmes, con las de él, mucho menos originales y dictadas ya casi siempre por un criterio meramente editorial" (62; "In his latest conversations with her, the difference in their opinions had become painfully clear to him; hers were sharp and firm, whereas his were less original and dictated almost always by simple editorial criteria"). Diego publishes books written by others. There is no deep dialogue between father and daughter. Diego has nothing to narrate, and Isabel has nothing to hear except practical problems for which concrete solutions can be found. She gives Diego use of her room in case he can work there more freely. Diego reflects:

> "Hay gente que nace para sufrir y otra para hacer sufrir," decía con frecuencia Agustina. Jaime se parecía a la madre, era del grupo de los que tienden a sufrir. Isabel, en cambio, era lógica, despegada y segura, como lo había sido él hasta hacía poco tiempo. (68)

> "Some people are born to suffer and others to make people suffer," Agustina often said. Jaime resembled his mother; he was from the group that tended to suffer. Isabel, however, was logical, unconcerned, and sure of herself, as he had been up until a short time ago.

But those who suffer find relief in telling the story of their misfortunes, whereas those who cause suffering wind up alone in this novel.

The Listener as Pivotal Character

This family romance soon expands to include Luisa, the young maid who recently arrived from a village near Madrid. The descriptions offered by the former maid, Pura, whom Luisa has come to replace, give Luisa her first notion of what the household and its inhabitants are like. Luisa shows interest in these stories of others: "[L]os perfiles apenas atisbados de sus moradores y aquella complicada urdimbre de historias incompletas y contradictorias lograban encender su interés y desviarlo de la atención hacia su propio problema" (86; "[T]he barely glimpsed profiles of the inhabitants and the complicated intrigue of incomplete and contradictory stories fired her interest and distracted her from her own problem"). Luisa's role is similar to that of the reader; like the reader, the young maid enters a new world, one that begins to unfold before her eyes on a Saturday night when Diego takes her to Madrid. Her previous life and experiences remain behind, but they later merge with the narrative and alter its course.

Under the pretext of working as a servant, Luisa has gone to Madrid to see Gonzalo, with whom she fell in love the summer before. His letter, which she reads when she is alone, resembles Diego's letter to Agustina. Expressions are repeated in both: for example, "ten confianza en mí" (42, 101; "have faith in me"). Luisa associates Gloria, spread out on her splendid bed, with the "muñecas de plástico" (114; "plastic dolls") that Gonzalo tells her about in his letter. She can't help imagining Gonzalo in a bed like that, next to a woman like that—a fantasy that later is realized in the novel.

Shortly after Luisa arrives at the house, she finds consolation for her sadness in Jaime, who in this way reciprocates the comfort that he received from her earlier: "Nada le gustaba tanto [a Jaime] como encontrarse en el umbral de una situación propicia, como esta de ahora, a la comunicación con un desconocido que daba muestras de desvalimiento" (125; "Nothing pleased [Jaime] more than finding himself on the threshold of a promising situation, like this one, for communicating with a stranger who shows signs of helplessness"). But there are visible faults in the lines of communication. Even when Jaime feels compassion for others, his ability to help is restricted because of his close attachment to his mother. He establishes a connection between this scene and the previous one with Agustina: "Pensó, por contraste, en los estragos irreparables del llanto sobre el otro rostro de mujer que este mismo pañuelo había limpiado la noche antes . . ." (127; "In contrast, he thought about the irreparable ravages that tears had left on another woman's face, which this same handkerchief had wiped away the night before . . ."). The handkerchief is a sign uniting the two women. But Jaime both shortens and lengthens the distance between Luisa and Agustina. Although Agustina, the maternal figure, is projected onto Luisa, there is a considerable age difference between the two. Agustina's troubles seem "irreparable" to her son. Luisa's difficulties, on the other hand, turn out to be passing. He observes on the young woman's face after her tears end "una luz que anunciaba la sonrisa" (127; "a light that announced a smile"). He recites the following lines: "*La primavera del futuro / es toda de hojas nuevas para ti*" (128; "The spring of the future / is all filled with new leaves for you").

Like Agustina, Luisa has a story to tell, and the compassionate Jaime seems like the ideal interlocutor: "[T]rató de organizar un posible resumen de aquella narración siempre diferida" (129; "[S]he tried to organize a possible summary of her always deferred story"). But she never manages to articulate her story for Jaime, producing instead another interior monologue. It is the reader, then, who perceives what Jaime cannot. In her monologue, Luisa alludes to the difficulties she has in structuring her tale, but perhaps the greatest obstacle comes from her intuiting that the attention Jaime can give her has limits, that he can't fulfill the role of the desired interlocutor.

Luisa is no less a complicated character than Agustina, Jaime, and others in the novel. The imaginary identification with Gloria takes place when Luisa observes her on the bed: "daría cualquier cosa por dormir en una habitación así, aunque sólo fuera una noche . . ." (113; "She would give anything to sleep in a room like this, even if it were for only one night . . ."). Luisa momentarily succumbs to the charms of the lady of the house playing out her movie star role (here we should remember that Gonzalo is a filmmaker). Luisa also has points in common with Diego, who like her laments the difficulty of giving shape to his story: "pero se trataba de fragmentos aislados y lo difícil estaba en la vertebración de unos con otros, en la estructura" (135; "but they were isolated fragments, and the difficulty resided in making links among them, in the structure"). Yet linking is possible to the extent that the fragmented characters connect among themselves by finding original words, which can serve to replace the "palabras estáticas que nos sustituyen" (133; "static words that stand in our place").

Political Divisions, Family Divisions

The family problems in Diego's home are revealed in one of his monologues. While sleepily perusing Francoist newspapers in his study, Diego remembers Isabel, who "cada día estaba más al tanto de las cuestiones políticas" ("was more and more interested in political issues") and whose opinions, in his view, "se habían radicalizado en exceso" ("had become excessively radicalized"). Isabel, allied with "muchos amigos periodistas, abogados y hasta obreros" (140; "many friends who were journalists, lawyers, and even workers"), represents the struggle against the regime, then close to its extinction, whereas her father has backed away from opposing the system. Because his attitude is that of a person who has tired of life, who opts for remaining on the sidelines of political discussion, Diego is unable to take sides with either Gloria or his daughter in the argument that erupts between the two one day over a family meal. Gloria's conservative mindset becomes evident here. The relationship between Gloria and Diego, despite their contempt for bourgeois values (mainly for traditional marriage), shows its negative side. Gloria, the supposedly liberated woman, accepts the oppression of a dictatorial regime.

Unlike Gloria, Diego at this point is conscious of the inauthenticity of his life. Nothing seems to matter to him anymore: "pensaba . . . que qué difícil era convivir al mismo tiempo con Isabel y Gloria, que de qué forma tan estúpida se consumen las horas del día, . . . que no conseguiría nunca escribir una novela" (141;

"he thought about how difficult it was to live with Isabel and Gloria at the same time, how stupidly the hours of the day were consumed, . . . how he would never manage to write a novel"). In sum, we see the intrusion here of literary forms more in harmony with the "existential novel" or with so-called social realism, a writing style in vogue years ago and one that Martín Gaite herself practiced.[3] A close connection is established between not being able to write a novel and not participating actively in the world of family and politics that surrounds us. But Diego's failure is counterbalanced by the writer's triumph; her novel (similar to the one that Diego planned) succeeds in imagining an interlocutor who truly listens and who thus communicates to her the necessary strength to write.[4]

Female Relationships in Two Novels

Luisa's announcement of her pregnancy seems, above all, to be a means of capturing Isabel's attention. But Isabel is not a desirable interlocutor. The love story behind the pregnancy doesn't interest her. When Luisa says, "¡Tengo miedo de que [Gonzalo] me haya olvidado, mucho miedo, mucho más que de estar embarazada!" ("I'm afraid that [Gonzalo] has forgotten me, very afraid, much more so than of being pregnant!"), this response follows: "A Isabel se le ensombreció la expresión. Se estaba acordando de su madre" (166; "Isabel's expression darkened. She was remembering her mother"). In Isabel's eyes, her mother, Agustina, is a negative model from which Isabel tries to make Luisa turn away, precisely because she sees the similarity between the two women: "'Ojalá no llegues a los cincuenta años como ha llegado ella,' le había dicho Isabel . . ." (186; "'I hope you don't become the kind of fifty-year old that she has . . . ,' Isabel said to her").

Isabel resembles Ena, Andrea's magnetic, privileged friend in *Nada*. The two young women openly rebel against their mothers, who were victims of unrequited love with men—the sadistic Román in *Nada*, the fickle Diego in *Fragmentos*. The behavior of both Ena and Isabel—*despegada* ("unconcerned") and *segura* ("sure")—serves as a defense against the humiliation that their mothers suffered. At the same time, Ena and Isabel differ from the two women their age: Andrea and Luisa, respectively. The compassionate nature of both Andrea and Luisa likens them to the maternal figures from whom Ena and Isabel seek to distance themselves. Luisa's sympathy for Agustina is apparent from the beginning; Andrea's compassion for Margarita, Ena's mother, takes a more difficult path and is achieved only after a long, dramatic conversation between the two.

The divergences between *Nada* and *Fragmentos* are also of interest. Margarita, in her maturity, manages to overcome her feelings of disillusionment, whereas Agustina commits suicide. Isabel has a masculine equivalent in her father, Diego, who nevertheless develops in a negative direction. We are left to wonder, given these parallels, what destiny awaits a woman like Isabel when she, in turn, reaches age fifty.[5]

Although three decades separate their publication, *Nada* and *Fragmentos* posit a similar thesis. Andrea and Ena complement each other in the same way that Luisa and Isabel do. Ena and Isabel surpass Andrea and Luisa in their capacity to face life energetically, but Andrea and Luisa exceed Ena and Isabel in generosity and compassion.

After her disappointment in love, Luisa decides to return to her village and speak with Víctor there: "hablar con él, que me quiere mucho y es al único que le he contado un poco mi historia" (196; "to speak with him, who loves me very much and is the only one to whom I have told a little bit of my story"). She continues to carry her tale, and Víctor, who was once Diego's listener and in love with Agustina, turns out to be the man best able to assume the role of interlocutor. But once the two learn of Agustina's suicide, they journey to Madrid together: Luisa says, "Quiero verlos, a Isabel, a Jaime, a todos. . . . Me pueden necesitar" (200; "I want to see them, Isabel, Jaime, everyone. . . . They might need me").

The ending of the novel resembles the beginning, when Luisa also arrives in Madrid from her village. On that occasion, Diego and Agustina accompanied her. But Agustina gets out of the car first when they reach the city. Luisa now thinks back on that moment: "miró el lugar por donde había desaparecido de la vista de sus ojos, para siempre, aquella figura esbelta y altanera" (202; "she looked at the place where that svelte, haughty figure had disappeared forever from her sight"). The two adjectives describing Agustina are surprising. We might say that in her mind Luisa has assimilated Agustina into Isabel. The fusion of mother and daughter, and of their dramatically different ways of being, points to a human ideal, one that Luisa embodies in the novel better than any other character.[6] Even though, like Agustina, she has been abandoned by a man, she will not repeat the maternal figure's destiny. She doesn't wallow in her misery but reacts immediately against it. She forgets her own story and goes back to Madrid, not on the trail of an amorous adventure that leads nowhere but motivated instead by the desire to help others.[7]

The emotional problems that Martín Gaite's and Laforet's characters face are much the same. The manner in which the two novels depict reality, however, varies widely—and in so doing provides an opportunity to learn about the authors' respective realities. *Nada* depicts Spain during the first years after the war, a miserable Spain (with pockets of prosperity such as the haute bourgeoisie of Barcelona) that certainly does not overlap with the social framework of *Fragmentos*. In Martín Gaite's text a generation has passed and the country has undergone a substantial transformation. Customs have changed and now, at the dawn of democracy, are linked fully to middle-class life: marriages are dissolved to a degree unheard of before; children live with only one parent (curiously, in *Fragmentos*, the daughter lives with her father, the son with his mother); homosexuals, like Jaime, have greater visibility; and drug dealers, like Salvador, Isabel's friend, also make an appearance. Yet the affective problems that the characters face transcend from one novel to the other. It is especially noteworthy that the author of *Fragmentos*, a fifty-year-old woman (like her character Agustina), shows toward the daughter figures (Isabel and Luisa) a depth of compassion and understanding similar to what *Nada*'s young author, closer in age to Andrea and Ena, feels for the mother figure.

On the other hand, the considerable literary mastery of Laforet and Martín Gaite manifests itself through very different strategies. In this regard, the passing of time is significant. The manner in which the two novels depict reality varies as much as or even more than the reality itself. Luisa is a character who would be difficult to explain in strictly realist terms. We never see her acting as a maid, and her relationship with Gonzalo doesn't define her either; it is her relations with other characters that prove to be of interest to the reader. She is attracted above all to Agustina's story, in which she sees a reflection of her own. From there she goes on to identify with Jaime, always willing to hear his mother's tales of woe. But Luisa also resembles Diego in his always frustrated desire to relate his intimate story. She finally displays cold-bloodedness, like Isabel, when she helps Salvador escape, as well as strength in combating her misfortunes instead of sinking into them, as Agustina does.

In Luisa, the fragments of others join together; opposites are able, potentially at least, to be reconciled through her. It is also through her that a union takes place between the readers of the novel and its author, who in Miguel de Unamuno's words creates herself by creating her readers—that is, making them at once interlocutors and possible narrators of their own stories.[8]

NOTES

Parts of this essay were published in my "Hacia la estructura de *Fragmentos de interior*," in Servodidio and Welles's *From Fiction to Metafiction*. All translations are my own.

1 According to Patricia Waugh, "[metafiction] suggests, in fact, that there may be as much to be learnt from setting the mirror of art up to its own linguistic or representational structures as from directly setting it up to a hypothetical 'human nature' that somehow exists as an essence outside historical systems of articulation" (*Metafiction* 11).

2 The characteristics of the "existential novel," as Gonzalo Sobejano enumerated them, may be observed in Diego (even though Martín Gaite is younger than the writers Sobejano includes in that literary movement): "alienación del individuo respecto a sí y a la colectividad en que pulula más que participa, . . . exploración del camino auténtico a través de sucesivos tanteos, experiencia de largos conflictos o súbitas conversiones, vivencia del fracaso" (*Novela española* 209; "alienation of the individual with respect to himself and the community in which he bounces around more than he participates, . . . exploration of the authentic path through successive attempts, experience of long conflicts or sudden conversions, feelings of failure").

3 There is, however, no essential contradiction between traditional realism and metafiction. As Linda Hutcheon says, "Reading and writing belong to the processes of 'life' as

much as they do to those of 'art.' . . . In this light metafiction is less a departure from the mimetic novelistic tradition than a reworking of it" (95).

[4] Martín Gaite's words are of interest in this context: "sólo se contará bien [una historia] cuando se imagine el gesto de quien va a escucharla al calor del entusiasmo comunicativo . . ." (*Cuento* 159; "[a story] is well told only when one imagines the gesture of the person who will listen to it with the warmth of communicative enthusiasm").

[5] Martín Gaite expresses the dangers of the unconcerned (*despegada*) attitude in *Las ataduras* ("Binding Ties"): "Nunca está uno libre; el que no está atado a algo, no vive" ([1960] 45–46; "One is never free; he who is not tied to something isn't living").

[6] Carol Gilligan shows the importance of this theme: "It is precisely this dilemma—the conflict between compassion and autonomy, between virtue and power which the feminine voice struggles to resolve in its effort to reclaim the self and to solve the moral problem in a way that no one is hurt" (285).

[7] In Ruth El Saffar's words: "[Luisa] emerges in the novel as the strongest character, since she has been able to escape illusion while not destroying her capacity for caring for others" ("Liberation" 188).

[8] As a precursor of metafiction, Unamuno deserves to be remembered here. As he affirms in the prologue to *La novela de Don Sandalio, jugador de ajedrez* ("The Novel of don Sandalio, Chess Player"): "diré que mi propósito era entrometerle y entremeterle al lector en él [el relato], hacer que se dé cuenta de que no se goza de un personaje novelesco sino cuando se le hace propio, cuando se consiente que el mundo de la ficción forme parte del mundo de la permanente realidad íntima" (1118–19; "I would say that my goal was to thrust the reader into the story, to make the reader aware that you enjoy a character in a novel only when you make him your own, when you agree that the fictional world forms part of the world of permanent intimate reality"). At the same time, Unamuno asks that our "permanent intimate reality," enriched by the fictions of others, be returned to the "world of fiction." Thus the narrator of *Don Sandalio* writes to Felipe, his interlocutor, "Ahora te me vienes con eso de que escriba por lo menos la novela de Don Sandalio el ajedrecista. Escríbela tú si quieres. . . . Y tú mismo mientras así le sueñes y con él dialogues te harás novelista" (1181; "And now you're asking me at least to write the novel of don Sandalio the chess player. You may write it if you want. . . . And as long as you dream him and dialogue with him, you yourself will become a novelist").

THE CANONICAL NOVEL *EL CUARTO DE ATRÁS / THE BACK ROOM*

The Back Room: Teaching Translation, History, Literature, and Culture

Joan L. Brown

There are many compelling reasons for students to enter the vaunted "back room" of Carmen Martín Gaite's most celebrated novel, whether in English or in Spanish. *El cuarto de atrás* (1978) won Spain's National Prize for Literature in 1979 and has since entered the Spanish literary canon. During a night-long conversation with a mysterious man dressed in black, a woman with the initial C—who exactly resembles the author—retrieves long-suppressed memories of growing up female in Franco's Spain. The curtain that conceals a mental back room, full of recollections that were censored for decades, is pulled back by a skilled interviewer who may not exist.

Helen R. Lane's expert English version of the novel, *The Back Room* (1983), allows readers to engage with the text and enjoy it. At the same time, students learn about translation as interpretation, history as a contested field, literature as a kaleidoscope of techniques, and culture as a gendered experience. Spanish history, especially that of the Spanish Civil War (1936–39) and its long aftermath (1939–75), is brought to life in a conversation between the protagonist and her visitor. This conversation functions as a laboratory for learning about literary genres and techniques. The fantastic, metafiction, memoir, intertextuality, and historiography are all vividly presented in the context of female culture and popular culture in postwar Spain.

Instructional Contexts

Spanish, Transatlantic, and European Literature Courses

I have taught *The Back Room* in English in several different courses, using techniques that I also use when I teach *El cuarto de atrás* in Spanish. In a course on the contemporary Spanish novel, this work is presented with other canonical titles by male and female authors from Spain. In a course on contemporary Hispanic literature by women, Martín Gaite's novel is contextualized by works by women writers from other regions of Spain and by Latin American women writers from Mexico, the Caribbean, and the Southern Cone. For a course on contemporary European literature by women, *The Back Room* is read in concert with novels from other regions of Spain as well as from France, Italy, and Germany.[1] All these literature-in-translation courses are taught at the intermediate level and are open to any undergraduate who has taken a first-year English course. Because there are no other prerequisites and the courses are cross-listed with other programs and departments, they attract students throughout the university.

In English as in Spanish, my courses are designed to encourage active student engagement and independent critical analysis. In every course, I give introductory lectures covering three topics: background on the country in which the work is set, the biography and bibliography of the author, and additional information necessary for an understanding of the text. Each course revolves around intensive class discussion and also includes individual and paired oral reports; question sets for individuals, pairs, and small groups; short individual response papers; collaborative projects; an hour-long exam on each work (composed of objective identification questions and analytic essays); and a term paper with a seminar in which students summarize their papers for the class and respond to questions from their peers.

Teaching *The Back Room* from a Sociocultural Perspective

I find a sociocultural approach in the classroom the most rewarding lens through which to view literature by women, as long as this lens is not used as a filter for stereotyping (Brown, "Teaching"). My version of a sociocultural approach separates the cultural production of women as a muted group within the dominant mainstream culture. It views literature by women as foreign, socially and culturally, in the same way that literature from another country is perceived as foreign. It supplies supplementary information to make this literature accessible to those who do not have direct experience of that nationality or gender. My approach is inclusive; I make cultural differences explicit instead of expecting those without firsthand experience to intuit them. This method fosters a classroom environment that is nonjudgmental and welcoming.

As I argued in "Teaching the Expanding Canon," there are at least four primary cultural differences to consider when establishing a sociocultural context for literature by women: the limited roles available to women in a traditional society, the norms that govern female psychosexual development for both heterosexuals and lesbians, the effect of aging on women's status and self-perception, and the gender-based conflicts inherent in the role of the woman artist. *The Back Room* is an ideal text for exploring all four: it features a woman who was socialized in a rigidly confining environment in which sexuality was repressed and women's status was ascribed (according to their social roles) rather than achieved (through accomplishments of their own). The woman, having entered middle age, observes signs of physical deterioration (of sight and hearing) that undermine her confidence. Although she has triumphed over many gender constraints, succeeding professionally while also fulfilling the maternal role, she still reverts to some of the stereotypical tropes for male-female behavior that she learned from romance novels and films of her youth.

Teaching about Translation through The Back Room

At a time when there are smartphone applications for instant translation, students may be unaware that literary translation is an art or that a translator's decisions can be open to discussion. The instructor's task is not merely to scout the terrain for students, pointing out obstacles they should be aware of, but also to equip them to read a translation critically. Lane, the translator, had the benefit of consultation with the author while she worked, and her translation captures many nuances of the original. (The *New York Times* noted that Lane "deserves congratulations for her graceful translation" [T. Talbot 20].) A competent translation such as Lane's gives students an opportunity to learn about translation as interpretation, through a critical reading.

To introduce the notion of translation as a series of choices, I discuss the concept of "instrumentalities," or the translator's tool kit, for replicating aspects of the original in another language.[2] A door that provides entry to this topic is an examination of small flaws in Lane's translation, flaws related to outdated word choices. This archaic lexicon makes C sound old-fashioned. In the Spanish original, C's language is contemporary, whereas in the English translation she sometimes uses stuffy language and antiquated idioms. Expressions such as "topsy-turvy," "in a jiffy," or "to make mock of" are obsolete in American colloquial speech, leading the reader to wonder who would talk that way. My answer is that it would not be the linguistically up-to-date protagonist of this novel, nor the author whom she represents. Students understand this translation defect immediately when they are shown examples.

Lane's obsolete English colloquialisms make C seem less relevant, less compelling, and less articulate than she is, an effect that is especially inappropriate for an author who did not erect barriers between spoken and written narration. I believe that C's uncharacteristically outdated expressions in English are a reflection of Lane's own lexicon, Lane being an American woman in her sixties who, one can speculate, did not live in a household filled with young people, as did the author. Lane's word choices seem to be an instance of what Kornei Chukovsky called the "self-portrait of the translator," which unwittingly inserts itself into an author's text (18). Lane evidently read C as a woman close to her own age (Martín Gaite was only four years younger) who therefore would have an older person's manner of speaking, but this assumption says more about Lane than it does about Martín Gaite.

To raise students' consciousness about the translator as a person with his or her own identity and to illustrate the larger concept of translation as interpretation, I encourage my students to read as translators. I advise the class that C's language was never dated and invite students to propose alternatives (other English words that the translator might have used, such as "suitcase" for "valise") whenever they come across language that strikes them as outdated.[3] This participatory exercise changes their perception of C, making her seem more approachable and more interesting. It also changes their perception of the text, leading to a somewhat proprietary sense of involvement, as they open the translator's tool kit and begin to tinker.

Teaching about History, Literature, and Culture through The Back Room

An overarching goal of mine when teaching this novel in English or Spanish is to help students appreciate how the fantastic elements facilitate a realistic memoir and why this seemingly contradictory combination is so effective. As I have explained in "A Fantastic Memoir" and in *Secrets from the Back Room* (ch. 10), a fantastic conversational partner is perhaps the only suitable companion for a journey back to the 1930s and 1940s in Spain. The region to be explored is both real and imaginary, because it includes what the adult thinks she remembers of childhood. And this area is not readily accessible. For Martín Gaite and her generation, the memories stored in the "back room"—which she described in an interview as a "secret region full of jumbled contents" (*Secrets* 161)—are both painful and well sealed, owing to personal repression as well as governmental censorship that lasted nearly four decades.

The man in the black hat, a consummate literary critic who is free from the constraints of the real world (and who shares drugs that may loosen the tongue), enables the narrator to enter her mental back room. He makes possible a realistic memoir about an unreal, almost unfathomable time, yielding a novelistic sum that is much greater than its parts. Because the life in question belongs to a writer and cultural historian, these memoirs brim with reflections on literature, history, and culture. To orient students' reading experience, I share the author's comments about the novel while she was writing it, contained in a letter that she sent me in January 1978:

> I'm managing to create an atmosphere that is quite magical and original, and I suspect that this book will be one of my most unusual and difficult

> to classify. Memoirs? Fantastic story? Reflection on the work of an author? I don't know, maybe a little bit of everything. I'm sure that critics will be perplexed, but I like it, precisely because it's so odd.[4]

As we read the novel, each class begins with a student's five-to-ten-minute oral report synthesizing the main elements (characters, plot developments, stylistic characteristics, and what the student perceives to be the major themes) of the day's reading. The report serves as a refresher and also allows those who may not have comprehended the text fully to have questions answered by a peer. After the summary, the same student supplies a question or topic related to the reading and leads the class in a discussion of it.

The Back Room *as a Resource for Teaching Spanish History*

Early in our study of the novel, I distribute and discuss a historical time line of key events in the author's lifetime. These include the periods of the Spanish Civil War, the Franco era, the transition to democracy (1975–82), and the constitutional monarchy from the transition to today. It is important for students to learn that *The Back Room* was the author's first work after the Franco dictatorship ended and that in it she is retrieving generational memories that could not be expressed earlier. As an ancillary prereading, I assign her "Autobiographical Sketch." For students in the honors section of the course, who must fulfill additional reading and writing requirements, and as extra credit for others, I assign Ana María Matute's "A Wounded Generation," an essay that provides insight into the generation of Spanish authors who experienced the war from a child's perspective. Although I fill in the events in Martín Gaite's life from the time the "Autobiographical Sketch" was written in 1980 until her death in 2000, my focus is on the period covered by *The Back Room*.

Images are invaluable for conveying some of the horrors of living through a civil war, especially experiences such as bombings, bomb shelters, and food-distribution lines, that relate to the novel. I show historical footage from the mid-century United States television program *War in Spain*, composed of scenes of the Civil War from beginning to end (Burton, Hughes, and Cronkite).[5] More recent documentaries include *The Spanish Civil War*, by Films for the Humanities and Sciences; the excellent trailer for this English-language film can be accessed on that organization's Web site (ffh.films.com). I may show brief compilations of war images that are on *YouTube*. I also share images of the author throughout her life, using the album of beautiful photographs interspersed in her poetry collection *Poemas*.

To bring Martín Gaite into the classroom, I show a number of film clips. Examples are the short film she made about her home town of Salamanca when she was in her fifties ("Salamanca") and the DVD *Carmen Martín Gaite: In Search of Conversation*, which shows her in her sixties. Parts of the central interview on this DVD are also available on the Films for the Humanities and Sciences Web site (as a trailer) and on *YouTube*; *YouTube* also has videos from the same period that show the author reading her poetry. Students who do not know Spanish will not understand what she is saying, but Martín Gaite's charismatic stage presence, her expressive yet subtle gestures, and the emotion in her voice are eloquent.

Literary Techniques and Genres

For students to understand the role of literature in the novel, they must grasp four critical concepts—fantastic literature, metafiction, intertextuality, and historiography—which I define for them through a presentation and a handout. Tzvetan Todorov comes first: since he appears in the initial chapter of *The Back Room*, students immediately encounter some of these concepts and are curious about them. I explain Todorov's definition of the fantastic as a never-resolved hesitation shared by the character and the reader. I further note his distinctions between the fantastic and its bordering genres, in which seemingly fantastic elements are explained logically.[6] This definition also clarifies a metafictional reference in the novel, to C's "The Spa" ("*El balneario*" [1954]). The man in black applies Todorov's definition of the fantastic to her prizewinning first novel and criticizes C for dissipating the all-important ambiguity that defines the genre. He tells her that she should have "dared to walk along that tightrope until the end of the story" instead of explaining the fantastic elements as part of a dream (47).

To illustrate the concept of metafiction, I have students maintain a running list of all references to literature that appear in the novel, beginning with Todorov's book (in the first chapter) and ending with the idea that literature exists to recover what has been lost (in the last chapter). When they finish the novel, we compare lists, and I supply any references that they have missed. The concept of intertextuality is explained with reference to the cockroach in chapter 1, which suggests associations with Franz Kafka's "Metamorphosis." If students have difficulty distinguishing between metafiction and intertextuality, which are not unrelated, examples help them grasp the difference.

To show that historiography or history writing is less objective than many historians make it seem—historiography is introduced when the author recalls real events and shares her mistrust of history books and newspapers—I try to communicate a sense of what it is like to live under a dictatorship. Images of Franco from *No-Do* newsreels (the abbreviation for *Noticiarios y Documentales* ["Newsreels and Documentaries"]), available on *YouTube*, reinforce his ubiquitous presence and control of the media. In addition to these film clips, I play four or five minutes of a recording of Franco giving a political speech. I use a CD that accompanies the book *Voces de España* ("Voices of Spain"), produced and edited by Frank Smith. I distribute the anthology's transcription of the speech in Spanish and my own translation into English. Even without the transcript, the dictator's bombastic tone is intimidating and disturbing, especially when played loudly.

Hearing Franco's voice highlights the powerlessness of the listener—the same trapped role that the author and her contemporaries were forced to assume for most of their lives. Since few if any of my students have lived under a dictatorship, I share some of my experiences from the 1960s in Spain under Franco and in Portugal under Salazar. My memories of intimidation include soldiers with machine guns on street corners as well as isolated incidents, such as one involving a man who frequented the café where we did our homework after school. One day, perhaps after one beer too many, the man began to volubly criticize the dictator. Within minutes his wrists were gripped by two men in suits, who forcibly led him away; we never saw him again.

My goal is to make palpable the oppression of the victors, who wrote the history of the Spanish Civil War as a glorious crusade that evoked the Reconquista ("Reconquest") and censored any competing version of reality. This information helps students understand the significance of Martín Gaite's rebuttal of the official story of Francoist history in *The Back Room*, a subject that David Herzberger has illuminated in *Narrating the Past*. Through the subversive genre of fantastic literature, the author retrieves uncensored memories that refute the propagandistic history foisted on her generation. Fantasy also enables Martín Gaite to avoid a boring litany of distant names and events—a format typical of the many retrospective testimonials that appeared after Franco's death.

The Back Room *as a Resource for Teaching about Culture*

Using *The Back Room* to explore Spanish culture of the postwar era is both natural and enjoyable, especially when the professor brings in props. Martín Gaite functions as an anthropologist to her own culture, using the same trained eye in her fiction and her nonfiction studies of social mores (Brown, "Carmen Martín Gaite" 87). To help students understand her memoir of female acculturation, I bring in small squares of the four fabrics that she names in the first chapter. I ask students to divide into pairs and give each pair a set of the four squares, along with a sheet containing definitions of *shantung*, *piqué*, *moire*, and *organdy*; their task is to match each fabric, marked with a number, to its definition.[7] The dictionary descriptions are soon revealed to be useless. For example, shantung is "a fabric in plain weave having a slightly irregular surface due to uneven slubbed filling yarns" ("Shantung"). Although fabric identification proves elusive, the exercise brings home the author's point about the necessity of acquiring specialized information as part of female socialization, and students enjoy the tactile experience. On the first set of identification questions, which function as pop quizzes and prepare students for the hourly exam, question 10 consists of four small squares of fabric stapled to the page. Students need not get the names right but must understand that, in Martín Gaite's youth, knowing the names of fabrics was part of women's socialization. As the author puts it,

"Not to be able to recognize fabrics by their names was as scandalous as to call neighbors by the wrong names" (*Back Room* 5).

Another mystifying cultural allusion is to paper hair curlers, featured in a detailed description in chapter 2. I was taught how to make these curlers by the author and can comfortably demonstrate them on a willing volunteer. An instructor can simply have a student with shoulder-length hair try to execute the technique, either alone or with the help of a classmate. A woman's hairstyle is given a literary connection when the author recalls seeing the dust-jacket photograph of the lovely young woman who won Spain's first Nadal Prize for literature, noticing that she defied convention by wearing her hair (naturally) straight.[8]

To show students that the author actually did complete her project of writing a nonfiction cultural history of postwar Spain—one of two projects she mentions in *The Back Room*, the other being a fantastic novel—I bring in her 1987 *Usos amorosos de la postguerra española* (*Courtship Customs in Postwar Spain*). The charming cover of the Spanish paperback shows a young woman listening to a record and dancing with a homemade male mannequin while consulting a book. I also bring in Margaret E. W. Jones's superb translation of this volume. For honors students and as extra credit for others, I assign the third chapter, "The Legacy of José Antonio," which details the Servicio Social ("Social Service") administered by the Sección Femenina ("Women's Section") of the Falange, the official state political party under Franco. This service was required of all young women. After students have read about it in chapter 5 of *The Back Room*, I show the opening scenes of Alfred Hitchcock's film *Rebecca*, which they find mesmerizing, and bring in a cardigan (*una rebeca* in Spanish, named after the heroine's attire). Students are not particularly charmed by the singing of Conchita Piquer, but I play one or two of her songs for them anyway. The images of Piquer that accompany her songs on *YouTube* are riveting.

Other classroom use of what language teachers call realia includes distributing a variety of items, such as a copy of the magazine *Lecturas* along with one of the Latin American women's magazine *Vanidades* (which published similar fiction), a copy of a Servicio Social compliance document from 1966, and stern-looking images of Queen Isabella wearing a cape contrasted with carefree images of the American actress Deanna Durbin in shorts. I show a photograph of game birds hanging in a country kitchen with a recipe from Julia Child and pass around a can of stewed partridge in a box with a drawing of the bird on it, purchased at a local supermarket in Spain. As they immerse themselves in these cultural referents, students become engrossed in the novel as well.

Student Collages to Synthesize The Back Room

As a culminating project for their exploration of *The Back Room*, students work in pairs to create collages that synthesize their reading experiences. Their collage can take one of two forms: it can reflect the contents of the novel, or it can depict their own memories of growing up, just as the author uses the novel to describe hers. When students are halfway through the book, I have them choose a collage partner; I then distribute poster boards and glue sticks. I also bring in Martín Gaite's posthumously published book of collages, *Visión de Nueva York* ("Vision of New York"), and pass it around as an inspiration. While most students compose collages of magazine and Internet images that relate to *The Back Room*, featuring cockroaches and old-fashioned typewriters and flaps leading to back rooms, a few in each cohort will document the milestones of their own lives. I find that these personal collages are the most surprising and poignant.

Students bring their finished projects to class on the day that we review for the exam on this novel. They take turns presenting their collages to the group. As part of the exam review, I distribute a summary of the principal motifs in each chapter, for small-group and whole-class discussion. I prefer to give this outline to students after they have finished the novel. I use prereading questions, class discussions, and identification questions for individuals or pairs to highlight motifs when they are most fully developed in the text. Others might distribute this outline at the outset, to use as a reading guide.[9]

Students are empowered to enter *The Back Room* by reading as translators and knowledgeable critics. They learn about relations among history, memoir, and fiction. They discover how the genre of fantastic literature can facilitate a realistic memoir of a traumatic and surreal time. Through the parallel that the author establishes between the forfeited back room of her childhood home (used as a playroom before the war) and the elusive back room of the mind, students gain insight into war, remembrance, and loss. They come to understand postwar Spanish history as a narrative constructed by the victors, censorship and intimidation under a dictatorship, tactics of evasion when rebellion is impossible, and the effects of time on memory. Students acquire information about female culture in postwar Spain, including social norms and rituals for women. Popular culture also is explored, especially the films and songs that encoded alternatives to the behavioral restrictions imposed by the Franco regime.

Once they have analyzed *The Back Room*, students can relate Martín Gaite's memoir to their own lives. Whether assessing the impact of world events (including war) on their lives or remembering key experiences from childhood, they engage with the novel in ways that are personally meaningful. Perhaps the best proof of the hold that it has on them is that in every course, and regardless of the other works in that course, *The Back Room* is the one most likely to be chosen for term papers. After entering the special realm of Carmen Martín Gaite's back room, students inevitably want to linger.

NOTES

All quotations in this essay use Lane's 1983 translation, in its current edition by City Lights Press (2000). For ease of reference, I ask students to pencil in the original seven chapter numbers, which were inexplicably omitted from the City Lights edition.

[1]The other works on the syllabus for the contemporary Spanish novel course are *Nada*, by Carmen Laforet (the English translation has the same title); *La familia de Pascual Duarte* (*The Family of Pascual Duarte*), by Camilo José Cela; *La Plaza del Diamante* (*The Time of the Doves*), by Mercè Rodoreda (*La Plaça del Diamant* in the original Catalan); and *Tiempo de silencio* (*Time of Silence*), by Luis Martín-Santos. These readings are followed by *The Back Room* and a twenty-first-century novel that students select from a changing group of four or five works. In this course as in others, Martín Gaite's novel is used to mark the introduction of history, metafiction, memoir, and the fantastic in the Spanish novel after Franco's death. Inevitably, the twenty-first-century novel that students read (such as *Soldados de Salamina* [*Soldiers of Salamis*], by Javier Cercas, or *El pintor de batallas* [*The Painter of Battles*], by Arturo Pérez-Reverte) reflects Martín Gaite's influence in these areas. My course on contemporary Spanish fiction by women includes the same novels by Laforet and Rodoreda along with Ana Matute's *Primera memoria* (*School of the Sun*), which directly precedes *The Back Room*. Following Martín Gaite's novel are Esther Tusquets's *El mismo mar de todos los veranos* (*The Same Sea as Every Summer*) and Rosa Montero's *La función Delta* (*The Delta Function*), again capped by a twenty-first-century addition chosen by students.

Although the contents of my course on contemporary Hispanic fiction by women change often, I always begin with literature from Spain and end with Latin American literature, so as not to overshadow the censored Spanish texts. *The Time of the Doves* followed by *The Back Room* constitute a unit on the Spanish Civil War from a woman's perspective; Adelaida García Morales's novellas *El sur* (*The South*) and *Bene* (contained in one volume) illustrate life for a young woman after the war, with a fantastic strand in *Bene*. The Spanish works are followed by three books from different regions of Latin America. From Mexico I have successfully taught short stories, poetry, and essays by Rosario Castellanos (*A Rosario Castellanos Reader*, edited by Maureen Ahern, spans all genres and emphasizes feminist social criticism); a long novel by Elena Garro (*Los recuerdos del porvenir* [*Recollections of Things to Come*], which interweaves history and fiction); and a short novel by Elena Poniatowska (*Querido Diego, te abraza Quiela* [*Dear Diego*], which inserts real-life references into a fictionalized context). From Puerto Rico, two works by Rosario Ferré are of high interest to students: *Papeles de Pandora* (*The Youngest Doll*), an anthology—of mostly short stories and some poetry— that has fantastic elements, and the novel *La casa de la laguna* (*The House on the Lagoon*), a saga covering Puerto Rican history. From Chile the magical realist fiction of María Luisa Bombal, contained in *La última niebla* (*"New Islands" and Other Stories*), suggests connections with Martín Gaite's fantastic novel, as do Isabel Allende's *Cuentos de Eva Luna* (*Stories of Eva Luna*), set in Venezuela. In the course on contemporary European fiction by women, other works include *The Time of the Doves* from Catalonia and novels by Natalia Ginzburg, of Italy (her novelized historical memoir *Lessico famigliare* [*Family Sayings*] makes for fascinating comparisons with *The Back Room* in the area of reconstruction of childhood memories); Marguerite Duras, of France (*Moderato cantabile* [*Four Novels* includes "Moderato cantabile"], which relates to issues of women's self-determination);

and Christa Wolf, of Germany (*Kassandra* [Cassandra], a retelling of a traditional myth from a different perspective).

2This term comes from Edith Grossman, who explains that instrumentalities "further the purposes of the fiction, the revelation of character, the progress of the action" (9).

3I have never taught the novel to a class in which some students read the English version while others read the original (though in Spanish literature courses some students report that they read both versions to ensure comprehension, using the English version as a personalized dictionary). In a literature-in-translation course, students who choose to read the work in Spanish could become resources for class discussion of English equivalencies, allowing the professor to elicit additional interpretation of the translator's choices. One method for obtaining this input would be to choose a contested Spanish quotation from the novel and ask students who read Spanish how they would render it in English. Their versions could then be compared with the published English translation.

4This translation is mine. Martín Gaite wrote, "Estoy consiguiendo un clima bastante mágico y original y me da la impresión de que será uno de mis libros más insólitos y difíciles de clasificar. ¿Memorias? ¿Relato fantástico? ¿Reflexión sobre la tarea del escritor? No sé, de todo un poco. Seguramente desconcertará a los críticos, pero a mí me gusta, precisamente por lo raro." This letter will be published in its entirety in volume 7 of the author's complete works (*Obras completas*), edited by José Teruel.

5When showing *War in Spain*, an episode of the series The Twentieth Century, it is necessary to help students observe and question the strong Cold War bias of its narrator, Walter Cronkite. He denigrates the Soviet Union, impugning the country's efforts in the Spanish Civil War, saying that the Soviets cynically supplied insufficient help to Spanish Republicans in order to further their own agenda. His commentary reflects United States mistrust of the Soviet Union during this period. When this bias is clarified, students can assess the film as a period piece while benefiting from its footage of the war. Instructors who wish to spend more class time transmitting the visual archive of the Civil War, and who can run PAL-format DVDs, can show the 2006 series *La guerra filmada* ("The Filmed War"). Sponsored by the Spanish Ministry of Culture, it features thirty-seven international documentaries and newsreels, including the footage that appears in *War in Spain* and much more.

6Students are introduced to the notion that two modes of fiction exist: the mimetic and the fantastic. Todorov's three categories for the fantastic are the truly "fantastic," in which ambiguity is sustained and explanations for irrational events are not advanced; the "marvelous," in which explanations for seemingly fantastic elements exist but belong to the realm of the supernatural; and "the uncanny," (the genre of "El balneario" ["The Spa"]), in which events "may be readily accounted for by the laws of reason" (*Fantastic* 46) but nevertheless evoke the surprise, shock, and unease that are associated with fantastic literature. The fantastic and the uncanny both appear in Martín Gaite's work, where they point to the need for subversion—both personal and literary—in the face of repression.

7Although the colors of these fabrics can vary according to availability, white piqué is a nice touch, since in "The Black Hat" (chapter 2), C recalls wearing a white piqué suit when she visited Amarante, Portugal, as a young adult.

8Though unnamed in *The Back Room*, the woman was Carmen Laforet, who won the prize for her first novel, *Nada*.

[9]The outline begins with the dedication to Lewis Carroll and the epigraph by Georges Bataille. Chapter 1, "The Barefoot Man," contains the motifs of insomnia, first memories of childhood, ruminations about the letter *C*, popular culture and female culture (fabrics, the magazine *Lecturas*, short novels by Elisabeth Mulder, romantic names, American movie stars of the 1940s, songs known as boleros), pills, Grandmother Rosario's sewing basket, Todorov's *Introduction to Fantastic Literature*, and the letter from an unknown man. Chapter 2, "The Black Hat," features the late-night phone call, the cockroach, the initial interview, the storm, "The World Turned Topsy-Turvy," the pages next to the typewriter, fantastic literature, "The Spa" and a real trip to a spa in 1944, history in books and newspapers, romantic novels, C's trip to Coimbra, the Servicio Social and the Women's Section, the game of going to the bomb shelter, the back room of her home in Salamanca, Carmencita Franco, hair curlers and female standards of beauty, and the war and postwar years. Chapter 3, "Come to Cúnigan Soon," contains a stay in the kitchen, courtship customs in postwar Spain, a rebellion against order, memories of the Madrid of her youth including visits to her grandparents' house, Cúnigan, dressmakers (seamstresses vs. "modistes") and the theater, the dual meaning of the back room, the menacing "bad end," and Queen Isabella as a role model (with the Women's Section magazine *Y* named for her). Chapter 4, "Red Light," has motifs of the white pebbles in an enchanted forest, the pills in the little gold box, the game "red light–green light," her father's black Pontiac, the murder of her Uncle Joaquín, norms of conduct for women, the death of Franco, and a phone call. Chapter 5, "A False-Bottomed Valise," contains a conversation with Carola; information about Alejandro; letters signed by C; popular culture in the form of the movie *Rebecca*, the magazine *Y*, and Conchita Piquer and her boleros; the "decent young women of the new Spain"; the false-bottomed valise; and her 1963 novel *Ritmo lento* ("A Slower Rhythm"). Chapter 6, "The Island of Bergai," contains motifs of Robinson Crusoe and the literature of evasion, scarcity and the transformation of the back room, women's romance novels and the protagonists' names Esmeralda and Alejandro, and friendship personified by the author's young companion (identified in "An Autobiographical Sketch" as Sofía Bermejo, which explains the "Ber" in "Bergai"). Chapter 7, "The Little Gold Box," features a conversation with her daughter, the presence of the little gold box, a new perception of cockroaches, and one hundred and eighty-two pages.

El cuarto de atrás, the Fantastic, and the Peninsular Survey Course

Dale J. Pratt

Teachers who may wish to include Martín Gaite in their syllabi but cannot devote more than three or four class sessions to her work can fit *El cuarto de atrás* (*The Back Room*) into a larger course on the fantastic and Spanish literature. I have used *Cuarto* as the culminating text in my survey course on Peninsular literature for the last ten years. Although this course is taught exclusively in Spanish at my university, the approach is also applicable to a survey of Spanish literature in English translation. In Brigham Young University's Spanish curriculum there is only one course devoted to a panorama of Spanish literature, a sad constraint that has in the past made for long lists of canonical texts and authors we "should read," each of which received only scant attention. Students taking this course generally have had an introduction to Hispanic literature course and perhaps our course on Iberian culture. Although intermediate to advanced in their speaking abilities, most find the seven-to-eight-page final paper assignment a daunting challenge. Previously I had an additional problem teaching this course: we would run short of class time, and the semester would wrap up just as we arrived at the twentieth century.

The Fantastic in Spanish Literary History

As a metafictional text combining personal memoir, narrative self-consciousness, and theorizing about the fantastic, *Cuarto* supplies a useful means of organizing discussion of Spanish literary history around questions of the marvelous, the uncanny, and the fantastic. Although of course many great texts from Spain have little to do with the fantastic, questioning any text's relation to the fantastic fosters exploration of all plays, poems, and narrative texts and their interpretive horizons. Despite Kathleen M. Glenn's assertion that "before the twentieth century fantastic elements were relatively infrequent in Hispanic literature" ("Martín Gaite" 165), texts ranging from the *Poema de Mio Cid* (1140; "Poem of El Cid") and Gonzalo de Berceo's *Los milagros de Nuestra Señora* (1240?; "Miracles of Our Lady") through Saint Teresa's *Libro de la vida* (1562–65; "The Book of Her Life"), Miguel de Cervantes's *Don Quijote* (1605, 1615), and Lope de Vega's *El caballero de Olmedo* (1620; "The Gentleman of Olmedo"), to José Zorrilla's *Don Juan Tenorio* (1884), Benito Pérez Galdós's "La novela en el tranvía" (1871; "The Novel on the Streetcar"), Emilia Pardo Bazán's "La santa de Karnar" (1891; "The Holy Woman of Karnar"), Antonio Machado's "La tierra de Alvargonzález" (1912; "Alvargonzález's Land"), and Miguel de Unamuno's "Mecanópolis" (1913) share in varying degrees an engagement with the supernatural or uncanny. Literature, paradoxically both the definer of and replacement for the real, ever deals with questions at the core of the fantastic. As Tzvetan

Todorov explains, "[O]n the one hand, it [the fantastic] represents the quintessence of literature . . . on the other hand, though, it is only a propaedeutics to literature" (*Fantastic* 168).

Cuarto explicitly and repeatedly cites Todorov's *The Fantastic* and self-consciously undertakes to become a fantastic text through investigation of his themes of the self. This engagement with the fantastic serves as a heuristic invitation for students as they look back on Spanish literary history. The reading and critical thinking in *Cuarto* model our department's desired outcomes for students of this survey course. *Cuarto* also models serious grappling with theory and can encourage students to use new theoretical tools to examine Todorov's structuralist methodology.

El cuarto de atrás *as the Culmination of a Literary Survey*

Undergraduate students in general find *Cuarto* a difficult read. The first chapter begins in medias res as the narrator wavers on the edge of sleep. Present and past flow together in her mind—"by intertwining the real with the fantastic, the author perfectly illustrates the confusion of real and unreal which characterizes all childhood memories" (Brown, "Fantastic Memoir" 19). Recollections are falsely or incompletely perceived as the narrator jumps between the idealized plots of the romantic novels she read as an adolescent and episodes that really occurred. Moments rich in symbolism (the stacks of books throughout her apartment, the sewing basket filled with knotted threads, the tripping over Todorov's book, the cockroach) mingle with jumbled memories of life in Franco's Spain; snippets of musical, cinematic, and literary texts; references to Martín Gaite's other writings; dialogue between the narrator and the mysterious man in black; and the confusing telephone conversation in chapter 5 between the narrator and Carola, who perhaps has dialed a wrong number. The text celebrates its ambiguity, thereby frustrating the efforts of the naive reader who seeks a unitary, definitive reading. Additionally, male students sometimes report difficulty identifying with the female narrator.

All these challenges make the book immensely rewarding to students who learn to read it. Part of the pleasure of this text derives from its realistic depiction of the world of childhood. The novel also evokes the awkwardness and role-playing of the adolescent, who mixes diverse elements of pop and traditional culture in repeated experiments in forming and living a life. Stephanie Sieburth expresses the feeling: "[I]f I could talk to Carmen Martín Gaite . . . I would thank her for capturing in such a compelling way the spark that songs and films can ignite in an individual, sparks that constitute new reasons for living and new ways of living" (237). The young male reader coming into contact with the stream of the narrator's memories can indeed learn to feel wonder at a different way of experiencing the world.

My survey course culminates in the reading of *Cuarto*. Texts from different centuries dialogue with each other—Jorge Manrique's fifteenth-century

Coplas (*Couplets for the Death of His Father*) with Gustavo Adolfo Bécquer's nineteenth-century "El rayo de luna" ("The Moonbeam"), Calderón's seventeenth-century *La dama duende* (*The Phantom Lady*) with José de Espronceda's nineteenth-century *El estudiante de Salamanca* ("The Student of Salamanca"), don Juan Manuel's medieval story of the wizard don Yllán with Galdós's modern "La novela en el tranvía," mirroring the intertextual and allusional dialogues in *Cuarto*. Martín Gaite's novel speaks to them all. Its quotidian setting and concern with seemingly trivial details complete the modern decentering of the supernatural begun in the Renaissance, yet leave room in the back for wonder, enchantment, and strange visitors in the night. All this is a welcome reassurance for the modern reader beset with the challenges of climate change and economic uncertainties (at a time when the phrase "We need a miracle" has retained its sincerity and urgency). *Cuarto* also records an adolescence lived under Franco and interrogates what constitutes valuable history, how to preserve it, and why. The novel playfully reveals the processes of creativity involved in writing literature and assigning meanings, from the perspective of a mature, accomplished woman.

El cuarto de atrás *and Todorov's Theory of the Fantastic*

Cuarto is a fantastic novel, with the interesting twist that it cites theory about fantastic literature. Many critics have discussed the place of Todorov's book in the novel.[1] Against them, Debra A. Castillo dismisses Todorov's presence in the novel as a red herring. In a highly illuminating discussion of the motif of the never-ending story, she asserts, "[T]he fantastic form fails to account for the power of the novel," and, "[W]e can approach the power of the text only by removing the formal constraints that mark the limits of the literary product—for such an analysis Todorov is a decoy rather than an aid" (815). But Glenn suggests that the relation between Todorov's book and *Cuarto* "is comparable to that which exists between the novels of chivalry and *Don Quijote*. Martín Gaite has chosen to play with and go beyond Todorov's analysis of the fantastic, but his analysis has been indispensable as a point of departure" ("*El cuarto de atrás*" 150–51). Unlike fantastic texts written in earlier centuries, *Cuarto* knows and remembers Todorov, hence the substantial critical energy expended to discern or deny his influence on the book. Part of our class discussion revolves around the debate over his role in *Cuarto*, following points made by Castillo, Glenn ("Martín Gaite"), and Joan Brown ("Fantastic Memoir"). Perhaps the best way to address the issue is to examine how the novel creatively misremembers Todorov, making *The Fantastic* a map of an idealized world much like the island of Bergai or the fanciful Cúnigan remembered from the narrator's childhood.[2]

Todorov approaches the fantastic as a fulcrum between the uncanny (an ostensibly supernatural event in a text later explained and resolved, however tenuously, according to rational principles) and the marvelous (an inexplicable event later accepted as truly supernatural). The fantastic arises during the moment of hesitation in the face of a supernatural or inexplicable event, hesitation elicited in the reader and in one or more of the characters. The reader, who until this point has understood the world of the text to be governed by laws of the real world, must decide whether or not that world is so governed. The ascription of rational explanations (e.g., an illusion involving coincidence, tricks, or misperceptions, or an imaginary experience involving a dream, drugs, or madness) moves the event into the category of the uncanny, and the reading can proceed. If no such explanation can be found, the reader must endure the ambiguity until the text finally does give an explanation or else entertain the idea that the world of the text is actually one in which miracles occur (see 24–40). A modern example of the uncanny familiar to students is the animated television series *Scooby Doo*: a crook dresses as a monster or fakes a ghost haunting—to drive down real estate prices, for instance—a scheme thwarted by the gang when Velma explains the supernatural occurrences and Freddie unmasks the culprit. On the other hand, everyday use of magic clearly marks J. K. Rowling's Harry Potter series as marvelous. The resolution of a fantastic moment alters all that has gone before, as in M. Knight Shyamalan's *The Sixth Sense* and *Unbreakable*; in each, a dramatic discovery profoundly changes the viewers' understanding of the film's world and their interpretation of the film's narrative. If a text never resolves the doubt about the apparently supernatural occurrence, it constitutes a rare example of a purely fantastic text like that of Julio Cortázar's "La noche boca arriba" ("The Night Face-Up"), in which a man experiences two competing realities, a hospitalization following a motorcycle accident and a ceremony in which Aztecs prepare to sacrifice him to their gods.

Todorov sees the fantastic as arising during the eighteenth century and ending early in the twentieth (166); he notes, however, that examples of the supernatural can be found throughout the history of literature (34). The dates he gives for the heyday of the fantastic are really those of the uncanny, corresponding to a time when efforts to rationalize the supernatural were seen as fruitful, not heretical. To incorporate his theorizing into a panoramic view of Spanish literary history involves stretching the limit of his definition of the fantastic to include texts ranging from "El romance del Infante Arnaldos" ("Lord Arnaldos") in the fifteenth century through *El caballero de Olmedo* in the seventeenth century to *Cuarto* in the twentieth. Although the most tension exists between the fantastic and the supernatural, with the possibility of the uncanny being an afterthought, such an approach opens a wealth of possible reading experiences for the undergraduate.

Cuarto is a fantastic novel; the presence of a completed manuscript where none existed before suggests supernatural action. But Todorov avers that the twentieth century no longer needs the fantastic: "[P]sychoanalysis has replaced (and thereby has made useless) the literature of the fantastic" (160). My students rebel at this idea; indeed, a glimpse at the marquee of the nearest cineplex shows that the fantastic remains alive and well in the modern imagination. What *Cuarto* accomplishes, though, is a revalorization of the psychological as fantastic terrain; it blurs any divisions among the author's memories, the interview with the man in black, and the process of writing the novel in such a way that exploration of the psychological ineluctably leads to the fantastic—not from the fantastic to the psychological, as Todorov would have it.

The supernatural operates in *Cuarto* on three levels. First, it brims with fantastic elements: the mysterious midnight visitor, the pathetic fallacy of the thunderous stormy night, the narrator's conversation with her younger self in the mirror, and most important, the increasing number of manuscript pages beneath the visitor's hat, pages that culminate in the completed *Cuarto* (see esp. Glenn, "Martín Gaite"; Brown, "Fantastic Memoir"). But for the novel to be truly fantastic, the reader must experience doubt as to the supernatural character of events, and the novel assiduously proffers possible rational explanations: it could all be a dream, the visitor's late arrival (and Carola's call) could be coincidental, and the papers in the typewriter and in the stack could somehow be a trick by the man in black. By suspending the rules of so-called realistic fiction and underscoring its own fictionality, the novel as metafiction becomes supernatural. Its new reality is what Linda Hutcheon terms "process mimesis" as opposed to the "product mimesis" of nineteenth-century realism (39–47). Metafiction causes the reader to hesitate à la Todorov. Also, life itself under Franco assumed an unreal character. In essence, what is supernatural about the novel is that people could experience childhood and adolescence during the Franco years and that now, after Franco's death, childhood could be treasured or mourned through storytelling. Brown explains:

> [F]or Martín Gaite's generation of Spanish children, childhood memories are necessarily unreal because they deal with an era which is without parallel. The fantastic mode intensifies the bizarre nature of the period in which the narrator grew up. By approaching the real facts of the war and the postwar era through the fantastic mode of narrative, the author subtly and effectively underscores the fantastic aura of the past four decades.
> ("Fantastic Memoir" 19)

It must be remembered that the narrator's world in *Cuarto* is far removed in place, time, and historical context from those of today's North American undergraduates, many of whom have only the vaguest idea of who Franco was. This distance makes the world of the narrator even stranger to them.

At the end of *The Fantastic*, Todorov makes an important shift: "[The question is] no longer 'what is the fantastic?' but '*why*' is the fantastic?" (158). I include this question on the final exam for my survey course. The students' best answers involve the recovery of postwar reality and an interpretation of the image of the white pebbles and bread crumbs from Charles Perrault's fairy tale "Hop o' My Thumb" (or "Little Tom Thumb"; the Spanish "Pulgarcito" is rendered as "Tom Thumb" in Lane's translation of *Cuarto*). They discuss the tale as invoked by the man in black (*Cuarto* 94 [*Back Room* 102] and 103 [112]) and by the narrator (120 [138] and 138 [162]). The white pebbles represent the dates, the facts of official history, stories sought in newspaper archives; the crumbs represent the subjective, the personal anecdotes, the atmosphere of postwar Spain and the feelings of those inhabiting it. Interestingly, the man in black creatively misreads Perrault's tale, in which Tom Thumb first leads his siblings home from the woods by leaving a trail of white pebbles. Prevented from gathering pebbles the next time, he spreads bread crumbs, but the birds eat them, leaving him hopelessly lost in the woods. The man in black reverses the order—unsuccessful bread crumbs the first time, pebbles the second time—though metaphorically he considers that the crumbs make the more successful, less confining trail; his revision of the tale is neither noticed by the narrator nor made explicit in the narrative (94 [102]). The man in black does not value the white pebbles of history. Unlike in Perrault's tale, the crumbs lead to home, to the narrator's childhood. History clearly is as linguistic a construct as fiction, but the narrator eschews the archives of written language in favor of the more personal, oral language of recounted memory (103 [114]). This bread-crumb mode of history writing becomes fantastic as we recall Todorov's concluding chapter, which evokes a Kafkaesque, generalized fantastic in which "the 'normal' man is precisely the fantastic being; the fantastic becomes the rule, not the exception" (173). The fantastic in *Cuarto* arises naturally through the narrator's ambiguous, semi-Proustian recollections of an unreal reality, whose seemingly Faustian bargain with the man in black opens the floodgate of memory.[3]

Techniques for Teaching the Novel to Undergraduates

I have students read *Cuarto* about three weeks before the end of the semester.[4] We spend four class periods discussing the novel. Initially I gave reading quizzes but learned that even the most disciplined students were having difficulty with the book and could not perform well on the quizzes. Now I provide a small study guide, which includes brief encyclopedia articles on metafiction and on the Civil War and Franco, a list of names and texts mentioned in *Cuarto*, Glenn's article "Martín Gaite" (not to be read until they have completed the first two chapters of the novel), and a set of study questions and discussion topics they are to prepare for class (see the appendix to this essay). We outline what the narrator and the man in black say to each other and what is happening in the rest of the text—for instance, where the narrator stands in chapter 3 (the kitchen), what she was supposed to read in the 1940s (the journal *Y*, from the Women's Section of the Falangist party) as opposed to what she and her friends enjoyed reading (romance novels), and what happened on the trip to Burgos. We divide into small groups and then report after examining important images such as the white pebbles and bread crumbs, the back room (in all its many forms), and the growing stack of manuscript pages.

On the last day, we discuss the relations among metafiction, official history, and memoir and address the role of Todorov and the fantastic in the text. By the third or fourth day on *Cuarto*, even the doubting Thomases in the back have something to say about *Cuarto*'s place in Spanish literary history. The final paper assignment requires them to compare *Cuarto* with two other texts we have read from different periods. This assignment often brings splendid results. For instance, students have compared images of women in *Cuarto*, in María de Zayas's *La fuerza del amor* ("The Strength of Love"), and in Zorrilla's *Don Juan Tenorio*; silences in *Cuarto*, in sonnets by Góngora, and in Saint Teresa's *Vida*; narration of the miraculous in *Cuarto*, in Juan Manuel's don Yllán story, and in *Don Quijote*; and authenticity in *Cuarto*, in Unamuno's "Mecanópolis," and in Manrique.

Building Up to El cuarto de atrás *in a Literary Survey Course*

Our discussions of Martín Gaite's novel come after a semester of studying the supernatural and the fantastic, when the students have been equipped to deal with Todorov's theory and what a modern fantastic novel might look like. I follow Todorov's usage for the terms "marvelous" (the supernatural accepted), "uncanny" (the ostensibly supernatural explained rationally) and "fantastic" (the hesitation in the face of the apparently supernatural, never resolved by acceptance or explanation) in describing the texts for this course. We read each text on its own terms; our discussions run far beyond a merely mechanical application of Todorov's theory of the fantastic. The first day of class, I present them with "El romance del Infante Arnaldos" as an example of a fantastic text according to Todorov. The opening lines of the poem set the text in a quotidian reality, albeit far removed from the one known to my students. Reference to the magically infused "mañana de San Juan" ("The Evening of Saint John" [my trans.]) foreshadows the possibility of the fantastic without removing Arnaldos from his routine hunting. The appearance of the strange boat made of exotic materials presages something special, but the reader has yet to hesitate in the face of the ostensibly supernatural. As the mariner's voice sounds across the waves, it appears to have magical effects—"que la mar ponía en calma / los vientos hace amainar" ("The waves stood still to hear him, / The wind was soft and low")—and the reader begins to doubt the normality of the scene. Arnaldos himself wonders at the situation: "por tu vida, el marinero / dígasme hora ese cantar" ("Tell me, for God's sake, sailor, / What song may that song be?"). The end of this version of the poem gives no explanation for the strange happenings. Students speculate on the identity of the mariner and on the content of his song and realize that there is no answer to their questions. A brief overview of how Todorov distinguishes among the uncanny, the marvelous, and the supernatural leads the students to conclude that "El romance del Infante Arnaldos" is indeed a fantastic text, because the doubts as to whether these events mark the supernatural are never resolved.

Students may object that, in the Renaissance world of the original audience of the text, such happenings might more readily be accepted as miraculous. Discussion segues naturally to inquiries into the reading expectations of the medieval audiences of the *Poema de Mio Cid* and Berceo's *Los milagros de Nuestra Señora*, the next texts on the calendar. The Cid's heroics—such as his splitting in two, from helmet to waist, the Moorish Rey Búcar and especially the episode with the lion—set the Cid apart from the normal world only by degree, not by category, so he is not fantastic. Berceo's texts—we read "La casulla de San Ildefonso" ("Saint Idelfonso's Chasuble"), "El sacristán impúdico" ("The Shameless Sacristan"), and "El romero de Santiago" ("The Pilgrim to Santiago")—deal openly with the marvelous. Don Juan Manuel's "Lo que contesçió a un deán de Santiago con don Yllán, el grand maestro de Toledo" ("What Happened with don Yllán, Wizard of Toledo, to a Dean of Santiago") more explicitly questions the reality of the world of the text, as the dean appears to live out his life and steadily rise in power and church authority, until as pope he once again denies don Yllán's request for a position for his son. Don Yllán breaks the illusion of the world in which the dean has lived the last years of his life, and readers see that it has all been a dream, or a spell of Yllán's doing, a test of the dean's integrity. Patronio displays his own magic, rivaling Yllán's, in the way he tells the tale from the dean's perspective, thereby bewitching the readers into thinking that what transpires has actually occurred in the real world. Although by the end of the story readers guess at the mechanism of Yllán's magic, there is no doubt about its marvelous nature. The virtual world created by Yllán (and by the narrator, Patronio) shares several elements in common with *Cuarto*—an ultimately self-conscious fictionality, the questioning of false or tenuous memories, and a wizard-like intermediary between an oneiric world and the real one.

Texts such as Manrique's fifteenth-century *Coplas por la muerte de su padre*, Garcilaso's sixteenth-century sonnets, or the sixteenth-century picaresque novel *Lazarillo de Tormes* do not participate in the fantastic. The apparition of Death in Manrique is strictly allegorical, and Garcilaso's poetic world and *Lazarillo*'s starkly realistic one provide counterexamples to the supernatural and allegorical realms of Saint Teresa's *Vida* (chs. 28–31) and San Juan's and Fray Luis de León's sixteenth-century poetry. Likewise with the baroque poets, on whom we spend several days. The question of the fantastic seems to fade at this point. Todorov's discussion of poetry and allegory (ch. 4 of *The Fantastic*) nevertheless facilitates discussion of the workings of language in Góngora and Quevedo, both of whom treat the supernatural in many of their poems, albeit not as a springboard to the fantastic.

Cervantes's "El retablo de las maravillas" ("The Marvelous Puppet Show") shows the power that an illusory, ideological construct like *pureza de sangre* ("purity of blood") gains over a group invested in the illusion (an issue that will return with the official discourse in *Cuarto*). A brief foray into *Don Quijote* helps students see, for the first time in the course, the workings of the uncanny. The narrator recounts the episode of the fulling hammers (pt. 1, ch. 20) without explaining, until the end of the episode, the strange effects. Don Quijote and Sancho hear a tremendous noise in the night. The knight bravely resolves to discover the source, while the squire in fear hobbles Rocinante. Morning light breaks the spell when they come upon the fulling hammers, which are instruments used to pound woolen cloth, not giants or warriors. The talking bronze head (pt. 2, ch. 62) is another example, although by this time readers have become accustomed to the trickery and never really wonder at the possibility of the supernatural. The Clavileño—famous flying wooden horse—episode (pt. 2, ch. 41) is not uncanny, because readers see the machinations of the duke and duchess, but it helps illustrate the uncanny if the students are asked to view events from Sancho's perspective.[5]

Calderón's *La dama duende*, through dramatic irony, explores the tensions between the servant's credulous belief in the marvelous and the master's baroque skepticism when confronted with the Phantom Lady's inexplicable ability to enter their rooms. The play also broaches issues of feminine identity and discourse. These issues are reiterated in Zayas's purely fantastic seventeenth-century "La fuerza del amor." At the end of the story, while doña Laura hangs over a bone pit at midnight, her brother, don Carlos, awakens and sets off to rescue her. On reaching the outskirts of town, near the bone pit, his horse stops in the road until don Carlos realizes that Laura is nearby and in peril.

Lope de Vega's *El caballero de Olmedo* embodies the fantastic in ways reflected in texts from later centuries, including *Cuarto*. In the third act, after don Alonso has spoken with his own shadow, a strange laborer sings the famous folk song about the death of the knight of Olmedo *before* don Alonso's murder. Both the audience and the characters view these events as fantastic. The intertextual insertion of the folk song mimics the self-consciousness of *Cuarto* and Galdós's uncanny story "La novela en el tranvía," in which a crazed narrator links into a murder plot snippets of stories he overhears, dreams, or reads on scraps of newspaper.

The nineteenth century brings Zorrilla's *Don Juan Tenorio* and Espronceda's *El estudiante de Salamanca*, both texts of the marvelous. Coupled with Mariano José de Larra's allegorical "Día de difuntos de 1836" ("Day of the Dead, 1836"), they emphasize Spanish Romanticism's pessimism and preoccupation with death. The motif of the quest for the *belle dame sans merci*, reiterated in Bécquer's marvelous "El monte de las ánimas" (205–16; "The Mount of the Souls") and "Los ojos verdes" (217-26; "The Green Eyes") and metaphorically in the marvelous "El *Miserere*" (279–91; "The *Miserere*"), gets a feminine inversion in Pardo Bazán's fantastic tale "La santa de Karnar," in which a young girl recovers her health on visiting a supposedly saintly living skeleton, a woman who eats nothing but the Eucharist. This brief feminist story deeply influences students' take on *Cuarto*, "La fuerza del amor," and even Saint Teresa's writings.

By sheer dint of grappling with a score of texts, students in a survey of Spanish literature course arrive at their own theory of reading and its importance. *El cuarto de atrás* affords the opportunity to teach them about the Civil War; the Franco era; the transition to the post-Franco era; memoirs; women's storytelling; and the nature of fiction, metafiction, and the fantastic. Given the intertextual presence of Todorov's book in *Cuarto*, the inclusion of the novel in a survey of fantastic literature seems natural. Other fantastic texts are possible capstones (Torrente Ballester's too lengthy *Don Juan*, for example), but *Cuarto*'s engagement with themes of reading, intertextuality, history, women's issues, and the encounter with the other links it to texts throughout the Spanish canon. According to Brown and Elaine Smith, *Cuarto* "is nothing less than a complete actualization of its creator's theory of literature" (69). It is a model for students to study, interpret, and creatively read and misread. Beyond that, it represents the culmination of past trends in Spanish fantastic literature while breaking new ground, an ideal novel upon which to hang our hat.

NOTES

In this essay, for *El cuarto de atrás* I am using the Siruela 2009 edition; for *The Back Room*, references are to Lane's translation.

[1] Brown, "Fantastic Memoir"; Cibreiro; Durán, "*El cuarto de atrás*"; Glenn, "Martín Gaite" and "*El cuarto de atrás*"; Ordóñez, "Reading"; Palley; and Spires, "Intertextuality."

[2] Brown explains, "[T]he ways in which Martín Gaite interrelates the fantastic and the real, both thematically and technically, give rise to a work which is much more effective and much more remarkable than either of its constituent elements would be separately. The fantastic and the real are more than complementary; each facet actually is enhanced by the symbiotic relationship they share" ("Fantastic Memoir" 17).

[3] The man in black acts more as analyst than muse. Brown and Elaine Smith assert that "the man in black accomplishes in one evening what it takes psychiatrists years to do. He has forced the narrator to face painful memories, and, in doing so, has removed their sting or, in psychiatric jargon, their 'negative cathexis.' The memories he has conjured up are, indeed, painful ones of war, deprivation and murder, but once the two characters have talked about them, their power to wound is diminished" (68).

[4] After reading Pardo Bazán's "La santa de Karnar," we jump to *Cuarto*, returning to Machado's "La tierra de Alvargonzález" and Unamuno's "Mecanópolis" and "El otro" to conclude the semester.

[5] The only purely uncanny text we read is Bécquer's legend "El rayo de luna" (247–62). At midnight in the ruins of a Templar monastery on the outskirts of Soria, Manrique begins to follow a beautiful woman. After a fruitless chase, he repeatedly seeks her in Soria, until finally after months he returns to the same monastery at midnight. He goes mad when he realizes that what he had thought was a beautiful woman was really the moonlight on the leaves.

APPENDIX: UNDERGRADUATE STUDY QUESTIONS FOR *EL CUARTO DE ATRÁS*

Who is the man in black? What is he like?

When does the interview begin? Why so late?

What does the narrator think of the man in black as an interviewer?

What might the cockroach symbolize?

How do the prints hanging on the wall relate to what happens in the novel?

List the various moments that lend a fantastic quality to the narration. What are the possible explanations for apparently supernatural happenings?

What types of texts did the narrator consume as an adolescent? How did they affect her and her friends? Whose roles did they emulate and why? What songs did they sing?

Which memories are most important to the narrator?

How do the epigram by Georges Bataille and the dedication to Lewis Carroll relate to what transpires during the interview?

What does the novel teach us about how we should read?

What do the white pebbles and the bread crumbs represent?

What are the effects of the pills from the golden box?

What images does the narrator associate with the name Franco?

Describe the members of the narrator's family, nuclear and extended. How has the war affected each of them?

In remembering the important scene in Burgos as her father and uncle attempt to recover the requisitioned car, how does the narrator's understanding of the event *now* differ from what she experienced in the moment?

What are the various meanings of "el cuarto de atrás"?

Is *Cuarto* a fantastic novel?

How is the fantastic mode related to the themes of recovering memories, writing personal history, and surviving a politically repressive regime?

What possible meanings derive from the scene when the narrator trips over Todorov's *The Fantastic*?

Much of the novel takes place in the narrator's mind. Write out or mark in red in your book the actual sentences the narrator and the man in black say to each other.

Where does the novel manuscript come from? How does it get written?

In what ways does *Cuarto* reiterate or modify the *ubi sunt* ["Where are they now?"] theme from Jorge Manrique's *Coplas*?

Compare the function of the self-consciousness and intertextual elements of *Cuarto* with those of Lope's *El caballero de Olmedo* (the *cantarcillo*) and Galdós's "La novela en el tranvía."

Compare the bread crumbs image with the plight of doña Ángela in Calderón's *La dama duende*, the feminism of Laura in María de Zayas's "La fuerza del amor," and the strange state of "la santa" in Pardo Bazán's "La santa de Karnar."

How does *Cuarto*'s feminine discourse respond to or resolve the problems outlined in the earlier texts?

What are the aspects of "herstory" that seem most vital in the novel?

In the end, is the interaction between the narrator and the man in black a Faustian bargain? What are the results of the interview? What does the narrator have that she did not have before?

Teaching *El cuarto de atrás* in the Context of History and Historiography

David K. Herzberger

El cuarto de atrás can serve as a prime example for students of how history and fiction cross paths. Martín Gaite was trained as a historian, and she has framed her most prominent novel with a strong sense of the historical and infused the novel with a thoughtful reflection on how the past is always constructed by the stories told about it. Her approach to time and narration in *Cuarto* provides the opportunity to teach the novel in two complementary ways: through the reading of Spanish history of the twentieth century, which gives students context both for the period referred to in the novel and for the time in which the work was published, and through the reading of *Cuarto* as a transgressive narrative, in that it stands in opposition to the historiography of the Franco regime. In this essay I concentrate on the latter (in both my undergraduate and graduate courses this approach has elicited the most thoughtful responses from students), but I do not disregard completely the former. Though my courses are taught in Spanish, the historical approach could be implemented in English as well, with information about the Francoist construction of history translated or synthesized by the instructor.

The Novel's Complex Context

To get at the heart of *Cuarto*, students must engage it in the complicated context of fiction, history, memory, intertextuality, and dissent. While the referential base of the novel remains important, the textual strategies and intertextual connections linking it to historiography should be foregrounded. First, students should read a general history of twentieth-century Spain (e.g., pertinent parts of Raymond Carr's *Spain, 1808–1975* or his more general *Spain: A History*), or instructors should present an overview. In my classes, there is both reading and overview, and in my lecture I emphasize the political and social conflicts of the Civil War and their roots in the late eighteenth and nineteenth centuries. Students must understand above all that, although Franco won the Civil War and imposed his will on Spain through raw military power and brute force, his victory could not be solidified and sustained over the long term without the construction of a political, economic, legal, and institutional infrastructure.

In the context of history, most relevant to the teaching of *Cuarto* is the Francoist use of the past to represent both the Civil War and his regime as the authentic and inevitable outcome of Spanish history. Because it is not feasible—there is no time—to have students explore in detail the myriad ways used by the regime to exert control over the meaning of history, instructors may offer a synthesis of critical ideas on the topic from works by Gonzalo Pasamar Alzuria,

Elías Díaz, Paul Preston and Ann Mackenzie, Rafael Valls Montes, Noël Valis, and me (*Narrating*).

At the same time, in order for students to have direct exposure to Francoist historians, they should be assigned shorter essays that represent the regime's understanding and construction of Spanish history. Three pieces that afford an overview of the general strategies and perspectives employed in the 1940s and 1950s are by the Francoist historians Florentino Pérez Embid, Vicente Palacio Atard, and Rafael Calvo Serer. In each of these essays students should be encouraged to look for ways in which the author proposes a single understanding of Spanish history linked to the Franco regime, emphasizes the regime as a manifestation of the authentic traditions of Spain, and speaks to the destiny of Spain by connecting Francoism to the origins of the nation.

Strategies for Narrating the Past in History and in Fiction

For students to understand fully how *Cuarto* speaks to history and dissents from Francoist historiography, it is useful to engage them in a discussion about how fiction and history are at once different and similar. This aspect of teaching *Cuarto* is difficult, because it is overtly theoretical. Students should first be given an overview of current thinking on the narrative and referential issues related to telling the past—either through reading selected passages of, for example, Hayden White (esp. *The Content of the Form*) or Paul Ricoeur (volume 1 of *Time and Narrative*) or through the instructor's presentation of the principal ideas of these writers. Once students have this theoretical foundation, it is helpful to initiate a discussion of how narrative creates meaning in storytelling. The instructor should also underscore the ethical foundations of history as a discipline that sets out to get things right but that is vexed by the contingencies of knowing and representing the past in a narrative form. Students might then be asked to discuss Francoist historiography in relation to the ideas of White or Ricoeur, with emphasis placed on the suppositions about knowledge, narration, representation, and power. In other words, they should be able to articulate what Francoist historians set out to do and what strategies they used to achieve the desired end.

For the teaching of *Cuarto*, Ricoeur's insistence that time is the ultimate referent of all narrative provides direct entry into the novel, to its link with history in general, and especially to its multilayered response to basic premises of Francoist historiography and the construction of historical meaning. Instructors might offer in this context a summary of chapter 7 of White's *Content*, which presents a good analysis of Ricoeur.

Francoist Historiography and Its Objectives

A major impetus of Francoist historiography came from the regime's desire to portray the flow of history before the Franco years as narrowly causal in relation to the present, so that Francoist Spain would be viewed as an inevitable outcome. One objective is to solidify the single meaning of the past that the regime created to justify its existence; another is to suppress dissent from this mainstream historiography. When Francoist historians insist on maintaining "el sentido permanente de la historia [de España]" (Pérez Embid 149; "the permanent meaning of the history [of Spain]"), or when they argue that there is an eternal Spain rooted in permanent and unchanging values, history metamorphoses into myth, which in turn, as Frank Kermode has proposed, embodies "a series of radically unchangeable gestures" (39). Jo Labanyi's study of myth and history during the Franco years (*Myth*) can serve as a guide here, introduced to students through a brief lecture or by having them read chapters 1 and 2 of her study.

Historical Time in the Novel

The Francoist idea of unchangeability and atemporality becomes a principal point of reference for Martín Gaite in her novel. Students should be asked to record, as they read, all references to time and to Franco's domination over everything related to its passing. For example, as the narrator watches the funeral of Franco on television and observes the images of his daughter, Carmencita, she is struck by the powerful presence of the dictator throughout her own life:

> Franco es el primer gobernante que yo he sentido en mi vida como tal, porque desde el principio se notó que era unigénito, indiscutible y omnipresente, que había conseguido infiltrarse en todas las casas, escuelas, cines y cafés, allanar la sorpresa y la variedad. (115)

> Franco was the first real ruler in my life that I was ever aware of as such, because from the beginning it was clear that he was the one and only, that his power was indisputable and omnipresent, that he had managed to insinuate himself into all the houses, schools, and cafés, do away with spontaneity and variety. . . . (132)

Franco is a synecdoche for the paralysis of historical time:

> [N]o soy capaz de discernir el paso del tiempo a lo largo de ese período, ni diferenciar la guerra de la postguerra, pensé que Franco había paralizado el tiempo, y precisamente el día que iban a enterrarlo me desperté pensando eso con una particular intensidad. (116)

> I am simply not capable of discerning the passage of time all during that period, or differentiating the war years from the postwar ones. The thought came to me that Franco had paralyzed time, and on the very day that they were about to bury him I woke up, with my mind focused on that one thought with a very special intensity. (133)

As the narrator watches Carmencita during the burial of her father, it strikes her that she has shared a lifetime with the aggrieved daughter (they are the same age). This realization leads her to reflect again on Franco's influence over time:

> [P]ara ella [Carmencita Franco] era simplemente su padre, mientras que para el resto de los españoles había sido el motor tramposo y secreto de ese bloque de tiempo. . . . y [que] cayeran como del cielo las insensibles variaciones que habían de irse produciendo, según su ley, en el lenguaje, en el vestido, en la música, en las relaciones humanas, en los espectáculos, en los locales. (119)

> [F]or her [Carmencita Franco] he was simply her father, whereas for all other Spanish he had been the devious and secret motive force of that block of time . . . and the imperceptible variations that inevitably came about, merely because of the passage of time, in language, in dress, in music, in human relations, in public entertainment, in places, seemed to have simply fallen from heaven. (137)

Rebutting Francoist Historiography through Memory and Narration

Once students have seen how Martín Gaite portrays the temporal numbness wrought by Francoism, they should explore how *Cuarto* seeks to open time (and history) to the creative power of narration. The narrator asserts that the past must be scrutinized anew:

> "[L]o van a enterrar", pensaba, pero lo pensaba al margen de consideraciones políticas, preguntándome . . . cómo había sido ese bloque de tiempo, lo pensaba desde el punto de vista del escondite inglés. . . . Fue cuando me di cuenta de que yo, de esa época, lo sabía todo, subí a casa y me puse a tomar notas en un cuaderno. Es el cuaderno que estaba buscando antes. (119–20)

> "They're going to bury him," I thought, but it was a thought quite far removed from any political considerations. . . . I was asking myself . . . what this block of time had been like. I was thinking of it from the point of view of the game of Red Light. . . . It was then that I realized I knew about that period. I went upstairs to my apartment, and began to jot things down in a notebook. That's the notebook I was looking for a while ago. (138)

Through memory (i.e., the "things" that she records in her notebook), Martín Gaite creates the foundation for the writing of *Cuarto*, and students can now see how the novel stands against specific aspects of Francoist historiography. Two examples from *Cuarto* make the point, one related to the narrator's indoctrination by the Sección Femenina, the other linked to the teaching of history in textbooks from her school years.

Students should be familiar in general terms with the Sección Femenina and its role in the lives of young Spanish women in the 1940s and 1950s (Scanlon is useful here for background information). But its specific pertinence to historiographic readings of *Cuarto* is revealed in the narrator's memory of how Isabel la Católica was promoted as a model for Spanish women by the Sección Femenina and how she was portrayed as mother of the nation. For the Francoists, the queen was a cynosure for authentic Spanishness, which was imposed on young women through the mythic representations of her life:

> Se nos ponía bajo su advocación, se nos hablaba de su voluntad férrea y de su espíritu de sacrificio, había reprimido la ambición y el despotismo de los nobles, había creado la Santa Hermandad, expulsado a los judíos traicioneros, se había desprendido de sus joyas para financiar la empresa más gloriosa de nuestra historia. . . . (86)

> We were placed beneath her advocacy, we were given talks about her iron will and her spirit of sacrifice, we were told how she had held the ambition and the despotism of the nobles in check, how she had created the Holy Office, expelled the traitorous Jews, given up her jewels to finance the most glorious undertaking in our history. . . . (90–91)

It is important for students to understand that the regime establishes a historical link between Queen Isabel and the young women of contemporary Spain. This link not only locates women and their duty to country as part of an obligation that goes back to the origin of Spain but also makes the past a necessary bridge to the future. In other words, young Spanish women are the destiny of Spain. It is Isabel who points the way: "Isabel la Católica jamás se dio tregua, jamás dudó. Orgullosas de su legado, cumpliríamos nuestra misión de españolas . . ." (87; "Queen Isabelle never gave herself a moment's respite, never doubted. Proud of her legacy, we would fulfill our mission as Spanish women . . ." [91]).

A Challenge to the Content and Form of Official History

Once students have absorbed the precepts of the narrator's view of writing about the past and fully grasp her mistrust of time as it was portrayed by Francoist historians, they will understand in a more complex way why she rebels against the mission assigned her by Spanish history. It is not simply because, as a teenager, she did not want to attend the classes at the Sección Femenina; she also rejected their historical meaning. Her rebellion thus occurs not only against the content of the history proposed by the regime (e.g., the role assigned her through the historical interpretation of Isabel), but also against what White calls the "content of the form." In opposition to a single-voiced story that is rigid and unyielding in its view of Spain and its history, she chooses multiple voices and narrative techniques, which favor disorder and ambiguity over certainty. The narrator notes:

> Bajo el machaconeo de aquella propaganda ñoña y optimista de los años cuarenta, se perfiló mi desconfianza hacia los seres decididos y seguros, crecieron mis ansias de libertad y se afianzó la alianza con el desorden que había firmado secretamente en el piso tercero del número catorce de la calle Mayor. (87)
>
> As a consequence of the brainwashing of that mawkish and optimistic propaganda of the forties, my mistrust of resolute and self-assured individuals became more marked than ever, my eagerness for freedom grew, and the alliance with disorder that I had secretly signed in the apartment on the [third] floor of No. 14 Calle Mayor turned into a near-unbreakable pact. (92)

Her desire for disorder, which in reality is a desire for freedom, operates on many levels. It forms the narrative foundation of *Cuarto* through metafiction and Tzvetan Todorov's view of the fantastic, shapes Carmen's mistrust of official history, and gives substance to a different way of understanding the past:

> [M]iraba en mi infancia los santos del libro de historia, ni los acontecimientos gloriosos ni los comportamientos ejemplares me parecían de fiar, me desconcertaban los reyes que promovían guerras, los conquistadores y los héroes, recelaba de su gesto altivo cuando ponían el pie en tierra extraña, defendían fortines o enarbolaban cruces y estandartes. (87–88)
>
> I would . . . look at the saints in the history book, neither glorious exploits nor exemplary conduct struck me as trustworthy models of behavior. Kings who stirred up wars, conquistadors and heroes disturbed me. I was suspicious of their prideful attitude as they set foot in foreign territory, defended forts, or planted crosses and flags. (92–93)

The narrator's rejection of official history also stems explicitly from what she was taught in school, for it is during the early years of her education when the past begins to shape her present and future. Students in the American classroom should know how schools configured the concept of Spain for young Spaniards in the 1940s and 1950s. A valuable (and entertaining) account is offered by Andrés Sopeña Monsalve in his *El florido pensil* ("The Delightful Flower Garden"). Part 3 of the book offers insight, laced with irony and humor, into how during the Franco years schoolchildren were exposed to a historic Spain filled with heroes, Christians, and conquests and how all the past served as prelude to the glorious rule of Franco. Valls Montes's study *Interpretación de la historia de España* ("Interpretation of the History of Spain") can give students a sense of how history was taught in Spanish schools during the 1940s and early 1950s, when Martín Gaite was a student.

The memory of how the narrator was taught history and of its imposition on her life widens the gap between what she was required to learn about the Spanish past and what she came to believe about it. She notes that "entonces aborrecía la historia y además no me la creía, nada de lo que venía en los libros de historia ni en los periódicos me lo creía" (54–55; "at the time I scorned history, and furthermore I didn't believe it, I didn't believe a word of what was recounted in history books or in the newspapers" [49]) and, later:

> Le escucho pensando en Isabel la Católica, en la falaz versión que, de su conducta, nos ofrecían aquellos libros y discursos, donde no se daba cabida al azar, donde cada paso, viaje o decisión de la reina parecían marcados por un destino superior e inquebrantable. (93)

> I keep thinking, as I listen to him, of Isabel la Católica, of the deceptive version of her conduct put before us in those textbooks and those speeches, where no room was left for chance, where each step, journey, or decision of the queen appeared to bear the mark of a superior and inevitable destiny. (100)

Most significant, the evocation of history in the context of her memories makes the past a slippery terrain for her, open and indeterminate, and representable only in a discourse conjured from the creative disorder of the back room. Students should therefore be able to see the link between the title of the novel and writing about the past in one of the key passages:

> [E]l libro sobre la postguerra tengo que empezarlo en un momento de iluminación como el de ahora, relacionando el paso de la historia con el ritmo de los sueños, es un panorama tan ancho y tan revuelto, como una habitación donde cada cosa está en su sitio precisamente al haberse salido de su sitio, todo parte de mis primeras perplejidades frente al concepto de historia, allí, en el cuarto de atrás, rodeada de juguetes y libros tirados por el suelo. (93)

> I must begin the book on the postwar period in a moment of sudden enlightenment like this one right now, tying together the march of history and the rhythm of dreams. It is such a vast panorama and such a topsy-turvy one, like a room where each thing is in its proper place precisely because it is out of place. All this goes back to my initial perplexities in the

> face of the concept of history, there in the back room, surrounded by toys and books strewn all over the floor. (100–01)

Recovering the Past through Memory, Metafiction, and the Fantastic

What students should learn from their reading of *Cuarto* in the context of Francoist historiography is precisely what the narrator herself learns from the writing of her novel. Two implicit questions configure the work as a whole: What prompted her to write in the first place? What does she seek to show about herself as well as about Spain and its past? Two quotations from the novel suggest the narrator's answer to these questions and provide a summary of the work's main propositions. First and above all, the narrator's intention grounds her writing in time, which as with Ricoeur affords the principal rationale for the commingling of history and fiction in her narrative. As the narrator puts it at the beginning of the novel, "¿Qué busco ahora? Ah, ya, un rastro de tiempo, como siempre, el tiempo es lo que más se pierde . . ." (38; "What am I searching for now? Ah, yes, the track of time. As always, time is what gets lost most often . . ." [25]).

It is this desire to recover time and history for the richness of their meanings rather than for the power of their myths that sets the narrator to writing about the past. Although openness, uncertainty, and polisemy lie at the heart of her investigation of the past through memory, metafiction, and the fantastic, she inserts herself into history in a way that allows the individual as well as the nation to bear multiple and complex meanings:

> [N]o somos un solo ser, sino muchos, de la misma manera que tampoco la historia es esa que se escribe poniendo en orden las fechas y se nos presenta como inamovible, cada persona que nos ha visto o hablado alguna vez guarda una pieza del rompecabezas que nunca podremos contemplar entero. (144)

> We are not just one being, but many, exactly as real history is not what is written by putting dates in their proper order and then presenting it to us as a single whole. Each person who has seen us or spoken to us at a certain time retains one piece of the puzzle that we will never be able to see all put together. (170)

As a result of their reading of *El cuarto de atrás* in the context of history and historiography, students should have a deeper understanding of how narrative gives meaning to the past, how those who control this meaning acquire and use power, and how it is possible to dissent from the given meanings of history through the opening of the past to new forms of narration and to new stories about it.

NOTE

References are to the 2009 Siruela edition of *El cuarto de atrás*. All English translations of the novel come from Helen R. Lane's *The Back Room*.

El cuarto de atrás and the Intellectual Work of Student Writing

Emily C. Francomano

El cuarto de atrás (*The Back Room*) is a dense and multifaceted tour de force, and one of the many ways that we can describe it is that it is a book about reading and writing, about reading as a writer and writing as a reader. Debra Castillo notes, "[T]he novel's central concern with the forms of writing and the function of memory has remained constant in Martín Gaite's subsequent work," particularly in *El cuento de nunca acabar* ("The Never-Ending Story"), a prolonged narrative meditation on literary creation (815). These concerns of *El cuarto de atrás* are also central themes in postmodern fiction and literary criticism. As the novel—if indeed we can call it a novel—delves into the intellectual, creative, and quasi-mystical craft of writing, it weaves the experiences of reading and writing into a reflection on culture, literary theory, and psychology. This essay discusses using *El cuarto de atrás* as a springboard for discussions and writing assignments designed to develop students' analytic engagement with the text and with their own reading and writing. Although these writing activities may certainly be adapted for classes working with *El cuarto de atrás* in translation, I designed them for a writing-intensive advanced Spanish literature class, as part of a larger vision of the teaching of writing as an intellectual activity in classes where most students are, while advanced, still second-language (L2) learners. They are "write to learn" exercises, in that students learn that they can produce meaningful and effective texts in the discipline of Spanish literary and cultural studies. At present, foreign language and L2 writing research is a growing field that, though still predominantly attuned to the context of English as a second language (ESL) and to a vision of writing as transcription, has begun to embrace the idea of L2 writing as intellectual work.[1]

Teaching the Novel in an Advanced Literature Course

I teach *El cuarto de atrás* in an upper-level undergraduate course called Contemporary Spanish Women Writers. The course is taught entirely in Spanish, and all readings are in Spanish, with the exception of relevant critical essays unavailable in translation. *El cuarto de atrás* is the second of six or seven texts (novels, short stories, and essays) read in the course, and it follows Martín Gaite's *Entre visillos*. Other authors studied in the course over the past few years are Esther Tusquets, Almudena Grandes, Rosa Montero, Clara Sánchez, Ana María Moix, Paloma Díaz-Mas, Lucía Etxebarria, Laura Freixas, Adelaida García Morales, and Eugenia Rico. Together, the two novels by Martín Gaite serve as an introduction to many of the issues that emerge throughout the semester, including but not limited to traditional and nontraditional gender roles in Spanish society during Franco's regime, the transition, and beyond; feminist literary criticism;

psychoanalytic theory; postmodern literary concerns, particularly metafiction, inter- and transtextuality, and reception; expectations for women's writing; and female-authored fiction as a commodity. I generally allot six seventy-five-minute class periods to Martín Gaite's two novels, which in addition to announcing many of the recurrent themes of the course, demonstrate the author's stylistic range.

Class size is generally small, about a dozen students; they are usually Spanish, comparative literature, and womens' studies majors, for whom the course fulfills a requirement, and they differ widely in their competency in Spanish and in their exposure to Spanish culture. Some are heritage speakers, others Spanish majors who have just completed semesters or years abroad, others advanced students whose linguistic competencies are entirely school-based. As is often true when students move from lower-level language classes to literature and culture courses, spoken and written accuracy varies greatly.

Contemporary Spanish Women Writers is a writing-intensive course in which students write weekly reading journals of 250–500 words, later choosing two entries to be revised and expanded into three-to-five-page response papers; the final written assignment is a ten-to-fifteen-page research paper. The journals are not graded but commented on, and spelling, grammar, and syntax errors are circled. If students cannot self-correct when these errors are pointed out, they are encouraged to come see me during office hours. In addition to these writing assignments, which are completed outside the classroom, students do frequent in-class writing.

El cuarto de atrás is a challenging book even for advanced students who have completed a semester abroad. Despite the difficulties it poses, each semester students say it is one of their favorite books read in their literature classes. The novel takes place on a proverbial dark and stormy night in the apartment of C, a writer, who is our narrator and author figure. In the first scenes, C trips over Tzvetan Todorov's *The Fantastic* and meets a large cockroach in her kitchen, signaling for us that we are in literary-critical territory from the outset. She then receives a mysterious visitor, the man in black, whose black glinting eyes are cockroach-like; she recognizes but cannot place him. He has come at midnight to interview her, perhaps psychoanalyze her, perhaps even to seduce her, if not all of the above. Never sure if she is dreaming, reading, remembering, or writing, C speaks with her visitor all night long about writing, reading, fiction, history, literary theory, and life during and after the Spanish Civil War. She is interrupted only by a phone call from another C—Carola, the suspicious lover of one Alejandro, who may or not be the man in black. The conversation between C and the man in black is stimulated by iced tea, served by the narrator, and small round pills proffered by the visitor. Throughout, C describes her desire to chart what she calls the *migas* ("crumbs") of history, the feelings and sensations of living through particular times, rather than the hard and cold facts or *piedrecitas* ("little stones"), likening herself to the heroine of a fairy tale, lost in the woods, who leaves a trail of crumbs (138). The novel ends when C awakes to find a sheaf of typed pages composing a completed novel, begins to read it, and promptly falls back asleep.

The novel is about—among other things—what Donald M. Murray has called "the complicated and intertwining processes of perception and conception through language" (375). Murray explores these intertwining thought processes in the context of an essay urging teachers of writing to consider them in the classroom.

The Teaching of Writing

My approach to the teaching of writing in the advanced second-language classroom stems from recent research and theory in college writing programs, particularly the work of James Slevin in *Introducing English*.[2] Slevin looks at the teaching of writing as "a response to the difficulty of writing" and as part and parcel of teaching historical and contextual reading:

> Such reading prompts interesting writing that serves to develop critical reflection, especially when students choose areas of their own to investigate in this manner. Such literacy helps students develop a clearer sense of writing not just as a process but as a form of production operating in history. . . .

Slevin's image of politically and historically engaged reading in the (English) composition classroom, while a physical and linguistic world away from *El cuarto de atrás*, provides an apt description of how Martín Gaite's persona C reads and writes in the novel. She (C) writes as "a form of production operating in history, a way of entering and shaping the world" (141).

My approach is also guided by several core beliefs about the nature of the interrelated activities of reading, discussing, and writing about literary texts, each of which enriches and depends on the other. I believe that reading complex cultural texts enhances linguistic competency and transcultural competencies.[3] I believe that a process-oriented approach to writing can be used in a classroom context where most students are reading, speaking, and writing in a second or foreign language. Finally, I believe that informal writing can play an important role in the development of ideas, writing skills, and individual style or voice in writing. Engaging with writing intellectually and not as transcription encourages students to take ownership of the language of instruction, be it academic or writerly English or academic Spanish, which may never be perfect but can and will communicate intellectually and convincingly.

Although some professors object to using class time for writing, I have found that there can be great benefits from informal writing in an advanced literature class in a second or foreign language. I agree with Murray not only that "we should certainly allow time within the curriculum for pre-writing" but also that "we should work with our students to help them understand the process of rehearsal to allow them the experience of rehearsing what they will write in their minds, on the paper, and with collaborators" (380).

Informal writing in class that involves jotting down ideas, speaking and rereading them out loud, and listening to others serves as a rehearsal for writing, thinking, and speaking in a second or foreign language. In-class writing can thus make it easier for students to participate in class and seminar discussions and make it less daunting for them to approach the task of writing outside the classroom.

Discussions of writing in the L2 or FL classroom traditionally and systematically focused on the production of correct forms, on writing as transcription rather than on writing as composition or intellectual work. In an advanced Spanish literature class, accuracy of transcription is of course still important, as most students are students of language as well as students of literature. Nevertheless, as Trisha Dvorak reports and as many instructors know from experience, advanced student L2 writing is "relatively impervious to teacher correction of form" (152). Data on composition development show that—perhaps counterintuitively—grammatical accuracy and written fluency improve "in the presence of feedback on content, and student writing does not improve following even repeated feedback on grammar . . . it appears that the most important contribution of the teacher to the process of learning to write is that of being a good reader" (156). Editing of grammar and syntax can, and according to Dvorak, "must be left for the final step in the process" (160).

Writing, and particularly writing in a second language, can be an alienating exercise that inhibits students. As Dvorak asserts, "[I]f foreign language writing instruction is to be effective, it must find a way to be a satisfying rather than an intimidating experience for students" (156). In-class writing activities and informal writing assignments give students a chance to work with the linguistic conventions necessary for writing in the discipline, in Spanish, in situations where the stakes are low. In other words, they know they won't be graded on their accuracy. In in-class writing, they won't be graded at all. By putting ideas into writing quickly and without the threat of grading based on accuracy hanging over them, they may also follow the compositional processes of skilled writers in both first and second languages. Many proficient writers "explore and clarify their ideas first, then attend to language-related concerns," not the other way around (153). Students can try out new vocabulary and rehearse crafting sentences containing terms from class discussion. Because accuracy of transcription is important in advanced classes, in-class writing can alert teachers to some common or entrenched errors of transcription, so that the teachers can devote some time to showing students how to correct them.

Writing Exercises Developed for El cuarto de atrás

Over the past few years I have used three writing exercises inspired by *El cuarto de atrás*. These exercises, and the reading strategies from which they stem, are continually evolving in my teaching practice. They reflect the kinds of writing assignments that Martín Gaite's text itself suggests as it progresses through its meditation about the transformation of memory and imagination into fiction and metafictive tale. In addition, they are designed to make students think about and perhaps even experience the kind of creative and intellectual processes that Carmen Martín Gaite depicts in her book.

1. Automatic Writing: "La anarquía de los objetos" / "The anarchy of objects"

This in-class exercise corresponds to students' reading of the first chapter, "El hombre descalzo" ("The Barefoot Man"). In early passages of the chapter, C gives readers an inventory of the objects in her room. Each object has its own story to tell and leads her in new narrative directions, which will then be taken up throughout the novel. The room assumes the role of privileged site for memories of growing up female in the Spanish postwar years. A description of the sewing box of C's grandmother serves as an initial image of the remembering mind and of the process of unpacking memories in order to record them. The image weaves together many associations of childhood in the postwar years, of the traditional women's work of sewing, which is of course related to storytelling, and of the deceptive nature of appearances. The sewing box is not merely a container for needles and thread but also the repository for a chaotic collection of articles, each pertaining to a particular moment in the writer's memory and imaginative process. Writing in *El cuarto de atrás* involves C's imposing control on this mass of objects through the acts of conversing, remembering, and recording that occur throughout the novel. The narrator's concentration on the sewing box and its contents, which include pharmaceutical products, bring readers' attention to the altered state of heightened observation and to the mnemonic, metaphoric, and metonymic properties of the room and its contents:

> Sigo bajando los ojos. Más libros, formando dos paredes encima del radiador, y entre ellas, sujetándolas, la cesta de costura que fue de la abuela Rosario. Casi no cierra de puro llena, no puedo comprender cómo caben dentro tantas cosas; siempre acudo a ella en casos de perplejidad, aquí acaba viniendo a parar todo, seguro que, al abrirla, me acordaré de lo que venía a buscar. . . . De la tapadera de mimbre entreabierta escapan carretes, enchufes, terrones de azúcar, dedales, imperdibles, facturas, un cabo de vela, clichés de fotos, botones, monedas, tubos de medicinas, allá va todo, envuelto en hilos de colores. (26)

> I look farther downward. More books, forming two walls above the radiator, and between them, holding them in place, the sewing basket that belonged to Grandma Rosario. It is stuffed so full it almost won't shut. I am unable to fathom how so many things can fit inside it. It's a foregone conclusion that when I open it I'll remember what I was in the midst of searching for. . . . From the half-open wicker lid there come spilling out spools of thread, electric plugs, cubes of sugar, thimbles, safety pins, bills,

> a candle end, snapshots, buttons, coins, bottles of pills, everything imaginable, all tangled up in colored thread. (11)

The sewing box is a mini *cuarto de atrás*, a back room introduced before readers are introduced to the actual back room: a playroom, refuge, and metaphor for the creative mind. Castillo observes, in reference to Martín Gaite's *Cuento de nunca acabar*, "Its elements are constitutive, not of the autobiographical 'I,' but of the writing self, the textured self of the text upon text of the narrative dream. This box . . . serves as a textual allegory for that other 'cajón de sastre que era nuestra cabeza' (*Cuento* 169)" ("the hodgepodge, literally the tailor's drawer, that was our brain") (826). As Martín Gaite remarked in her 1981 interview with Marie-Lise Gazarian Gautier:

> Alude a un cuarto concreto de mi infancia, el cuarto de jugar, que estaba en la parte de atrás de mi casa de Salamanca. Pero también hay un simbolismo, porque en la mente humana existe una especie de cuarto trasero donde se almacenan los recuerdos, un cuarto donde todo está revuelto y cuya cortina sólo se levanta de vez en cuando sin que sepamos cómo ni por qué. Y como precisamente en esta novela, a causa de la visita del hombre vestido de negro, se levantó esa cortina y los recuerdos de la infancia me anegaron, de ahí el doble sentido del título: por una parte, una alusión a la infancia y, por otra, a la memoria que el desconocido me avivó con su visita misteriosa e inesperada.
> ("Conversación con Carmen Martín Gaite en Nueva York" 11)

> The title alludes to a specific room from my childhood, the playroom, which was at the back of my house in Salamanca. But it is also symbolic, because there exists in the human mind a sort of back room where memories are stored, a room where everything is mixed up and whose curtain is lifted only once in a while, without our knowing how or why. Just as in this novel, because of the visit from the man in black, the curtain lifted and I was flooded by childhood memories, that is where the double meaning of the title comes from: on the one hand, an allusion to childhood, on the other, the memories sparked by the stranger with his mysterious and unexpected visit.

In class, we read these passages from the novel and the interview aloud and comment on the resonances between them, and we compare the scene described by C in the first pages of the novel to the painting *Harmony*, by Remedios Varo, which was felicitously chosen for the cover of the 1989 Destino edition of *El cuarto de atrás*. This painting also appears in both the Spanish and English versions of Janet A. Kaplan's books on the artist. In Kaplan's words, the painting depicts a composer:

> An androgynous figure whose features mirror Varo's own [who] sits in a medieval-looking study filled with the tools of the alchemist. Taking

> objects from a treasure chest—geometric solids, jewels, plants, crystals, handwritten formulas—the composer places them as notes onto a three-dimensional musical staff, creating from a chaos of possibilities the order that is music. (178)

After students view the image, I ask them to close their books and prepare for a short exercise designed to give them some idea of the process Martín Gaite describes and of the way that objects can tell stories. Memories of discrete objects may seem simple, but, as the student writers quickly see, in the process of remembering, such objects show themselves to be enmeshed in webs of relations and in historical and social contexts: they are *piedrecitas* ("little stones") surrounded by *migas* ("crumbs") (*Cuarto* 94).

I ask students to close their eyes, imagine their own room, either a dorm room or a room in their childhood home, and focus on an object in it. Then I ask them to open their eyes, place their pen or pencil tip on their paper—or fingers on the keyboard—and write about the object, beginning with a description and proceeding to its history and associations. Students see almost immediately that narratives emerge from this reflective process. Starting to write with the body, even before thinking of the first word, is an important part of the exercise, because the physical stance communicates to the brain that it is time to write (Mayo).

I limit the writing to ten minutes, time enough to demonstrate to students how many words can flower from a single object in memory. I ask them to reflect on this experience. As their responses indicate, many students spend the first few minutes wondering what to write, but once they begin writing, it can be difficult to stop as memories crowd upon memories. Martín Gaite relates this very experience in *El cuarto de atrás*. That the narrative seems to flow effortlessly, without external organization or revision, is the author's metafictive ruse. The novel, magically, mysteriously produced by the end of *El cuarto de atrás*, may have begun as the product of a poetic fugue, but it has been carefully constructed.

As a follow-up to the automatic writing in class, which may give students a sense of what it is to enter into a creative fugue, I encourage them to return to what they wrote in class for their weekly journal assignment.

2. "Es difícil escapar a los esquemas literarios de la primera juventud" / "It is difficult to escape the literary stereotypes of one's earliest years": Reading with and against the Grain of Master Plots

In one of the many metafictive moments in *El cuarto de atrás*, C remarks to herself, as she stares into the eyes of her interlocutor and her heart begins to beat wildly, romantically, "[E]s difícil escapar a los esquemas literarios de la primera juventud, por mucho que más tarde se reniegue de ellos" (122; "It is difficult to escape the literary stereotypes of one's earliest years, however hard one tries later to renounce them" [141]). She is thinking about the *novela rosa* ("romantic novel") and about how the situation in which she finds herself might so easily become a love scene thanks to the powerful pull of a familiar genre. Martín Gaite, like so many other contemporary women writers, engages the stories and genres that have provided women with morals and models throughout history. She does so through a continual critical process of rereading and rewriting much beloved but psychologically and socially prescriptive and proscriptive texts, which make romantic love and marriage the twin central axes of women's self-realization. The *novela rosa* is a constant shadowy and not-so-shadowy presence in *El cuarto de atrás,* the man in black being the antithesis of the romantic hero: he encourages C to talk about literature, politics, ideas, and history—themes that have no place in the thoughts and speech of the interchangeable Esmeraldas and María Victorias of the *novela rosa.* I refer to the essay "Los malos espejos" ("Distorted Mirrors"), first published in 1972 and included in the collection *La búsqueda de interlocutor y otras búsquedas* ("The Search for a Conversational Partner and Other Searches"), in which the author described the universal search for one's own reflection in the mirror of a person free from preconceived notions.

After discussing the *novela rosa* and the marriage plot in terms of the narrative expectations of genre and the reception of female readers, students begin to write by identifying the *esquemas literarios* ("literary trajectories") of their own childhoods. For North American students, these plot lines are often fairy tales interpreted by Disney, such as "Beauty and the Beast."

This in-class writing exercise consists of two parts. In the first, I ask students to take a few minutes to write an interpretation of a familiar fairy tale with the grain, and we share two or three of these interpretations. For example, if we read "Beauty and the Beast" with the grain of the story, we can take a comfortable and socially prescriptive lesson: looks are only skin deep, so when looking for love, we must look beyond physical appearances. Frogs may really be princes. But if we resist the compelling flow of the marriage plot and read against the grain, the story can have darker implications. Students spend another few minutes writing resisting interpretations. As a student once remarked, "'Beauty and the Beast' can also be read as a text that teaches women to put up with bestial men." Reading against the grain can present a challenge to students who prefer to give "the right answer," and it is my hope that this exercise helps them see that the right answer might not necessarily be the true one.

This exercise, which blends a close reading of part of chapter 4 with brief, informal, in-class writing and discussion, can be continued in journal entries that consider the effect these master plots and narratives have on students' own views of the world and, especially for students in the first weeks of a class on women's writing, on their expectations as readers of fiction written by and for women.

3. "Escribir es parir" / "Writing is like giving birth": Metaphors of Writing

The third writing exercise takes as its focus one of the central images of *El cuarto de atrás,* the typed manuscript, which appears as if by magic during the passage of the long night of wakeful dreaming, conversation, and remembering. In the opening pages of chapter 2, "El sombrero negro" ("The Black Hat"), C sees a page bearing words from the first chapter of *El cuarto de atrás* and rearing out of her typewriter, which is now open, though she is sure that she left it closed: " '[A]l hombre descalzo ya no se le ve.' ¿Cuándo he escrito esto?" (36; " 'The barefoot man has now disappeared from sight.' When did I write that?" [24]).

Later, page 79 takes the place of this page in the typewriter, and a pile of pages appears, significantly under the black hat doffed by the mysterious interlocutor. C's reaction to the mysteriously proliferating pages is paralysis and "surprise verging on terror" (trans. mine):

> No puedo continuar. Acabo de fijarme en el folio que asoma por encima de la máquina y me he quedado paralizada; ahora ya la sorpresa roza casi el terror. . . . Inicia el folio, copiada entre comillas, y no hay escrito nada más, excepto un número en el ángulo superior derecho, el 79. Pero bueno, estos setenta y nueve folios, ¿de dónde salen?, ¿a qué se refieren? El montón de los que quedaron debajo del sombrero también parece haber engrosado, aunque no me atrevo a comprobarlo. (91)
>
> I am unable to go on. My attention has been arrested by the top of the sheet of paper peeking out above the roller of the typewriter and I am standing there paralyzed. I am so dumbfounded I am almost terrified. . . . The page begins with it, copied between quotation marks, and there is nothing else written on the page, except for a number in the right-hand corner: 79. But then where are the rest of these seventy-nine pages? What are they about? The pile of papers underneath the hat seems to have grown bigger too, though I don't dare check to see. (98)

Finally, when C wakes, she sees that a book manuscript has literally taken the place of Todorov's book on the fantastic and that the 182 numbered pages bear the title "El cuarto de atrás" (177; 215). The novel, and with it Martín Gaite's metafictive wile, thus comes full circle. The book itself is the product of the fantastic. Writing, reading, conversing, remembering, waking, and dreaming are all bound together in the manuscript that has magically appeared, its contents no longer stored in that "back room of the mind" described by Martín Gaite in the interview with Gazarian Gautier.

This exercise can be done when students have finished or almost finished the novel. It can be done in class or as a journal assignment. Students read another quotation from Gazarian Gautier's interview with Martín Gaite:

> Se suele decir que escribir es una tarea muy ardua, y en algunos aspectos lo es, por los problemas que plantea al escritor. Pero es, sobre todo, juego y aliciente, como una apuesta para vencer, sortear esos problemas, para

> burlarlos. Creo que siempre que un escritor se ha divertido haciendo lo que hacía, ha logrado divertir a los demás. Yo aspiro a que quien lea mis libros se divierta por lo menos la tercera parte de lo que yo gozo al escribirlos. Pero si, en cambio, se toma la tarea de escribir como algo abrumador y obligatorio, el texto resultante acusa esa actitud compulsiva y sale más rígido, menos fluido. Hay quien ha llegado a sostener que escribir es como parir. Lo han dicho los hombres, claro, que no tienen ni idea de lo que es parir. Creo que a una mujer nunca se le ocurriría hacer una metáfora tan disparatada. (10)

> They often say that writing is a very arduous task, and in some ways it is, because of the problems it sets for a writer. But above all it is play and incentive, like a dare to solve those problems, to get the best of them. I think that whenever a writer has enjoyed what he was doing, he has entertained others as well. I strive to give the reader of my books at least one-third of the fun that I have writing them. But if on the other hand one considers the task of writing as something overwhelming and obligatory, the resulting text shows that compulsory attitude and comes out more rigid, less fluid. There are those who have even said that writing is like giving birth. Clearly, this has been said by men, who don't have the slightest idea of what giving birth is like. I think a woman would never have come up with such a nonsensical metaphor.

Martín Gaite takes on one of the oldest metaphors about writing, that of literary creation as giving birth. As she notes, it is generally used by male authors. It traditionally and ironically serves a paradigm in which men create works of art and literature, their children or stepchildren in Cervantes's twist on the theme, while women procreate (Freixas 121–30). Martín Gaite's comment also makes a mordant point about the desire of literary critics and the press to impose biological metaphors of artistic creation on women writers.

I ask students to consider both Martín Gaite's quotation from the interview and the miraculous, painless birth of the book imagined in *El cuarto de atrás*. After class discussion, they take five minutes to write other metaphors for the writing process in general and for their own writing in particular. As with the other exercises, they can continue to develop this theme in their journals.

El cuarto de atrás *as a Springboard for Student Writing*

Many other passages from the novel can serve as material for informal writing assignments. Just as *El cuarto de atrás* is fertile ground for discussing postmodern literary theoretical concepts, such as metafiction and intertextuality, it is also an ideal text for inviting students to consider the intellectual work of writing. In-class writing not only lowers the stakes of writing in a second language; it also serves as a rehearsal for formal writing and speaking, as student writers develop their own distinctive writerly and analytic voices. Even for students who may never achieve complete transcriptive accuracy, informal writing is a space in which they can expand their transcultural understanding, by thinking through and articulating their opinions in the target language.

In my experience, students can write at a very high level of critical engagement in a second language: they can write creative nonfiction, play with master plots, and craft metaliterary metaphors. It is challenging and time-consuming to do in-class writing, but it results in better undergraduate research and better formal writing. *El cuarto de atrás* and other self-reflexive texts, whether modern or premodern, help us design reading-and-writing activities that transform students from passive readers into information gatherers who understand content and form and can summarize cogently. The classroom cannot be *el cuarto de atrás*—we do not have the luxury of spending long midnight hours in conversation, aided by little round pills—but it can provide students with the alternative realities of Martín Gaite's narrativized memories and fictions and with receptive interlocutors.

NOTES

For *El cuarto de atrás*, the Siruela 2009 edition is used. Translations of the novel are Lane's, except as noted. Other translations are my own.

1 On the subject of L2 writing, see Dvorak; Manchón and De Haan; and Valdés, Haro, and Echevarriarza.

2 My approach also draws on Bean, though I do not quote him in this essay.

3 The MLA Ad Hoc Committee on Foreign Languages advocates that instead of seeking "to replicate the competence of an educated native speaker," the goal of language and culture studies in higher education should be to educate students "to function as informed and capable interlocutors with educated native speakers in the target language," to be able to "reflect on the world and themselves through the lens of another language and culture," and to reach a level of "transcultural understanding" that includes the "ability to comprehend and analyze cultural narratives that appear in every kind of expressive form" (236–37).

Teaching *El cuarto de atrás* with Nonfiction Works by Martín Gaite at the Graduate Level

María Fernández Babineaux Lamarque

I include Carmen Martín Gaite's works in two graduate courses: in Stylistics and Literary Theory and in Modern Peninsular Literature. Both are part of the curriculum to complete a master's degree in Spanish at Texas A&M University, Commerce. In each course, I combine selections from Martín Gaite's volumes of nonfiction with her best-known novel, *El cuarto de atrás* (*The Back Room*). In the Peninsular literature course, the author's nonfiction is also used to elucidate other frequently taught novels from twentieth-century Spain. Though each of the two graduate courses emphasizes a particular critical lens—narratological for one, sociocultural for the other—the technique of pairing nonfiction texts by the author with *El cuarto de atrás* can be deployed in both.

Graduate students are frequently asked to use theory and contextualize it for research papers. However, they are rarely taught how to independently apply the theories they learn in class to a novel. I have found that selections from the works of Gérard Genette, Paul Ricoeur, and Martín Gaite can involve them in that application. An understanding of how these theoretical works are exemplified in the novels they read in a course allows students to more readily carry out their own analyses. In particular, Martín Gaite's fiction and nonfiction together show how her ideas are developed in her novel. Writing a short paper every week gives students practice exploring theoretical contextualization as they prepare for a culminating research paper. At the same time, the short papers contribute to their formulation of ideas for class debates and help them develop ideas that they will explore in the research paper.

A *Literary Theory and Narratology* Course

In my graduate theory course, I use *El cuarto de atrás* along with *El cuento de nunca acabar* ("The Never-Ending Story"), Ricoeur's *Time and Narrative*, Genette's *Figuras III* (*Figures III*), and Catherine Bellver's "*El cuarto de atrás* and the Role of Writing."

El cuarto de atrás is covered in three two-hour-and-forty-minute weekly class sessions. Student reading assignments for the first session are the novel and Ricoeur's "The Circle of Narrative and Temporality" (1: 3–90). I explain the notion of temporality in *El cuarto de atrás*, drawing on his concepts of *intentio* and *distentio* and demonstrating how they are actualized in Martín Gaite's text. The novel starts as a continuation of a narration: ". . . Y, sin embargo, yo juraría que la postura era la misma . . ." (19; ". . . And yet I'd swear that the position was the same . . ." [1]). Time's displacement is therefore introduced at the beginning of the novel, and it continues throughout the text, guiding readers to a resolution that takes them back to the starting point. But readers cannot immediately superimpose both temporalities of the novel on the narrated time. To help them understand both, the first part of the novel must be kept in mind in order to resolve what will exist in the future. Ricoeur calls this "distentio," or the parallel impression of the reader's memory and the expectation of the past in the present, and the temporality oscillates between memory and expectation (1: 16).

This temporal interplay is crucial to readers' comprehension of *El cuarto de atrás*. According to Ricoeur, the mind is poised among expectation, memory, and attention as images are introduced by the narrator. The expectation left in the first part of *El cuarto de atrás* is supported by readers' attention to the events that follow. The narrator's memories build the transit through the present, which is also the future of this past. These operations are called "intentio," as the past increases proportionally while the future diminishes. At the end of the novel, the future is entirely absorbed by and merges with the past, as the narrator reads from her mysterious manuscript:

> ". . . Y sin embargo, yo juraría que la postura era la misma, creo que siempre he dormido así, con el brazo derecho debajo de la almohada y el cuerpo levemente apoyado contra ese flanco, las piernas buscando la juntura por donde se remete la sábana . . ."
> ¡Qué sueño me está entrando! (177)

> ". . . And yet I'd swear that the position was the same. I think I've always slept this way, with my right arm underneath the pillow and my body turned slightly over onto that side, my feet searching for the place where the sheet is tucked in . . ."
> How sleepy I'm getting! (215)

The narration is truncated by the writer's exhaustion—her tiredness from and of writing. At the beginning of the novel, this same passage shapes a circular temporality that has no exact resolution, as explained by Ricoeur.

For the second class, students are required to read Genette's *Figuras III*. We discuss the notion of narrator as posed in chapter 5. The protagonist in *El cuarto de atrás*, named C, is a self-conscious, second-level narrator.[1] Her conversation with *el hombre vestido de negro* ("the man dressed in black") both constitutes the plot and is embodied in it. The man as C's interlocutor has a double function. The content of their conversation functions as diegesis (narration) for an extradiegetic reader;[2] as actual material it functions intradiegetically, for intradiegetic readers of C's unfinished novel or novel in progress. The positions of narrator, author, and interlocutor are exchanged throughout the novel. Inasmuch as they are objects in the narrative, they serve as metadiegesis, a narrative that analyzes narrative from within.

The homodiegetic narrator (a character in the story) in *El cuarto de atrás* is also a good example of a metanarrator (one who tells a story about a story). C questions her place in the narration—for example, in the scene in chapter 2 in which the man in black scrutinizes the role of literature as a means to escape logic and create alternative worlds. In this encounter, their first, C and the man in black engage in a discussion about literature as a "refugio" (56; "refuge" [49]) or a simple "desafío a la lógica" ("defiance of logic" [50]). Her inquiring into why she writes is a recurrent theme: an analysis of the purpose of literature for the writer.

For the third class, students read *El cuento de nunca acabar*, part 1, chapters 1–3, 5–7, and Bellver's essay. In *El cuento*, Martín Gaite theorizes about writing and its difficult paths. According to her, it involves an understanding of the power of what is said and of the force that words carry in the reconstruction of an event, a person, or a story. The process entails the personal and cultural baggage of both writer and reader, baggage that can transform the initial text into many texts. She points out that every detail affects the building of a story. In her own writing, she recounts that the production of a novel takes shape from notes collected by her over time and divided by topic. She later replaces them with the "cuaderno de todo" ("notebook for everything"), which contains a chaos of ideas, "desordenado y revuelto" (60; "disorganized and tangled").[3] These ideas will be shaped by readers and listeners, who reproduce them under their own imprint.

Chapters 5 and 6 of *El cuarto de atrás* have the metaphoric names "La maleta de doble fondo" ("A False-Bottomed Valise") and "La isla de Bergai" ("The Island of Bergai"). In them, the narrator discusses literature and its numerous meanings and twists. The multiple bottoms of a specially constructed suitcase point to the creation of numerous worlds within the world of the book. For Martín Gaite, literature immerses readers progressively and maps their outlook on the world. It provides not only new eyes to observe but also new blueprints to interpret the surroundings. In chapter 5, C is woken by the ringing of the phone. The caller is a stranger who introduces herself as Carola, and she is looking for her husband, Alejandro. As this conversation begins, C looks at Tzvetan Todorov's words in his book on fantastic literature, and during her long talk with Carola, she has memories of her childhood. She realizes that Carola has very likely mistaken her for another person called C, a person who resembles her in many ways. Images mix with Todorov's thoughts: "el tiempo y el espacio de la vida sobrenatural no son el tiempo y el espacio de la vida cotidiana" (126; "the time and space of supernatural life are not the time and space of daily life" [145]). Martín Gaite intermingles a past episode with her friend in school, the writing of her novel, her memories of Franco's regime, and the uncanny conversation with a woman who is sure that C is the lover of her husband, Alejandro, presumably the man in black. All four things have Todorov's words as their underlying base. Physically, there is the false-bottomed suitcase that Carola finds in her attic. The many spaces that it holds allow more content than that held by an ordinary suitcase. In this chapter, different mental scenarios, like the things that Carola finds in the suitcase, are linked.

A Modern Peninsular Literature Course

I examine five novels in the modern literature graduate course: *Nada*, by Carmen Laforet (1945; 2008); *Primera memoria*, by Ana María Matute (1960; *School of the Sun*); *La familia de Pascual Duarte*, by Camilo José Cela (1942; *Pascual Duarte's Family*); *Tiempo de silencio*, by Luis Martín-Santos (1960; *Time of Silence*); and Martín Gaite's *El cuarto de atrás*. I include her *Usos amorosos de la postguerra española* (1987; *Courtship Customs in Postwar Spain* [2004]) as one of the primary texts for this class, along with one critical essay for each novel. Although the course is conducted entirely in Spanish, all its texts are available in English, so the readings could also form the basis for a course on twentieth-century Spanish literature in translation.

Students analyze the novels through a theoretical and historical approach. The evolution of the representation of women in the fiction produced by men and women in Spain in the Franco era (and immediately thereafter) is the object of our analysis. Students read each novel with one chapter of *Usos amorosos* and a selection of theoretical and critical texts. For instance, *Nada* is read with chapter 4, "La otra cara de la moneda" ("The Other Side of the Coin"), which is about the humor magazine *El codorniz* ("The Quail") and resistance to traditional gender roles under Franco. *Primera memoria* is read with chapter 2 of *Usos amorosos*, "En busca del cobijo" ("In Search of Protection"), which deals with the reduced social options open to women who adhered to conventional expectations. *Pascual Duarte* is combined with chapter 5, "Entre santa y santo, pared de cal y canto" (given the Spanish title in *Courtship Customs*, the refrain appearing as "Even male and female saints need a thick wall to separate them" [84]), which discusses women's education, explores the concept of masculinity that was imposed on men, and explains the dichotomy between "good women" and "loose women" that was ingrained in them. *Tiempo de silencio* is combined with two chapters: 8 ("El tira y afloja" ["Advance and Retreat"]), which is about women's training to catch a man and how little the sexes actually knew about each other thanks to stringent courtship codes, and 9 ("Cada cosa a su tiempo" ["Everything in Its Time"]), which considers the sanctioned stages of male-female relationships. Other theoretical lenses are nationalism, new historicism, irony, parody, and intertextuality in these works.

El cuarto de atrás is read in two two-hour-and-forty-minute weekly class sessions with chapter 3 of *Usos amorosos*, "El legado de José Antonio" ("The Legacy of José Antonio"), in which Martín Gaite describes the infamous Servicio Social ("Social Service"), which was led by Pilar Primo de Rivera, José Antonio Primo de Rivera's sister.[4] The Servicio Social was a mandatory program for single or widowed women aged fifteen to thirty-five. They were taught to be ideal wives and companions for their men. For the Falange the only three serious duties a woman could perform were loving her husband, sewing his clothes, and bearing him all the children that God commanded. Passivity and submissiveness were the most important qualities that a woman could display under Franco, and the Servicio Social was the institution created to reinforce and disseminate this ideology.

In *El cuarto de atrás* C refers on several occasions to the strict rules of the Servicio Social. In chapter 3, "Ven pronto a Cúnigan" ("Come to Cúnigan Soon") and during her conversation with the man in black, she tells how she abhorred this oppressive and totalitarian government program, how she rejected the Servicio Social dictates and the figure of Isabel la Católica, who was the symbol of sacrifice and a model for Spanish women. The magazine *Y* was one of the vehicles of indoctrination that the regime used.[5] The popular saying "Mujer que sabe latín no puede tener buen fin" (84–85; "A woman who knows Latin can come to no good end" [88]) encompassed the idea of education as nondesirable for women at that time. C casts off the patterns and models of the Servicio Social, the magazine *Y*, and other voices that advocated "alegría y actividad" (85; "happiness and activity" [89]) in women as the foundational characteristics of a splendid wife. C explains how these repressive dogmas affected her:

> Bajo el machaconeo de aquella propaganda ñoña y optimista de los años cuarenta, se perfiló mi desconfianza hacia los seres decididos y seguros, [y] crecieron mis ansias de libertad . . . (87)
>
> As a consequence of the brainwashing of that mawkish and optimistic propaganda of the forties, my mistrust of resolute and self-assured individuals became more marked than ever, [and] my eagerness for freedom grew . . ." (92)

The ways in which chapter 3 of *Usos amorosos* is exemplified in *El cuarto de atrás* give students an understanding of the political context in which the novel was produced and of the strict gender roles enforced by Franco's regime. I have also found it helpful to assign the reading of Todorov's *The Fantastic*, chapter 3 ("The Uncanny and the Marvelous"), and Sigmund Freud's *The Uncanny*. For further discussion of *El cuarto de atrás* as a representation of the genre of the fantastic, I also assign one of the many critical essays that analyze this novel: Joan Brown's "A Fantastic Memoir: Technique and History in *El cuarto de atrás*."

Requirements, Evaluation, and Grading

Students are quizzed every class on the reading material assigned for it. They are also asked to submit a response paper for every class, in both courses. In the response paper, they analyze one aspect of the novel that interested them. The ideas developed in this assignment are usually used by students to contribute to class discussion. They tend to examine the works structurally (narrator, space, time, discourse, tropes, and metaphors) and theoretically from various perspectives. They frequently engage in feminist readings of the work. Other analyses have explored the masculine voice versus the feminine voice, the role of literature, the role of biography (comparing C with the author of *El cuarto de atrás*), the notion of authorship, the inner exile of the writer, the text as a testimonial, and memory and history. The final paper should be based on one of the novels read in class. Before it is written, students must explain their thesis to the class and provide supporting arguments. This presentation leads to a debate and defense of their thesis. The resulting feedback and suggestions determine if students need to revise their plan for the final paper.

In my experience, graduate students enjoy parallel readings of Martín Gaite's *El cuarto de atrás* and some of her nonfiction works, a combined approach that helps them understand theory by asking them to use it in a direct, accessible manner. The simultaneous reading of selected works of fiction and nonfiction helps them understand a range of theoretical ideas and track those ideas in the fictional works. Because these classes are structured on the model of a workshop, students are able to practically apply various theoretical tools to the texts. In their final presentations, they propose and defend a thesis, demonstrating that they have learned how to integrate the theory learned in class into their own analyses.

NOTES

All Spanish quotations are from the 2009 Siruela edition of the novel and from Helen Lane's English translation of the book.

[1] Within the main narration, another narrator of short embedded passages is inserted. This second-level narrator holds a self-conscious perspective toward the novel, revealing to readers that the story is an invention. Her remarks on the storytelling process highlight the gap between fiction and reality, a common feature of metafiction.

[2] Two reader figures, a term used by Genette (*Figures III* 255–56), are notable: the fictive (extradiegetic) reader, who operates at the level of the narrator, and the fictional (intradiegetic) reader, who operates at the level of the action.

[3] A substantial collection of excerpts from these notebooks was published in the posthumous anthology *Cuadernos de todo*.

[4] José Antonio Primo de Rivera was the founder of the political party Falange Española, whose fascist ideology was the foundation of Franco's regime. He was executed after being found guilty of rebellion by the Republicans. After his death, he became "el Gran Ausente" ("The Great Absent One") and an important icon of Francoism (*Usos amorosos* 55; *Courtship Customs* 55).

[5] Other magazines published at the time besides *Y* were *Chicos* ("Young People") and *Mis Chicas* ("My Girlfriends"). Saturated with political proselytism and attempts to indoctrinate, they each made their ideology and agenda clear.

Fairy Tales and Rewriting: Teaching *Caperucita en Manhattan*

Lissette Rolón Collazo

A motif in the fiction of Martín Gaite is the revisiting of classics of so-called children's literature, a genre that shaped her as a reader and eventually as a writer. Her contributions to children's literature, especially her 1990 novel *Caperucita en Manhattan* ("Little Red Riding Hood in Manhattan"), are accessible and resonant for students. In this essay I contextualize the novel, then describe a teaching methodology that approaches it as a vehicle for both literary analysis and the student rewriting of fairy tales. Creative rewriting may sound daunting, but I have found that with instructor support—for example, grounding the activity in the critical tools afforded by narratology—students can achieve it successfully. The task can also be particularly instructive and enjoyable given the students' interest in a novel that reworks a familiar fairy tale in quite subversive terms.

Martín Gaite's Children's Literature

As early as the first post-Franco phase of her narrative (i.e., 1976–85 [Rolón Collazo, *Figuraciones*]), Martín Gaite cultivated her own versions of children's stories, which until fairly recently have been dismissed as popular literature. The first of her stories of this kind, *El castillo de las tres murallas* ("The Three-Walled Castle," about a mother and her daughter who fights for social justice), was published in 1981.[1] The second, *El pastel del diablo* ("The Devil's Pie," in which the young heroine seeks freedom and wisdom), appeared in 1985.

Collected in the volume *Dos cuentos maravillosos* ("Two Fantastic Tales"), they established a pattern in later fairy tales by Martín Gaite: the protagonist oscillates between identification with or attachment to the immediate surroundings and a social cause,[2] then escapes into a fictive or magical space.

The classical fairy tale that *Caperucita en Manhattan* rewrites was first recorded by Charles Perrault at the end of the seventeenth century, and "Little Red Riding Hood" may have more versions than any other.[3] In the written representations of the oral tradition, a girl leaves her home and encounters a stranger in the woods. In Martín Gaite's version, a young American girl, Sara Allen, encounters a wolf in a different sort of forest: New York City. Although the novel is set in the United States, it has not yet been translated into English.[4]

In *Castillo*, *Pastel*, and *Caperucita*, an exceptional woman subverts the representation of women in traditional fairy tales. The socialization process in Martín Gaite's stories challenges generic convention in that the woman is transformed by liberating qualities and acts. The publication of *La Reina de las Nieves* (1994; *The Farewell Angel* [1999]) completed her venture into the realm of children's literature, though it was a novel for adults. *Reina* analyzes elements of the genre as pre-text and creates new representations that resist both the hegemonic culture and the original texts. Although, unlike *Caperucita*, *Reina* is not exactly a rewriting of a tale—in this case, of Hans Christian Andersen's "Snow Queen"—the evocation of an original functions as a pre-text for the narrative.

A Narratological Approach to Caperucita en Manhattan

Theoretical underpinnings of *Caperucita* involve the formal analysis of narrative (narratology), in particular the narrative of folktales. Once the concepts of this approach have been transmitted, students can apply them to their own, original narratological exercise. This task is geared to students who have reached an advanced level of language competency, in teaching contexts that can range from high school to upper-level undergraduate and graduate Spanish courses.

Regardless of level, this approach fulfills many goals. In a Spanish language class, it provides activities for the development of comprehension (primarily aural and reading skills) and production (oral skills related to textual analysis, critical reactions, and opportunities for both essay and creative writing). Critical thinking skills, for which questioning is perhaps the quintessential exercise, also are reinforced. In a course on literary criticism or cultural theory, this approach can combine narratology and feminism, or it can be included in a course devoted to Russian formalism, structuralism, or feminist theories.

An Introduction to Narratology

Narratology is one of structuralism's most vigorous branches. Its premise is that every narration has a profound structure that has been conventionally agreed on. The field's purpose is to identify, decipher, and explore the elements of that structure. The pioneers of this field took as their point of departure the distinction between *fabula* (the story) and *syuzhet* (the plot, the telling of the story) made by the Russian formalists, along with the findings of Vladimir Propp in his studies of popular and traditional tales.

Propp's classic *Morphology of the Folktale* developed the concept of function to enrich the conventional analysis of characters. The dramatis personae, Propp argued, should be studied from the standpoint of the functions they perform in the development of the narration. He classified the actions and roles of the characters according to these functions, though not all popular narrations exhibited all the functions.[5] His organizational scheme overstresses the binary of hero and villain. Furthermore, for both hero and villain masculine identity is the default. It is also assumed that the hero plays the most active role among the dramatis personae and that his culminating marriage is heterosexual. These conventions of the hegemonic culture, as feminist critics have long noted, perpetuate social expectations and socialization in line with traditional gender roles.[6]

But Propp's taxonomy is just one of several possible models for narratological analysis. Other currents in narratology shift emphasis to the elements of the *fabula* or story (events, actors, time, place), to the elements of the *syuzhet* or plot (sequences, rhythm, frequency, focalization), or to the fictional discourse (as outlined by Bal).

The distinctions among *fabula*, *syuzhet*, and text are significant. The first refers to narrative content in chronological order; the second points to the narration per se and the way in which it is presented by the narrator or narrators; the third encompasses many dimensions, including kinds of narrator, description, and commentary and levels of narration. Each discourse or text constitutes a possible version of the *fabula*.

Claude Bremond, Gérard Genette, and Roland Barthes proposed other models and typologies of study that either emphasize certain elements or consider global features of the narration (e.g., the function of narrations in society). Bremond recommends studying narrations from the standpoint of the transformation of characters (their improvement or degradation [90–94]). Barthes develops a model that studies narrations in terms of three fundamental elements: narrative function, action, and discourse. In his *Figures III*, Genette offers a model that studies narration using the elements of presentation and focalization (revising the New Critics' notion of point of view), among others.[7]

Narratology has launched debates about the art of storytelling and its social functionality, about typologies and their convenience and inconvenience, and about the analytic developments that its descriptive scrutiny can and does enable. Mieke Bal, insisting on narratology's extraordinary potential as a method for identification and description, has urged critics to take the findings of narratological studies as points of departure for interpretations that take into account social constructs such as gender, race, and class (17).

The inventory of analytic questions that can be derived from narratology is extensive. Some of the more frequent questions are: Who speaks? Who is the addressee? When and where does the speaking take place? How much does the speaker know? Who sees? What are the events? How does the story begin and end? Which characters participate, what are their functions, and what transformations do the characters undergo? What kind of presentation is chosen, and what difference does that choice make? What is the relation among event, commentary, and description? Other questions depend on the aspect or element that a given analysis engages. Narratological analysis, therefore, is useful to elucidate any kind of narration, from story to advertisement to movie to political campaign. Every text that tells a story is a narration.

Before or during class discussions on narratology, students may be asked to investigate core concepts using any bibliographical resource, from the library or the Internet. They might search for information about structuralism, narration, narratology, Propp, Barthes, or Genette. Mini research projects and in-class presentations can complement the instructor's synthesis of concepts.

A Brief Narratological Analysis of Caperucita en Manhattan

A pedagogical narratological analysis is necessarily geared to enriching students' understanding of a text within the constraints of a course syllabus. This goal can be achieved by limiting the analysis to a study of the main players in *Caperucita*, along with their functions and the social and cultural implications that Martín Gaite's variation evokes with respect to Perrault's "Little Red Riding Hood." In narratology, characters are called actors and actresses, and their actions and the scenes in which they participate are emphasized (Propp uses the term "dramatis personae" [25–65]; Bal, "actors or actresses" [33–45]; Greimas, "actants" [67–70]). With a study of its actresses, I demonstrate how *Caperucita* problematizes the hero-villain binary implicit in Propp's model of functions while at the same time developing new subjectivities for women and alternative models of socialization.

Sara Allen, a ten-year-old girl who lives in Brooklyn, takes advantage of the absence of her parents to visit her grandmother, Rebeca, in Manhattan. To get to Morningside, where Rebeca lives, Sara travels through Central Park. There she meets Miss Lunatic, a marvelous woman who does not appear in Perrault's version, and Mr. Woolf, a rich businessman who owns a gigantic pastry shop and is sad because his strawberry pies have lost their popularity. Miss Lunatic inspires Caperucita's solitary trip and her conquest of fear in order to achieve freedom, while the wolf ends up being assisted by the girl instead of becoming a predatory villain.

According to Propp's classificatory system, Martín Gaite's narration contains many of the functions of folktales. But the most interesting functions in the novel are those that modify or altogether invert classic models. Some transform the hero-villain binary, while others do not ascribe heroism to an exclusive character: for example, Miss Lunatic shares with Sara the status of heroine. Mr. Woolf, far from being the wolf who besieges, tricks, and eats his victims, becomes the recipient of Sara's and Rebeca's affection and the provider of the girl's dreams. Grandmother Rebeca and Mr. Woolf fall in love, and Sara achieves both the trip and the freedom she has desired. Miss Lunatic reveals that she is Madame Bartholdi or the Statue of Liberty, one of the circumstances that confer heroism on her.

The Propp functions that posit evil, failure, or punishment of the villain are inverted. Mr. Woolf does not harm Sara and is not vanquished or punished. Sara does not return home (at least not at the diegetic or story-world level), does not get married, and does not ascend the throne. On the contrary, she cultivates solitude and undertakes a journey to freedom that knows no return. Martín Gaite's Little Red Riding Hood is a heroine who does not submit to any of the social expectations for a girl her age.

What are the cultural implications of the changes that *Caperucita en Manhattan* introduced to Perrault's version of the tale? With the exception of Vivian Allen (Sara's mother) and her friend (Mrs. Taylor),[8] in Martín Gaite's version the main actresses—Sara, Rebeca, and Miss Lunatic—constitute alternatives to the hegemonic roles assigned to women: they are free of social constraints and committed to the problems of the city. For María Soliño, *Caperucita* is centered around nontraditional feminine figures:[9]

> In this new female-centered text, older women are beautiful, active members of society worthy of love and romance, and not just evil old hags. Little girls such as Sara grow happily and normally by exploring the exciting world that lies outside their windows. But most importantly, the females in *Caperucita en Manhattan* love and help each other. The spokeswoman for traditional patriarchal society, the mother Vivian Allen, is written out of the text early on in the novel. (88)

Whereas Vivian Allen perfectly reproduces the role of homemaker and heterosexual wife while rejecting Sara and Rebeca, since they seem to be always "pensando en otra cosa" (33; "thinking about something else"), Sara resists becoming like her mother. She enjoys reading, looks for adventure and freedom, and accepts solitude joyfully:

> . . . Sara tenía que quedarse a solas para conocer la atracción del impulso, la alegría de la decisión y el temor del acontecer. Venciendo el miedo que le quedara, conquistaría la Libertad. (158)

> . . . Sara had to remain alone in order to experience the attraction of impulse, the joy of a decision, and the fear of things happening. Overcoming the fear that remained, she would conquer Freedom.

Rebeca lives alone in Morningside, has been married several times, was an actress at a music hall, knows very well how to tell stories, and is bored by cooking (68). This figure, who bears some similarity to Broadway artists, becomes the inspiration and the object of emulation of the heroine. Sara's encounter with her grandmother without a third party present (a previous visit included Sara's mother) is the main motive for Sara's journey.

But the subjectivity that Sara ultimately imitates is that of Miss Lunatic (Madame Bartholdi and the Statue of Liberty). In this female character, who corresponds to the typology of the fairy in folktales, Martín Gaite fuses escapism and involvement in social issues. The mysterious old woman, at first dressed as a beggar, devotes herself to helping others with her supernatural powers.

Caperucita en Manhattan is an example of the possibilities of liberation and subversion of the children's literature genre. A narratological analysis of Martín Gaite's rewriting of "Little Red Riding Hood" reveals liberating variations or inversions of narrative functions related to gender. As Jack Zipes has shown in "The Potential of Liberating Fairy Tales," these stories can transform the codes of socialization of classical narrative functions, and they can enable subversive social strategies. Through the representation of emergent women who transcend Propp's functions or problematize the hegemonic hero-villain binary, Martín Gaite contributes to this process of transformation and supports initiatives that promote alternative subjectivities and roles for women.[10] Instead of warning about the dangers of the forest and thereby reinforcing women's relegation to the domestic sphere, *Caperucita* invites women to achieve freedom by overcoming fear and the social prohibitions that seek to restrict and isolate them.

The ECA Methodology

The methodological strategy known as ECA (exploration, conceptualization, and application) is the basis for the organization of my pedagogical unit on *Caperucita en Manhattan*. This strategy, developed by Ángel Villarini, allows for the development of skills while drawing on students' previous knowledge. It also recognizes students as active agents in the process of teaching and learning.

During the exploration phase, students display their intuitive or formal knowledge and insights about the material under discussion. They also identify the skills to be developed. The conceptualization phase develops the historical, intellectual, and analytic contents of the material (in this case, of narratology). In the application phase, students extend their acquired knowledge to other texts; at the same time, they evaluate their own and others' critical applications. This exercise also allows them to extrapolate skills from narratology to improve their linguistic and cultural competencies.

With respect to the analytic goals of this methodology, the unit features the critical application of various basic concepts of narratology (actor-actress, function, hero, villain), an exercise in creative rewriting inspired by Martín Gaite's rewriting of "Little Red Riding Hood," peer-to-peer discussion and exchange, and the formulation of a brief response essay in which students assess the social and cultural implications of some of their classmates' versions of fairy tales.

Description and Objectives of the Creative Rewriting Exercise

Once students are familiar with some of the fundamentals and possibilities of narratology and have identified the innovative elements in *Caperucita en Manhattan*, they are in a position to undertake a creative exercise. Depending on the level of their language skills, preparation for the exercise might include distribution of bilingual vocabulary lists, a basic summary of Propp's functions in Spanish, a portfolio of sample stories by prior students, or perusal of Spanish-language picture-book fairy tales, whose occasionally harsh endings will surprise many students. Although I use such supportive material separately for students, this exercise also could be carried out collaboratively in pairs or small groups, which would add brainstorming and consensus-building tasks. Writing cues could also be converted into discussion topics if the instructor wishes to shift the focus from written to oral expression.

The exercise has four steps. First, students are asked to create a narrative structure based on one to four of Propp's functions. The concept of *fabula* or story should be emphasized here. They should write a brief description of what happens associated with each function. This structure should be given in the chronological order of events. Second, students are asked to create a narration using the chosen functions and the described events. The concept of *syuzhet* or plot is paramount here. Students must make sure that the sequence, pace, actors and actresses, and elements of the narration are organized in a manner different from the chronological one. Their organization will depend on their own creative plan and on the desired effect on readers. In the third step, students read and react orally to their peers' stories. At this time they are asked to take notes on one or more of the other students' versions. Finally students are asked to write a brief essay (two to three pages) answering the following question about one or more peer essays of their choosing: What are the sociocultural implications of this story?

My approach to teaching Martín Gaite's *Caperucita en Manhattan* is built on the premise that both the formal analysis of literature and creative rewriting can serve as foundations for the development of students' linguistic and sociocultural competencies. Specifically, this approach strengthens comprehension and production in Spanish while generating awareness of both the formal and the social dimensions of literature. Notable aspects of the social dimension are the cultural influence of categories, characteristics, and roles associated with gender. For advanced learners of Spanish, *Caperucita* is a text that enables the transmission and application of critical concepts. The powerful fascination that this novel and fairy tales in general hold for students can be harnessed to inspire both analysis and creativity in Spanish.

NOTES

I thank Beatriz Llenín Figueroa for translating this essay.

[1]For criticism on this text, see El Saffar, "Carmen Martín Gaite"; Brown, *Secrets* 166–71.

[2]Soliño finds that the theme of Martín Gaite's first story for young people is socialist: "*El castillo de las tres murallas* has a rather obvious socialist message. The local townspeople are starving, and in spite of the high taxes they pay Lucandro, he prefers to leave his best farmland fallow while they strive to survive by farming rocky hillsides. Altalé at an early age becomes the champion of these people by openly defying her father and giving the peasants land" (95).

[3]On the medieval oral versions of "Little Red Riding Hood," see Ziolkowski. A Spanish version of Perrault's tale is in Álvarez. On the cultural implications of the multiplicity of folktale versions, see Zipes, *Trials*.

[4]*Caperucita en Manhattan* has been translated into Italian, German, Japanese, and many other languages (Martinell Gifre, *Al encuentro* 88).

[5]Propp identified thirty-one functions in the folktale. Among them are an interdiction is given to the hero; the interdiction is violated; the villain reconnoiters; the villain attempts to deceive the hero in order to take possession of him or his belongings; the hero, deceived, unwittingly helps his enemy; the villain causes harm to a member of the family; the hero leaves home; the hero is tested, interrogated, attacked, and so on, which prepares the way for his receiving either a magical agent or a helper of some kind; the hero and the villain join in direct combat; the hero is branded; the villain is defeated; the initial misfortune or lack is repaired; the returning hero is pursued; the hero, unrecognized, arrives home or in another country; the hero is given a difficult task; the task is accomplished; the hero is recognized; the hero is given a new appearance; the villain is punished; and the hero marries and ascends the throne.

[6]For another critique of narratology that focuses on gender, see Lanser.

[7]Other theoreticians of narratology who propose complementary or alternative models are Greimas; Todorov ("Structural Analysis").

[8]After what Mrs. Taylor hears on television advice shows, she suggests that Vivian take Sara to a psychiatrist (33, 45).

[9]Martín Gaite begins this phase with what might be called a hybrid narration, straddling the folktale and the novel. The publication of *Reina* shows an inclination toward the novel, although many resonances of children's literature persist.

[10]Some critics who address this issue are Stone; Zipes, *Don't Bet*; and Kolbenschlag. See also Bottigheimer.

The Practice of Literature: "In Search of an Interlocutor" through Carmen Martín Gaite's *Nubosidad variable*

Randolph D. Pope

> We ought not to confine ourselves either to writing or to reading; the one, continuous writing, will cast a gloom over our strength, and exhaust it; the other will make our strength flabby and watery. It is better to have recourse to them alternately, and to blend one with the other, so that the fruits of one's reading may be reduced to concrete form by the pen.
>
> —Seneca, Letter 84 to Lucilius

Before I propose here my method to actively read a novel by Carmen Martín Gaite in an advanced-level course that involves a considerable amount of writing, I must face my difficulty in writing about this topic. Since I have not only read her work but also am privileged to have known her, I can hear her admonishing me—marginally, without stressing it, yet firmly—to drop my professorial self and engage directly in conversation with her and with her work. To converse does include the fairly constant evaluation going on in our minds, but it also must part with critical distance: it requires engagement. For some, the concept of engagement lost its luster after the politics of existentialism and Marxism, and even of Christian thought à la Jacques Maritain (Christian existentialism), a politics that collapsed by becoming too rigid and that was overcome by historical events.

But engagement is central to Martín Gaite's presentation of experience—not as conceptual rigor but as personal encounter. Meeting and communicating with a person one cares about, recognizing the uniqueness of this communication, and keeping the unique dialogue alive are the main adventures of much of her work. They are adventures because they involve risk (one may be disappointed), involve leaving the comfortable rut (movement away, distancing), and there are obstacles along the way, as when one tries to reach a hidden treasure or goes on a spiritual quest. Martín Gaite explained the difficulty of finding someone with whom one could talk not at but with: "La del interlocutor no es una búsqueda fácil ni de resultados previsibles y seguros . . . porque no da igual cualquier interlocutor" ("Búsqueda" 26; "The search for an interlocutor is not easy nor does it offer predictable or sure results . . . because not every interlocutor is the same").[1] My purpose in teaching is the creation of interlocutors and the engagement of readers.

A Writing-Intensive Seminar with Personal Engagement

Among the many good reasons for teaching any literary text are to improve students' linguistic skills, to increase their familiarity with another country and historical period, and to develop their ability to read critically. I find that requiring from students a good amount of regular writing helps them consolidate their grammar and syntax (no easy task), expand their vocabulary, and refine their ability to formulate and analyze challenging ideas. For Martín Gaite, writing was always more than a labor to perform well; it was a personal activity that could expose her. I want students to learn from her example, to open up and enter into a real conversation.

My seminars are clearly labeled as ones in which personal writing will be required. But student privacy is ensured: no information contained in what students write will be revealed in class, and I promise that at the end of the semester all files containing their writing will be deleted from my computer. I have discovered, teaching several courses in which this confessional approach is encouraged, such as seminars on European autobiography, that having students hand in a printed copy makes them cautious, as does my returning in class their pages with my comments. We take advantage of electronic pseudo-intimacy: they send me their weekly texts as attachments before midnight of a certain day (most texts come in a few minutes before twelve), and I send my comments back also late at night. I stress often that they are writing primarily not for me but for themselves.

The Text Reading the Reader: Analyzing and Emulating the Author's Strategies

The predominant mode of criticism today is to use literature as part of a web of information to gain a critical insight into a culture. This goal is definitely praiseworthy, yet it folds into itself an obliviousness to the uniqueness of literary accomplishment. Critical insight can be an important reminder of the values that lead to positive social change, but typically it remains at the level of conceptual understanding, reaffirming the critics-readers in their laudable stand without examining further the possibility of action. Martín Gaite's novels and essays work against the grain, resisting being consumed as entertainment or even as information, questioning our way of living, displaying all the subversive strength of the essay and of fiction. They are a superb example of what Roland Barthes suggested as the text reading the reader, by making him or her complicit in its own writing.[2] How does Martín Gaite accomplish this, and how can we use her strategies not only to analyze her writing but also to emulate her?

Teaching Nubosidad variable*: Reading, Writing, and Rescue*

Nubosidad variable (*Variable Cloud*) is a novel about writing and friendship.[3] Because it is long, it is appropriate at the undergraduate level only for an advanced seminar where one can devote several weeks to it. It is electrifying to get involved with this novel, to encounter it by writing alongside it, by imitating its process. I follow the strategy proposed by Seneca: Do not confine the activity to either reading or writing, but rather entwine them: "Nec scribere tantum nec tantum legere debemus" (276; "We ought not to confine ourselves either to writing or to reading" [278]).

This novel tells the story of two women, Sofía Montalvo and Mariana León, who for many years were schoolmates and best friends, until they both fell in love with the same fellow university student, Guillermo. They went their separate ways, and each knew nothing of the other's life. Sofía, especially talented at writing, dropped out of the university and married a businessman, Eduardo, with whom she has three children. Mariana became a psychiatrist and lives alone. She has no children and is now in a tumultuous and unsatisfactory relationship with one of her patients, who appears to be bisexual. Both Sofía and Mariana reminisce about the time they were in school and anticipating what was to come. They think of each other, imagining their reunion: "Un tema recurrente en esas historias era el de nuestro reencuentro cuando fuéramos mayores, después de haber estado largo tiempo separadas por circunstancias de la vida" (58; "A recurrent theme in those stories was our meeting again when we were older, having been separated for years by force of circumstance" [48]). Beyond the prophetic nature of these stories, we see their wisdom in accepting the difficulties of life while keeping a beacon of hope.

Sofía and Mariana meet at the inauguration of an art exhibit and rekindle their friendship by deciding to write to each other. One will send a letter, the other will write a notebook, but both will reflect on their lives in the warmth that their friendship provides. There is a wonderful quality about this friendship, which in its cultural and historical context may be viewed as feminine. The women are open, interested in each other, considerate of each other's family. The relationship flows, not trapped by a pose or competitive impulse. Guillermo, Sofía's husband, Mariana's present lover, and Sofía's male children are shadowy figures in a stale background that has become toxic.

Writing will release in Mariana and Sofía the courage they need to rescue their lives. Mariana will take time away from her patients; Sofía will distance herself from her husband. By meeting with each other, they manage to find themselves. In the final pages of the novel we see them happily reunited, reading what they have written, far from their jobs and families, perhaps ready to attempt a new beginning in which they can support each other. They present a model that I offer my students, not only to analyze but also to try for themselves. Very clearly Martín Gaite states that writing is a way to deepen an understanding of ourselves and improve our lives.

To live well, I believe, is an art that can be learned. Most of our students, despite their ear pods, buzzing phones, and *Facebook* entourages, are under great stress and live on an emotional roller coaster. I want to restore for them one of the ancient functions of literature: the use of stories as models for the care of the self. Michel Foucault reminds us:

> No technique, no professional skill can be acquired without exercise: nor can the art of living, the *technē tou biou*, be learned without an *askēsis* that should be understood as a training of the self by oneself. This was one of the traditional principles to which the Pythagoreans, the Socratics, the Cynics had long attached a great importance. (208)

This training involves both reading and writing, activities that are contemplation of the self fired by imagination, where not only what has happened may be seen thoroughly but also what could have been and what might be. Foucault tells us of the practice of keeping notebooks with "a material and a framework for exercises to be carried out frequently: reading, rereading, meditating, conversing with oneself and with others" (210)—not just to know but also to know how to act. Mariana and Sofía use writing as a form of conversation with the self and with others. I encourage students to start their own search in writing, parallel to Martín Gaite's. They are sure to have a friend from whom they have grown distant and whom they can propose as an interlocutor. Their first step should be to enter the novel as a fellow writer, in a search that makes the novel matter.

Overcoming Obstacles to the Search for an Interlocutor

Many of the obstacles to this search are presented in the novel. One obstacle is the fear of what we might find in ourselves. In my course on European autobiography I offer students the option of writing a scholarly paper or writing entries of their autobiography during the semester. Most choose the autobiography assignment, believing at first that it will be easier, but without fail a few weeks later several show up at my office crying—I am not exaggerating—because autobiographical writing proves too painful: it dredges up the ugly and rightfully forgotten. Furthermore, since I encourage students to share their recollections with their families, they get versions that differ from theirs and sometimes passionate denials or corrections. As Mariana says, many of the questions that arise "eran porqués sin respuesta; yo misma en el fondo no quería buscarla, tenía miedo de hurgar en lo que habría podido darme una respuesta fea" (25; "they were questions that had no answers; deep down, I didn't want to find one, I was afraid of rooting around in things that might produce an answer I didn't want to hear" [15]).

Another obstacle is the difficulty of devoting time to the self. Mariana is busy with her patients, Sofía with her husband and children. Both need to get away, to carve out for themselves the required silence and solitude. Mariana simply takes off, leaving a temporary replacement, Josefina Carreras, in charge. Perhaps the name Carreras ("races, sprints") signals the intensely busy life Mariana leads, with no time for what Foucault outlines as the main objectives of good care of the self: "withdrawing into oneself, getting in touch with oneself, living with oneself, relying on oneself, benefiting from and enjoying oneself" (211).

Our students usually do not have time for a retreat, for hours of contemplation, or for productive conversations deep into the night. I request therefore a short piece of meditative writing every week, one double-spaced page, no more than two. I respond to it with commentary that has the tone of a conversation. The first few pieces that come in are cursory and detached, weak and with all the defects of a successful scholarly paper—there is no risk and no personal exploration. My task, as in any writing course that encourages self-revelatory prose, is to make students comfortable with speaking in their own voice and challenging their reading with their life experience. I admit that I am not sure which elements of this methodology are crucial to effecting a change in student writing—whether it is my comments urging students on or simply that they become more adept with practice. I do know that this technique inevitably produces a transformation: soon students are engaged in real writing and connecting the novel with their own lives.

I try not to overintellectualize when dealing with sensitive topics. Not all professors will agree that the risk of confronting sensitive topics should be taken, believing that our defense mechanisms are there for a reason. Certainly, a writing-intensive seminar such as the one I describe can be conducted without delving into the personal. The risk I seek to confront is one that Martín Gaite recognizes in *Nubosidad variable*, when a patient challenges Mariana's approach to knowledge, her epistemological strategy:

> No digo que no hayas bajado alguna vez [a los pozos de oscuridad de la sexualidad], pero como un submarinista cauto y sofisticado, protegido por artilugios de seguridad respiratoria, que tiene buen cuidado de revisar previamente para que no le fallen. Es lo que hacéis generalmente los profesores. Por eso vuestras aportaciones al esclarecimiento de los problemas confusos son correctas pero insuficientes. Precisamente el erotismo es como una marea que rompe los diques de lo inteligible. Y tú quieres entender sin arriesgarte a dejarte anegar por esa marea. (108)
>
> I am not saying that you may not have descended sometimes [into the obscure wells of sexuality], but as a cautious and sophisticated scuba diver, protected by contraptions for safe breathing which you have carefully checked beforehand to make sure they will not fail. That is what you professors usually do. That is the reason why your contributions to illuminating confusing problems are correct but insufficient. Precisely, the erotic is like a tide that breaks the dams of the intelligible. And you want to understand without risking that you could be overwhelmed by that tide. (my trans.)[4]

How can I wear protective scuba-diving gear and at the same time encourage my students to have the daring of Martín Gaite? When did we decide that a literature class was a space for nothing shocking, personal, or questionable? We may easily speak about the evils of the Franco dictatorship, the gender or class oppression in the nineteenth century, and so on, but it is not easy to turn the flashlight on ourselves. Yet, I would claim, it must be done, within the limits of the legal, the possible, and tolerable. Those who keep their armor on will remain in the traditional professorial stance, adducing information that is correct but sadly insufficient.

The Transformative Power of Diary and Letter Writing

Martín Gaite provides one of the most convincing statements I have seen in contemporary Peninsular literature of the importance of diary and letter writing as a strategy not only to explore the self but also to change it. In this sense she is connecting with an ancient tradition described by Pierre Hadot in *What Is Ancient Philosophy?*, where he explains how the early stages of philosophy were concerned less with understanding ideas than with living a good life. It was only around the first century BC that "philosophical teaching itself essentially took on the form of textual commentary" (150). Earlier, "the goal was to become better; and discourse was philosophical only if it was transformed into a way of life" (173). I am, in this respect, old-fashioned: I want to know how the reading of *Nubosidad variable* can be transformed into a way of life, how it can be applied to improve the art of living. Hadot laments that with the institutionalization of learning the excitement of learning was resolved into puzzles to be solved and quizzes to be aced. The ties between learning and life were dissolved:

> It must be admitted that there is a radical opposition between the ancient philosophical school, which addressed individuals in order to transform their entire personality, and the university, whose mission is to give diplomas which correspond to a certain level of objectifiable knowledge. . . . The goal is no longer, as it was in antiquity, to train people for careers as human beings, but to train them for careers as clerks or professors—that is to say, as specialists, theoreticians, and retainers of specific items of more or less esoteric knowledge. (260)

Martín Gaite insisted that writing about the self was transformative. It is a paradox that a text fixes into words what is actually fleeting and mutable, vital in its power to change: "El alma humana se parece a las nubes. No hay quien la coja quieta en la misma postura" (126; "The human soul is like the clouds; you never catch it in the same position twice" [114]). For this reason the writing in my courses takes place weekly, focused on the encounter between text and self, with the hope that when the writing is collected at the end, its variety will affirm creatively and positively that we are not stuck in one position. Like the characters in the novel, we can move on into life, armed with the strategy of writing to take care of ourselves.

A good friend of mine once called Martín Gaite, expressing the desire to meet her. Martín Gaite responded that she did not have time for new friends. When I heard this, I was shocked. Then I realized that her response revealed a profound respect for the other, for the time and the giving it takes to become a true interlocutor. Teaching her work requires giving of oneself, being generous with one's time. Hadot writes about Socrates, "[W]e have encountered a personality which, by its mere presence, obliges those who approach it to question themselves" (29–30). Similarly, Martín Gaite and her work raise questions always directed toward understanding ourselves better and living a better life. She knew that a better life was not about trivial happiness. It was a constant quest, which she exemplified in both life and text. My obligation is to pass along this quest to my students.

NOTES

[1]Translations are mine unless otherwise noted. Translation page numbers refer to Margaret Jull Costa's *Variable Cloud*.

[2]In *S/Z*, Barthes questions the statement "I read the text," affirming, "it is not always true. The more plural the text, the less it is written before I read it" (10). The same idea is found in his *Pleasure of the Text* (24–25 and esp. 62).

[3]Although my courses are taught in Spanish, the availability of this novel in English opens up the possibility of using this methodology in a literature-in-translation course.

[4]In *Variable Cloud*, the "wells of sexuality" ("pozos de sexualidad") are rendered more generally as "wells of darkness" (97).

French Feminism(s) and *Écriture Féminine*: Teaching *Nubosidad variable* in a Graduate Seminar

Ofelia Ferrán

In 1998, as a beginning assistant professor, I taught my first graduate seminar: Contemporary Spanish Women Writers. The class was small: five students, all women, signed up. I remember the course fondly. The reduced size of the class and the enthusiasm we all shared for the course material led us to have wonderful, engaging discussions. We read novels and short stories published by Spanish women authors between the 1960s and the 1990s, and Carmen Martín Gaite's 1992 novel *Nubosidad variable* (*Variable Cloud*) was the last reading of the course.

I remember thinking then how lucky I was to have a job that allowed me to share with others not only the literature I loved to read but also the theoretical texts, ideas, questions, and concerns that I enjoyed exploring and thinking about, as well as to find that students could become equally passionate about both. I believe that Martín Gaite herself would see this joyful classroom experience as one measure of her success as an author, since her work unfailingly elicits such a response.

Feminist Theory in a Graduate Seminar on Spanish Women's Writing

The seminar included readings in feminist literary theory—mostly, but not exclusively, French feminist literary theory, which I saw as providing rich, if debatable, theoretical frameworks for engaging with women's writing. I was interested in having the students confront the theoretical readings critically. The goal was not to have them read the theory in order to then dutifully find examples of one idea or another in the literary texts we read but rather to understand how literary and theoretical texts helped elucidate each other. I was particularly interested in exploring the usefulness, and also the limitations and possible pitfalls, of the various articulations of "*écriture féminine*," or uniquely female writing, that are present in French feminism.

I wanted the class to read the various definitions or descriptions of *écriture féminine* in such authors as Luce Irigaray, Hélène Cixous, and Julia Kristeva and to try to understand where their ideas came from, how they evolved, what kinds of assumptions underlay the theoretical concepts, and what problems might accompany those assumptions. We explored how calls for an *écriture féminine* might be seen as problematic if they implied that some essential, universal feminine nature was represented in women's writing. We also considered how they could be empowering if *écriture féminine* was understood as multiple expressions of a utopian practice that did not necessarily represent the feminine as preexisting but sought to create it through an experimental poetics—one that grew out of a critique of the concrete limitations to women's expression in a patriarchal system.

I also assigned other kinds of feminist theoretical writing in the course, especially writings produced in Spain. Many of Martín Gaite's theoretical and critical writings, despite her claim to the contrary, are clearly feminist. Finally, the seminar included readings about the history of feminism and of women's lives in contemporary Spain, in order to place the literary production of women in the contexts of the development of a women's movement and of women's changing social, political, economic, and cultural conditions.[1] In the end, the course sought to unsettle ideas of what feminism is or can be, as much as it intended to have students learn about one particular constellation of theoretical approaches that could prove useful in analyzing literature produced by women. In this essay I do not provide a systematic review of French feminisms, because such overviews already exist.[2] I refer only to specific concepts and ideas that we explored in the seminar, particularly with relation to Martín Gaite's novel. Since both the novel and many relevant theoretical materials are available in English, this approach could also be used in advanced courses taught in translation.

Foundational Theories for Analyzing Women's Writing

We began by reading Sigmund Freud's "Femininity," excerpts from Irigaray's critical rereading of Freud's essay in "The Blind Spot of an Old Dream of Symmetry," from *Speculum of the Other Woman*, and sections of her *This Sex Which Is Not One*. We also read Jacques Lacan's "The Mirror Stage as Formative of the Function of the I" and several other excerpts from his *Écrits* in which he develops his theory of the imaginary and the symbolic. We read selections of Kristeva's *Revolution in Poetic Language* in which she presents her theory of the semiotic and the symbolic, as well as Cixous's "Sorties" and "The Laugh of the Medusa." We spent time with the original texts by Freud and Lacan because I wanted students to understand how critics like Irigaray, Kristeva, and Cixous developed their theoretical models as responses to, and subversions of, previous dominant discourses.

From Irigaray's reading of Freud's "Femininity" we saw how the norm of sexual development in a phallocentric model is that of a boy and how a girl is presented as a boy who lacks a penis and is thus secondary and inferior. Irigaray reveals how a girl in Freud's model serves merely as a mirror that reflects the normal development of a boy. A girl, for her "normal" sexual development, must do something a boy does not have to do: turn against her first object of affection, her mother, in order to establish the bond with her father, through the oedipal complex, that will guarantee a stable heterosexual social order.

From Lacan's writings we saw how the "normal" development of a girl is based on distancing herself from her mother, in passing from what Lacan calls the imaginary into the symbolic realm, which for him is linked to the acquisition of language and the acceptance of the Law of the father. We explored how Kristeva develops her notion of the semiotic realm, in opposition to the symbolic, as a way to reestablish a connection with the maternal space that, in both Freud and Lacan, is repressed in order to establish a girl's normal development.

In Cixous's writings too we noticed the valorization of the maternal as one of the tropes guiding her reflections of what *écriture féminine* might look like. We explored how her call for an *écriture féminine* that writes a woman's body grows out of Cixous's deconstruction of the binary oppositions on which patriarchal thought is based, such as mind/body, culture/nature, in which woman is always associated with the negative side. A practice of *écriture féminine* deconstructs such binaries not only by affirming that which was debased in patriarchal thought (e.g., the body) but also by staunchly presenting itself as a practice that cannot be perfectly theorized or fixed, one that is in perpetual movement and flux.

We noted how for all three theorists, albeit in very different ways, such a revolutionary practice of writing somehow passes through, as Kari Weil summarizes, "woman's discovery of her repressed desires and more specifically, her repressed pleasure of *jouissance*," where *jouissance* is understood as an intense and intensely transgressive orgasmic pleasure (165). Because the patriarchal repression of a woman's body and desire is fundamentally based on a repression of the maternal, we also took note of how, for these French feminists, "the first step, then, is for woman to imagine her relation to her mother's body, in order to reverse the devaluation of her origins and her 'imaginary' within culture" (168).

Student-Led Integration of Theory and Practice

My graduate course was structured to encourage an active and critical reading practice in which theory helps us understand literature but in which—just as important—literature helps us interrogate theory. A key technique for implementing this approach is student leadership of class inquiry. My preferred methodology is collaborative, with students working together in pairs. Each pair chooses theoretical readings in which it is particularly interested, then teaches part of a class in which these readings are connected to the novel being read—an activity that is quite different from a student presentation. While the professor provides the theoretical and sociocultural scaffolding students need to build their analyses and shape the sequence of their contributions, it is the graduate students who originate much of the discussion content. In fact, they are responsible for developing the pedagogical strategies and activities to be used during the part of the class they teach. These strategies can range from small group work to full class discussion, from a detailed review of specific theoretical concepts from the day's readings to a creative group activity in which students work with the concepts in a less structured manner. As the class read *Nubosidad variable*, many of the theoretical ideas of feminism helped us understand the development of the two main characters in the novel, Sofía and Mariana, and the various roles that writing plays in their lives.

Writing, Reading, and Redemption in Nubosidad variable

Women, Writing, and Reading

Although Shoshana Felman is not a French feminist, I begin my synthesis of graduate-level exploration of Martín Gaite's novel with a quotation from her *What Does a Woman Want? Reading and Sexual Difference*, which can be helpful in getting students to think about the connections among women, writing, and reading in the novel:

> *None of us, as women, has as yet, precisely, an autobiography*. Trained to see ourselves as objects and to be positioned as the Other, estranged to ourselves, we have a story that by definition cannot be self-present to us, a story that, in other words, is not a story, but *must become* a story. And it cannot *become* a story except through the *bond of reading*, that is, through *the story of the Other* (the story read by other women, the story of other women, the story of women told by others), insofar as this story of the Other, as *our own* autobiography, *has as yet precisely to be owned*. (14)

Nubosidad variable shows how two women help each other, through the bond of reading and by becoming each other's much-needed interlocutor, to develop the stories that constitute their autobiographies. These stories are unavailable to them insofar as each woman, in a different way, is radically estranged from herself. The estrangement has much to do with the kinds of repression of the female experience that French feminists have demonstrated is at the heart of patriarchal society. Martín Gaite's novel explores the repression and alienation of her two female characters but also underscores the concrete political, social, and economic developments in Spanish society of the 1970s, 1980s, and 1990s that contributed to them.[3]

Sociocultural Criticism of 1990s Spain

Set in the early 1990s, the novel opens with the image of Sofía, a middle-aged housewife waking up in the morning to the light coming in from her bedroom window. Her husband, Eduardo, is taking a shower in the adjacent bathroom, and the sound creates an increasing sense of unease in Sofía, who is trying to hold on to the images of a dream she had that night. In her dream, she and her estranged friend Mariana, whom she has not seen in years, were together in a field that she eventually recognizes as the landscape of one of her favorite novels, which she had been reading before falling asleep: *Wuthering Heights*. After a curt exchange in which the emotional distance between husband and wife becomes apparent, Eduardo, stumbling over the novel with his expensive Italian shoe, exclaims, "¿No comprendes . . . que seguir leyedo *Cumbres borrascosas* es quedarse enquistada?" (17; "You must be in a bad way if you're re-reading *Wuthering Heights* at your age" [7]).[4]

This beginning highlights the different value systems of husband and wife: while Eduardo, the successful businessman, revels in the power and social status that his newly acquired wealth gives him, metonymically represented by his expensive Italian shoes, Sofía wishes to escape the reality of a money-oriented world through novels and dreaming. It is no coincidence that the family maid says of Eduardo, "[S]e da un flash a Mario Conde" (73; "He looks like your typical executive" [63]). Readers of the English translation miss out on the "typical executive" qualities embodied by the man mentioned in the original: Mario Conde was president of the powerful Banesto financial group in Spain and the epitome of the new, handsome, rich, aggressive, and successful Spanish businessman of the 1980s and early 1990s—until he was found to have mishandled enormous sums of money, a transgression for which he was first fired and later imprisoned. Through this comparison of Eduardo with Mario Conde, Martín Gaite criticizes a superficial, money-obsessed society, one from which Sofía has grown increasingly estranged, as she has grown increasingly estranged from her husband.

Eduardo, in turn, criticizes her interest in reading novels as "quedarse enquistada," or being regressive (literally, "stunted"), because it underscores her lack of interest in the material world he has made central to his identity and reveals her lack of interest in fulfilling the role she was expected to play in their marriage: the trophy wife who admires her husband without reservation, who contributes to his social and economic advancement by hosting parties, and who serves as a constant mirror of his success. Eduardo's characterization of Sofía's reading as "quedarse enquistada" brings to mind Irigaray's warning that "the rejection, the exclusion of a female imaginary certainly puts woman in the position of experiencing herself only fragmentarily, in the little-structured margins of a dominant ideology, as waste, or excess, what is left of a mirror invested by the (masculine) 'subject' to reflect himself, to copy himself" (*This Sex* 30). Sofía will indeed end up as a kind of "waste" in her husband's life, because, as she eventually discovers, he has long had an affair with a beautiful younger woman, one who dutifully fulfills the role of flattering mirror.[5]

Sofía will not play the supporting role of mirror to her husband's desires and needs:

> Me niego a corresponder, a representar el papel de esposa de alto status, que esconde su cansancio tras una sonrisa, lleva la batuta en conversaciones sin fuste, pasa bandejitas y se siente pagada de su trabajera

> con la típica frase: "Has estado maravillosa, querida", que le dirige el marido cuando se van los invitados, ninguno de los cuales se ha divertido un pelo. (73)

> I just refuse to play the game, to play the part of the status wife who hides her tiredness behind a smile, who calmly takes the lead in trivial conversations, passes little trays around and finds sufficient reward for all her hard work in the words: "Darling, you were wonderful," spoken by her husband once the guests have departed, none of whom have enjoyed themselves in the least. (63)

Writing as Liberation

This rejection by Sofía of the role socially expected of her marks her as a type of woman that Martín Gaite effectively analyzed in her book *Desde la ventana* ("From the Window"). In the chapter entitled "Mirando a través de la ventana" ("Looking through the Window"), she explains how many women, dissatisfied with the constraints that society imposes on them, feel "sed de ventana" (51; "a thirst for windows"). For many such women, "la vocación de escritura, como deseo de liberación y expresión de desahogo, ha germinado muchas veces a través del marco de una ventana. La ventana es el punto de enfoque, pero también el punto de partida" (51–52; "the call to write, as a desire for liberation and an expression of relief, has often emerged through the frame of a window. The window is the focal point, but also the point of departure"). Trapped in the routine of their lives, they look out the window and imagine themselves free. It is already clear that Sofía experiences "la vocación de escritura, como deseo de liberación y expresión de desahogo" as a reader of novels that help her escape a daily reality she finds stifling. Soon it will be as a writer of her own texts that she will experience, much more deeply, the liberation that writing provides, allowing her, in the words of Felman, to finally own her own story.

At a party she attends the same day the novel begins, Sofía runs into Mariana, whom she dreamed about the night before. They reestablish their old friendship, which she always believed ended when she began to go out with a young man who turned out to be Mariana's boyfriend. But Sofía discovers through their new relationship that it was Mariana's sense of inferiority in the face of Sofía's exuberant imagination and capacity for poetic and literary creation that led to the rift—even before the incident with the young man.

Writing as Pleasure

It is precisely that imagination, the joy of playing with words, of inventing new worlds through language, the sense of *jouissance*, that they will both come to experience in the writings they exchange throughout the novel, writings that bring them together again and enable each to survive her existential crisis.

Mariana mentions the joy of literary creation that Sofía continues to exude, explaining, after some small talk at the party where they meet, that "si quería seguir tu arrebato verbal necesitaba recuperar cierta fe infantil que tú no has perdido y yo sí, creer en la transformación del local, lograr que se operara el milagro poético de su nueva investidura" (31; "if I wanted to keep up with your verbal flow, I'd have to recover the childish faith that you haven't lost but which I have, and be able to believe in the possibility of transforming a place and allowing the poetic miracle of its new incarnation to take place" [21]). This "milagro poético" continues to emerge after they take leave of each other, because Mariana, a psychoanalyst, tells Sofía, as she tells many of her patients, that Sofía must write to give free rein to her imagination. When Sofía asks if she can send Mariana her writing, Mariana agrees, little suspecting that this advice, meant to help her friend, would ultimately also lead to her own salvation.

The novel's chapters consist of Sofía's writing exercises in the form of diary entries dedicated to Mariana alternating with Mariana's letters to Sofía. The choice of diary entries and letters is no accident: Martín Gaite, in the chapter "Buscando el modo" ("Searching for the Way") in *Desde la ventana*, says that these two genres have often been used by women because of their private nature and because in them the interlocutor, whether real or invented, is usually present and "es la búsqueda apasionada de ese 'tú' el hilo conductor del discurso femenino, el móvil primordial para quebrar la sensación de arrinconamiento" (59; "it is the passionate search for that 'you' that is the guiding thread of feminine discourse, the principal motive for breaking the feeling of being cornered"). Again, writing becomes a way to combat the frequent sense of entrapment in women's lives, and it does so partly through the explicit seeking of an ideal interlocutor, which Sofía and Mariana finally find in each other. They do not meet again until the end of the novel, but through their writings they share a growing sense of *jouissance* that ultimately enables each to break with the past and envision a better future.

The connection between writing and pleasure is often evoked in their writings. Sofía, having started her writing assignment for Mariana, reflects:

> Yo he deseado pocas cosas con la fuerza con que deseo en este momento volver a ver a Mariana, donde sea, cuando sea (sé que va a pasar), y poderle decir: "Mira, te he traído de regalo este cuaderno"; así que me gozo en irlo llenando despacio, esmerándome en la letra. Eso es como estar ya con ella también ahora según lo escribo, un anticipo de felicidad que conjura la muerte del tiempo. Y da también gusto en sí. . . . (76)
>
> I have desired few things with the intensity with which I now long to see Mariana again, wherever, whenever (I know it will happen), and to be able to say to her: "Look, I've brought you my homework as a present"; so I enjoy slowly filling up this new notebook, taking care over my handwriting.

> It's like being with her already even as I write, an anticipation of happiness that wards off the death of time. It's a pleasure in itself. . . . (66)

Desire is the spark that engenders writing, and the writing produces an intense pleasure, such as when Sofía states, thinking of the blank notebook she is slowly filling, "[M]e gozo en irlo llenando despacio, esmerándome en la letra," or when she further notes that this process "da también gusto en sí" (76; "I enjoy slowly filling up this notebook, taking care over my handwriting. . . . It's a pleasure in itself" [66]). Later, Mariana also explains that "mi patria es la escritura" ("writing is my homeland") and highlights how she experiences "el gozo de inventarla" (143; "the pleasure of inventing it" [131]). This pleasure that both women experience in writing is akin to the *jouissance* of *écriture féminine*.

Writing the Body

This *jouissance* is also linked to the body. Mariana remembers how Sofía, as a child, played with words, invented stories, especially when they spent the night at each other's homes, talking the night away:

> Y la noche, como todo lo que nombrabas, se convertía en personaje de cuento. Era el duendecillo Noc, lo sentías revolotear con sus alas irisadas y negras, bajar dulcemente hasta ti, hasta tu boca abierta, y meterse en tu cuerpo; te desataba los lazos de la lengua, irrumpía casa adentro por los pasillos de los pulmones, del corazón y de los intestinos, y notabas cómo a su paso iba apagando los interruptores que dan calambre y encendiendo los que dan luz de luna. (58)

> [A]nd the night, like everything else you mentioned, became a character in a story. It was the goblin, Noc; you could hear him fluttering his dark, iridescent wings, flying gently down towards you, towards your open mouth, into your body; he untied the knots in your tongue, rushed inwards down the passageways of your lungs, your heart and your intestines, and you noticed that as he passed he switched off all the switches that gave you cramp and switched on the ones that provided moonlight. (48)

The almost sexual description of how this "duendecillo Noc," the magic teller of tales that Sofía invented, enters her body and lights it up with moonlight, points to the way that her imagination and later her writing are literally embodied, in a process akin to orgasmic pleasure and fullness. One can hear echoes here of Cixous's description of an *écriture féminine* in which "I, too, overflow; my desires have invented new desires, my body knows unheard-of songs. Time and again I, too, have felt so full of luminous torrents that I could burst" ("Laugh" 246).

Endless transformations and metamorphoses characterize Sofía and Mariana's writing. This fluidity is matched by fragmentation. What Sofía creates brings to mind her joy as a child in breaking words up to make them mean new things, a practice she remembers fondly:

> A ella le gustaba inventar palabras y desmontar las que oía por primera vez, hacer combinaciones con las piezas resultantes, separar y poner juntas las que se repetían. Las palabras un poco largas eran como vestidos con corpiño, chaleco y falda, y se le podía poner el chaleco de una a la falda de otra con el mismo corpiño, o al revés, que fuera la falda lo que cambiase. (114)

> She used to enjoy inventing words and taking to pieces words she'd heard for the first time, making different combinations with the dismantled pieces, breaking them up and putting together the pieces that occurred more than once. Long words were like dresses with a bodice, a waistcoat and skirt and you could add the waistcoat of one to the skirt of another that had the same bodice or, the other way round, you could swap the skirt. (103)

Sofía has a great sense for the materiality of language, and the fragmentation with which she played as a child she now explores not only in her writing but also in the collages she produces, another form of expression based on the breaking down of existing images to produce fragments that allow her to see and express the world, and herself, in ever new ways.[6]

Writing as Reawakening

As they continue writing about their lives, writing their bodies, both Sofía and Mariana find the strength to face the things that have been holding them back and repressing their desires and drives. Sofía finally leaves Eduardo and moves temporarily into the apartment in which she once lived with her parents and which is now taken over by her three children. On her first night there, she has a dream about her mother and becomes one with her. She was long estranged from her mother, resenting the way her mother passively accepted the traditional, submissive role of wife. In the dream, Sofía experiences how easy self-alienation becomes in the patriarchal society that she, just like her mother, has had to endure, and she identifies with her mother for the first time. She explains later to her daughter:

> [M]e he desdoblado en ella, acabo de acordarme, ¡es que era ella!, . . . No me había pasado nunca eso con mamá, se salía de mí como si yo la pariera, de verdad, alucinante. Y pensaba con sus frases y revivían sus recuerdos. (381)

> I was walking along the corridor as if I were her. Yes, I've just remembered, part of me split off into her, I *was* her! . . . It's never happened to

> me before with Mama, it was almost as if I'd given birth to her, really, it was incredible. (364)

Sofía has not just dreamed of her mother but also has become her, given birth to her, and this new connection is a necessary step in her liberation from a world that entrapped Sofía and made her suffer. The novel reflects the need for a connection with the maternal that the French feminists assert as necessary "in order [for woman] to reverse the devaluation of her origins and her 'imaginary' within culture" (Weil 168). Through this new connection to her mother, we can see that much of Sofía's writing and artistic creation through collages, in which Sofía breaks down preexisting images or words to create new, unexpected ones, can be understood as forays into the semiotic, in Kristeva's terminology, that maternally defined realm of disruptive pulsions and drives that can disrupt and transgress the established and fixed order of the patriarchally defined symbolic.

At the end of the novel, Sofía goes to visit Mariana in the south of Spain. Mariana has gone there to escape her own entrapment in a life that appears to be perfect (she is a successful psychoanalyst) yet hides many painful contradictions and inconsistencies. For years she tried to write an academic essay on eroticism yet failed because she could not relate to her topic in any way that was not overly rational. As she complains, "[M]i trabajo sobre el erotismo empezó a despedir un tufillo a rancio, a caldo de cerebro" (108; "[M]y work on eroticism began to smell slightly rancid; it acquired a whiff, which it's never quite lost, of something cooked up in the brain" [97]). Through her letter writing to Sofía, however, Mariana discovers how to let go of her need to control and classify everything and allows herself to be open to contradiction and inconsistency. She finally realizes that, to be able to write on the topic of eroticism, "[l]o que quizá tendría que hacer es atreverme con un texto poético donde diera rienda suelta a todas estas contradicciones, con una novela quizá, y dejarme de tanto psicoanálisis" (193; "[p]erhaps I should take a chance and write a poetic text, a novel perhaps, where I could give free rein to all these contradictions and abandon all this psychoanalysis" [181]). Mariana too is learning how to break out of the straitjacket of the symbolic and enter the dynamic realm of the semiotic, through writing.

The last scene of the novel is a clear image of writing as *jouissance*. The two friends sit together in a seaside bar, enjoying the wind blowing and rain falling around them; they laugh as they write and share their writing with each other. They are combining their texts into one, a new text that readers are given to understand is the novel they have just read. Sofía and Mariana are finally able to own their autobiographies. Through writing and reading, they have become the active creators of their lives, a transformation that reflects what Martín Gaite, in *La búsqueda de interlocutor* ("The Search for an Interlocutor"), describes as the fact that "cuando vivimos, las cosas nos pasan; pero cuando contamos, las hacemos pasar; y es precisamente en ese llevar las riendas el propio sujeto donde radica la esencia de toda narración" ("Búsqueda" 24; "when we live, things happen to us; but when we recount them, we make them happen; and it is precisely in that capacity of the subject to hold the reins that the essence of all narration resides").

Carmen Martín Gaite's novel goes beyond *écriture féminine* by providing a concrete and scathing critique of the forces in contemporary Spanish society that repress women's lives and desires. But her writing also embodies what Weil describes as a positive effect of *écriture féminine,* inasmuch as "French feminists used *écriture* as a weapon not to represent the feminine but to create it through experimental poetics. By creating the feminine in their own work, they hoped to provoke women to participate in reimagining their lives and their world" (169). It is to be hoped that Sofía and Mariana are not the only ones empowered by being able to "reimagine their lives and their world" through reading and writing—that the readers of Martín Gaite's novel, including students who read and engage critically with it in a class, will be empowered too.

NOTES

[1] Pilar Folguera's *El feminismo en España* is a good collection of articles on the development of feminism in Spain. Sonia Núñez Puente's *Una historia propia* provides an overview of the development of women's social conditions in contemporary Spain. Mercedes Carbayo-Abengózar's *Buscando un lugar entre mujeres*, Rosario Ruiz Franco's *¿Eternas menores?*, and Martín Gaite's own *Usos amororos de la postguerra española* (*Courtship Customs in Postwar Spain*) describe women's changing social conditions in contemporary Spain.

[2] Toril Moi's *Sexual/Textual Politics*, the relevant sections of Maggie Humm's *Reader's Guide to Contemporary Feminist Literary Criticism*, the appropriate entries in Elizabeth Wright's *Feminism and Psychoanalysis: A Critical Dictionary*, Ann Rosalind Jones's "Writing the Body," and Kari Weil's "French Feminism's *Écriture Féminine*" are among the most helpful works. The anthology *New French Feminisms* is a classic collection of representative texts (Marks and Courtivron).

[3] Salvador Oropesa's "*Nubosidad variable*" and the section on the novel in Carbayo-Abengózar's *Buscando un lugar entre mujeres* help students understand the elements of Spanish society that Martín Gaite is criticizing in her novel.

[4] English translations of passages from *Nubosidad variable* are from *Variable Cloud*, by Margaret Jull Costa. All other translations from Spanish are mine.

[5] Mirrors play an important role in the novel, serving as narrative structuring devices as well as metaphors that make various points, not just the idea of woman being a mirror for man. The many ways mirrors function in the novel is a worthy topic for discussion with students. Janet Pérez's "Structural, Thematic, and Symbolic Mirrors" is helpful here, as is Lee-Ann Laffey's "Frente al espejo." Jenijoy La Belle's *Herself Beheld* is a good general study of the use of the mirror metaphor in women's writing.

[6] On the role of collages in the novel, see Kathleen Glenn's "Collage, Textile." Fuencisla Zomeño's "La constitución del texto femenino" and Pérez's "*Nubosidad variable*" show how the novel presents women's attempts to produce women-centered writing.

Teaching *La Reina de las Nieves*: Metafiction, History, and Student Writing

Vilma Navarro-Daniels

A topic-based, writing-intensive seminar I taught on metafiction in film, narrative, and drama in post-Francoist Spain proved to be a particularly rewarding course for me and for my students. Developed at Washington State University for advanced undergraduate students of Spanish, the course was taught entirely in Spanish and required students to read, write, and take part in discussions in the target language. The class met twice a week in sessions of seventy-five minutes each, over fifteen weeks. Students were expected to read the assigned material as well as critical articles about the works discussed in class. They were also provided with detailed viewing and reading guides that contained background information, ancillary readings, and links to relevant texts and images, along with discussion topics for small groups. Among the literary works studied in the seminar, I included one novel: Carmen Martín Gaite's *La Reina de las Nieves* (*The Farewell Angel*).[1]

My pedagogical approach to *Reina* combines analysis of its extratextual aspects and exploration of its literary features. Though its publication date was 1994, it was begun fifteen years earlier and is set in the late 1970s, so it is a transition novel. Through the eyes of Leonardo Villalba, one of the characters, students can ramble through Madrid and learn about the social, political, and cultural life during the Spanish transition to democracy. Leonardo is a misfit in what later became known as post-Francoist Spain. The character uncovers the pretense of community, showing how people have been abandoned and isolated. Leonardo is critical of a society that displays a facade of success while refusing to face its past. At the same time, the novel's status as metafiction invites students to think about the nature of fiction making.

Since the students enrolled in this seminar were still acquiring the language, writing was an essential component of the learning process. Each student had to conduct a research project and write an essay based on it. I provided a list of films, short stories, novels, and plays created in Spain during the late transition and after—all having a strong metafictional aspect. I trained my students in the use of the *MLA International Bibliography* and other helpful databases. I made guidelines available to them for their search and collection of information and for the organizing and writing of their essays. These guidelines covered the formulation of a defensible thesis, the place of the thesis in currents of existing criticism, the use of critical tools and different sources of information, the organization of the research paper, and the formal presentation of the paper. Students had to write a proposal for their final project, which was due by the middle of the semester.

Another course assignment was an individual oral presentation in Spanish based on an article dealing with a film or literary work on the syllabus. Students had to explain the main ideas of the article in their own words and apply them to the assigned work. Each student also wrote two four-page take-home essays consisting of responses to a choice of questions dealing with the material studied up to that point in the semester. Cues for essay responses included quotations from critics on subjects related to fiction and its creation, which the student could use as a point of departure for independent critical analysis.

The seminar was divided into five units: an introduction and a unit for each author and genre (film, short fiction, novel, drama) covered in the course. Martín Gaite's *Reina de las Nieves* was the focus of the fourth unit of the seminar. After studying and discussing two films and three short stories, students turned to the novel, searching for its metafictional devices and their possible meanings. Placing Martín Gaite's work two-thirds into the semester gave my students time to read the entire novel.

At the beginning of the semester, we devoted several classes to metafiction. I also furnished my students with the historical, political, social, and cultural context for post-Francoist Spain. The works were approached from the perspective of the seminar's main topic: the connection between fiction and reality. Although all the works have complex metafictional features, they also provide, in many different forms, a representation of Spanish society, and the personalities of their characters are not far removed from those of the readers.

The Novel's Historical Frame

According to Teresa Vilarós, the first stage of the transition begins in either 1973, the year of the assassination of Luis Carrero Blanco, head of the Spanish government in the waning years of Franco's dictatorship, or 1975, the year of Franco's death. The end date is 1981, the year of Antonio Tejero's frustrated military coup, which resulted in a defense of the democratic system by King Juan Carlos. For Vilarós, in 1981 democracy had yet to be assimilated by Spanish society, but the defeat of the coup rallied popular support and led to the consolidation of democratic institutions. The second part of the transition extends from the political victory of the Socialist Party in the general elections in 1982 to the signing of the treaty of Maastricht in 1993, an agreement that allowed Spain to become fully integrated into Europe. One year earlier, several important cultural events promoted an image of Spain as a completely modern and European nation—among them the Universal Exhibition in Seville, the Olympic Games in Barcelona, the election of Madrid as the Cultural Capital of Europe, and the presentation of the keys of Sepharad to the Jewish community (1–3).

We studied how in the later stage of Spain's democratic consolidation, the decentralization of historical thinking—that is, the abandonment of metadiscourse as the model for explaining the past, a model used in the first part of the transition—was accompanied by new developments in literature and cinema (15, 24). Literary and cinematic characters grew increasingly fragmented, even distorted, as they listened to the discourse of others to invent themselves (218). In the works we analyzed in this course, characters generally have discarded all political categories of self-definition; instead they resort to the language of cinema, literature, journals, and letters—in other words, to a language that fictionalizes life. But this fictionalization is directed not inward but outward, toward the new Spanish society, thus becoming a critique of the modernization of the country. It reveals and explores social problems, such as unemployment, drug addiction, violence, isolation, alienation, poverty, racism, and homophobia.

Metafiction as a Theoretical Base

Metafiction has been seen as a mode of writing that distances fiction from life, a mode that "tends to point back at the work itself" and "designates fiction itself as the primary referent" (Spires, *Beyond the Metafictional Mode* 9), but in our seminar we modified that view. Our premise was that metafiction, instead of positing a disconnection between life and literature, actually explores and creates reality through the process of making fiction. We analyzed works in which fiction, according to Patricia Waugh's model, integrates both reality and the devices that we use to shape our perceptions of the real ("What Is Metafiction"). Although our seminar opened with a discussion about what critics such as Linda Hutcheon have called the "narcissistic" side of metafiction, given that the text turns back on itself, we also considered that a work's self-reflection is never directed solely inward; because it must also move outward, it is referential, as David Herzberger has demonstrated ("Split Referentiality").

Works and characters with metafictional features are not entities locked in a universe made entirely of language and isolated from the world; rather, they preserve a bond with life (Herzberger, "Split Referentiality" 422, 428–29). This bond is expressed through many creative strategies used by characters when assuming the role of writer, reader, actor, film director, or singer. A metafictional work focuses our attention on it as fiction—not to distance itself from the real world but to show us how the processes of creating fiction and creating life complement each other. The way in which characters live is intrinsically bound to their roles as readers, writers, or performers. They understand themselves, they interpret their own history, and they project themselves into the future using fiction as their point of departure. The act of writing, reading, acting, inventing a plot, or even lying is what allows them to attain reality.

Metafiction in La Reina de las Nieves

According to Waugh, metafiction must be understood as a dynamic concept. She notes its self-referential nature but also emphasizes the implications it has for the extratextual or real world:

> *Metafiction* is a term given to fictional writing which self-consciously and systematically draws attention to its status as an artefact in order to pose questions about the relationship between fiction and reality. In providing a critique of their own methods of construction, such writings not only examine the fundamental structures of narrative fiction, they also explore the possible fictionality of the world outside the literary fictional text.
> ("What Is Metafiction" 2)

Self-reflexiveness is an exploration of fiction through the making of fiction (2). In Martín Gaite's novel we see this self-reflexiveness in the allusions to painting, literary language, and literary works—in the multiple intertexts that shape the plot and the main characters. The title's direct reference to the story by Hans Christian Andersen is accompanied by allusions to works by Henrik Ibsen, Albert Camus, Erich Fromm, William Shakespeare, Gaston Bachelard, Ramón del Valle-Inclán, Michel de Montaigne, Mircea Eliade, Leopoldo Alas (Clarín), Karl Philipp Moritz, Miguel de Cervantes, Adelbert von Chamisso, Paul Verlaine, and Constantine Cavafy, among others. Through these references, Martín Gaite makes reading a main theme of the novel.

Julia Kristeva maintains that "any text is constructed as a mosaic of quotations; any text is the absorption and transformation of another. The notion of intertextuality replaces that of intersubjectivity, and poetic language is read as at least double" (*Kristeva Reader* 37). My students examined how the "absorption and transformation" of Andersen's story takes place in Martín Gaite's novel. They read the fairy tale in English and discussed the similarities and differences between the two narrations. They were amazed when they understood how *La Reina de las Nieves* is constructed as an ongoing dialogue with other works, which are brought into the novel, transformed, and provided with new meanings. Their original meanings are not lost but remain even as they are transformed. Such coexistence produces what Kristeva identifies as an ambivalent duality: "[T]he writer can use another's word, giving it a new meaning while retaining the meaning it already had. The result is a word with two significations: it becomes ambivalent. This ambivalent word is therefore the result of a joining of two sign-systems" (*Kristeva Reader* 43–44).

The metafictional nature of Martín Gaite's novel is highlighted by two characters who are writers, well-versed readers, and literary critics. Sila and Leonardo often realize that they are following models from literature and art. They are so deeply influenced and shaped by those fictional beings that they cannot establish a clear dividing line between themselves and them. The discourse they use is full of references to fictional texts. Waugh states that our creation of our identities and what we call reality is based on fiction:

> If, as individuals, we now occupy "roles" rather than "selves," then the study of characters in novels may provide a useful model for understanding the construction of subjectivity in the world outside novels. If our

> knowledge of this world is now seen to be mediated through language, then literary fiction (worlds constructed entirely of language) becomes a useful model for learning about the construction of "reality" itself.
> ("What Is Metafiction" 3)

Intertextual Referents and Ekphrasis in the Novel

The characters of *La Reina de las Nieves* discuss literature, film, and the act of artistic creation. Such conversations include Leonardo's journals; Sila's book of essays about vertigo; Leonardo's talks with his grandmother, his father, and his friend Mónica; and Sila's encounter with the old schoolteacher, who is an outstanding storyteller. Among the intertexts summarized for students in handouts are Camus's novel *L'étranger* (*The Stranger*) and essay "Le mythe de Sisyphe" ("The Myth of Sisyphus"), which express his ideas on life and the absurd.

I devoted an entire class to the discussion of the enigmatic presence in the novel of Caspar David Friedrich's *Wanderer above the Sea of Fog* (1817–18; it is sometimes called "The Wanderer above the Mists" and known in Spanish as "Caminante sobre un mar de niebla"). We viewed and analyzed Friedrich's painting, which is described in the novel both directly and obliquely. In the painting, a solitary man stands on a rocky promontory looking out over a vast, misty terrain, empty except for low-lying vegetation and boulders, with mountains looming in the distance; his back is to the viewer. We discussed the connection between the man in the painting and the main characters in the novel. Students saw that the painting is crucial to understanding Leonardo and Sila and the longing for freedom, authenticity, and infinity that sometimes seems to overwhelm them. This desire brings them close to a nature that conveys the solitude of Romantic heroes. Martín Gaite uses Friedrich's painting to create a Romantic interpretation of Leonardo and Sila, as Nuria Cruz-Cámara has shown ("Re-creación").[2]

In her essay "Los amores malditos" ("Damned Loves"), Martín Gaite explains her idea of the Romantic hero as one who has been separated from society or who voluntarily assumes that isolation (312). Yet a deep bond unites the Romantic hero with nature:

> [E]l aislamiento de los personajes románticos, empeñados en saciar a solas su sed de totalidad y fusión con la Naturaleza, es lo que los asoma al abismo de la perdición. Encarcelados en la soberbia de su propio "yo" no son capaces de hallar en tan estrecha cárcel sino contradicción y desdicha.
> (313)

> [T]he isolation of Romantic characters—determined as they are to seek solitary satisfaction of their longing for oneness and fusion with Nature—takes them to the abyss of ruin. Imprisoned in the pride of their

> own "I," they are unable to find within the confines of such prison anything other than contradiction and despair. (my trans.)

Martín Gaite, discussing how nature is represented in Romantic literature and painting, alludes to the work of Friedrich:

> Paisajes invernales, casas desmoronadas, tempestades, cementerios, playas desiertas son motivos en la imaginería romántica que insinúan el imperio de lo inabarcable por el hombre. Ese hombre, en las pinturas de Friedrich, por ejemplo suele contemplar de espaldas, con ademán desolado y estático aquello que no abarca ni penetra. Estas figuras son símbolo de la incertidumbre y la desolación de quien ha perdido irremisiblemente el paraíso. (313)
>
> Winter landscapes, dilapidated houses, storms, cemeteries, deserted beaches are recurrent motifs in Romantic imagery, which point to the immensity of that which can never be encompassed. The man depicted in Friedrich's paintings, for example, always with his back to us, contemplates with a transported and desolate expression something that he can neither contain nor fathom. These figures are symbols of the uncertainty and desolation of one for whom paradise is irretrievably lost. (my trans.)

The qualities identified by the author are evident in other Friedrich paintings that we view and discuss in class.[3]

The incorporation of Friedrich's painting puts *La Reina de las Nieves* in the ekphrastic tradition. Ekphrasis is "a literary mode . . . [that] *is the verbal representation of a graphic representation*" (Heffernan 298–99). In Martín Gaite's novel, it is a verbal representation of Romantic paintings, which in turn depict a landscape that expresses the sublime. The sublime is an experience "born out of the encounter between consciousness and the world" that implies an "emotional transport" and "the feeling of an ineluctable immersion in the alluring vastness of nature" (Levine 377). The sublime landscape is characterized as "tragic, sinister, diabolical, but superb; savage, fantastic, lugubrious, and yet delicious; terrifying, terrible, astonishing, but colossal and grandiose" (378). Romantic painters frequently placed in it one of their typical figures: the lonely traveler, so common in the works of Friedrich. Martín Gaite surrounds her characters with sublime nature. Early in the novel, Sila is introduced to the reader as a traveler who wanders and explores the cliffs from where she contemplates the enraged sea, which is the perfect setting for the solitude she desires.[4]

These examples point to what Waugh considers the main assumption in metafiction: the understanding of the world as if it were a book ("What Is Metafiction" 3), a thing to be written. Extratextual reality therefore does not stand apart from fiction: if human experience of the world is mediated or indirect, because it must be narrated or told to be understood, then it is a construct

(16, 18). The concern about fiction is tied to the question of "how human beings reflect, construct and mediate their experience of the world" (2).

According to students' evaluations, the seminar was highly successful. The inclusion of different literary genres and film, as well as the challenge of conducting a research project about a work of their choosing, sustained their interest. Students also appreciated the introduction to literary theory. They were particularly enthusiastic about the realization that abstract concepts can be concretized in films, narrative, and theater.

Through brief, weekly written student reports summarizing class discussions, I was able to monitor what students assimilated from class. They also used their reports to raise questions about specific points, questions that later were addressed in class. They felt that the seminar gave them the opportunity to practice and improve their Spanish reading skills as well as their spoken and written Spanish, while they learned about film, literature, and post-Francoist Spanish society. These goals were achieved in the course of the promotion and practice of critical thinking and in an atmosphere that encouraged students to express their ideas even in the face of disagreement by others. They came to understand that their positions had to be based on ideas and knowledge rather than mere subjective impressions, likes, and dislikes.

Unquestionably this type of course is demanding in terms of preparation, selection of materials, and adaptation of abstract concepts to the level of the students. Inclusion of *La Reina de las Nieves* made the seminar particularly challenging. Reading this long novel requires effort and commitment from a nonnative speaker. Nevertheless, the pedagogical strategies I chose gave my students the tools they needed to approach the text. I would add this observation: the novel emotionally touched them. Young learners identified with Leonardo and Sila and with their existential concerns. Because of this emotional connection, *La Reina de las Nieves* richly fulfills the expectations of our advanced students of Spanish.

NOTES

[1]The availability of the novel in English makes it a viable option for courses on Spanish literature in translation or Spanish cultural history. The other texts in my seminar were Carlos Saura's film *¡Ay, Carmela!*; Ignacio Martínez de Pisón's short stories "El filo de unos ojos" ("The Edge of His Eyes"), "La muerte mientras tanto" ("Death in the Meantime"), and "El rey de bastos" ("King of Clubs"); Pedro Almodóvar's film *Tacones lejanos* (*High Heels*); and Paloma Pedrero's play *La isla amarilla* ("The Yellow Island").

[2]Chapter 1 of her *El laberinto intertextual* is entitled "La re-creación del romanticismo en *La Reina de las Nieves*," an earlier version of which appeared in the journal *Symposium*.

[3]Relevant images in other paintings by Friedrich are the twisted, snowy tree trunks in *Winter Landscape* (1811); the solitary man among tall trees in *The Chasseur in the*

Forest (1813); the two small figures by the ocean's edge in *Two Men by the Sea* (1817); the view of the sea from immense cliffs that dwarf two men and a woman in *Chalk Cliffs on Rügen* (c. 1818); the tall woman facing the horizon in *Woman before the Rising Sun*, also known as "Woman before the Setting Sun" (1818–20); the two men in a forest looking at a sliver of moon in *Two Men Contemplating the Moon* (1818–20); the two women on a terrace staring out at immense spires and boat masts in *The Sisters on the Balcony* (c. 1820); the woman in a long dress looking out a window in *Woman at a Window* (1822); the two men contemplating a vast expanse of seashore at what appears to be low tide in *Evening Landscape with Two Men* (1830–35); and the four people on boulders in the water as a full moon rises in the distance in *Moonrise by the Sea* (c. 1821). These paintings can be viewed at the *Web Gallery of Art*.

[4]Cruz-Cámara reviews theories of the sublime with regard to gender, arguing that Martín Gaite subverts traditional masculine formulations of Romanticism ("Re-creación").

Analyzing *Los parentescos* and Preparing Students for Creative Writing

Isabel Estrada

Carmen Martín Gaite's final and unfinished novel, *Los parentescos* (2001; "Familial Relations"), lends itself both to in-depth analysis of its form and content by the instructor as well as to the creative application of that analysis by the student. Instructors may discuss the novel's narrative strategies, contextualize its representation of Spanish society at the beginning of the twenty-first century, and convey basic notions of narrative fiction. But a literature class need not end with the acquisition of knowledge. If students are asked to write a conclusion to this unfinished work in the style of the author, they will be forced not only to use their knowledge but also to reflect on it. In my experience, creative writing exercises improve in a long-lasting way students' processing and appreciation of Spanish literature and language. Such an exercise works best in an upper-level undergraduate course taught in Spanish, because the novel's length and narrative complexity require advanced reading and writing skills.[1]

In the first-person narration of *Los parentescos*, the protagonist, Baltasar (Balti), remembers his life, starting from the age of four. When the novel opens, he is seventeen, and his story tells how he learned from the difficult relationships of his family—a late-twentieth-century Spanish family that breaks with tradition and whose bonds are formed and reformed by divorces and second marriages. A unit on Martín Gaite's novel could be included in a course on literature and culture of democratic Spain or one on Spanish literature since 1975 (a key year, marking the beginning of Spain's transition to democracy).

In courses that meet for seventy-five minutes twice a week, students would need two weeks to read and analyze the entire novel. The four class sessions devoted to the novel begin with an introductory lecture on sociocultural and political context and on Martín Gaite. Next is an instructor-led unit on narrative techniques, followed by students' analytic application of them through two work sheets. As a culminating activity, students use their knowledge of narrative and of the novel to compose original endings to the work.

The lesson plans presented here distinguish between the roles of instructor and student. As the lessons progress, the instructor's role gradually diminishes, while the student's expands. That is, the instructor guides students until they have processed the relevant concepts and are able to apply them to their writing.

First Class Session: Contextualization of the Novel

I firmly believe that lectures are an essential component of all balanced lesson plans, because students need basic reference information before they can feel confident forming opinions about literary texts. Before they begin to read *Los parentescos*, the instructor should consider lecturing on the sociopolitical aspects that inform the novel: the changing nature of gender relations in democratic Spain, the end of *patria potestad* (legal rights of men over women and children), the legalization of birth control, the legalization of divorce in 1981, and the limited legalization of abortion in 1985. This background will help students understand the absence of a nuclear family in the novel and the fluidity and instability of the relationships in Balti's family.

A brief presentation of the author's place in literary history as well as her stylistic trademarks will help guide students' reading. Beginning in the 1950s, Martín Gaite's work reflected social change in Francoist and democratic Spain. She is the only woman whom literary historians include in the group of writers known as the generation of the 1950s.[2] The most noteworthy features of her writing are the representation of family structures, the importance of communication, reflection on the role of language in the learning process, and use of the bildungsroman. My introductory lecture, no more than forty minutes long, covers these points concisely.

Because a monotonous presentation will lose the students' attention, I usually include a clip from Martín Gaite's interview with CUNY TV that illustrates the theme of the necessity of communication. The interview, conducted by José María Conget and Raquel Chang-Rodríguez (Martín Gaite, Interview [1996]), portrays the author as an appealing personality with an unforgettable hat.[3] She reflects on communication failure not only as a theme in her narrative but also as a phenomenon of large cities—in other words, she situates the concerns of her work in a global framework. Students can relate the need to communicate to their own lives. The viewing takes no more than fifteen minutes.

At the end of class, I distribute two work sheets that structure much of the second and third classes. I briefly give students instructions on how to prepare their work sheet responses so that they can actively participate in class.

Second Class Session: Narrative Techniques

Shlomith Rimmon-Kenan's *Narrative Fiction: Contemporary Poetics* is especially useful for teaching narrative techniques, being a succinct and clear manual. First published in 1983, it is digitized and available in many library collections. With the aim of establishing the spatial and temporal parameters at play in the beginning of the novel as well as the nature of the narrator, I prepare a guide that introduces the narrative elements that students should identify in the text, and I describe the narration's act of communication using this diagram:

AUTHOR→ {(NARRATOR)→TEXT→(NARRATEE)→} READER[4]

The curly brackets separate the real world from the fictional world, and the elements in parentheses may or may not appear in the fictional world. In my experience, not all my students are capable of distinguishing between author and narrator, but having a woman author and an adolescent boy narrator helps. (In my courses, this brief presentation does not last more than ten minutes.)

The two work sheets contain explanations of the role of the narrator and give examples of temporal structures, adapted again from *Narrative Fiction*. The goals of the work sheets are twofold: to have students analyze the relation between the narrator of *Los parentescos* and the fictional world it describes and to have them understand the temporal structure of the novel—a basic element of this bildungsroman. The first handout presents the various functions of the narrative voice (Rimmon-Kenan 86–103), and students are asked to identify them in the novel.

Work Sheet 1: Relevant Functions of the Narrative Voice

Because the purpose is to diminish the role of the instructor as the lesson plans progress, the class is divided into three parts. I recommend that, first, instructors explain the work sheet and offer their own responses. Then they can divide the class in two and assign each group one of the items on the handout. Students can then be asked to compare their responses and use them to create, in ten to fifteen minutes, a minipresentation that they will share with the entire class. The third part of the class is dedicated to these minipresentations, following the order of these work-sheet elements:

1. Description of Space and Setting

> The narrative voice can describe setting in a brief and straightforward manner, but it can also assign symbolic meaning to spaces. Notice how Balti describes domestic spaces. Does his description seem sterile? Can you find other nonliteral meanings assigned to domestic spaces?

Symbolic meanings of setting are common in Martín Gaite's work. Examples are in her novel *El cuarto de atrás* (*The Back Room*) and the story "La trastienda de los ojos" ("The Room behind His Eyes"). In *Los parentescos*, we are told, "Las puertas prohibidas dan a jardines en sombra de donde sube la nostalgia de lo incomprensible" (135; "The forbidden doors lead to shadowy gardens that give rise to nostalgia for the incomprehensible").[5] We see the poetic use of domestic space by an adult narrator who describes his childhood from the perspective of the present. "The incomprehensible" refers to the beginning of his learning process, a process that has been concluded in the present of the narration.

2. Physical Description of the Characters

> It is important to consider the attitude of the narrative voice toward the characters. The narrative may limit itself to very basic description, but it

> may also use descriptions of appearance that express an opinion about a character's personality or emotional state. Look for passages in the novel in which the narrator alludes to the inner life of a character by means of descriptions of appearance.

Students should observe how the narrator, a four-year-old child at the beginning of the novel, interprets the world of appearances. For example, "yo sé que mi padre está hecho polvo, desamparado, se lo noto en la cara. Es como si se le hubiera corrido el maquillaje o se le viera la cicatriz de algún lifting" (105; "I know that my father's falling apart, he's defenseless, I can see it in his face. It's as if his makeup had run, or as if a scar left by a face-lift were suddenly visible"). Both sentences show that Balti perceives his father's emotional state. His learning process is revealed not only through his interpretations but also through his rhetorical use of simile, in language appropriate to an adult.

3. Selection of Information

> The narrative voice decides what elements of the story merit being narrated, thereby establishing a hierarchy among its elements. Look for moments when the narrator's omission of information stands out.[6]

Students should pay attention to the artificiality of narrations and notice how the narrative voice guides us in our interpretation of the work. For example, "[El misterio del paso del tiempo] [m]e ha servido para arrancar a contar cosas de la boda de mis padres. Que tampoco importa la boda en sí, sino por lo que vino luego. Y también por lo que había enterrado antes, que no es poco" (40; "[The mystery of the passing of time] has served to get me started describing my parents' wedding. Which in itself is not important; the wedding is important only because of what happened after. And also because of what I buried before, which is not irrelevant"). The novel begins with Balti's parents' wedding when he was four, and from this point on he narrates the circumstances that led his parents to this union as well as how the union later deteriorated. As he grows, he establishes bonds with his half brothers and half sisters, gradually expanding these emotional ties until he becomes an adolescent who understands the complexity of family relations in Spain in the year 2000.

4. Descriptions of the Characters' Personalities

> Describing characters, a narrator may choose to communicate only what the narrator sees. But if there is explanation of the way the characters act, then the narrator's intervention is more visible. If in addition the narrator makes value judgments, then the narrator is establishing authority over the characters. Look for textual examples in which Balti describes the members of his family and explain how he relates to them.

A narrator can direct the views of readers in many ways. It is important to analyze how Balti's perceptions, both of his family and of himself, evolve in the course of the book. Balti expresses consciousness of himself and his narration: "[L]levo tres meses largos haciendo arqueología de mi transformación en niño locuaz partiendo de mudito" (80; "For three long months, I have been excavating my transformation from mute to talkative child"). That the talkative child reflects on language itself and on his narration can be described as a metafictional exercise by the author.

5. Omniscient Narration

> The narrative voice occasionally offers information about what a character did *not* think, say, or know. By knowing what others do not, the narrator has total control over the narrative. Search for examples of this control in the text and explain their function in the context in which they appear.

The world of a work of fiction includes information not available to all its characters. The narrator, revealing that information to us, thereby creates a special link between narrator and reader. In the following example, this link is particularly evident: "Lo que no le dije es que me estaba volviendo un experto en tocarme el cuerpo y que daba mucho gustito" (232; "What I did not say is that I was becoming an expert in touching my body, and that it gave me great pleasure").

6. The Narrative Voice Comments on Plot or Narration

> The narrative voice calls attention to the text as artifice.[7] Such commentary represents the highest level of visibility of the narrator. Identify passages in the text in which Balti refers to his own narration and explain what effect it has on your reading.

In the construct that is narrative, the suspension of disbelief is broken when the narrator calls attention to the text as artifice. Students should be given the concept of willing suspension of disbelief. A good illustration is the rhetorical question that Balti poses to himself: "Tengo diecisiete años, ¿de qué me sirve retroceder a cuando tenía cuatro y luego ocho y luego quince?" (81; "I am seventeen years old. What's the point of regressing to when I was four and then eight and then fifteen?"). This question is relevant on two levels. At the level of content, Balti is reflecting on his maturation. At the level of narration, the author is reminding us of the experimental, metafictional narratives of 1970s literature.

Students have now identified several important narrative elements. The next work sheet focuses on the temporal structure of the narrative and is designed for the third class, in which student participation is increased.

Third Class Session: Temporal Structure and the Reader's Role

The third class is divided in two parts and focuses on student participation and group work. The first part utilizes a work sheet; the second is organized around the instructor's presentation of relevant theory.

> *Narrative Time*
>
> Narrative time can be:
> 1. Linear in chronology
> 2. Nonlinear in chronology
>   Prolepsis: the narrative jumps forward in time, and events from the future are given with no reference to the events that preceded them.
>   Analepsis: the narrative jumps back in time (definitions adapted from Rimmon-Kenan 43–58).
>
> Outline the temporal structure of the novel. Take into account that its final chapter is unfinished. Do you think that it was Martín Gaite's intention that the last chapter written be the final one? Consider that the novel's end focuses on the same temporal frame as the beginning, for example.

Students should see that the novel does not progress chronologically. They therefore need to learn the technical terms *flashback* and *flash-forward* in order to refer to the temporal structure of the novel. These concepts help them reexamine the novel and compose a possible ending in keeping with the author's narrative strategy. Students should be asked to rearrange the events in the novel and discuss the implications of Martín Gaite's use of time. By examining the structure of the novel, they gain a better understanding of the protagonist's development as well as of the process through which his family relationships become comprehensible to him.

The narrative is circular. Although we know that Martín Gaite left the novel unfinished, so the circularity may be unintended, the published text is all we have to work with. *Los parentescos* begins with the first encounter between Balti and Olalla on the morning of Balti's parents' wedding, and the girl's energy strongly attracts him. Olalla, two years older, turns out to be the daughter of Balti's mother's first husband. Olalla may also be the cause of that marriage's disintegration. The final chapter of the novel is called "La raya invisible" ("The Invisible Line") and is an allusion to a game that Olalla invented. Martín Gaite wrote only the beginning of this chapter before her death; it centers on an analepsis that returns to the moment in which the two children met and contains a letter that Balti never sent to Olalla. In it, he expresses his admiration for her; the letter is his first act as narrator.

Theorizing the Role of the Reader

The absence of chronological order in *Los parentescos* allows instructors to discuss the role of the reader. To this end, the chapter entitled "The Reading Process: A Phenomenological Approach," from Wolfgang Iser's *The Implied Reader*, is enlightening (274–94). In my experience, students are not accustomed to reflecting on their role as readers or on the indeterminacy of the text, and Iser's seminal work helps them understand their fundamental role as givers of meaning. They should know that critics have theorized the reader's role such that a text has no fixed meanings and is not determined by authorial intentions. Of particular importance is the idea that "the convergence of text and reader brings the literary work into existence"; that is, the literary work is created through the dialectical relation between the text and each individual reader (275). Iser contends that the reader has to "fill in the gaps" of a text (280).

Fourth Class Session: Creating an Ending

The class is divided into groups of four and asked to complete the following tasks. First, each group should spend about ten minutes brainstorming to create an ending for the unfinished chapter, which will be an ending for the novel as well. Students must review the novel and the concepts they have learned in previous classes. When the group has decided on the ending, they should spend fifteen to twenty minutes writing. Normally, during this activity, I walk around the classroom answering any questions the groups may have. When the writing is finished, the instructor will read an ending aloud and invite the whole class to comment on it. During this reading aloud, the instructor has the opportunity to point out and correct grammatical errors. Students, even in advanced literature courses taught in Spanish, tend to appreciate such brief reviews of grammar.

The creative diversity of the different endings composed by the student groups will illustrate Iser's theory about the active participation of the reader. Each group should explain to the class which of the novel's narrative and temporal elements guided their writing of the ending. Meanwhile, the rest of the class, in their reading of the narratives composed by their classmates, perform the work of literary critics.

NOTES

[1]An analytic approach to *Los parentescos* would be quite different from the one I describe in this essay. It would rely more on the secondary literature. I would expect students to have some awareness of reader reception theory, for example, and might assign selections from the work of Wolfgang Iser and of Stanley Fish.

[2]Josefina (Rodríguez) Aldecoa (1926–2011) was in close contact with this group of friends and would later write about the same era. Because she did not begin writing in earnest until the 1980s, she is not customarily included in the mid-century literary cohort.

[3]The interview is available online at www.cuny.tv/show/charlandoconcervantes/PR1000847.

[4]This is a simplified version of Rimmon-Kenan's diagram. The original terms "implied author" and "implied reader" might confuse students at this level (87).

[5]All translations of *Los parentescos* are mine.

[6]The work sheet can include examples from other texts that highlight different levels of perception and intervention expressed by the narrative voice. For example, the narrator selects information in the first line of *Don Quijote*: "En un lugar de la Mancha, de cuyo nombre no quiero acordarme . . ." (Cervantes [1955] 35). Edith Grossman translates this as, "Somewhere in La Mancha, in a place whose name I do not care to remember . . ." (19). In her essay "Tiempo y lugar" ("Time and Space"), Martín Gaite observes, "Dice Miguel de Cervantes que no quiere acordarse, pero es evidente que se acuerda . . ." (*Pido* 386; "Miguel de Cervantes says that he doesn't care to remember, but it is clear that he remembers").

[7]A wide variety of self-referential passages from *Don Quijote* could help to illustrate this point.

POETRY, THEATER, AND TELEVISION

Teaching the Poems of *A rachas*: Themes and Forms

Josefa Álvarez

The Evolving Stages of Carmen Martín Gaite's Poetry

Although Carmen Martín Gaite attained her greatest literary recognition as a narrator and essayist, throughout her life she occasionally ventured into the genre of poetry. In fact, it was with poetry that she began her writing career, as a young adult in her native Salamanca. She never thought seriously about publishing her poems until her friend Jesús Munárriz, a poet and the proprietor of the Hiperión publishing house, asked her to compile them for publication. Thus was born *A rachas* ("In a Gust of Wind") in 1976, a volume whose title suggests that Martín Gaite's poetic side was not central to her persona.

The book has gone through successive iterations. In the first edition, she assembled poems from her young adult years—from the 1950s—along with additional poems written afterward and grouped under the heading "Poemas posteriores" ("Later Poems"). In 1979, a second edition of her poems appeared, which differed from the first only in a few formal revisions. In 1986, a third edition was augmented by six poems from her youth that she managed to rescue from old notebooks and by three new poems included at the end. The author continued to write poetry, and in 1993 a new edition was published, once again expanded, under a new title: *Después de todo: Poesía a rachas* ("After All: Poetry in a Gust of Wind"). A subsequent volume of selections of Martín Gaite's poetry, featuring a CD with recordings of her readings of these poems, was published in 2000.[1]

Because her poems were written throughout the various phases of her life, and because *A rachas* follows an apparent chronological and autobiographical progression, "it is almost as though Martín Gaite had published a diary" (Brown, *Secrets* 140). This progression leads us to analyze the content and form of the poems by considering the volume's individual segments in its most complete edition, *Después de todo*.

The accessible language of Martín Gaite's poems allows instructors to work with them at various stages of instruction, beginning at intermediate levels of Spanish language learning. In this essay I propose a way of introducing some of the poems in 200- and 300-level college courses on Spanish literature and provide ideas for teaching Martín Gaite's poetry in a 400-level course. I offer concrete pedagogical suggestions and resources and discuss and analyze each segment of *Después de todo*. To assist those who are considering teaching the author's poetry, a listing of the poems discussed here—including the form and main themes of each—is given in the appendix to this essay as a reference.

Teaching A rachas *at the Intermediate and Advanced Levels*

I have taught Martín Gaite's poetry in two literature courses: Approaches to Reading Texts, in the Syracuse University program in Spain, and Introduction to Spanish Literature 1, at Le Moyne College. The students in both courses were at the high-intermediate level, having completed at least four semesters of Spanish. I selected a few short and easy-to-understand poems to review the most important topics of each poetic phase. Because of their apparent simplicity, I selected "Tiempo de flor" ("Time of Flowers"), a good example of the romantic and nostalgic poetry of the author's youth, and "Por el mundo adelante" ("Onward into the World"), a perfect text to illustrate the restrictions and suffocation of this time period, the first twenty years of Franco's dictatorship, as well as the author's search for her identity. From her later poems, I used "El escondite inglés" ("Red Light–Green Light"), to introduce the topics of memory and life's fleetingness, and "Coplas de amor y desgarro" ("Couplets of Love and Anguish"), to analyze her older, more jaundiced perspective on love. Finally, I chose the late poem "La última vez que entró Andersen en casa" ("The Last Time That Andersen Came Over"), to explore the theme of loss.

Before reading a poem, I encourage discussion about its title, introduce images connected with its vocabulary or content, and match some of its words with their meanings, synonyms, or antonyms. If students do not know vocabulary, I promote the use of dictionaries. Organizing the students into pairs or small groups promotes verbal interaction in the classroom.

Next I read the poem's text aloud. Often we can listen to the author's reading (when the poem is one that she recorded for the collection *Poemas*) and compare our recitations with hers to better understand the spirit of the poem.

Sometimes I use the author's recording in specific activities, such as removing five or six words in the text and asking the students to replace them using their knowledge of the words' contexts. While they listen to the poem, they review their results. A fruitful technique is to omit a few verse-ending words and play with the rhyme, if present.

I always request that students look carefully for the poetic voice (an "I," a "he" or "she," a "we") and for those who are addressed (a fictitious "you," a split poetic "I," a hostile "you" that refers to the environment, to cite some examples). It is also useful to map the meaning of the poem's words or lines to a set of interpretation choices. Such activities help the student see a poem's structure and understand its meaning. It is important to pay attention to the verbal forms and their changes in Martín Gaite's poems and to decide whether they have a function. For example, "Por el mundo adelante" resorts to three different tenses in order to detail the past, present, and projected future of the poetic "I." We also need to be attentive to changes in point of view.

I ask the students to isolate the poems' figures of speech, separate them into different levels (phonic, morphosyntactic, lexical-semantic), and point out the more meaningful ones. For example, in an alliteration (at the phonic level) in "Nubes" ("Clouds"), one can feel the wind changing the clouds' shapes with the repetition of *s*: "Bisontes negros / ensenadas de iris . . ." (*Después de todo* 21; "Black bisons / rainbows' inlets").[2] Parallelism and anaphora (at the morphosyntactic level) are used to emphasize key ideas in "Callejón sin salida" ("Blind Alley"): "Y no puedo volver / y no quiero volver" (24; "And I cannot come back / and I do not want to come back"). Personification (at the lexical-semantic level) heightens the Romantic tone and emotional intensity of "Nubes": "Mi tierra tenía sed" (21; "My land was thirsty"). After identifying these rhetorical devices, students are ready to formulate their own interpretations, grasp what a poem is doing, then summarize its theme or subject. I compare their summaries and encourage them to reach a consensus through small-group and whole-class discussions. Finally, we study the external poem structure (the versification) and proceed to read the poem aloud again, giving emphasis to significant pauses, words, or figures of speech.

Comparing the author's poetry and prose is productive for intermediate and advanced students alike. A useful strategy is to introduce some of her passages or short stories and have students consider how her poems treat the same topics. I use two anthologies for this exercise: *Antología de Carmen Martín Gaite: Traer a cuento* ("Anthology of Carmen Martín Gaite: Bringing Up Stories"), edited by Julián Moreiro, and *Cuéntame* ("Tell Me"), edited by Emma Martinell. The poems of Martín Gaite's first youth may be read with the short story "La chica de abajo" ("The Girl from Downstairs"), which features the same provincial environment of the author's 1958 novel *Entre visillos* (*Behind the Curtains*) and of her poem "Por el mundo adelante." The story contains symbols (the opened window, closed and warm places, tolling bells) and associations (the Romantic connection between feelings and nature, the blending of dreams and reality, the negative connotation of awakening from a dream) that are evident in the early poems. It also gives the social background of postwar Spain and previews two major topics of Martín Gaite's work: the importance of an interlocutor for good conversation and the symbolism of the back room.

In 400-level courses, I assign poems that are more difficult, such as "Convalecencia" ("Convalescence") and "Domingo por la tarde" ("Sunday Afternoon"). They are excellent for studying the theme of youth and can be combined and compared with Martín Gaite's contemporary Jaime Gil de Biedma's "Domingo" ("Sunday").

At advanced levels, I like students to focus on a specific topic—for example, the metapoetical verse that is common among poets of the Spanish generation of the 1950s. It is interesting to compare Martín Gaite's poems with those of other Spanish women poets (Elvira Lacaci, Pilar Paz Pasamar) and male poets of her time (José Ángel Valente, Gil de Biedma). The metapoetic theme has resonance also with excerpts from *El cuarto de atrás*: in chapter 1, ". . . y esta cama grande, rodeada de libros y papeles en los que hace un rato buscaba consuelo…" (16; ". . . and this big bed surrounded by books and papers in which I was seeking consolation a little while ago . . ." [5]). Also relevant to the theme is Martín Gaite's nonfiction, such as "Ponerse a leer" ("Beginning to Read"), in *La búsqueda de interlocutor* ("The Search for a Conversational Partner").

The poems "Espiga sin granar" ("Unripe Wheat Spike") and "Jaculatoria" ("Brief Prayer"), difficult for students at lower levels but quite interesting for advanced learners because of their metaphoric value, illustrate the construction of subjectivity. "Todo es un cuento roto en Nueva York" ("Everything Is a Fractured Story in New York") is an indispensable text to read with Margaret Persin's essay "Carmen Martín Gaite's *A rachas.*" The instructor can begin with images of New York City and close with the projection of Edward Hopper's painting *Hotel Room*. The poem might be analyzed with "Madrid la nuit" ("Madrid Night") and "Farmacia de guardia" ("All-Night Pharmacy").

Several Web pages provide information, recordings, graphic resources, interviews, and articles about Martín Gaite's work. Instructors are welcome to access links provided on my personal Web site, where I present additional ideas and sample activities for working on Martín Gaite's poetry in Spanish literature classes (http://cor.to/poesia-gaite).

The Themes and Forms of Martín Gaite's Poetry

Poemas de primera juventud ("Poems of First Youth")

As Munárriz indicated in an editorial note, the author's first poems transport us to the provincial world of her youth, evoking Spain's generation of the 1950s in their expression, rhythm, and music. I teach her work in this context, using Andrew Debicki's *Spanish Poetry of the Twentieth Century* and Sharon Keefe Ugalde's *En voz alta* ("Speaking Out Loud").[3] Debicki demonstrates how the

Spanish poets of Martín Gaite's generation in "their formative years were . . . greatly affected by the rigidity and hypocrisy of their first post–Civil War decades" (99). For women poets, this social order had special implications. Women were relegated to the least favored role in a hierarchical gender system that anchored them to archaic models of submission and isolation. Ugalde shows that for this reason many poems by women were a way of crying out in the face of the suffocating routine of their lives (20).

The poetic voice in many of Martín Gaite's early works confronts an "[o]ther which is multiple" that limits and restricts her (Persin, "Carmen Martín Gaite's *A rachas*" 96). In the poems "Callejón sin salida" and "Certeza" ("Conviction"), this other appears in the *vosotros* (the familiar, plural form of "you") who have "walled her in" (*Después de todo* 36). She opposes this restraint and makes clear her intention to escape. In "Por el mundo adelante," reality traps her "como un pulpo" ("like an octopus"), and her rebelliousness finally demands, "Abrid ya las ventanas / . . . / Quiero huir de los ámbitos / calientes y tapiados" (25; "Open the windows already / . . . / I want to flee these hot, walled-in confines"). The author uses antithesis, such as that of windows and walled-in confines, to show the strong opposition between the inner wishes of the poetic voice and the surrounding world that constrains her. Like her generational colleagues (Debicki 109), Martín Gaite creates symbolic meaning from real points of reference. She uses walls, doors, windows, and balconies as elements that represent being locked away when they refer to closed environments or that suggest freedom when they are open. Catherine G. Bellver, in her study of Spanish women poets of the 1920s and 1930s, affirms that for them "the element of possession—of both the self and the other . . . connotes autonomy and power, qualities indispensable for self-assertion" (*Absence* 13). This statement is equally true of Martín Gaite's early poetry: her youthful impulse places her poetic feminine self at the center of a hostile world, but Martín Gaite believes herself capable of leaving that world in search of broader horizons.

Self-confidence emboldens the poet to venture forth, with a mobility that in the past was reserved for men (Bellver, *Absence* 44), and to set out alone. Traditionally, the solitary state was negative for women, linked to "trágico abandono" (Ugalde 49; "tragic abandonment"). The poet moves on, "alegre y sola . . . / por el camino mío que he encontrado" (24 ["Callejón sin salida"]; "happy and alone . . . / along the road I have found") or insists on wanting to leave by herself (25 ["Por el mundo adelante"]). She reaffirms herself fully in her chosen solitude, laying claim to it as a path to growth and personal development. Solitude is the key to individual freedom, to the possibility of leaving the window open and passing through it to new worlds and experiences.[4] Women's silence is also seen as positive and strong instead of negative and powerless. These new definitions of solitude and silence pertain to a new woman, whom the author envisions in poems such as "Espiga sin granar," where a mirror constructs identity, as Persin notes in her detailed analysis of the poem (*Getting* 100). Identity is further created through the act of writing. Martín Gaite and the poets of the generation of the 1950s, self-aware of and explicit about the poetic process, frequently insert metapoetic reflections into their poems.[5] For the female poets of this cohort, writing becomes a refuge from societal restrictions (Ugalde 48). In the *silva* "Luna llena" (*Después de todo* 29; "Full Moon"), the *silva* being one of Martín Gaite's favorite verse forms,[6] the poet addresses the moon, recalling all the clichés by poets and lovers who alluded to it without ever penetrating its mystery. By using the first person plural, she includes herself in this group, feeling connected to this "largo río subterráneo / de palabras marchitas / que viene desde Safo y Rosalía / a morir en mi boca" (29; "long subterranean river / of withered words / that come from Sappho and Rosalía / to die in my mouth"). She thus identifies herself as heiress to a tradition of women poets who have their own voice. "Rosalía" refers to the Galician poet Rosalía de Castro (1837–85), who exemplifies the approach to women's writing that is born from looking out from an interior refuge, represented by the image of a window and a woman who watches from it without being seen (*Desde la ventana* 51–55).

References to poetic masters appear in many poems of the author's youth. In "Luna llena" and in "Batalla perdida" (*Después de todo* 46; "Lost Battle"), the poet speaks of an inscrutable landscape that no lyric word can render. She echoes Juan Ramón Jiménez, who was intent on finding "el nombre exacto de las cosas," (136; "the exact names for things"), and much of the vocabulary and content of the poem recall Jiménez (Persin, "Carmen Martín Gaite's *A rachas*" 94).[7] Like him, Martín Gaite is obsessed with the inexorable passing of time. In her "Días azules" (34; "Blue Days"), days are likened to grapes that fall from their bunch one by one.

With a melancholy tone that evokes another influence from her youth, the poems of Antonio Machado, she proclaims, "¡He dormido tan cerca / del reloj de pared!" (34; "I have slept so close / to the clock on the wall!"). This swift passage of time is noted in several compositions on love, whether dealing with love's pleasures or its absence. In "Otro otoño" (37; "Another Autumn"), the personified season of the year calls out to the glass (a metonymic device for "window") of the poetic I. The poem's tone is also linked to Rosalía de Castro and to those nameless things that she sought in the Galician countryside, a topic echoed in *Desde la ventana* (53). These romantic suggestions of the inescapable passing of time and of love fulfilled, awaited, or lost are important topics of these first poems, whose "starry-eyed perspective never reappears in any of the author's subsequent writing" (Brown, *Secrets* 142).

In these as in subsequent poems, Martín Gaite opts for the artistic use of spoken language, as is typical of her generation, filling each work with colloquial, stock phrases such as "cada palo que aguante su vela" (*Después de todo* 72; "you made your bed, now lie in it"), "a palo seco" (92; "on its own"), or "amigos topados a voleo" (68; "friends run into by chance"). Martín Gaite's poems feature words associated with her Castilian homeland and the countryside (*risco*, *matorral*, *cigüeña*, *cierzo*; "crag," "bush," "stork," "north wind") and with places and objects characteristic of small provincial cities (*faroles*, *fuentes*, *plazas*, *callejas*, *iglesias*;

"street lamps," "fountains," "plazas," "narrow streets," "churches"). Sometimes, to achieve an effect, she combines those common words with words that are not (*estertor*, *postrera*, *enjugar*, *yerma*, *agorero*, *intangible*, *trémulo*; "death rattle," "very last," "wipe away," "wasteland," "prophet of doom," "intangible," "quavering"). These juxtapositions give her poetry a tone rich with contrasts, particularly between the external routine of life and the poet's interior musings.

Blank verse—poetry without rhyme but with considerable rhythm—is the common structure in this first poetic stage, with a predominance of hendecasyllabic (eleven-syllable) and heptasyllabic (seven-syllable) lines. There is an abundance of metaphors and similes that refer to nature, and there is ample use of personification. In poems such as "Me pesas como un fardo" (27; "You Weigh on Me like a Bale"), Martín Gaite uses various forms of repetition to emphasize the slow and predictable pace of provincial life. Among her devices are anaphora (repetition at the beginning of phrases), epanalepsis (repetition at regular intervals), and chiasmus (inversion of syntactic elements). A circular (ring) structure is evident in poems such as "Tiempo de flor" (19) and "Rastro borrado" (23; "Erased Traces"). This device either emphasizes an idea or expresses the monotony of existence.

Poemas posteriores ("Later Poems")

The later poems were written after the author turned forty. Several of the topics in her earlier compositions return in them but are usually treated in a new way. The later poems echo the medieval Spanish lyric tradition. An example is the frequent use of octosyllabic couplets and such other characteristic stanzas and verses as the *pie quebrado* ("half line"), which was used by Jorge Manrique in his *Coplas por la muerte de su padre* ("Ode on the Death of His Father") and in the marquis of Santillana's *serranillas*. Martín Gaite's newer work opens with the poem "Jaculatoria" (53–54), written in octosyllabic rhymed verse. The lyric voice is directed to a "you" that seems to be the poet's reflection in the mirror. What the poet seeks is not so much the construction of an identity as its preservation, in the face of many obstacles. This poem features a chorus, another typical device of medieval poetry, of "No te mueras todavía" ("Do not die yet"), to reinforce its theme.

Love returns as a central theme in these midlife poems, although from the perspective of disillusionment, skepticism, and irony. It comes hand in hand with memory and remembrance, whose weight is greater from this point on. A good example of this weight is found in the four-stanza poem "Descarrilamiento" ("Derailment"). Combining heptasyllabic and alexandrine lines with the half lines of each (resp., pentasyllabic and heptasyllabic), the poet uses rhythm to evoke a train derailment, which is the metaphor for a couple's breakup. The lyric voice, which represents the author, tries to establish a conversation with a fictitious interlocutor, but this unsuccessful effort leads to the same question that begins the poem, "¿Cómo pudo ocurrir el descarrilamiento?" (59, 60; "How could the derailment happen?"). Overwhelming disenchantment is communicated by this circular structure.

Joan Brown observes how these love poems explore in detail "the complex stages of reaction to the end of a love affair . . . from surprised hurt, to plaintive anger, to resignation and, finally, equanimity" and relates them thematically to the novels *Retahílas* ("Yarns") and *Fragmentos de interior* ("Inner Fragments"), in which the feminine protagonists, like the author herself, live through the dissolution of a marriage. From Brown's perspective, the culmination of this reflection on the different phases of love is "Diez coplas de amor y angustia" ("Ten Couplets of Love and Anguish"), where all are considered (*Secrets* 144–45). These wry verses are marked by subtle irony and humor, devices employed by members of Martín Gaite's generation to combat feelings of sadness and helplessness (Tusón 53). In these couplets Martín Gaite has a clear intertextual referent: medieval Galician-Portuguese *cantigas de amigo* ("songs for friends"). The poetic voice addresses a *tú* (familiar "you"), the lost love, as did the feminine voices of the *cantigas*. The author knew these poems well and identified them with women's laments despite their male authorship *(Desde la ventana* 59).

If the poems of Martín Gaite's youth were written in a provincial setting, her later poems were written in an urban setting where loneliness is a constant. In "Madrid la nuit," the poet exclaims, "Tienes frío, estás solo y hay que esconder el miedo" (*Después de todo* 69; "You're cold, you're alone, and you must hide your fear"). The masculine gender is the neutral form, and the addressed *tú* universalizes the experience of being in a great Spanish city where the night is spent meandering from place to place with friends encountered by chance. Finding an interlocutor is the only thing that can conquer the existential void. The poet exhorts, "Echa hilo a la cometa de la noche" (68, 69; "Let out the kite string of the night") at the beginning and end of the circular composition, the string being a constant metaphor for conversation, which the author believes is the best balm for solitude.[8]

The last poem in this group, "Todo es un cuento roto en Nueva York" (88–92; "All Is a Broken Story in New York"), utilizing the same metrical combination as "Madrid la nuit," unfolds in a great metropolis. Its view of the striking contrasts of New York City, the antithetical parallelisms of luxury and squalor, brings to mind Federico García Lorca's *Poeta en Nueva York* (1939–40; *Poet in New York*). The poetic I urges fictional readers to search for a woman whose reality they doubt, in a menacing city. Finally she invites them to find her in a painting by Edward Hopper, where she sits alone on a bed in an anonymous boardinghouse. In this ekphrastic text (analyzed by Persin, *Getting* 102–11), Martín Gaite turns to intertextuality with film, art, and literature to depict a woman alone in a room. Hopper's painting becomes the mirror in which the author regards her own mature reflection.

At this point in Martín Gaite's poetic development, metapoetic reflection returns, now questioning the usefulness of writing as consolation for the pain of existence, in poems such as "Libros y papeles" (71–72; "Books and Papers"), whose form is that of Manrique's couplets. Language is a vehicle for communication but also an obstacle to be overcome even as it constitutes the theme of the poem (Persin, *Poesía* 17), as in the revealingly titled "¿Qué hacer con las palabras?" (87; "What to Do with Words?").

Anxiety about the fleetingness of existence and the recollection of lost childhood are other recurring themes in this section. Through "El escondite inglés" (64; "Red Light–Green Light"), we grasp the metaphor for the rapid passage of time that the narrative voice in *El cuarto de atrás* explains with clarity in the chapter with this title (ch. 4). The poem repeats the refrain, "Una, dos y tres, / escondite inglés, / a esa niña de rojo, / ya no la ves" ("Red light–green light / One, two, three, / that girl in red / you no longer see"). The rhyme accompanies the disappearance of the girl when she becomes an adult. The brevity of the verse is in keeping with the flight of time, the object of the poem's reflection. In these later poems, and to a lesser degree in the final ones in *Después de todo*, rhymed verse predominates. The rhyme is normally consonant, and the meter (heptasyllabic, octosyllabic, hendecasyllabic) has greater variety than that of earlier works. Many of the later poems have an air of song acquired through repetition or a refrain, as in "Jaculatoria," "Amor nómada" (64; "Nomadic Love"), and "Libros y papeles."

Después de todo ("After All")

On reading the third and last grouping of poems, compiled in 1992 and published the following year, readers familiar with Martín Gaite's biography will find it difficult not to think of the death of the author's daughter, Marta, in 1985. These poems are the most intimate and personal of the collection. The theme of memory is present in the entire volume as a unifying, indispensable connection with life: as in her novels, memories belong to and unite those who share them (Martín Gaite, *Hilo* 113).

"La última vez que entró Andersen en casa" introduces, through its title and opening lines, *La Reina de las Nieves* ("The Snow Queen"), the novel dedicated to her daughter after her daughter died: "Me ha raptado—dijiste— / la Reina de las Nieves. / Pero esta vez no era literatura" (95; "'She has kidnapped me,' you said, / 'the Snow Queen.' / But this time it wasn't literature"). The poetic "I" in this *silva* addresses a "you" who confronts death's arrival. The reader sees both author and daughter at the moment of their farewell. We find the same intimate tone in "Quien motiva mi queja" (96; "The One Who Causes My Lament"), in which the poet bemoans the emptiness caused by the absence of an irreplaceable interlocutor, the one for whom she was always searching and whose words could comfort her. It is not difficult to imagine her deceased daughter as that missing person. In these poems, and in "Escrito en la cara" (102–03; "Written on the Face"), which is dedicated to the memory of the portrait painter María Antonia Dans, the poet recalls the meaningful words of a deceased loved one.

Common to many of these poems is what Ugalde has called the poetic re-creation of a matrilineal legacy, achieved at times by analyzing the relationship with a mother, grandmother, or daughter, and in some cases with an aunt or friend (83–84). The absence of these important feminine figures in the life of the poet is somewhat eased by her compositions, which recall the time in which the past and the present, daydreams and reality, were all blended in what Ugalde calls "la creación de un tiempo monumental" (85; "the creation of a monumental time"). Through that prism we are able to comprehend "El desorden antiguo" (100–01; "The Old Disorder"), in which by searching for objects from the past one tries to remember, or the final poem, "El cuarto de jugar" (113; "The Playroom"), which recalls childhood play that mingles imagination with reality and the magical back room that symbolizes the importance of interior spaces for this author (Moreiro 24).

Love reappears in this section, distorted as pain and the void left by its extinction in "Donde acaba el amor" (97; "Where Love Ends") and "Pájaro vegetal" (98; "Vegetable Bird"). With this emptiness comes the death of desire, which subtends the poem "Chispa de plata apagada" (105; "Desire Extinguished"). Alienating loneliness merges with this same theme in "Farmacia de guardia" (110; "All-Night Pharmacy"). The poetic voice finds itself in the middle of a telephone conversation which ultimately becomes an interior monologue, a common technique in Martín Gaite's last poems (seen also in "El desorden antiguo").

A rachas is a valuable and surprisingly accessible collection of poetry, written during several periods of the author's life. In addition to their intrinsic thematic and formal interest for students of Spanish language and literature, these poems contribute to a better understanding of Martín Gaite's universe, offering a closer look at some of her most intimate and enduring concerns.

NOTES

[1] Again responding to the encouragement of a friend in publishing, the head of a record company (Alberto Pérez of Avizor Records), *Poemas* highlights a CD of Martín Gaite's readings of thirty-five of her poems. The accompanying book presents the text of these poems along with two brief introductions (one by Pérez, the other by Martín Gaite). The volume is illustrated with photographs of the author over the course of her life. Twenty-six previously published poems are absent from this collection, and two previously unpublished poems—one from the 1970s and one from 1998—are included for the first time.

[2] English translations of Martín Gaite's verses were provided by Catherine Nock of Syracuse University. Translations of *El cuarto de atrás* are taken from *The Back Room*.

[3]Ugalde recognizes Martín Gaite as a member of the generation of mid-century yet excludes her from her anthology, ruling out authors who dedicate themselves principally to other genres (10).

[4]The female literary voice in *El cuarto de atrás* manifests this same appreciation of youthful solitude. In chapter 4, the author describes the "sensación incomparable de libertad" (103; "incomparable feeling of freedom" [*Back Room* 107]) when she is alone with her cousin in a hotel room in Burgos.

[5]One example of this self-awareness is González's "Palabra muerta, realidad perdida" ("Dead Word, Lost Reality"). See Debicki 126.

[6]A *silva* is a compound of *imparisílabo* ("unpaired syllable") verses of *arte menor* (eight syllables or less) and *arte mayor* (more than eight, including alexandrines of 7 + 7 syllables). It was frequently used by Antonio Machado.

[7]Many of Martín Gaite's early poems have the Romantic tone of the earliest Jiménez poetry. Explorations of nature and the nostalgia that its contemplation produces, with an awareness of the fleetingness of existence, evoke his "El viaje definitivo" (96).

[8]Regarding string as a metaphor of connection, note the title *Retahílas* ("Yarns") or the recurring allusions to conversation in *El cuarto de atrás*. See Sobejano, "Carmen Martín Gaite" 524.

APPENDIX: FORMS AND MAIN THEMES OF THE POEMS DISCUSSED

Title	**Form**	**Main Themes**
***Poemas de primera juventud* ("Poems of First Youth")**		
"Tiempo de flor"	*silva;* ring composition	melancholy over the loss of a young love
"Por el mundo adelante"	Anacreontic romance	environmental pressure; desire for freedom
"Callejón sin salida"	Anacreontic romance; ring composition	solitude in the pursuit of individual freedom
"Luna llena"	*silva*	metapoetic reflection (the poetic word does not represent reality); identity created through writing
"Batalla perdida"	*silva*	existential reflection on the passage of time
"Días azules"	Anacreontic romance; ring composition	unrelenting passage of time and loss of youth
"Espiga sin granar"	*silva*	female identity construction

Title	Form	Main Themes
***Poemas posteriores* ("Later Poems")**		
"Jaculatoria"	song in octosyllabic verse with consonant rhyme	preservation of one's identity
"Descarrilamiento"	*silva*; ring composition	love disillusionment after a breakup
"Coplas de amor y angustia"	octosyllabic couplets with consonant rhyme	skepticism about love when one grows old
"Madrid la nuit"	*silva*; ring composition	solitude and lack of communication in the city
"Todo es un cuento roto en Nueva York"	*silva*; ekphrastic poem	female solitude and lack of communication
"Libros y papeles"	series of *sextillas* ("sestets")	metapoetical reflection: language as vehicle for and obstacle to communication
"El escondite inglés"	series of *redondillas* in pentasyllabic verse	passage of time; loss of childhood and youth
***Después de todo* ("After All")**		
"La última vez que entró Andersen en casa"	*silva* with half verse	her daughter's death
"Quien motiva mi queja"	*pareados* ("pairs of verse")	emptiness and pain from her daughter's death; loss of an interlocutor
"El desorden antiguo"	*silva* with pentasyllabic half verse	poetic re-creation of a matrilineal legacy
"El cuarto de jugar"	heptasyllabic verse with consonant rhyme	remembrance of childhood
"Farmacia de guardia"	*silva*; dramatic monologue	loss of faith in life; loneliness

Teaching Carmen Martín Gaite's Play *La hermana pequeña*

Janet Pérez

My teaching of Carmen Martín Gaite's works has been largely on the graduate level—the one significant exception, a three-day *cursillo* ("short course") in October 2007 at the Universidad Carlos III (Madrid-Getafe), was composed of fourth-year undergraduates with a few beginning graduate students. The *cursillo* offered some three hundred students an orientation to concepts of gender, followed by a gender-studies-based survey of Martín Gaite's fiction and theater up to 1975. The *cursillo* was taught entirely in Spanish, as are my graduate courses at Texas Tech University. My graduate teaching of Martín Gaite occurs in two venues. One is a course on the twentieth-century novelistic canon, which covers twelve novels, only two of them written by women; the other is a course on twentieth-century women novelists, which covers twelve to thirteen novels. Both courses examine text, subtext, and context (history, politics, sociocultural climate, aesthetics). Of Martín Gaite's works, the novelistic canon class reads *El cuarto de atrás* (1978; *The Back Room*), sections of *Usos amorosos de la postguerra española* (1987; *Courtship Customs in Postwar Spain*), and extracts from *Esperando el porvenir* (1994; "Awaiting the Future"), and the course on women novelists reads *Entre visillos* (1958; *Behind the Curtains*) and *La hermana pequeña* (1999; "The Little Sister"). *Las ataduras* (1960; "Binding Ties") is assigned to a few volunteers, who lead discussions on its relation to the other texts, emphasizing gender issues. Both courses employ lecture, question, and discussion formats, and students write essays comparing and contrasting Martín Gaite's titles with those of two or three other novelists from the same period.

These courses have been taught at night for twenty-five years, facilitating attendance by nontraditional, nonresident students who teach at surrounding schools and colleges. Many drive three hours for the three-hour class, then drive home. The schedule isn't easy for them, but motivation is high. The women writers course begins with an introduction to concepts of gender, using Núria Pompeia's delightful cartoon book *Mujercitas* ("Little Ladies")—I give handouts, make *PowerPoint* presentations, or show overhead projections of especially appropriate cartoons. Students can keep the handouts, but the projections permit watching the cartoons while hearing explanations of gender roles and associated concepts that correlate well with the lives of many characters in both *La hermana pequeña* and *Entre visillos*.

The courses are reading-intensive: students must read a novel and supplementary material for each weekly class. They must also prepare for and participate in analytic discussions.

Women in the Works of Martín Gaite

Like most Spanish women writers of her generation, Martín Gaite rejected the label of feminist, yet women and women's condition loom so large in her writings that she herself observed in the prologue to her *Cuentos completos* (1978; "Complete Stories") that "Cuentos de mujeres" ("Women's Stories") would have been an equally suitable title, acknowledging an obsessive concern with women's condition from the beginning of her literary career (8–9). Obliquely referencing gender issues, she cites the inability of women to reconcile what they want from life with the lives they are living—the frustrated feminine quest for a more acceptable identity. Most likely Martín Gaite had not encountered gender studies as it is known in the United States, because it was still being introduced in Spain as recently as 2007. Yet her works provide a gallery of feminine gender types and role models—often models to avoid—and gender constructs provide a lens that brings the novelist's world into focus, revealing unexpected connections. Her fiction constantly deals with gendered problems, as do her essays, including the parodically entitled *Desde la ventana* (1987; "From the Window"). That collection offers meditations on women writers and women characters who evoke *la condición ventanera* ("the window lifestyle"), which restricted them to gazing outward on life's passing from domestic confinement. Women of different generations in her novel *Entre visillos* gaze from the window, from behind the curtains. Gender difference provides the underlying dynamics of her reconstruction of male-female relations in *Usos amorosos del dieciocho en España* (1973; *Love Customs in Eighteenth-Century Spain*) and *Usos amorosos de la postguerra española*, among her major essays, as well as in her novels.

Defining Gender

Gender is by no means synonymous with biological sex: as used in gender studies, the term *gender* signifies a social construct, the totality of social expectations, identity, and duties attached to human beings because they were born male or female. Gender appears early in children's lives, primarily as prohibitions: Girls don't fight, boys don't cry, girls mustn't shout, boys don't wash dishes, girls can't go out alone, boys don't play with dolls. Gender looms larger when young people choose careers, with injunctions such as, Girls should not be engineers, rocket scientists, or experts in cattle breeding, and boys should not be nurses, dressmakers, or nannies. Gender shapes personalities, appearances, and lives; it opens and closes doors.

In a hilarious but telling way, Pompeia's *Mujercitas* shows how patriarchal society molds and deforms normal, healthy, spontaneous, and autonomous girls, creating young women who are inhibited, timid, passive—self-abnegating, submissive servants of males whom the Franco dictatorship called *mujercitas* ("little ladies"). Pompeia's incisive cartoons provide sociological analyses of the dictatorship's modeling of feminine gender. Selected sketches work well to explain gender's impact on Spanish literature under Franco. As today's Spanish university students—most of them born after Franco's death in 1975—know little of his regime and its gender policies, Pompeia's sketches offer a crash course on gender for students in Spain as well as the United States.

Gender theorists such as Elizabeth Flynn and Patrocinio Schweickart stress the importance of formative reading for children and adolescents. Martín Gaite clearly understood the propagandistic function of readings prescribed for females by the dictatorship. In *El cuarto de atrás* and *Usos amorosos de la postguerra española*, she recalls the pleasure she took in reading prohibited books, noting that the regime and proper society considered it inappropriate—as in centuries past—that women should be writers.[1] She repeatedly decried the prudish, boring, unimaginative apologies for conformity in books that were imposed on girls and young women and instead created her own nonconforming, "tomboy" gender-role models for girls.

Gender Awareness in Martín Gaite's Work

The term *género* ("gender") that carries the meanings given to it by gender studies today is absent in Martín Gaite's work, as it is absent from the 2001 *Diccionario de la lengua española* (Real Academia Española; "Dictionary of the Spanish Language").[2] According to the *Feminist Dictionary*, *gender* refers to "the socially imposed dichotomy of masculine and feminine roles and character traits. Sex is physiological, while gender . . . is cultural." It is a division of women and men caused by "social requirements of heterosexuality, which institutionalizes male sexual dominance and female sexual submission" (174). Martín Gaite needed no foreign term, however, to resist the gender models imposed by a reactionary, patriarchal hegemony in Spain. Various critics have noted her predilection for an independent gender model that she termed *la chica rara,* the rebellious girl or tomboy, modeled on herself—one who rejects conventional restrictions imposed on girls, aimed at stifling spontaneity, creativity, and autonomy while urging them to be little ladies.[3] She recalls her rebellion against the official model of *encierro* ("female cloistering"), her decision to become a writer, her interest in the theater, her love for the countryside and dressing as a country girl. In *Esperando el porvenir*, a photograph shows her helping a friend who is barefoot and bare-legged while climbing a tree (127)—although in the Franco era, failure to follow rigid feminine dress codes could incur a fine. The regime deemed such behavior defiance. Smoking was soon added to the list of prohibitions (men could smoke in public but not women), along with receiving visitors alone or being out late.

Becoming an actress was another act of defiance under Franco. Both the writer and the character of the elder sister in her 1950s drama *La hermana pequeña* participate in theater; the sister's most significant transgression is her decision to forgo matrimony to become an actress. The elder sister is an alter ego or mask of the author. Martín Gaite participated in theater in her university years and enjoyed ignoring that prohibition. At that time, theater people were pariahs: "frecuentarlas suponía una especie de desafío a las normas" (*Esperando* 153; "associating with them was defying the rules").

Martín Gaite resisted the imposition of traditional feminine gender roles (wife, housekeeper, mother). She rejected and criticized readings that were gendered female: both the regime's promatrimony propaganda and the *novela rosa* ("romance novel"). Her critiques of such reading material appear in *El cuarto de atrás*, *Usos amorosos de la postguerra*, and *Esperando el porvenir*. Her short stories, especially the early ones, illustrate how traditional socialization and gendered education limited the educational and economic options of women and curtailed their autonomy. The stories contain portraits of defeat and despair: women must work for their own survival or that of their children or elders but fail for lack of education. Similar situations appear in the early novels and in *La hermana pequeña*. Yet Martín Gaite's novels and drama demonstrate that resistance is not futile. Women who struggle, stubbornly following their dreams to obtain some education, either experience success or make progress toward it.

Growing Up Female under Franco

Legal constraints on Spanish women of earlier generations, abolished by the Second Republic (variously dated from 1931 to 1936, when the Civil War erupted, or from 1931 to 1939, when it ended), were revived by the Franco dictatorship (1939–75). The author, born in 1925, juxtaposes her generation's situation with that of women from earlier centuries and finds frightening similarities. She is inspired to write by women's *encierro*, the restriction to domestic space (such as the convent or, in times past, the harem); by the systematic discouragement of female higher education combined with legal barriers to women's access to the workplace and public arena; by the limited, prescriptive reading material imposed on girls; by the vigilant oversight of parents and guardians; and by the single-minded preparation of females for marriage and motherhood. All these constraints required women to comply with the behavioral double standard and the legal status of being owned.

The Franco regime propelled Spanish women backward into the nineteenth century with its abrogation of suffrage and women's civil rights (both granted by the Republic) and with its Victorian regulation of women's dress, speech, education, and conduct. Girls were taught that the primary reason for their existence was to bear many children—repopulating a fatherland decimated by war, exile, and the imprisonment or execution of defeated Republicans. The spinster became an object of ridicule and, for marriageable females, fear. The only acceptable alternative to spinsterhood was the convent—for those who lost a husband or fiancé or had a religious vocation. Otherwise, marriage and motherhood were defined as a woman's God-given, patriotic duty.

Yet marriage was often not a viable option: census statistics from the period indicate that forty percent of women were without husbands. There were simply not enough men. It was both cynical and cruel to prepare women exclusively for the roles of wife and mother when so many could not possibly marry. Beyond the dead and the exiled, thousands upon thousands of supposedly eligible men were maimed, blind—unable to support a family. This context informs the texts of *La hermana pequeña* and *Entre visillos*, explaining Natalia's older sisters' panic as well as the courage of the play's elder sister.[4]

The Play

Many readers are familiar with *Entre visillos*, but the drama (produced and published in 1999 but written decades earlier) is not well known.[5] *La hermana pequeña*, like *Entre visillos*, presents sisters whose mothers have died and whose absent or deceased fathers have left conservative maiden aunts to raise them. Different feminine gender models and lifestyles are featured in both works, but ultimately the main characters reject them, opting instead for careers (the play's younger sister decides to study medicine). Secondary characters in both works illustrate negative—but indissoluble—matrimonial outcomes, while women seeking autonomy flee provincial capitals for Madrid. The adolescent female's quest for freedom and agency appears in all Martín Gaite's novels from *Entre visillos* to *Irse de casa* (1998; "Leaving Home"); hence several have been studied as quest romances.[6] *La hermana pequeña* encapsulates the battle between a feminine desire for liberty, or thirst for working out one's own destiny, and the obstacles of patriarchal gender constructs. Mercedes Carbayo-Abengózar stresses changing sociocultural contexts during the half century in which Martín Gaite wrote, noting that works of the 1990s portray realities for women that are different from those in works of the 1950s and 1960s.[7] Emma Martinell underscores the author's treatment of the feminine universe, with many scenes set in interiors (domestic space), as in *Entre visillos* and *La hermana pequeña* (Martín Gaite, *Hilo* 61–79).[8] Gender constructs and resistance to them provide the unspoken foundation for the play's action: successive paradigmatic feminine types appear, representing the conflict between patriarchally inscribed gender constructs and marginalized, nominally liberated alternatives.

The two half sisters—they have the same father but different mothers—have been separated for over a decade. Laura, older by some fifteen years, escaped her stepmother's vigilance, moving from the town of Huesca to Madrid to become an actress. Preadolescent Inés, her mother's only child, remained in provincial Huesca, chafing under conventionalism and taboos until her mother's death; then, against her aunts' advice, she traveled to Madrid to seek her older sister. Laura, in her late thirties, ekes out a bohemian existence in a tiny, unkempt apartment; after years of struggle, she has become established. Arrival of her tearful younger sister—innocent and inexperienced at twenty-two—unsettles Laura, who has no wish to raise a child. The play's title notwithstanding, the sisters are equally important: Laura dominates the first act, Inés the second, and they share the third. Experienced readers will recognize Laura as another *chica rara*. She possesses qualities that Martín Gaite acknowledges in herself in *El cuarto de atrás*: fondness for the theater and theatrical people, staying up until dawn, sleeping during the day, smoking cigarettes, ignoring social conventions, externalizing her rebelliousness by lounging in pajamas and living amid disorder.

Unlike wealthy, dissatisfied widows who have impeccable reputations but are hypocritically promiscuous, Laura scrupulously avoids emotional and physical entanglements. Gonzalo, Laura's former boyfriend, and his mother—personifications of the Franco regime's ideal, aristocratic family—spend their lives abusing drugs and alcohol, living the dolce vita. His mother and her wealthy friends, like the women separated from their wealthy husbands in *Entre visillos*, display lifestyles that would have been criticized in Laura or in the café singer Rosa in the novel—who are unmarried, not wealthy, and not aristocrats. Martín Gaite demonstrates that Francoist repression discriminated on the basis of class: upper-class girls could do things that middle-class girls could not.

Unable to take in her little sister, Laura accepts the offer from Gonzalo to lodge Inés with his wealthy, widowed mother. For nearly a year Inés is exposed to different gender role models, lifestyles, and opportunities. Both sisters reject repeated marriage proposals from Gonzalo, a wealthy but immature playboy, showing that neither woman lacks opportunities to marry. (Given the official distaste for spinsters, this circumstance made them more attractive characters when the play was written.)

Inés eventually decides against staying longer with Gonzalo's mother. She visits Laura to say goodbye and tells her that she will return to Huesca to prepare to enter medical school. The audience sees real understanding and affection between the sisters, and the final act introduces humor and much metatheatrical language—figurative references to curtain calls, *desenlace* ("denouement"), and Laura's wondering whether certain outcomes, like marriage, are bad theater. The second and third acts subvert regime stereotypes—the myth of marriage happily ever after (also illustrated in *Entre visillos*), the myth of the unattractive, maladjusted, discontent *soltera* ("old maid") driven to spinsterhood by her inability to attract a man.

When teaching *La hermana pequeña* or other works by the author, I employ context, much of it provided by Martín Gaite herself, to enrich students' experience of the text. My goals are to educate them about the Franco dictatorship, post–Civil War literature (with emphasis on the novel), and women's condition as revealed in literature. Martín Gaite courageously offered observations, without editorializing, on such sensitive topics as wife abuse and the neglect and abandonment of wives and children—problems still very real today. Gender equality was part of the original framework of the European Community's overarching organization (the community was more receptive to gender concepts than national governments were). Gender justice, given Spain's double standard and the spousal abuse rampant today, still eludes Spanish society, which has not fully addressed the problems of women and equity, or of women and power—some of which became prominent only after the author's death. Yet throughout her life Martín Gaite was concerned with the struggle to improve women's condition. I want my students to understand the how and why of that struggle.

NOTES

Translations from Spanish are mine, unless otherwise indicated.

[1] In *Esperando el porvenir*, Martín Gaite recounts, "Escribir era entonces . . . un atributo muy desnudo de prestigio. Yo recuerdo que tardé muchos años en atreverme a poner 'escritora' en mi pasaporte . . ." (38; "Writing then was totally bereft of prestige. I remember it took me many years to dare put 'writer' on my passport").

[2] Few scholars of Martín Gaite have used the term *gender* in studying her works. Ordóñez ("Decoding") comes closest, employing the term *sex roles* rather than *gender roles*. See Pérez ("Carmen Martín Gaite").

[3] The nonconforming, rebellious girl in the fiction of Martín Gaite has been extensively studied by Brown, beginning with her dissertation (see her *Nonconformity*).

[4] Many students are unaware of the historical persecution of unmarried women, who were burned for centuries as witches or (in Victorian England, 1880–1930) were forced to emigrate to the colonies. Nina Auerbach, writing in a decidedly postfeminist age, comments that the "Victorian old maid herself is a social construction" (ix), an observation applicable to the situation of spinsters under Franco who were treated with hostility and scorn—even by many women writers (see Pérez, "Portraits").

[5] *La hermana pequeña* was the first play that Martín Gaite wrote, but the first one produced was her dramatic monologue *A palo seco* (1985; "On Its Own"), staged in 1987 (Martinell, Introduction 16). The author's program notes (for the 1999 *estreno* ["opening night"] at Madrid's Centro Cultural de la Villa), which became the prologue for the printed edition, indicate that the drama was written many years before but give no date. José Teruel gives the date of composition as 1959 ("Nota" 52). The director, Ángel García Moreno, receives praise from the author for situating the action in the late 1950s and replicating period clothing and decorating styles (Martín Gaite, *Hermana* 9).

[6] See Pérez, "Portraits" and "Presencia." Curiously, few critics focus on Martín Gaite's second period (her novels of the 1990s), while much scholarly attention has been given to *El cuarto de atrás*. Other critical volumes, including that of Servodidio and Welles, were too early to contain studies of gender roles or the novels of the 1990s.

[7] Carbayo-Abengózar notes these traits in the author's writing of the 1950s and 1960s: existential anguish, solitude, failure, and dissatisfaction—mostly suffered by women. In the author's writing of the 1960s and 1970s she finds a more psychological exploration of gender problems and women's struggle against restrictive roles. My research indicates that Martín Gaite's concern for gender issues pervades her entire work and traces Spanish women's changing gender roles throughout the second half of the twentieth century.

[8] Martinell never mentions gender but addresses the author's understanding of the feminine universe and her concern with feminine cloistering.

The Pleasures and Perils of Bringing *Celia* into the Classroom: Teaching the Television Adaptation in a Course on Childhood and Youth Culture

Jessamy Harvey

Spanish children's literature remains undervalued on the global stage, seldom translated and therefore absent in the lineup of icons of childhood such as Carlo Collodi's Pinocchio, the wooden puppet who yearns to be a real boy; Astrid Lindgren's unconventional Pippi Longstocking; Johanna Spyri's kindhearted Heidi; or Lewis Carroll's curious Alice. But Celia, who has charmed Spanish-speaking children and adults alike with her fantastic imagination and outspokenness, as well as with the chaos that her ingenuous words and actions inevitably generate, is still unknown outside the world in which she was created. This character first appeared in the children's section of the magazine *Blanco y negro* ("Black and White") in 1928, then became the child-to-woman heroine of a series of books for children authored by Encarnación Aragoneses Urquijo (1886–1952), who wrote under the pseudonym Elena Fortún.

The seven-year-old Celia was the classic literary icon of modern Spanish childhood. Many women writers who grew up between the 1930s and the 1950s have openly identified themselves with her—for example, Pepa Blanes Noguera, a self-confessed "Celiadicta" (4; "Celiaddict"), and Carmen Martín Gaite, who considered Celia her "amiga del alma" ("soul mate") of childhood and declared that she inspired her to become a writer ("Crecimiento" 531). Martín Gaite talks about Celia in essay anthologies such as *Tirando del hilo* ("Unraveling the Skein") and *Pido la palabra* ("May I Have the Floor?").[1] With José Luis Borau she wrote the script for the television series *Celia*, originally broadcast on RTVE (Spanish public television) in 1993.[2]

Both Fortún's classic *Celia lo que dice* ("What Celia Says") and this television adaptation are taught in an undergraduate course that I devised to interrogate the categories of childhood and youth in modern Spanish culture. Although undergraduate students are now familiar with the practice of interpreting the production and reproduction of cultural knowledge through three dominant categories (gender, class, and race), this course aims to get them to take another category into account: age. Identifying age as a cultural category that is not fixed or easily defined but instead shifts over time and place helps students shed preconceived notions and find strategies to recognize the constructed nature of childhood—as Philippe Ariès, in *Centuries of Childhood*; Dianne Gittins, in "The Historical Construction of Childhood"; and Josette Borderies-Guereña, in "Niños y niñas en familia" ("Boys and Girls in the Family"), have demonstrated. Certainly children and young people have been the subjects of such established disciplines as psychology and education, but this course draws from a relatively new academic field of inquiry, often called childhood studies, as well as from the more established field of youth studies, as understood by Neil Campbell, in *American Youth Cultures*, and Alan France, in *Understanding Youth in Late Modernity*.

Although childhood studies has no set methodological approach, academics working in this field consider what exactly is meant by childhood, their intention being to shed light on cultural assumptions made about it. A new paradigm emerged in the 1990s that considers the ways in which children have voice and agency (Prout and James's "A New Paradigm for the Sociology of Childhood?" is especially relevant), but the section of the course focusing on the textual and audiovisual character Celia considers how childhood is an adult construction, one that appears both natural and accessible—Have we not all been children? Do we not all know children?—but is not so straightforward.

Teaching Celia *to Continuing Education Students*

This upper-level undergraduate course is taught at Birkbeck, a higher education institution with a distinctive student body, as it provides evening and mainly part-time degrees for adults who live and work around London (what in the United States is known as continuing education). Our students come from a wide range of national, ethnic, social, and often nonconventional educational backgrounds and can be in their early twenties or beyond retirement age—a diversity that is both productive and challenging. Since one of the course's primary questions is, What is childhood?, the differences among students encourage an exchange of many perspectives and may unsettle received ideas about childhood and its presumed opposite, adulthood.

When students grasp that childhood is a historical and social construction, they can begin to understand how different media use strategies to address children; they can also begin to analyze critically Fortún's portrayal of family, society, and culture in Spain on the cusp of and during the Second Republic (from 1931 to 1939) as well as how and why the *Celia* television series of the 1990s makes more visible Fortún's sociopolitical engagement with her period. Students read Martín Gaite's essay "Pesquisa tardía sobre Elena Fortún" ("A Belated Inquiry into Elena Fortún"), now included as the foreword to the Alianza edition of *Celia lo que dice*, and thereby develop an understanding of how the scripts for the television series can be interpreted as the result of one woman writer's creative involvement with the work of a literary predecessor.[3]

Because students encounter the theoretical problems of children's literature before they read *Celia lo que dice*, then go on to view the television adaptation and approach Martín Gaite's foreword critically, this essay follows that order.

Celia and Issues of Authorship, Readership, and Power

One of the first questions that we work through in relation to Celia on the page and on the screen is, Who is speaking to whom, and why? (Rose 59). The question generates discussion on issues such as authorship, readership, audience, and adult-child power relations. For this meeting, students have been asked to read extracts from Jacqueline Rose's now classic essay "The Case of Peter Pan." Because this text is demanding, I give a brief introductory lecture on what Rose is trying to do. Kenneth Kidd writes, "Put reductively, the big debate in children's literature studies is whether or not children's literature is really children's literature, since, after all, it is nearly always written by adults" (119). As Rose and others note (Lesnik-Oberstein; Honeyman), children's literature is problematic because it conceals a power imbalance (between the adult writer and the child reader) and does not acknowledge that the child reader is being presented with the adult writer's idea of what a child should be. I illustrate Rose's appraisal of the act of writing for children as a form of child seduction by discussing the prologue to *Celia lo que dice*, where Fortún writes in the third person describing Celia's personality, position in the household, and looks. Fortún concludes:

> Celia siente la necesidad de decirlo todo, y va a contar todos los menudos incidentes de su vida inquieta, que para los que tengan su edad serán claros y transparentes, y un poco absurdo para las personas mayores, tan intolerantes e injustas casi siempre. Escuchad. (48)
>
> Celia feels the need to explain everything and is going to narrate all the minor events of her restless life, which for those who are her age will be clear and transparent and a little absurd for the grown-ups, who are almost always so intolerant and unfair. Listen.

Celia as a Chica Rara *or Odd Girl*

The novel begins, "Me desperté asustada, y oí como si un gato estuviera arañando las maderas del balcón. ¡Los Reyes Magos!" (49; "I woke up frightened, and heard a noise as if a cat were scratching the floor of the balcony. The Three Wise Men!").[4] If one were to practice Rose's "hermeneutics of suspicion" (Kidd 122), this switch from third to first person must be viewed critically. The narrator's voice does not appear again until the conclusion of the novel, so there is no obvious mediation between Celia and the reader, to whom she speaks directly. Students should not fall into the trap of seeing her as a representation of the average child (inquisitive, fidgety, adventurous, imaginative). She is a nonconformist, what Martín Gaite called a *chica rara*—hence her attraction. On the page and on the television screen she is under constant pressure to behave, to be clean, calm, and unobtrusive—and she fails. With Celia, Fortún disturbs the dominant representation of Spanish girlhood, that of the little girl as excellent daughter, precursor to perfect bourgeois womanhood, and inaugurates a new type of heroine in Spanish literature.[5] Does Fortún's switch to the first person allow young readers scope to think through their own positions in relation to adult power, as Martín Gaite maintains Celia did for her child self, allowing her as reader to criticize adults for being boring and bossy ("Pesquisa" 8)? The narrative arc is not a positive one—for example, toward emancipation or self-discovery—but neither is it subversive; rather it is one of gradual exclusion.

Celia lo que dice, given that it is a compilation of short stories from a magazine, has a fragmentary, episodic quality, though the narrative progresses through one year, from the Feast of Epiphany until the return of winter, during which year Baby, Celia's little brother, Cuchifritín, is born. Although Celia is the viewpoint character, the story is also about a wealthy Madrid household. The family may be nuclear at heart, but to function it requires an army of servants, retainers, and other satellite support, not just the domestic staff but also the janitor's family. Celia gives her expensive Christmas presents to Solita, the illiterate and overworked janitor's daughter, because King Balthazar told Celia that rich girls should share with poor girls. After her first fashionable haircut, she snips off the pedigreed cat's fur to update its looks and upsets her mother. She plays at traveling around the world in a car (the bathtub) with her infant brother but, in re-creating a storm, drenches them, endangering Baby's life. These episodes unsettle most of the adults around her, as readers gradually gather from the dialogue, even though Celia does not understand the responses of the adults. Increasingly, as one episode follows the next, students become aware that while Fortún may be making us laugh with her portrayal of a rebellious or subversive little girl, there is an underlying tragic thread running through the narrative.

Because adult students are short on time, having to juggle work with their family and social commitments, the class is split into groups to enable them to familiarize themselves with, update one another on, or read a selection of the short chapters, which although peppered with colloquialisms are accessible to advanced Spanish-language learners. These chapters have appealing titles, such as "Promesas sin cumplir" ("Failed Promises"), "Es pecado mentir" ("It Is a Sin to Lie"), and "¡Ha llegado el niño!" ("The Baby Has Arrived!").

Students perceive that Fortún is actually writing about an isolated, neglected, and misunderstood girl, whom the housekeeper calls an "inclusera" (248; "a foundling"), whose imagination upturns the household continuously, and who eventually tries her mother's patience (her father is generally more sympathetic, until Celia endangers his son's life) and gets banished to a boarding school (forever, as the subsequent books make clear; Celia never lives with her mother again). What is it that displaces Celia—the birth of her brother? her failure to conform to her mother's ideal? her mother's refusal to put her daughter's emotional well-being first at the cost of her own ambitions? A telling sentence in "Promesas sin cumplir," as Martín Gaite notes ("Pesquisa" 19), hints at this conflict, for when Celia's mother is asked to clarify why she is so busy, she says that she must "escribir dos o tres cartas y salir a las seis a tomar el té con mis amigas del Lyceum" (70; "write two or three letters and go out at six to have tea with [her] girlfriends at the Lyceum"). Martín Gaite's foreword makes clear that the Lyceum Club Femenino, a cultural center for women, is a "nido del feminismo español" (20; "incubator of Spanish feminism"). This chapter shows that there is a deep tension in the text between a child's emotional needs and female emancipation (Fortún herself was an active member of this club); it also sparks students' interest in the sociohistorical setting, which is explored more fully in the second class session, on the television adaptation.

Celia on the Screen: Heritage Television

Although it is not my aim to have students interpret the television series as a faithful adaptation of the book or a straightforward re-creation of the period that preceded the Second Republic, it does help to bring that time to life. In filming, careful attention was paid to period costumes and the staging on Madrid streets of traditions such as Saint Anthony's Day or Carnival. Even when the camera follows Celia, viewers can overhear adults conversing among themselves about the rapid and tumultuous changes taking place in Spanish society (noted by Martín Gaite in "Pesquisa," by Nash, and by Payne). Students are introduced to the concept of heritage films and how they selectively reconstruct the past through a process of inclusion and exclusion to offer a cohesive and hegemonic vision of national identity, culture, and history for consumption in the present—a construct explored by Núria Triana-Toribio. As John Caughie has argued, the phenomenon of film crossed over into television (208; see also P. Smith). The *Celia* television series was not made specifically for children; it was broadcast in prime time on Tuesday evenings, presenting all the characteristics of the quality classic serial or adaptation that was being produced for television across Europe in the 1980s and 1990s.

We examine various clips. An especially interesting one can be found in the second episode, based on the chapter "El hada en el sotabanco" ("The Fairy in the Attic"). Viewing this scene, students become aware that Celia, although she still answers out loud and asks repeated questions, often expresses her subversive ideas in voice-over. Although still the main focus of the camera, which frequently frames her face in close-up and is therefore at the height of a child, she is shown silently moving about, unseen by the adults but observing and judging them. She returns to the family apartment, having followed the maid to an attic where a destitute old woman, who was the previous janitor's wife, lives. Disgusted by the meager meal offered the woman and desiring to be someone other than a useless and superfluous child, Celia sets about raiding the pantry: "[Y]o no le voy a subir sobras a Doña Cándida" ("I am not going to take Doña Cándida leftovers"), thereby highlighting the hypocrisy of the affluent classes.

Moments earlier, the camera captures her slipping out of view and unobserved into the pantry, but it stays in the room and remains focused on the servants talking. One says, "[P]ues si ponen el divorcio, las bodas van a perder mucho" ("If divorce is decreed, weddings will be devalued"), and Doña Benita replies, "¡Pero que van a poner! ¡Si no se atreverán!" ("As if they would! They wouldn't dare!").

Martín Gaite and Borau scripted direct allusions to historical context, giving the adaptation an overtly sociopolitical slant with the intention of presenting to a now democratic Spain the recovery of the Republican period, suppressed during the regime. Although Fortún made no allusions to the changing legal status of women (the reference to the lyceum aside), she was certainly critical of her contemporaries. She repeatedly pointed to the disparity between the wealthy and the poor, and her protagonist yearned to bridge the gap between the haves and have-nots. After raiding the pantry and using the netted fabric to dress up as a fairy, in the book and on the screen Celia pops upstairs to give food as well as her savings to Doña Cándida. One might be tempted to interpret Celia as simply another child figure who serves as witness to adults' failings and then offers solutions that lead to familial and social harmony, but Fortún complicates matters by showing that Celia's actions are misunderstood. When Celia presents herself as a fairy, for example, Doña Cándida sees instead a figure from the Catholic roster: Saint Polonia. Fortún depicted a Spain fragmented along the lines drawn by urbanization and modernity through beliefs, customs, and everyday life practices. Celia is no redemptive child Romantic visionary but yet another social actor; she is locked in her own perspective, that of fantasy.

Teaching the television adaptation helps make more evident the social turbulence and historicity of the book, but the cultural politics of this re-creation of the past in the democratic 1990s must be taken into account. This questioning approach should be used when students are asked to read Martín Gaite's writings, like "Pesquisa," about Celia. This essay—unlike the television series, which is a collaborative work—may appear to simply offer us a window to the past, but it can be unpacked further.

Fortún and Martín Gaite

Curiously, Celia overshadowed her creator, to the extent that Fortún disappeared from public memory after her death, until the literary recovery led by Marisol Dorao. This academic researcher not only found an unpublished manuscript, "Celia en la revolución" ("Celia during the Revolution"), which narrates the adolescent Celia's experiences of the Spanish Civil War, but also wrote the only full-length biography of the author, *Los mil sueños de Elena Fortún* ("The Thousand Dreams of Elena Fortún"). Martín Gaite records her indebtedness to Dorao in her own process of recovery:

> A la niña que yo fui no le importaba nada de Elena Fortún, pero a la mujer que soy ahora nada puede gustarle tanto como seguir el rastro a aquella señora que sin duda llevaba una niña dentro y me la regaló para que jugara con ella. ("Pesquisa" 36)

> The girl I once was did not care a bit about Elena Fortún, but the woman I am now loves nothing more than to follow the trail of that lady who, without a doubt, had an inner child and gave her to me as a gift to play with.

The work by Martín Gaite on Fortún is described perceptively by the French scholar Marie Franco as a virtual encounter between women writers across a temporal and historical gap and also as a "jeu de miroirs" (221; "game of mirrors") in which the adult Martín Gaite exchanges her childish self-identification with Celia for a conflation with Celia's creator, "parler d'Elena Fortún, parler de soi" (232; "to speak about Elena Fortún, to speak about herself"). Franco notes a strategic management of history in "Pesquisa" to erase the significance of the Civil War and the dictatorship in the development of both a personal and a collective Spanish identity, to emphasize instead the continuities between the emancipatory character of the Second Republic and the contemporary democratic period. If students can be encouraged to read Martín Gaite's prologue not merely as a source of background information to contextualize *Celia lo que dice*, they begin to appreciate the dialogue across generations and think about the implications of this creative engagement.

Working over three class sessions on a book for children, on its adaptation by Martín Gaite for television, and on an essay by her can lead students to focus on the large question of the politics of recovery. Recovery involves not only a lost writer, a beloved fictional soul mate, a literary classic, and a historical period but also a phase of life and the question of the complex investments of adults in the concept of childhood.

NOTES

Translations from Spanish and French are mine.

[1] In *Tirando del hilo* [2007], José Teruel, the volume editor, offers a scholarly inventory of the author's works about Elena Fortún, reporting that Martín Gaite's fascination with her predecessor lasted throughout her life (524). In addition to the essay "El crecimiento de Celia" ("The Growth of Celia"), *Tirando* contains the essay "Celia: Raíces y frutos" (607–11; "Celia: Roots and Results"). Teruel explains that four relevant, undated essays in *Pido la palabra* are versions of lectures that the author delivered in 1992 at the Fundación Juan March. Their titles are "Elena Fortún y su tiempo" (39–58; "Elena Fortún and Her Times"), "Elena Fortún y sus amigas" (59–79; "Elena Fortún and Her Friends"), "Arrojo y descalabros de la lógica infantil" (80–101; "Daring and Defeats of Juvenile Logic"), and "Interpretación poética de la realidad" (102–21; "A Poetic Version of Reality").

[2]*Celia* remains accessible, as do many of Spain's quality television series, because it is distributed in DVD format by Divisa (www.divisared.es). Additionally, RTVE put it online (www.rtve.es/television/celia/). Information about the series and its cast of more than eighty actors, led by the young Cristina Cruz Mínguez (and with Ana Duato as her mother), is available on the movie database *IMDb*. Teruel notes that thirteen episodes of the series were written by Martín Gaite, though only six were filmed. The original air dates of the six programs were between 5 January and 9 February 1993 (Martín Gaite, *Tirando* [2007] 524).

[3]Students work only on the first book of the series and therefore focus on the first two episodes of the television adaptation, so they miss a fleeting screen appearance of Martín Gaite herself. She plays a nun singing in the choir in the final episode, which, as Marie Franco points out, problematically materializes or embodies—I would suggest inserts—the ghost of a passionate reader in the televisual narrative (225).

[4]The evening of 5 January, preceding Epiphany, is when the three wise men deliver presents for Spanish children. It is the equivalent of Christmas Eve in the United States.

[5]The type appeared earlier in British and American children's literature: the child who "is at odds with everything and everyone, [and] finds the world a quite nonsensical place" (Baker 90).

SELECTED ESSAYS

Teaching Carmen Martín Gaite as a Feminist Thinker

Roberta Johnson

Carmen Martín Gaite was not only a foremost Spanish novelist of the post–Civil War era; she was also a leading intellectual. She held a doctorate from the University of Madrid, writing her thesis on courtship practices of the Spanish eighteenth century, and she wrote subtle and provocative essays on a variety of topics. Her essays, many of them first published in periodicals and later collected in volumes, can be used in classes on Spanish language, literature, literary theory, and culture. Her literary theories provide insights into the way narrative works; her historically oriented books are useful background for eighteenth-century or post–Civil War Spanish literature and culture. As Constance Sullivan and others have pointed out, Martín Gaite's essays are invariably literary. Their lively language, which contains many concrete examples and useful vocabulary, is a good model for students. Thus the essays are fine choices for undergraduates who are learning to read, write on, and discuss sophisticated topics in Spanish and for graduate students who are studying literary theory in addition to literature. I focus here on how Martín Gaite's nonfiction can assist in exploring Spanish literature and culture from a feminist perspective. In order of their publication, I treat *La búsqueda de interlocutor y otras búsquedas* (2000; "'The Search for a Conversational Partner [an Interlocutor]' and Other Searches"), *Usos amorosos del dieciocho en España* (1972; *Love Customs in Eighteenth-Century Spain* [1991]), *Usos amorosos de la postguerra española* (*Courtship Customs in Postwar Spain* [2004]), and *Desde la ventana* (1987; "From the Window").[1]

The courses in which I have taught works by Martín Gaite from a feminist perspective are Introduction to Literary Analysis, with advanced composition and conversation components ("Las ataduras" [1960 (Harper); "Binding Ties"]); Survey of Modern Spanish Literature (the novelette *El balneario* [1954; "The Spa"] and essays from *Desde la ventana*); Post–Civil War Spanish Fiction, for undergraduates and graduates (*El cuarto de atrás* [1978; *The Back Room* (1983)] and chapters from *Usos amorosos de la postguerra*); undergraduate and graduate Literature and Film of the Spanish Civil War (*El cuarto de atrás* and chapters from *Usos amorosos de la postguerra*; I include Javier Cercas's *Soldados de Salamina* [2001; *Soldiers of Salamis* (2004)] as a contrast to Martín Gaite's feminist Civil War memory novel); Contemporary Spanish Women Writers, for undergraduates (*El cuarto de atrás* and chapters from *Usos amorosos de la postguerra* and *Desde la ventana*); and Spanish Feminist Theory, for graduates (*Usos amorosos de la postguerra*, *Desde la ventana*, and *El cuarto de atrás*). Courses that I have not taught in which Martín Gaite's feminist works could be incorporated are second-year language classes that introduce reading, writing, and conversation; culture courses that focus on Spain; and courses in English on feminist theory from several countries (fortunately, *Usos amorosos del dieciocho en España* and *Usos amorosos de la postguerra española* are available in English translation).

Since feminism as a concept is an important topic for discussion in many of my courses, I begin with Martín Gaite's position on feminism as a social movement and as a personal identity. A number of critics have noted that Martín Gaite was averse to considering herself and to being considered a feminist. For example, Caroline Wilson finds "huellas de su recelo hacia el feminismo" (75; "traces of her distrust of feminism") in her attitude toward North American academic feminist literary criticism.[2] Lissette Rolón Collazo points out that Martín Gaite was especially critical of militant, highly public feminism, which becomes routine and institutionalized, what Martín Gaite calls in *La búsqueda* "meros gritos exasperados que se diluyan sin eficacia ni relieve" ("Las mujeres" 98; "mere desperate shouting, which dissolves leaving no trace"). In 1974 she declared herself "antifeminista" ("an antifeminist"), saying that she aspired to freedom, but while feminists talked about freedom, they did not know how to use it: "la llevan como una pedrada para arrojársela a la cara a los demás" (qtd., from Villán, in Rolón Collazo, "Diálogo" 74; "they carry it like a stone to throw in others' faces").

Nearly all the critics who comment on Martín Gaite's resistance to the feminist label believe that much of her writing contains what would today be recognized as having a feminist purpose. As early as 1977, Phyllis Zatlin Boring had "no doubt that Martín Gaite is a feminist writer, fully conscious of women's restricted role in society and of the problems that role poses for the individual who wishes to develop herself fully as a person" (324). Sullivan finds that Martín Gaite's feminism becomes more evident over time; she notes "the increasingly clear feminism of her essays, while she continues to reject the label of 'feminist' to describe them" (42). Rolón Collazo affirms that "no hay duda que la condición de la mujer—más recientemente la escritura de mujeres—es una preocupación latente y persistente en la obra de la salmantina" ("Diálogo" 73; "There is no doubt that women's condition—more recently women's writing—is a latent and persistent preoccupation in the Salamancan writer's work"). Janet Pérez remarks that when Martín Gaite's work is viewed as a whole, gender is "the nucleus around which nearly every title revolves" ("Carmen Martín Gaite" 169). As Martín Gaite herself recognized, her feminist method is not overt:

> . . . lo que me ha pasado siempre es que he tenido una rebeldía muy poco agresiva, pero muy profunda, algo difícil de explicar, pero siempre he sido más rebelde de lo que he parecido y me han podido atribuir las personas que me conocen sólo superficialmente. Mi rebeldía no es de alharaca . . . le doy una vuelta a todo y acabo haciendo lo que quiero sin gritar. Yo voy procurando no desgastar la eficacia de mi protesta en palabrerías, sino procurando ir a mi modo. . . . Yo no sé si es táctica, pero procuro rechazar lo que veo que no me gusta, rechazándolo dentro de mí, diciendo yo eso no lo voy a hacer, pero no levantando una bandera y gastando pólvora en salvas . . . es que soy modosa muy modosa.
>
> (Aznárez 14; qtd. in Carbayo-Abengózar 50)

> . . . I have always had a deep, but very unaggressive, rebelliousness. It is rather difficult to explain, but I have always been more rebellious than I seemed, and people who do not know me well do not notice it. My rebellion is without fuss . . . I turn everything around and end up doing what I want without shouting about it. I try not to wear out the efficacy of my protest with wordiness; instead, I try to go my own way. . . . I don't know if it is a strategy, but I try to reject within myself what I don't like. I just say to myself that I am not going to do this or that, without raising a flag or wasting gunpowder on salvos. . . . I am very quiet, very discreet.

The importance of inner resolve versus exterior manifestations and pressures motivates Martín Gaite's thinking about women from her first essays to her last.

Martín Gaite's Views on Gender and Identity Formation

The Search for an Authentic Identity

A major area of Martín Gaite's feminist thought centers on the formation of the female self. Whether or not her ideas on identity formation were informed by her early reading in French existentialism (particularly Jean Paul Sartre and Simone de Beauvoir) is beyond the scope of this essay, but it is an interesting subject for exploration in graduate classes on Spanish or European literary or feminist theory.[3] At the heart of Martín Gaite's particular view of womanhood is the problem of forming an authentic identity; here one could find a connection with French existentialist thought, although Miguel de Unamuno, her Salamancan compatriot and youthful acquaintance, would be as likely a source. In this vein, I have assigned Unamuno's *Niebla* (1914; *Mist*) and Martín Gaite's *El cuarto de atrás* in the same twentieth-century Spanish fiction course, not only for the metafictional comparison but also for each author's focus on the self's relation to the other. In addition, the roles that Unamuno and Martín Gaite give women contrast in ways that provoke student discussion.

Martín Gaite's concept of identity formation emphasizes a natural inclination in the individual that is shaped (often to the detriment of the authentic self) by external forces; in *Usos amorosos de la postguerra española*, these forces are specifically Spanish and historically situated in the Franco era (1936–75). In this sense her theories coincide with the so-called social constructionists, like Judith Butler, who reject biological notions of gender.[4] On the other hand, Martín Gaite makes a number of statements that have occasioned some critics to place her within difference feminism, which includes the North American feminist theorists Carol Gilligan and Nancy Chodorow; the French thinkers Luce Irigaray, Julia Kristeva, and Hélène Cixous; the Italian group of Luisa Muraro's Diotima; and the Barcelona-based *Duoda* group of Milagros Rivera.[5] In a 1976 review of Steven Goldberg's *La inevitabilidad del patriarcado* (*The Inevitability of Patriarchy*), Martín Gaite registered skepticism about both social and biological explanations of gender:

> Está visto que la consolidada polémica sobre si las diferencias entre el comportamiento femenino y el masculino estriban en razones sociales o en razones biológicas está llamado a no terminar nunca y a aburrirnos hasta el infinito, a despecho de su presunto incentivo de variedad.
> (*Tirando* [2006] 59)

> Obviously the well-established polemic over whether the differences in feminine and masculine behavior arise from social or biological causes is destined to go on forever and bore us to death, in spite of its presumed encouragement of variety.

Ultimately, Martín Gaite's feminist philosophy is sui generis and cannot be classified according to standard groupings of feminist theories.

The Tyranny of Preconceived Images

In a cluster of essays, some from as early as 1961 and included in *La búsqueda de interlocutor*, her collection of essays published in 1973, Martín Gaite first articulated her ideas on the female self. "Personalidad y libertad" (1961; "Personality and Freedom"), outlining the problem of the authentic self without reference to gender, would be a good assignment for conversation classes or introductions to literature that need not focus on women or feminist perspectives.

Its central ideas inform most of Martín Gaite's feminist essays in *La búsqueda* as well as her book-length feminist works. The term *personalidad* is employed to mean something akin to the Greek persona or mask, a facade presented to others that may not correspond to the person's inner urges. She points out that in this construction of the self, the activities one pursues are designed to maintain an image, "dejándonos llevar hasta donde requiera su cumplimiento, sin preocuparnos de la figura que ese cumplimiento nos haga componer" (*Búsqueda* [2000] 85; "allowing ourselves to be led wherever its fulfillment requires without concern for the figure that this fulfillment leads us to create"). She gives the example of studying for good grades to make parents proud rather than for the sake of knowledge. Such practices create a jar that has a label but no contents (Martín Gaite is a master of the apt visual image, and she elaborates on the jar/person metaphor for more than a paragraph). Once we have raised expectations in others that we will behave in a certain way, we are reluctant to cause scandal or disappointment by acting in any manner that is not consistent with the image we have created. But we are not free unless we are able to ignore these preconceived images that provoke increasingly automated responses. Thus the personality and freedom we have sought are illusory.

Women and External Models

In "La influencia de la publicidad en las mujeres" (1965; "The Influence of Advertising on Women"), Martín Gaite's concern about external pressures on personality formation turns specifically to women.[6] One can use this essay as a stand-alone reading in conversation classes or in courses or course units that focus on Spanish women. The opening paragraph summarizes the theories about self-formation from her essay on personality and freedom and applies them to the specific case of advertising that targets women. Her astute sensitivity to language uncovers the ways advertising takes advantage of women's sense of inferiority and lack of importance to encourage them to buy products that might enhance their self-worth:

> A la buena disposición femenina para recibir de otro normas por las que regirse (tendencia fácilmente comprensible si se piensa en su pobre papel de comparsa a lo largo de la sociedad patriarcal), hay que añadir la circunstancia de que nunca una mujer se ha visto tan sedienta de afirmación y diferenciación, tan obsesionada por conquistar esa <<personalidad>>, que ha de valerle el aprecio de los demás, como en el seno de la sociedad actual, donde todos los letreros invitan al éxito, al amor y a la felicidad individual como metas absolutas y accesibles mediante recetas prácticas. (*Búsqueda* [2000] 90)

> To the feminine disposition to accept alternative norms by which to live (an easily understood tendency, if one thinks about women's miserable role as an extra throughout patriarchal society), one must add the fact that a woman has never been so hungry for affirmation and distinction,

so obsessed with acquiring a "personality," which others' appreciation can afford her, as in today's society where all the billboards invite one to be successful, to enjoy love and individual happiness, absolute goals achievable via practical recipes.

Advertisers insinuate themselves into women's empty lives by employing a confidential ("tú a tú" ["friend to friend"]) tone, and they exploit women's "latente mimetismo" ("latent mimicry") in order to "avecinarles lo más posible a los ídolos del cine o del dinero, antiguamente inalcanzables . . . al dejar vislumbrar los interiores de sus mansiones" (90–92; "bring them as close as possible to movie or millionaire idols, who used to be out of reach . . . by allowing a peek into the interiors of their mansions"). For Martín Gaite, the most egregious aspect of these strategies is their emphasis on men as women's only active realm. Thus advertising is a powerful means of maintaining the social status quo: "Resumiendo: el daño más notable que hace la publicidad a la mujer es el de colmar fraudulentamente su deseo de ser tenida en cuenta y escuchada, alejándola cada vez más de esa independencia liberadora de que tanto le habla" (94; "In summary: the most notable damage wrought by advertising directed at women is its fraudulent appeal to their desire to be taken into account and listened to, removing them further and further from the liberating independence about which these messages so often speak to her").

Martín Gaite applies her concept of female identity formation to specific examples in "De madame Bovary a Marilyn Monroe" (undated but perhaps written in the mid-1960s, when Marilyn Monroe's 1962 death was still a fresh memory; "From Madame Bovary to Marilyn Monroe"). Both Madame Bovary and Marilyn Monroe committed suicide because they lacked an authentic inner personality. Both attempted to respond to models of behavior that were imposed from without and could not escape these models when, having imitated them, they rejected them. Martín Gaite asserts that Madame Bovary's lovers did not interest her; Emma Bovary was attracted to the image of herself having lovers. She killed herself "porque su imagen se le había roto y porque ella no era capaz de buscar su identidad en otra imagen nueva y menos falsa" (110; "because her image was destroyed and because she was unable to search for her identity in another, new, and less false image"). The same thing happened to Marilyn Monroe when she married Arthur Miller in 1956: "su imagen se le debió romper y volver inservible" (110; "her image must have cracked and become useless").

Women and Solitude

"Las mujeres liberadas" (undated; "Liberated Women")[7] addresses the problem of women and solitude, what Martín Gaite calls in *Desde la ventana* "arma de dos filos" (26; "a double-edged sword"). If in "De Emma Bovary a Marilyn Monroe," she theorized that Emma Bovary's and Marilyn Monroe's inability to "aguantarse a palo seco a sí mismas" (*Búsqueda* [2000] 112; "put up with themselves alone")[8] was central to their not having developed an authentic self, in "Las mujeres liberadas" she considers the need to form relationships for the very Unamunian "anhelo de perdurar en otro" (102; "desire for self-perpetuation through another"). Here she takes what might seem a rather different view of women's relations to others. Women today can choose to leave marriage (although divorce was not yet possible in Spain) and live on their own (as Martín Gaite herself did after 1970). The author did not extend this option to her protagonist in the novella "Las ataduras," which, having been published in Spain in 1960, does not advocate separation for the unsatisfied woman. "Las ataduras" and "Las mujeres liberadas" can fruitfully be read in tandem; the essay makes explicit the implicit tension in the work of fiction between a woman's familial ties and the need for solitude.[9] In the essay, she notes that married women have always enjoyed higher esteem than single women, even in historical periods when a husband's authority seemed absolute. The married woman "se ha sentido más persona" (*Búsqueda* [2000] 97; "felt herself more of a person in her own right") than a single woman. This situation, along with other factors, has attracted women to marriage.

But married women's enhanced social status may not compensate for the lack of interpersonal communication in marriage. Women who leave marriage generally enter into a series of short-lived and unsatisfying relationships, because they are unable to endure solitude, although it is their only means of achieving independence. The ephemeral relationships are driven by the same need to possess and to survive through someone else that drives the impulse to marry. Martín Gaite concludes pessimistically that "[o] se asumen las ataduras o se asume la soledad" (*Búsqueda* [2000] 102; "one either accepts ties or accepts solitude").[10] She mollifies the dichotomy between relationships and solitude in the autobiography she wrote in 1980 for Joan Brown's foundational *Secrets from the Back Room*, in an undated lecture ("Mujer") included in *Pido la palabra* (2002; "May I Have the Floor?") and in *Desde la ventana.* By the time Martín Gaite wrote the autobiography, she had found a middle way: to live alone but avoid loneliness by privileging friendships: "Yo no le temo a la soledad, me he acostumbrado a ella y la aguanto bastante mejor que la mayoría de la gente que conozco, pero siempre estoy dispuesta a quebrarla cuando un amigo viene a perfumarla con su conversación y compañía" (*Secrets* 204; "I am not afraid of being alone, I have become accustomed to it, and I tolerate it better than most people I know. But I am always ready to break my solitude when a friend comes to perfume it with his conversation and company" [33]). In 1999, Carmen Alborch published her best-selling *Solas* ("Women Alone"), which made the same argument. When Martín Gaite wrote the essays that compose *Desde la ventana*, she no longer felt ambivalence about women and solitude: solitude was essential to forging a solid female self and to the female creative process. In "Buscando el modo" ("Searching for the Way") she develops an idea that she put forward at the end of "La búsqueda de interlocutor" in 1966: "la alegría de la razón que ha encontrado en soledad la expresión que buscaba" (32; "the joy of reason that in solitude has found the expression it sought"). In her 1986 lecture, she emphatically declares that innovation is impossible without the prior condition of solitude, and she believes that men and women respond differently to being alone, because their circumstances differ. Men, whose socially acceptable arena is the public sphere, welcome the solitude required for creative activity, while women, often denied daily contact with society in the workplace and elsewhere, are not as eager to give up opportunities for social engagement (*Desde la ventana* 48). In "La mujer y la literatura" (undated; "Woman and Literature"), published in *Pido la palabra*, Martín Gaite insists on the importance of "la soledad asumida voluntaria y orgullosamente" (327; "solitude accepted voluntarily and proudly") as a special trait of women who write.

Material for Conversation and Composition Classes

Any of the four essays from *La búsqueda* discussed above is ideal for conversation and composition classes. Martín Gaite herself noted that her language is often colloquial, and her ample use of idiomatic expressions offers students the opportunity to enrich their Spanish language skills. In fact, she coauthored a Spanish conversation textbook.[11] I have students bring lists of words and expressions (with definitions in Spanish) that they want to add to their personal Spanish vocabulary, and in class we compile a dictionary with a special section for idioms. My discussion questions focus on whether or not Martín Gaite's points about personality formation are specific to the Spain of her time or reflect student experiences in the United States today. Is there, as she proposes, a difference in the way external forces operate in identity formation of women and men? If there is a difference, is it a substantive difference or a matter of degree?

For the essay on women and advertising, students bring to class their own examples of advertising from contemporary magazines or Web sites that confirm or refute Martín Gaite's ideas about how advertising preys on women. Can students identify language or images that encourage women to think of themselves in a particular way that may not be natural for women and that encourages them to adopt a false identity? Students may also be asked to think of more recent examples of people with a well-known public image, like Marilyn Monroe, who have destroyed themselves, often by drug overdose (Elvis Presley, Jimi Hendrix, Jim Morrison, Janis Joplin, Kurt Cobain, Heath Ledger) and to discuss whether or not attempting to live up to an image they and others created led to that self-destruction.

Teaching Martín Gaite's Historical Feminist Writings

Usos amorosos of the Eighteenth and Twentieth Centuries

Martín Gaite's thinking about women in Spanish society took a historical turn in *Usos amorosos del dieciocho en España*, presented as a doctoral dissertation before it was published. In this book Martín Gaite locates the disintegration of the Spanish Golden Age honor code in the courtship practices of the eighteenth century. The honor code, by which a man's honor resided in the sexual purity of his female relatives, led to extreme preoccupation with guarding female chastity and to blood retributions for even perceived breaches. Her carefully documented account of *cortejo* (or *chichisveo*—there is no good translation for this upper-class custom in which a man who was not the woman's husband became her admirer and constant companion) hypothesizes that women gained an important amount of personal liberty through this custom, an opportunity for independent action they had not heretofore enjoyed.

A short selection from *Usos amorosos del dieciocho* (chapter 4 discusses marriage and the honor code) in a course on the history of Spanish literature or culture can facilitate the transition between the Golden Age and the modern era by providing insights into how literary representations of Spanish marriage customs moved from Pedro Calderón de la Barca's *El médico de su honra* (*The Physician of His Honour*) to Leandro Fernández de Moratín's *El sí de las niñas* (*The Maiden's Consent*). In addition, Martín Gaite's highly readable account of courtship customs in the Spanish eighteenth century can humanize a century that is often given short shrift in surveys of Spanish culture and literature, perhaps because its themes and styles seem less interesting to today's students. By introducing a selection from *Usos amorosos del dieciocho*, one can engage students in a discussion of how the eighteenth century moved Spain from a decaying empire to a modern nation and how courtship and marriage customs reveal major shifts in national cultures. The reading in *Usos amorosos del dieciocho* can also be paired with Benito Jerónimo Feijoo's "Defensa de las mujeres" (1726; "Defense of Women"), one of the earliest feminist treatises in Spanish.

Martín Gaite's historical feminism continues in *Usos amorosos de la postguerra española*. This masterpiece places the theories of female identity formation Martín Gaite developed in the 1960s and 1970s in the specific context of the early post–Civil War period (1939–53). It chronicles the many legal and social pressures exerted by the Franco regime and La Sección Femenina de la Falange (the Women's Section of the Falange, the fascist political organization founded by José Antonio Primo de Rivera), the dictatorship's arm for making women conform to traditional Spanish values, to force them into the traditional Spanish mold of mother, homemaker, and wife. The work introduces a new essay style that combines academic research (primarily in journals allied with the Franco regime and Sección Femenina) with personal reminiscence and anecdote. As Sullivan notes, this "boundary crossing" is extraordinarily engaging. So able is Martín Gaite in this much-quoted book to re-create the early Franco era through historical fact, vivid scene, and narrative technique that Robert Spires declares that Martín Gaite "helped me develop the capacity to imagine myself as an embodied or contextualized 'other.' The 'other' in my case, a Midwestern male, was experiencing life as a Spanish female" ("Embodied History" 141).

Paired with such Martín Gaite novels as *Entre visillos* (1958; *Behind the Curtains*) and *El cuarto de atrás* and with many other Spanish novels set in the

Franco era (e.g., Carmen Laforet's *Nada* [1945], Ana María Matute's *Primera memoria* [1960; *School of the Sun*], Mercè Rodoreda's *La Plaza del Diamante* [1962; *The Time of the Doves*]), readings from *Usos amorosos*, perhaps enhanced by *PowerPoint* images from Spires's article on *Usos* and cartoons from the popular Franco-era humor magazine *El codorniz* ("The Quail"), can help students achieve Spires's experience. I always assign at least one chapter of *Usos amorosos* (usually chapter 3, "El legado de José Antonio" ["The Legacy of José Antonio"], on the Sección Femenina) in undergraduate classes on the post–Civil War novel and most of the book in graduate classes on that subject.

Usos amorosos works its magic through various literary strategies and subtle irony that permeates everything. The feminist viewpoint is rarely stated overtly. For example, instead of railing against the Sección Femenina's lack of enthusiasm for women's higher education, Martín Gaite merely points out the silly, superfluous rhetoric in an article from a 1941 issue of *Medina*, a magazine published by the organization. She follows her one-sentence commentary with a telling quotation and leaves it to the reader to see the article's backward message about women's seeking a university education:

> Se han abierto de nuevo las puertas de las viejas y vetustas Universidades. Por ellas entra un tropel de muchachas con el semblante sano y la piel bronceada. . . . Su paso deja en el ambiente cálidos olores de algas marinas y de tomillos y espliegos. . . . ¿Podrán decir los que las contemplan que los estudios han borrado su feminidad? ¡No y mil veces no! La mujer es como la rosa, que por más cuidados que le dedique el jardinero, jamás podrá convertirla en clavel . . . nunca cambiarla de especie. (67)

> The doors of the venerable old universities have opened again. Through them passes a throng of wholesome-looking, tanned girls. As they pass by, they trail warm scents of sea breeze, of thyme and lavender . . . would those who look at them say that their studies have erased their femininity? No, no, a thousand times no! A woman is like a rose: no matter how carefully a gardener tends it, he will never be able to turn it into a carnation. . . . He can never change its species. (*Courtship Customs* 64)

I ask both undergraduate and graduate students to perform the same kind of close textual analysis with *Usos* that they do with literary works in order to discover Martín Gaite's feminist intent.

Underlying the entire book on postwar courtship customs is the theory Martín Gaite advanced in the feminist essays of *Búsqueda*—namely, that women's fundamental problem is lack of an authentic self and an unsatisfying attempt to live according to images imposed from without. In the Franco era, the image of the happily married woman predominated; she smilingly sat at the sewing machine, stood over the stove, or surrounded herself with children. There was no room in the public imagination for the single career woman or the married woman who combined career and motherhood. As a visual example of Martín Gaite's arguments in *Usos*, I show two images of Laforet. In one, a photograph taken about the time she wrote *Nada*, she is smoking and appears thoughtful and independent. The other, from a popular woman's magazine, shows her in a domestic setting with three of her children.

Desde la ventana: Women in Literary History

Martín Gaite claims never to have thought about women's writing as different from men's until she was introduced to North American feminist theorists and literary critics during her 1980 stay in New York. In 1986 she gave four lectures on the subject, which were published under the title *Desde la ventana*.[12] The lectures contain valuable perspectives on some of the classics of Spanish literature. The collection can accompany a survey of Spanish literature from the Golden Age to the early post–Civil War period. Each chapter addresses female authors (mostly in a particular historical frame). Chapter 1, "Mirando desde la ventana" ("Looking from the Window"), considers the Golden Age narrator María de Zayas y Sotomayor and the poet Sor Juana Inés de la Cruz and the nineteenth-century poets Gertrudis Gómez de Avellaneda and Rosalía de Castro. Martín Gaite situates these female authors within prevailing male attitudes toward women, which include disparagement of *ventaneras* ("women who like to look out the window"). She upturns the traditional male view of women's window gazing as a desire to be seen by pointing out that women may just enjoy the view or the opportunity to learn of events occurring outside the house. She considers window gazing a manifestation of women's need for interests beyond the boring domestic realm. She perceptively analyzes the literary and psychological functions of the window in women's literature. The window is "el punto de enfoque, pero también el punto de partida" (52; "the focal point, but also the point of departure") for some women's writing, because windows allow the oblique and hidden view of an exterior from an interior.[13] Martín Gaite believes this viewpoint is particular to women writers and not usually found in writing by men.

"Buscando el modo" centers on women writers' attempts to express their passions through writing. In Santa Teresa de Jesús's works Martín Gaite finds many characteristics she associates with the successful female writer: "aceptación de la soledad, mirada cauta y concreta, búsqueda de interlocutor, pasión incomprendida y desobediencia a los modelos propuestos" (61; "acceptance of solitude, a cautious and concrete gaze, search for an interlocutor, misunderstood passion, and disobedience to established models"). She locates the novelty of Santa Teresa's writing in its rough epistolary-like style full of repetitions and meanderings. She believes the epistolary form is particularly suited to women, because it gave women a way finally to express in writing their innermost emotions. "Buscando el modo" can be paired with readings in Santa Teresa's poetry or *Libro de la vida* (1562–65; *The Book of Her Life*) as well as with first-person novels by women (e.g., Laforet's *Nada*). For this segment, students would benefit from seeing clips or even an entire episode of Josefina Molina's 1983 Spanish television miniseries *Santa Teresa*, which was scripted by Martín Gaite.[14]

"El hombre musa" ("The Male Muse") is a splendid companion to units or courses on the Spanish Romantic period that traditionally emphasize the emotional states of male authors like Mariano José de Larra, El Duque de Rivas, José de Espronceda, José Zorrilla, and Gustavo Adolfo Bécquer, although Rosalía de Castro is now often included. Martín Gaite analyzes Castro's *El caballero de las botas azules* (1867; *The Gentleman of the Blue Boots*), a delicious entrée into women's roles in Spanish Romantic works. As Martín Gaite notes, Castro inverts the traditional female role as muse to the male writer by creating a male muse:

> Pocas veces se habrá enunciado de forma más acertada la mezcla de anhelos encontrados que despierta en el alma femenina la aparición del hombre misterioso. En ellos se resume un deseo fundamental y casi siempre insatisfecho que la mujer alberga en lo más recóndito de su ser: el de ser tenida en cuenta y apreciada no sólo como oponente amoroso, sino como interlocutor. (*Desde la ventana* 97)

> Rarely has the mixture of longings that the appearance of a mysterious man awakens in the feminine soul been so exactly expressed. The fundamental and almost always unsatisfied desire that the woman harbors in her innermost being is summarized in those longings: that of being taken into account and appreciated not only as an amorous opponent but also as an interlocutor.

Martín Gaite too employed a male muse figure in *El cuarto de atrás*, and I have students read the essay along with the novel in both undergraduate and graduate courses in order to stimulate their thinking about the roles of C and the mysterious male visitor in the novel.

"La chica rara" ("The Odd Girl"), the fourth essay included in *Desde la ventana*, focuses on the early post-Franco period and introduces the odd girl character—a character that Martín Gaite did not address in *Usos amorosos de la postguerra española*, which centered on social customs rather than literary types. "La chica rara" is an ideal companion piece to many Franco-era novels. She mentions Laforet's *Nada*, Dolores Medio's *Nosotros los Rivero* (1953; "We, the Riveros"), Matute's *Los Abel* (1948; "The Abels"), Martín Gaite's own *Entre visillos*, and Rodoreda's *La Plaza del Diamante*, but many more could be added, even recent novels such as Lucía Etxebarria's *Beatriz y los cuerpos celestes* (1998; "Beatrice and the Heavenly Bodies").[15] Martín Gaite's essay contrasts female protagonists such as *Nada*'s with those in *novelas rosas* (Harlequin-type romances), many of which were written by women who belonged to the Falange party or who subscribed to its goals for women.[16] Martín Gaite details Laforet's subversion of all the major tenets of the typical romance novel: the woman who feels complete only when she secures a strong, handsome, faithful man; the idealized romantic encounters between the woman and the man; and the happy ending in marriage after many trials and tribulations. The men in *Nada* are anything but ideal, and the young protagonist Andrea's potential couplings with one or another wealthy (if not strong, handsome, and faithful) man are frustrated, in part by her own rebellious nature and her recognition of the mismatch. The odd girl is not coquettish, and her life goal is not focused on the domestic sphere; quite the contrary, she prefers public spaces and often walks in the street alone. Novels whose odd girl protagonists do not conform to the social requirements of a young woman in search of a good husband radically undermine the happy ending in engagement or marriage. Sometimes the odd girl protagonist remains (happily) single or ends up in an unhappy marriage.

Teaching Martín Gaite's Works in a Graduate Course on Feminist Theory

I conclude this overview of teaching Martín Gaite as a feminist thinker by outlining a graduate course I have taught twice on Spanish feminist theory and in which several texts by her are central. Her theories of the female self and of women writers and characters demonstrate the uniqueness of Spanish feminist thinking. Although she, like many of her Spanish predecessors, draws on both Spanish and foreign (particularly Anglo-American) sources in her feminist thinking, she reaches positions that are unpredictable and her own. Because the course centers on the Spanish feminist tradition, I do not include texts by feminist theorists written in English, French, German, or Italian, which are generally taught in feminist theory courses in English departments or comparative literature programs. If feminist theory is taught as a unit in Spanish department graduate theory courses, it usually focuses on non-Hispanic thinkers. I speak of foreign theorists in lectures for purposes of comparison.

The course begins with Feijoo's "Defensa de las mujeres," which sets the stage for Concepción Arenal's logical, rational style of argumentation. I read in tandem Arenal's and Emilia Pardo Bazán's speeches on women's education from the landmark 1892 pedagogical conference on this subject, contained respectively in *La emancipación de la mujer en España*, a collection of Arenal's feminist writing, and *La mujer española*, Pardo Bazán's collected feminist essays. These speeches make evident the schism in these two early feminists' orientation—Arenal's emphasis on women's social role, Pardo Bazán's on the woman as individual. Pardo Bazán's novel *Los pazos de Ulloa* (1886; *The House of Ulloa*) affords an opportunity to discuss whether or not the author employs her ideas on women's education in her fiction. The following generation of feminists, including Carmen de Burgos (*La mujer moderna y sus derechos* [1927; "The Modern Woman and Her Rights"] and Margarita Nelken (*La condición social de la mujer en España* [1919?; "The Social Condition of Women in Spain"]), treats the social and legal obstacles to women's development and independence. Some of the fiction selections are Burgos's "El articulo 438" ("Article 438") and "La flor de la playa" (1920; "The Beach Flower") and Nelken's *La trampa del arenal* (1923; "The Sand Trap"). I also include Federico García Lorca's plays *Yerma* (1934) and *La casa de Bernarda Alba* (1936; *The House of Bernarda Alba*), which resonate with Spanish feminist ideas of the 1920s and 1930s. María Zambrano and Rosa Chacel, somewhat younger than Burgos and Nelken, emphasize the importance of a woman's inner being in ways that illuminate Chacel's *Memorias de Leticia Valle* (1946; *Memoirs of Leticia Valle*).

Martín Gaite's feminist thought picks up both Burgos's and Nelken's social emphasis and Zambrano's and Chacel's existential orientation.[17] *Usos amorosos de la postguerra española* addresses the social conditions in which Spanish women's inner development stagnated, while *La búsqueda* and *Desde la ventana* consider women's identity formation from within and their imaginative, creative potential. Martín Gaite's feminist theories frame analyses of Laforet's *Nada* and Martín Gaite's own *El cuarto de atrás*. The Martín Gaite readings lead nicely into the next unit on the debate that arose in the democratic era between equality and difference feminists (Celia Amorós representing the former, Milagros Rivera the latter). Some critics ally Martín Gaite with difference feminists. I conclude the course with Alborch's *Solas* and Juan José Millás's novel *La soledad era eso* (1990; "That's What Loneliness Was"), both born of the same transition to democracy that gave rise to that debate. These works remind us of Martín Gaite's concerns with women's interiority. The courses I have taught on this material were given at branches of the University of California, which operate on the quarter system (ten weeks). In a semester-long course, one could assign more literary readings to illustrate how Spanish feminist theory can provide useful points of discussion for Spanish literary texts.

Carmen Martín Gaite possessed a personality in the positive sense she sometimes uses the term in *La búsqueda de interlocutor y otras búsquedas*. Those of us who had the good fortune to spend time with her will never forget her warmth, her spontaneous wit, her creative imagination, and her humility. Because today's students unfortunately no longer have the possibility of meeting her, I try to give them a sense of her as a person by showing clips from an interview with her by Joaquín Soler produced by Radiotelevisión Española in 1981.[18] I select footage that relates to the work or works we are reading (for example, for "Las ataduras," her discussion of her youthful summers in Galicia and her relationship with her father). Her commanding presence and forthright responses to the interviewer are vivid evidence of her quiet feminism.

NOTES

[1] I do not include *El cuento de nunca acabar* (1983; "The Never-Ending Story") in this study, although Emilie Bergmann has convincingly demonstrated the important gender implications in Martín Gaite's essay on narrative theory. I refer the reader to her article. The most overtly feminist chapter in *El cuento*, "Las mujeres noveleras" ("Women Who

Make Up Stories"), would fit well in courses that include units on women and the Franco era in Spain. On the whole, however, *El cuento* (or selections from it) would work best in a course on general literary theory or as a companion piece to a specific novel or short story. It is a highly original consideration of the origins and function of narrative.

[2]Except as noted, all translations are mine.

[3]See Carbayo-Abengózar for a discussion of the influence of European existential thought on Martín Gaite and other writers of her generation (43–73).

[4]Sullivan notes that Martín Gaite employs "gender analysis before feminist theory had come to make distinctions between sex, sexuality, and gender and to prioritize the latter as a category of analysis" (45).

[5]Carbayo-Abengózar argues for reading Martín Gaite as a "difference" feminist (123–52).

[6]Betty Friedan's *The Feminine Mystique*, published in Spanish translation in 1965, possibly inspired this essay.

[7]The references to public feminist demonstrations indicate that the article was written in the late 1960s or early 1970s. Note that in 1970 Martín Gaite separated from her husband, Rafael Sánchez Ferlosio.

[8]Martín Gaite employs *a palo seco* ("alone" or "on its own") and other colorful idioms in her writings on women to enhance the idea of absolute solitude and the challenge women face in enduring it. See, for example, "enfrentándose a palo seco con la soledad" (*Desde la ventana* 60 ["Buscando el modo"]; "confronting solitude cold turkey"); "la de resistir a pie quieto la soledad en aquella habitación" (26 [Introd.]; "resisting solitude unflinchingly in that room"); "Con el tiempo pasa igual que con la soledad: únicamente metiéndose de lleno y a cuerpo limpio en sus fauces puede llegar a regalarnos su fruto, ese fruto tan duro de arrancar como de pelar . . ." (*Búsqueda* [2000] 129 ["Cuarto a espadas sobre las coplas de posguerra"]; "It is the same with time as with solitude: only by placing oneself wholeheartedly and completely in its jaws will it render us its fruit, a fruit that is as difficult to harvest as it is to peel . . .").

[9]"Las ataduras" was included in the textbook *Puntos de vista*, by Sandra Harper, an anthology of Spanish narratives with pedagogical apparatus (vocabulary, questions, discussion topics) that I used many times as an introduction to reading in fourth-semester Spanish classes.

[10]Other essays in *La búsqueda* relate to identity formation or the tension between solitude and companionship, but they are not woman-centered. "La búsqueda de interlocutor" (1966; "The Search for an Interlocutor") postulates the narrator's solitude and corresponding need for a narratee or destined recipient: "[N]unca habría existido invención literaria alguna si los hombres, saciados totalmente en su sed de comunicación, no hubieran llegado a conocer, con la soledad, el acuciante deseo de romperla" (28; [T]here would never have been any literary invention if people, their thirst for communication completely sated, had not through solitude experienced the acute desire to break that solitude"). Again we hear echoes of Unamuno, whose *nivolas* ("new novels") contain a great deal of dialogue and monologues with an invented interlocutor, such as the dog Orfeo. Martín Gaite's "Los malos espejos" (1972; "Bad Mirrors") explores the external pressures—bad mirrors—on identity formation; only in risking solitude can one discover something original.

[11]*Conversaciones creadoras: Mastering Spanish Conversation*, written with Joan L. Brown, is built around original minidramas in dialogue form.

[12]But in "La mujer en la literatura," she indicates that she had already intuited what she later learned was called gynocriticism in North American literary criticism. In the lecture, she makes an important point about the difference between male and female writing not included in the more historically focused *Desde la ventana*. Women, she believes, are not driven by reason and the need for full explanations in their writing: "En el fondo, la mayor diferencia entre el discurso masculino y el femenino . . . estriba en que un hombre, en un nivel de inteligencia parecido al de la mujer con quien discute, no se resigna a no entenderlo todo, a base de una clasificación por temas que en su mismo empeño de imponerse dialécticamente puede resultar artificial. Ella, en cambio, desconfía muchas veces del entendimiento como norma" (*Pido* 339; "Fundamentally, the principal difference between masculine and feminine discourse . . . resides in the fact that a man, whose intelligence level is similar to that of the woman with whom he is discoursing, does not resign himself to not understanding everything by means of a thematic classification whose very effort to impose itself dialectically can be artificial. She, on the other hand, often distrusts understanding as a norm").

[13]In her 1990 essay "Los incentivos de la ventana" ("The Window's Inducement"), reprinted in the 1992 edition of *Desde la ventana*, the author extends her analysis of women's window gazing to paintings, noting that "los caminos o paisajes entrevistos desde la ventana por una mujer siempre llevan a una aventura soñada" (136; "the paths or vistas glimpsed by a woman looking out the window always lead to an adventure of her dreams").

[14]The miniseries is currently available from Spanish public television (http://tienda.rtve.es), though the three DVDs must be converted from the European PAL format. From time to time the series is broadcast in the United States (with English subtitles) by the global Catholic television network EWTN.

[15]Brown's "The Nonconformist Character" reveals that Martín Gaite invented "odd men" as well as odd girls and women in the novels *Entre visillos*, *Ritmo lento*, and *Retahílas*. See also Nuria Cruz-Cámara on the odd girl character in Laforet's *La isla y los demonios* and Martín Gaite's *Entre visillos* ("'Chicas raras'").

[16]See Alicia Andreu for a discussion of Sección Femenina ideals embedded in the *novela rosa*.

[17]Andrew Bush's "Dwelling on Two Stories," which draws on Zambrano's ideas about space and psychoanalysis to elucidate Martín Gaite's posthumous novel *Los parentescos* (2001; "Familial Relations"), is a model of how Spanish feminist theory can be employed in analyses of Spanish fiction.

[18]The hour-long interview is currently available through *Google Videos*. Relevant portions also appear in the Films for the Humanities DVD *Carmen Martín Gaite: In Search of Conversation*.

Appendix A: Carmen Martín Gaite's Autobiographical Sketch

Introduction

Carmen Martín Gaite's autobiographical sketch came as a surprise to me. Our plan was that I would write a biographical chapter for my book *Secrets from the Back Room: The Fiction of Carmen Martín Gaite*, based on information that she supplied. At the beginning of June 1980, in Madrid, we embarked on interviews for this purpose. Armed with a tape recorder and a legal pad, I sat with her in the same red-wallpapered living room described in *The Back Room*. I asked questions, and she answered, sometimes at length, over the course of several days. Gradually she lost patience with the interview process. "I'll do it," she announced. "Come back tomorrow." The next afternoon, she handed me the manuscript that appears here: sixteen typed pages with handwritten insertions in ink and pencil. The Spanish original and my first English translation were published in 1987 in *Secrets*.

When she gave the pages to me, her essay did not bear a title. She referred to it as her autobiography but readily agreed that a better title would be "An Autobiographical Sketch," since it left open the possibility that she might someday write a full-length autobiography. Sadly, this did not come to pass. Martín Gaite did, however, write a one-sentence coda years later, when she included the sketch with her collection of reprints *Agua pasada* (1993; "Water under the Bridge"). In her introduction she explained its provenance and added an update that obliquely acknowledged the loss of her daughter in 1985: ". . . para un lector que no conozca mi biografía reciente, donde lea 'soledad' y 'muerte', puede estar seguro de que mi vivencia de esas dos nociones era aún bien incompleta" (11; "for those of you who are unacquainted with my recent life, where you read 'solitude' and 'death,' rest assured that at the time, my experience with these two phenomena was far from over").

The English translation that appears here is new. Having worked with Martín Gaite for another twenty years, and benefiting from reviewers' comments on the original translation, I am confident that the current translation is much closer to the author's lexicon, style, and spirit.

Un bosquejo autobiográfico

Carmen Martín Gaite

Nací en Salamanca, el 8 de diciembre de 1925, a las doce de la mañana de un día frío y soleado. Esto de nacer a mediodía y con sol parece presagio de buena fortuna, según dicen los nigromantes; pero en mi caso, y sin ánimo de quitarle méritos al sol, creo que todo lo bueno que me ha pasado en este mundo (y lo que, siendo menos bueno, haya sabido aceptar o convertir en mejor) se debe al amor a la vida y a la confianza que desde la infancia me inculcaron mis padres, ambos de una calidad humana excepcional. Aparte de su bondad natural y de su inteligencia, poseían ambos un particular y acusado sentido del humor que conservaron hasta la vejez, gracias al cual cualquier conversación mantenida con ellos jamás era convencional o rutinaria, sino algo muy vivo y divertido.

Mi madre era gallega, de Orense, hija de un catedrático de geografía, Javier Gaite y de su mujer Sofía Veloso, a ninguno de los cuales llegué a conocer. Mi madre había venido a parar a Salamanca porque sus dos hermanos varones estudiaban en aquella Universidad. Uno de ellos, mi tío Vicente, que era médico, conoció en una tertulia de café al joven notario José Martín, viudo y sin hijos, y se lo presentó a su hermana María, mi madre. Las chicas casaderas salmantinas veían en este viudo reciente y de brillante carrera lo que entonces se llamaba un buen partido, pero ninguna logró sacarle de sus casillas más que aquella bella gallega de dulce mirada que no tenía el menor interés de "pescarle". Se enamoraron y, tras un breve noviazgo, se casaron en Madrid—donde vivían mis abuelos paternos—el 19 de mayo de 1923. Se vinieron a vivir a Salamanca, donde él tenía su despacho y al año siguiente, en febrero de 1924 nació la primera hija de este matrimonio, mi hermana Ana María, en una casa de la calle de la Rúa, porque entonces no era costumbre que las mujeres fueran a dar a luz en el hospital.

Poco después, cuando mi madre ya estaba embarazada de mí, se mudaron a la casa donde yo nací, en la Plaza de los Bandos número 3, que fue nuestra vivienda hasta que a mi padre lo trasladaron a Madrid en 1950. Con motivo de aquella mudanza de la calle de la Rúa a la plaza de los Bandos, a mi madre estuvo a punto de caérsele encima un pesado armario de luna, que fue capaz de sujetar ella sola, desplegando una fuerza extraordinaria, únicamente en virtud del terror que le producía—según me contaba luego—la idea de que aquel accidente pudiera matarme a mí. Afortunadamente unos empleados de la notaría de mi padre acudieron a sus voces y nos salvaron a ambas de la catástrofe, razón por la cual miro siempre aquel armario como el emblema del primer peligro contra mi vida esquivado con buena estrella.

De la casa de la Plaza de los Bandos, en cuyo piso de abajo tenía mi padre instaladas sus oficinas, y que recientemente han derribado, tengo un recuerdo tan claro que parece que aún la estoy viendo. La he descrito en mi cuento "La chica de abajo" y también en mi última novela *El cuarto de atrás*, así como la placita provinciana y silenciosa a la cual daban los balcones de la parte delantera y donde tanto jugué con los niños de la vecindad. Entonces había pocos coches en Salamanca y no resultaba nada peligroso jugar en la calle ni patinar, ni montar en bicicleta, lo cual contribuía a fomentar en los niños esa tendencia suya hacia la expansión y la libertad que hoy la vida en las grandes ciudades aborta y dificulta.

Al colegio no fui. Mi padre era poco amigo de la educación impartida por frailes y monjas, y en Salamanca (ciudad de costumbres rígidas y de muchos prejuicios) colegios no religiosos y de cierta calidad no había prácticamente ninguno. Mi hermana y yo en la primera infancia tuvimos varios profesores particulares de dibujo y de idiomas y de cultura general, pero fue sobre todo mi padre quien nos aficionó personalmente al arte, a la historia y a la literatura.

Cuando terminaba su trabajo y subía a reunirse con nosotras, nos enseñaba muchos libros de estampas y de mapas que tenía en su biblioteca y era un placer para él contestar a todas nuestras preguntas, tarea en la que mi madre también metía baza, levantando la cabeza de las primorosas labores que siempre hacía y siguió haciendo hasta los últimos años de su vida, o del libro que estuviera leyendo. Aburridos nunca los recuerdo, le sacaban partido a todo lo que hacían y se lo pasaban muy bien uno con otro, pero nunca nos excluyeron a nosotras de su intimidad, sino que nos hicieron parte importantísima de ella. La mayor parte de los asuntos los discutían en nuestra presencia y nos llevaban a todos sus viajes. Jamás sentí esa sensación de desamparo o desvío que tienen algunos niños cuando sus padres desaparecen sin más explicaciones y los dejan a ellos en manos de institutrices o criadas, y mucho menos esa segregación implícita en la fórmula tradicional de "los niños no preguntan esas cosas". Nuestras preguntas infantiles siempre se veían atendidas.

En verano íbamos puntualmente a veranear durante dos o tres meses al pueblo de San Lorenzo de Piñor, a cinco kilómetros de Orense. Es una aldea en la montaña, donde también mi madre había pasado los veranos de su infancia y donde mi abuelo Javier había mandado construir una casa muy bonita con jardín y huerta, junto al camino. No tenía luz eléctrica ni agua corriente, pero a nosotros nos encantaba estar allí. En ese mismo pueblo veraneaban también los hijos de mi tío Vicente. Las temporadas pasadas allí fueron definitivas para mi vinculación con Galicia, que siempre he considerado como mi verdadera patria. Aprendí el dialecto de la región y muchas canciones populares, me volví indómita y poco melindrosa, trepé a los árboles y a las peñas, robé fruta, me monté en carros de heno de ruedas chirriantes y tirados por bueyes, me hice amiga de los niños de la aldea, asistí a procesiones y romerías, y—ya un poco mayor—allí aprendí a bailar, tuve mis primeros escarceos amorosos y escribí mis primeros versos. San Lorenzo de Piñor—donde no he vuelto desde hace muchos años, porque la casa luego se vendió—significa para mí la esencia misma de la juventud y de la libertad, allí están mis raíces y su paisaje abrupto y montaraz decora con frecuencia mis sueños. En este pueblo he situado algunas de mis narraciones como *Las ataduras* o *Retahílas*.

Mi padre, aunque no era gallego, también adoraba aquella tierra. Su padre era de un pueblo de Valladolid y su madre de Santander, pero él había vivido en Madrid desde los dos años y se consideraba madrileño. En Madrid donde había pasado toda su juventud y había cursado la carrera de Leyes, asistió a muchas tertulias de escritores y de artistas de principios de siglo y de ahí le venía su gran afición a la literatura, que cultivaba con bastante acierto. Versificaba con facilidad y, aparte de sus trabajos y conferencias de derecho, había escrito varios cuentos para niños, que nos leía, pero que nunca publicó. Pero sobre todo, escribía unas cartas graciosísimas, llenas de detalles, con una caligrafía preciosa, y era un narrador oral excepcional. A su padre, mi abuelo Gumersindo, que era representante de comercio, lo perdió cuando yo tenía cuatro años, así que casi no me acuerdo de él, y menos de mi abuela Dolores, una señora muy guapa, que había muerto siendo mi padre estudiante. Pero esta doña Dolores López tenía una hermana viuda, Carmen, que había vivido siempre con mis abuelos, la cual, al quedarse viudo su cuñado Gumersindo, se casó en segundas nupcias con él, porque además era hermano de su primer marido. Estaban ya casados, pues, hacía mucho cuando yo nací, así que la recuerdo como a mi verdadera abuela y como a tal la traté siempre. Me pusieron su nombre porque fue mi madrina. Esta señora conservaba, además de muy buena planta y empaque, un piso hermoso en la calle Mayor número 14, que es donde veníamos siempre a parar en nuestros frecuentes viajes de Salamanca a Madrid. La impresión que estos viajes y Madrid mismo producían en mi ánimo de niña provinciana y ansiosa de más amplios horizontes, está en parte recogida en mi novela *El cuarto de atrás*.

Poco antes de empezar la guerra civil española, mis padres decidieron enviar a mi única hermana Ana María—que ya estaba en edad de empezar el bachillerato—a estudiar al Instituto Escuela de Madrid. Era esta una institución que heredaba, tanto en sus métodos como en su orientación general, el espíritu liberal de la famosa Institución Libre de Enseñanza, que tomó auge a partir del krausismo; la educación era mixta—niños y niñas juntos, cosa que en Salamanca parecía tener una connotación de pecado—y la enseñanza religiosa no era obligatoria sino optativa. (Mis padres no eran beatos, aunque iban a misa, y nosotras habíamos tomado la primera comunión, ya bastante mayores y sin traje blanco.) Mi hermana se vino, pues, a estudiar a Madrid y vivía con mi abuela y dos criadas mayores en aquel caserón de la calle Mayor. El proyecto era el de que, dos años más tarde, yo hubiera venido a estudiar también a ese centro, pero la guerra que estalló en verano del 36, poco después de las primeras vacaciones de mi hermana, destruyó esos planes y tantos otros.

Toda la guerra la pasamos en Salamanca, con bastante miedo, debido a las ideas liberales de mi padre y a las de todos sus amigos, muchos de los cuales—entre ellos don Miguel de Unamuno—sufrieron persecución o cárcel por parte del General Franco, que tenía en Salamanca su Cuartel General y reprimió—como es sabido—cualquier conato de liberalismo. A mi padre no lo llegaron a encarcelar, porque no pertenecía a ningún partido político, pero siempre nos estaban aconsejando que no habláramos con nadie de sus opiniones antimilitaristas y la casa se había convertido en una especie de refugio, que reforzó nuestros lazos familiares. A un hermano de mi madre, Joaquín Gaite—discípulo y amigo de don Miguel de Unamuno—lo fusilaron en agosto de 1936 por tener carnet del partido socialista. De mi tío Joaquín, profesor de geografía, y de la influencia que tuvo en mi infancia he hablado también en *El cuarto de atrás*.

Hice todo el bachillerato en el Instituto femenino de Salamanca, un caserón destartalado y frío, cuyo ambiente he descrito en mi novela *Entre visillos*. Allí iban niñas de las más distintas clases sociales, pero la mayoría de condición modesta, entre las que coseché mis primeras buenas amigas, sobre todo Sofía Bermejo, hija de dos maestros que estaban en la cárcel, y que me aficionó a escribir diario. También empecé con ella una novela e inventamos la isla de Bergai. (Todo esto lo he contado en *El cuarto de atrás*.) En el Instituto tuve muy buenos profesores, entre ellos don Rafael Lapesa y don Salvador Fernández Ramírez, ambos académicos en la actualidad y a quienes la guerra había pillado por casualidad en Salamanca. Creo que a estos dos excelentes profesores les debo mi definitiva vocación por la literatura y el esmero con que me entregaba a los ejercicios de redacción, por el placer de hallar su beneplácito. De todas maneras, tanto mi padre como mi madre, también me fomentaban con decidido entusiasmo estas aficiones. También debo a mi paso por el Instituto de Salamanca la superación definitiva de una posible "conciencia de clase" y la tendencia a seleccionar mis amistades por afinidades ideológicas o sentimentales y nunca tendiendo a consideraciones de tipo social.

En 1943, en plena postguerra, empecé la carrera de Filología Románica en la Universidad de Salamanca. Consistía en dos cursos de estudios comunes a todas las ramas de Filosofía y Letras y tres cursos de especialización. En primero de "comunes" estábamos matriculados cuatro chicos y siete chicas. Uno de estos chicos era Ignacio Aldecoa, que llegó a ser uno de los más importantes prosistas de postguerra, y otro el poeta Agustín García Calvo, actualmente catedrático de Lenguas Clásicas en la Universidad de Madrid y excelente escritor. De ambos, así como del ambiente de la Universidad salmantina en aquellos años de postguerra he hablado en mi artículo "Un aviso: ha muerto Ignacio", escrito a la muerte de Aldecoa en 1969.

En la Universidad colaboré en la revista *Trabajos y días*, donde vieron la luz mis primeros poemas (algunos de ellos recogidos ahora en mi librito *A rachas*) e hice teatro universitario, bajo la dirección del profesor de Literatura don César Real de la Riva. Representamos, por ejemplo, en cursos sucesivos, varios entremeses de Cervantes y una obra de Shakespeare, *El mercader de Venecia*. El teatro me apasionaba casi tanto como la literatura y la tentación de llegar a ser actriz profesional se me insinuó en varias ocasiones, pero el ambiente de aquellos años y mi condición de jovencita burguesa no eran demasiado propicios para aquel sueño, que descarté sin pena porque, además, la literatura me tiraba más que nada. Leí muchas obras clásicas, tanto de teatro como de poesía y prosa, y devoré con especial fruición casi todas las novelas de la generación del 98 que mi padre tenía en su biblioteca. Y las de un escritor portugués poco conocido, pero que a mí me apasiona: Eça de Queiroz.

En verano de 1946 me dieron una beca para la universidad portuguesa de Coimbra y viajé por primera vez al extranjero, y además yo sola, cosa que me ilusionaba mucho, porque entonces no era costumbre que una chica viajara sin compañía. Portugal, tal vez por sus vinculaciones lingüísticas con Galicia, es un país que siempre me ha fascinado particularmente y me siento atraída por sus costumbres y su literatura. Estuve dos meses en Coimbra y conocí también Oporto y Lisboa. En ese período me nació el propósito de hacer la tesis doctoral sobre los cancioneros galaico-portugueses del siglo XIII y empecé a tomar notas para este trabajo.

En 1948 me licencié en Filología Románica y ese mismo año me dieron otra beca de estudios, esta vez para la Universidad de verano de Cannes. Fueron unas vacaciones inolvidables. Entré en contacto, durante aquellos cursos, con muchos autores franceses que no había leído, Sartre, Camus, Saint-Exupéry, Gide, Proust, etc., perfeccioné mucho mi francés y, sobre todo, conocí por primera vez, a mis veintidós años, el sabor auténtico de la libertad. Asistí a bailes en "boîtes", a batallas de flores, jugué a la ruleta. Me relacioné con estudiantes de otros países, exentos de prejuicios, me acosté a las tantas y decidí que no quería seguir viviendo en Salamanca. Nunca se me había planteado de forma tan clara la idea de abandonar mi familia y mi ciudad.

Cuando regresé a Salamanca, les dije a mis padres que me quería ir a Madrid a trabajar y a preparar mi doctorado, que Salamanca se me había vuelto un ambiente demasiado conocido y limitado, que me aburría.

De noviembre de 1948 a la primavera de 1949 viví sola en Madrid. Mi abuela había muerto hacía poco y algunos de los muebles de la calle Mayor se habían trasladado a un pisito pequeño que compró mi padre en Madrid, donde vivían las dos criadas viejas de la abuela, Paula y Marcelina, que eran como de la familia. Con ellas estuve viviendo durante ese tiempo, pero salía y entraba cuando me daba la gana y traía a muchos amigos a casa. Había reencontrado en Madrid a mi antiguo compañero de estudios Ignacio Aldecoa y él me puso en contacto con mucha gente que conocía y que empezó a ser mi grupo: Medardo Fraile, Alfonso Sastre, Jesús Fernández Santos, Rafael Sánchez Ferlosio, entre otros. Ninguno era muy buen estudiante ni soñaba con ser profesor, todos llevaban en la sangre el virus de la literatura y empezaban a colaborar en revistas madrileñas, *La hora*, *La estafeta literaria*, *Clavileño*, *Alférez*, *El español* y *Alcalá*. En contacto con este grupo de amigos, mis proyectos universitarios se fueron diluyendo y me relajé bastante en el trabajo de la tesis, que había comenzado sobre los cancioneros galaico-portugueses y que, poco a poco, me empezó a aburrir. A ello contribuyó también el hecho de que el viejo profesor a quien había elegido para que me la dirigiera, don Armando Cotarelo, era un hombre apático, que nunca me estimuló y al que sólo vi dos veces. Trabajaba sola, sin estímulo y como perdida en la Biblioteca del Consejo de Investigaciones Científicas. Empecé a escribir cuentos y artículos y a verlos publicados en alguna de las revistas mencionadas. Iba mucho al café, al teatro, a la taberna y de paseo con mis nuevos amigos, mucho menos universitarios que yo, mucho más bohemios, todos ellos buenos escritores. Conocí también a poetas, pintores, actrices y periodistas. Madrid me parecía una ciudad fascinante. Había decidido que quería vivir siempre allí.

Para ganar algo de dinero, trabajaba durante toda la semana haciendo fichas para un diccionario que estaba preparando la Real Academia Española. Me daban libros con palabras subrayadas y mi trabajo consistía en poner arriba de la ficha la palabra subrayada en mayúsculas y debajo una cita del contexto y la referencia al libro de donde procedía la frase. Me pagaban a 15 céntimos la ficha, pero como trabajaba muy deprisa, me podía defender. Con el primer dinero que cobré, me compré un vestido de terciopelo verde.

Por las mañanas iba a la Ciudad Universitaria porque estaba matriculada en unas asignaturas que eran necesarias para llevar a cabo el doctorado, pero no pude examinarme de ninguna porque a finales de curso, en mayo, cogí el tifus y me entraron unas fiebres altísimas. La penicilina no había llegado todavía a España y el tifus era una enfermedad muy grave. Vino mi madre a cuidarme y, como no mejoraba, me trasladaron a Salamanca en una ambulancia, por consejo de mi tío Vicente, que era el médico de la familia. Estuve casi cuarenta días en la cama, a punto de morirme, y deliré muchísimo. Aquel verano, después de sanar, empecé a escribir un libro que se titulaba *El libro de la fiebre*, donde, en plan poético y surrealista, trataba de rescatar las imágenes fugaces de mis delirios. Estaba muy entusiasmada y me parecía muy bonito, pero Rafael Sánchez Ferlosio, a quien se lo enseñé pocos meses después, cuando le volví a ver en Madrid, me dijo que no valía nada, que resultaba vago y caótico, así que sólo llegué a publicar unos fragmentos en *La hora*, me parece.

Ese mismo verano de 1949, mi padre decidió pedir el traslado a Madrid. En otoño se levantó definitivamente la casa de la plaza de los Bandos, nos mudamos, y a principios de 1950 ya vivíamos toda la familia en Madrid, en un piso de la calle de Alcalá, 35, donde vivieron mis padres hasta su muerte en 1978 y donde sigue viviendo mi hermana Ana María, que nunca se casó.

Durante esa primera etapa de mi vida en Madrid con la familia, daba clases en un colegio a niñas de bachillerato, de historia, gramática y literatura. Las niñas me querían bastante pero, como mis clases eran poco ortodoxas y además yo tenía un aspecto muy infantil, no me tenían respeto ninguno, armaban mucho alboroto en la clase y la directora me acabó echando. Entonces me puse a trabajar como escribiente en el despacho de mi padre por las mañanas. Tenía el despacho en el piso segundo de la calle de Alcalá, 35, y la vivienda la teníamos en el cuarto. No era un trabajo que me gustara mucho, pero me daba algún dinero, en espera de tiempos mejores.

En enero de 1950 me hice novia de Rafael Sánchez Ferlosio, dos años más joven que yo y mal estudiante, pero excelente escritor. Me dedicó su primer libro *Industrias y andanzas de Alfanhuí* y poco después se fue a cumplir el servicio militar a Tetuán. Nos escribíamos mucho y yo era la primera vez en mi vida que estaba tan enamorada y tan influida por alguien, había abandonado por completo mi proyecto de la tesis doctoral, así como el de hacer oposiciones para ganar una cátedra. Mi experiencia con aquellas niñas del colegio de la calle de Martínez Campos me había revelado que mis dotes para la enseñanza eran más bien escasas.

El 14 de octubre de 1953, me casé con Rafael Sánchez Ferlosio, que había terminado su servicio militar, pero no la carrera. Acababa de fundar con Sastre y Aldecoa la *Revista Española*, que económicamente fue un desastre pero que ahora es muy buscada por los estudiosos porque allí colaboramos todos los prosistas de la llamada "generación de los años cincuenta". Los consejos de Rafael y de Aldecoa me habían servido para abandonar el tono lírico de mis primeras composiciones y para ser más rigurosa y exigente en mi prosa. Mi cuento "La chica de abajo", que les había gustado mucho, es seguramente mi primera narración estimable y en ella ya están muchos de los elementos y temas que posteriormente elaboré mejor. Rafael y yo (a pesar de que él había conseguido un trabajo modesto como secretario de un ingeniero) pensábamos vivir de nuestras colaboraciones literarias.

Después de casarnos, pasamos unos meses en Roma, en casa de los abuelos maternos de Rafael, en la Piazza de Santa Maria sopra Minerva, donde él había nacido. Luego volvimos en otras muchas ocasiones a aquella casa. Los abuelos de Rafael eran una gente encantadora y me encariñé mucho con ellos; la abuela Ida me enseñó a cocinar, que yo no sabía, y se pasaba las horas muertas hablando conmigo. Viajamos también a Nápoles, Florencia y Venecia. Italia se me metió muy dentro y además me puso en contacto con la literatura contemporánea del país, que me influyó mucho, sobre todo Pavese y Svevo. También estuvimos en Paris.

Desde que me casé vivo en Madrid, en un séptimo piso de la calle de Doctor Esquerdo núm. 43, que mi padre nos regaló, y que tiene una gran terraza. (Lo he descrito con todo detalle en mi última novela *El cuarto de atrás*, durante la conversación con el hombre vestido de negro que me visitó una noche.)

Nunca tuvimos criada, nos repartíamos las tareas domésticas y trabajábamos con total independencia uno de otro. La misma independencia que manteníamos en todo, sin interferir nunca uno en las amistades ni en las manías del otro, y recibiendo continuamente a los buenos amigos. Él escribía sobre todo de noche, y yo también me volví bastante nocturna y muy poco esclava de los horarios. A ninguno nos gustaba el lujo superfluo ni las comidas de ceremonia, lo que más nos unía era el gusto por hablar y el sentido del humor, aunque él es más crítico que yo, más inadaptado y menos sociable.

En la primavera de 1954 obtuve el premio Café Gijón por mi novela corta *El balneario*. Tanto esta novela como todas las que escribí posteriormente no las leyó Rafael hasta que ya estaban terminadas. No quería dejarme influir por sus críticas, que muchas veces me desanimaban. Prefería que me las hiciese cuando el libro estaba ya en prensa.

En octubre de ese mismo año 1954, nació nuestro primer hijo Miguel, que murió de meningitis en mayo del año siguiente, cuando Rafael acababa de escribir *El Jarama*. Esta fue la primera vez que yo sentí en mi vida cómo el suelo le puede fallar a uno repentinamente debajo de los pies, cuando menos se espera, y comprendí visceralmente algo de lo que siempre había tenido una noción más bien abstracta: la esencia precaria, amenazada y efímera de la felicidad. La muerte de mi primer hijo me enseñó a no volver a conceder nunca importancia a los disgustos menores, fue el primer paso hacia la madurez, y deseé tener otro hijo como nunca había deseado nada en este mundo.

El 22 de mayo de 1956 nació mi hija Marta. No he tenido más hijos.

En 1957 terminé mi primera novela larga *Entre visillos* y la envié al premio Nadal, sin que nadie lo supiera, con el pseudónimo de Sofía Veloso (el nombre de mi abuela materna). Rafael había ganado ese mismo premio dos años antes con *El Jarama* y no quería que el hecho de ser yo su mujer influyera ni en pro ni en contra en el ánimo del jurado. Gané el premio Nadal el 6 de enero de 1958. Me enteré de la noticia por la radio, estando sola en casa con mi hija dormida en su cuna.

Como no se trata aquí de repetir la bibliografía de mi obra, que el lector podrá encontrar exhaustivamente ofrecida en la tesis de Joan Lipman Brown, que va a continuación, me limitaré a decir que el premio Nadal contribuyó a facilitarme la publicación de mis obras, ya que era el más importante que por entonces se concedía en España, y me reafirmó en mi propósito de seguir escribiendo siempre. Aparte de eso, suponía un notable respiro económico, porque la novela se vendió muy bien.

En los años siguientes simultaneé mis tareas domésticas, maternales y literarias, con un nuevo rebrote de afición al estudio. Empecé a estudiar sobre todo historia de España del siglo XVIII, período en el que tenía grandes lagunas de ignorancia. Solía ir a estudiar a la biblioteca del Ateneo de Madrid, que cierra a la una de la madrugada. Casi siempre iba a partir de las ocho, después de acostar a mi hija, y muchas veces, cuando sonaba el timbre para avisar el cierre del Ateneo, era yo el único lector nocturno de la sala. De esta vocación tardía de autodidacta nació mi interés por un personaje muy contradictorio, perseguido por la Inquisición, don Melchor de Macanaz, sobre el cual nadie había hecho un estudio serio. Por seguirle la pista abandoné mis trabajos literarios, me metí en archivos, hice viajes a Simancas y a Paris y, al cabo de siete años de tenaz pesquisa, había reunido los datos suficientes para una biografía que apareció en 1970. De paso, revolviendo aquellos papeles de archivo, se me había despertado simultáneamente la curiosidad por los usos amorosos del siglo XVIII, y al abandonar al viejo Macanaz, seguí investigando sobre este tema. Estas investigaciones desembocaron en un segundo trabajo, *Usos amorosos del siglo XVIII en España*, que, antes de publicarlo, pensé que podría servirme como tesis doctoral y para rematar así, aunque tardíamente, aquella carrera universitaria iniciada brillantemente en Salamanca y que había quedado truncada a mi venida a Madrid. No pensaba dedicarme a la enseñanza universitaria, pero siempre me ha gustado terminar las cosas que empiezo, así que en 1972, ya peinando canas, leí mi tesis doctoral en la Universidad de Madrid. En el Tribunal estaban mis antiguos profesores Rafael Lapesa y Alonso Zamora Vicente, este último como director de la tesis. Me concedieron el premio extraordinario de fin de carrera. Desde luego no dejaba de ser un caso el mío bastante extraordinario, por lo insólito.

Y aquí termina, por ahora, ese paréntesis de casi diez años en que me dediqué a la investigación. Sobre todo porque me había dado cuenta de una cosa: de que los archivos son algo muy absorbente y, como te metas en ellos sin condiciones, no te libras ya en vida del insensible veneno que segregan. Y yo tenía muchas ganas de volver a la literatura, que había abandonado desde la publicación de *Ritmo lento* en 1962.

Desde el otoño de 1970 vivo sola con mi hija Marta en la misma casa de doctor Esquerdo, que compartí diecisiete años con Rafael. Nuestra separación fue amistosa y nos seguimos viendo con mucha frecuencia. Viene aquí siempre que quiere. Yo a esta casa le tengo un gran cariño y nunca se me ha ocurrido mudarme a otra, en ningún sitio me encuentro tan a gusto como aquí. Mi hija está terminando ahora la carrera de Filología inglesa y ya hace traducciones y da clases en un colegio, donde parece que la respetan más que me respetaban a mí aquellas niñas del pasado. Mi hija es muy amiga mía, nos reímos mucho juntas y nos lo contamos todo.

Excepción hecha de un período de ocho meses en el año 73, en que tuve un empleo en la editorial Salvat, nunca he desempeñado trabajos atenidos a un horario fijo, y se puede decir que he vivido exclusivamente de la pluma, como era mi deseo. He hecho ediciones críticas, traducciones, prólogos, artículos, guiones de cine, adaptaciones de clásicos, colaboraciones para la radio, y hasta he cantado canciones gallegas en un teatro. Pero siempre he evitado, aun a costa de vivir más modestamente, los empleos que pudieran esclavizarme y quitarme tiempo para dedicarlo a la lectura, a la escritura y a otra de mis pasiones favoritas: el cultivo de la amistad. Los amigos son para mí la cosa más importante del mundo, la más gratificante y consoladora, y se requieren una delicadeza y un tino especiales para no perderlos. Creo que el secreto está en no tiranizarlos ni en exigirles más de lo que buenamente quieran darte, como y cuando puedan, en respetar su albedrío, en ser tolerante con sus defectos, y en no pretender acapararlos, poseerlos ni ejercer sobre ellos influencia de ningún tipo. Sólo así no se pierden y reaparecen siempre como un milagro, inesperado, porque sólo se tiene de verdad aquello que no se somete a las reglas de la obligatoriedad o de la posesión, lo que nace en el seno de la libertad. Yo no le temo a la soledad, me he acostumbrado a ella y la aguanto bastante mejor que la mayoría de la gente que conozco, pero siempre estoy dispuesta a quebrarla cuando un amigo viene a perfumarla con su conversación y compañía. Hablar con la gente de la más diversa condición y edad es algo que me encanta, y escuchar tanto o más que hablar. Supone una fuente inagotable de enseñanza y renuevo. Por un rato de buena conversación, lo dejaría todo.

Desde 1974 estoy enredada en un ensayo bastante ambicioso donde trato de analizar las motivaciones de la conversación y las diferencias entre la narración oral y la narración escrita. Creo que si siempre pudiera uno comunicarse con sus semejantes de forma adecuada y en el momento adecuado, no necesitaría escribir, la escritura es como un sucedáneo para paliar esta incomunicación que hoy padecemos. Pero este trabajo, que lleva el título previo de *El cuento de nunca acabar*, amenaza con ser demasiado fiel a su título porque no lo acabo nunca, abierto, como está, por naturaleza, a toda clase de interrupciones.

De octubre de 1976 a mayo de 1980 he ejercido de forma regular (todas las semanas) la crítica de libros en el periódico *Diario-16*. Esto me ha dado una visión más amplia de la literatura contemporánea española y extranjera, aportándome también nuevas ideas y enfoques que enriquecen *El cuento de nunca acabar*, al tiempo que lo interrumpen y demoran.

No sé qué más puedo decir de mí. Tal vez que tengo bastante buen carácter y que no soy derrotista: hasta en los momentos más negros trato de tener presente que siempre puede renacer la esperanza, mientras quede vida. Lo único terrible es la muerte.

Mi padre murió en octubre de 1978 y mi madre en diciembre de ese mismo año. Por quince días no se enteró de la concesión del Premio Nacional de Literatura a la novela mía que más le gustaba a ella, *El cuarto de atrás*. En la primavera del año siguiente a su muerte, 1979, asistí a un congreso de literatura española contemporánea celebrado en Yale y descubrí la ciudad más fascinante del mundo: Nueva York. Había algo de despedida de un mundo y de descubrimiento de otro en aquel viaje deslumbrador e inesperado que por una parte mitigaba la herida de la reciente pérdida de mis padres y por otra la acentuaba, cuando me daba cuenta de que ya nunca podría volver a escribirles para hacerles partícipes de mis impresiones. Nunca dejaron de alentarme en mi trabajo ni de compartir todas mis alegrías ni de esperar mis cartas, cuando estaba ausente.

Desde el hueco que me dejaron y dedicado a su memoria—que nunca me abandonará mientras tenga vida—escribo este esbozo biográfico donde he tratado de reflejar torpemente algo de la luz que a manos llenas me regalaron desde aquel mediodía luminoso y frío del 8 de diciembre en que se inclinaron a mirarme sobre la cuna. Mi madre contaba siempre que yo también los había mirado a ellos: que tenía los ojos completamente abiertos. "Como dos estrellas negras"—decía.

Madrid, junio de 1980

An Autobiographical Sketch

New translation by Joan L. Brown

I was born in Salamanca, on 8 December 1925, at high noon on a cold and sunny day. Fortune-tellers claim that being born at midday and with sunshine is a harbinger of good luck. Without wishing to detract from the sun, however, in my case I think that everything good that has happened to me in this world (as well as anything less good that I have been able to accept or convert into something better) has been due to the love of life and the confidence that my parents instilled in me from infancy. My parents were exceptional human beings. In addition to their natural goodness and their intelligence, each of them possessed a personal and very keen sense of humor, which they retained well into old age. Because of this, any conversation with them was never conventional or routine, but rather quite lively and entertaining.

My mother was Galician, from Orense. She was the daughter of Javier Gaite, a geography professor, and his wife, Sofía Veloso, neither of whom I ever knew.

My mother had come to Salamanca because her two brothers were studying at the university there. One of them, my uncle Vicente, who was a physician, was acquainted with the young notary José Martín, a widower without children, from a *tertulia* that met regularly at a local café.[1] Vicente introduced him to his sister María, my mother. The marriage-minded Salamanca girls saw what was then called a good catch in this recent widower with a brilliant career, but the only one who captivated him was that beautiful Galician with the sweet gaze who didn't have the slightest interest in "reeling him in." They fell in love and after a brief courtship were married in Madrid, where my paternal grandparents lived, on 19 May 1923. They settled in Salamanca, where my father had his office, and the following year, in February of 1924, their first child was born—my sister Ana María. She was born in a house on the Calle de la Rúa, because in those days it was not customary to give birth in a hospital.

Shortly afterward, when my mother was already pregnant with me, they moved to the house where I was born, 3 Plaza de los Bandos, which was our residence until my father was transferred to Madrid in 1950. During that move from the Calle de la Rúa to the Plaza de los Bandos, my mother was almost crushed by an extremely heavy armoire. She would tell me later that she was able to hold it back by herself, unleashing extraordinary strength, only by virtue of the terror that she felt when she realized that the accident might kill me. Fortunately some employees from my father's notary office ran to help when they heard her cries and saved us both. As a result I have always regarded that armoire as a symbol of danger, the first threat to my life averted with good fortune.

I have such a clear memory of the house on the Plaza de los Bandos, where my father had his offices on the ground floor, and that recently has been torn down, that it seems as though I can see it now. In my story "La chica de abajo" ("The Girl from Downstairs") and also in my most recent novel, *El cuarto de atrás* (*The Back Room*), I have described the house and the silent little provincial plaza that the front balconies overlooked, where I so often played with the neighborhood children. In those days there were few cars in Salamanca, and it was not the least bit dangerous to play in the street, or skate or ride a bicycle. This helped foster the fondness for space and freedom that children have, which today is frustrated and impeded by life in big cities.

I did not go to school. My father was hardly sympathetic to the education imparted by priests and nuns, and in Salamanca (a city of rigid customs and many prejudices) there were practically no schools offering a quality education that were not religious. In our early childhood my sister and I were taught drawing and languages and general culture by several private tutors, but above all it was my father who inspired us personally to love art, history, and literature.

When he finished his work and came upstairs to be with us, he would show us many books of illustrations and maps that he had in his library. It was a pleasure for him to answer all our questions, a task in which my mother also participated, raising her head from the delicate needlework that she always did and continued to do until the end of her life, or from the book that she was reading. I never remember them being bored; they made the most of everything they did and enjoyed each other's company. But they never excluded us from their intimacy, making us instead a very important part of it. They discussed most issues in our presence and took us on all their trips. I never felt that sense of abandonment or indifference that some children have when their parents suddenly disappear without explanation, leaving them in the hands of governesses or maids. Even less did I sense the segregation implicit in the traditional axiom that "children should be seen and not heard." Our childish questions were always answered.

Every summer we spent two or three months in the town of San Lorenzo de Piñor, five kilometers from Orense. It is a small village in the mountains, where my mother had also spent the summers of her youth. My grandfather Javier had had a lovely house built there, with a garden and an orchard, beside the road. It had no electricity or running water, but we found it delightful to be there. My uncle Vicente's children spent their summers in this same hamlet. The time I spent there was decisive in forming my ties with Galicia, which I have always considered my true homeland. I learned the dialect of the region and many popular songs. I became headstrong and something of a tomboy; I climbed trees and rocks, stole fruit, rode in hay wagons with squeaky wheels pulled by oxen, made friends with the children in the village, and took part in processions and pilgrimages. And—when I was a bit older—it was there that I learned to dance, had my first flirtations, and wrote my first poems. Although the house was later sold and I have not returned for many years, San Lorenzo de Piñor represents to me the essence of youth and liberty; my roots are there, and that steep and craggy landscape frequently appears in my dreams. I have situated some of my fiction, such as "Las ataduras" ("Binding Ties") and *Retahílas* ("Yarns"), in this village.

Although he was not Galician, my father also adored that land. His father was from a small town in Valladolid, and his mother was from Santander, but he had lived in Madrid from the time he was two years old, and he considered himself a native *madrileño*. In Madrid, where he had spent his entire youth and had completed his legal studies, he attended many *tertulias* of early-twentieth-century writers and artists, and from these grew his avocation of writing, which he cultivated quite successfully. Poetry came easily to him, and aside from his publications and lectures on the law he wrote children's stories, which he read to us but never published. He was an exceptional storyteller, but above all, he used to write extremely entertaining letters, full of details, in beautiful handwriting. He lost his own father, my grandfather Gumersindo, a commercial representative, when I was four, so that I barely remember him. I have even fewer memories of my grandmother Dolores, a very attractive woman who died when my father was a student. But doña Dolores López had a widowed sister, Carmen, who had always lived with my grandparents. When her brother-in-law Gumersindo became a widower, she married him—in a second wedding for both, since he also happened to be her first husband's brother. They had already been married for many years when I was born, and I remember her as my true grandmother and always treated her as such. They named me after her because she was my godmother. Besides maintaining a very impressive appearance and bearing, this woman also maintained a beautiful home at 14 Calle Mayor, where we always stayed during our frequent trips from Salamanca to Madrid. My novel *The Back Room* contains some of the impressions that those trips and Madrid itself made on me, as a provincial girl eager for broader horizons.

Shortly before the Spanish Civil War began, my parents decided to send my only sister Ana María—who was old enough to start high school—to study at the Instituto Escuela ("Institute School") of Madrid. In both its methods and its philosophy, this school inherited the liberal spirit of the famous Institución Libre de Enseñanza ("Free Institute of Education"), which had flourished from the inception of *krausismo*.[2] It was coeducational, with boys and girls together—something that in Salamanca seemed to have a sinful connotation—and religious instruction was optional rather than mandatory. (My parents were not devout, although they did go to Mass, and my sister and I had taken the First Communion, although at an older age than most children do and without wearing white dresses.) My sister came, then, to study in Madrid, and she lived with my grandmother and two elderly maids in that enormous house on the Calle Mayor. The plan was that in two years I would go to the same place to study. But the war, which broke out in the summer of '36, soon after my sister's first vacation, destroyed those plans and so many others.

We spent the entire war in Salamanca, living in fear, owing to my father's liberal ideas and those of all of his friends, many of whom—including don Miguel de Unamuno—were persecuted or imprisoned by order of General Franco, who had his general headquarters in Salamanca. As is well known, Franco repressed any hint of liberalism. They never went so far as to arrest my father, because he did not belong to any political party, but we were always told that we shouldn't discuss his antimilitary opinions with anyone. The house turned into a refuge of sorts, which strengthened our family ties. My mother's brother, Joaquín Gaite—disciple and friend of don Miguel de Unamuno—was shot and killed in August of 1936, for having a Socialist Party membership card. In *The Back Room* I have also spoken about my uncle Joaquín, a geography professor, and the influence that he had on my childhood.

I completed all of high school at the Instituto Femenino ("Girls' High School") of Salamanca, a cold, ramshackle mansion whose atmosphere I have described in my novel *Entre visillos* (*Behind the Curtains*). Girls of different social classes attended the high school, but most were of modest circumstances. From among them I gathered my first good friends, notably Sofía Bermejo. It was Sofía, the daughter of two teachers who were in jail, who initiated me into the pleasures of keeping a diary. I also began a novel with her, and together we invented the island of Bergai. (I have described all this in *The Back Room.*) At the school I had very good teachers, among them don Rafael Lapesa and don Salvador

Fernández Ramírez, both now members of the Royal Spanish Academy, whom the war had left stranded by chance in Salamanca. I think that it is to these two outstanding professors that I owe my literary vocation, as well as to the care that I devoted to my writing exercises, for the pleasure of earning their approval. In any case, both my father and mother strongly encouraged me to pursue these interests. Also as a result of my experience at the Instituto Femenino of Salamanca I overcame any potential "class consciousness" and developed the tendency to base my friendships on ideological or emotional affinities and never on considerations related to social standing.

In 1943, in the midst of the postwar era, I began my studies for a degree in Romance philology at the University of Salamanca. My academic program consisted of two years of courses that were general requirements for all areas of philosophy and letters, and three years of courses in my specialization. We were four boys and seven girls matriculated in the first year of "commons." One of those boys was Ignacio Aldecoa, who became one of the most important prose writers of the postwar era, and another was the poet Agustín García Calvo, currently a professor of classical languages at the University of Madrid and an excellent writer. In my article "Un aviso: Ha muerto Ignacio" ("A Bulletin: Ignacio Has Died"), written on the death of Aldecoa in 1969, I have spoken of both men, and also of the atmosphere of the University of Salamanca in those postwar years.

At the university I worked on the magazine *Trabajos y días* ("Works and Days"), where my first poems saw the light (some of them collected now in my little book *A rachas* ["In a Gust of Wind"]). I also acted in the university theater, under the direction of literature professor don César Real de la Riva; in consecutive years, for example, we performed several short plays by Cervantes and Shakespeare's *The Merchant of Venice*. The theater was almost as passionate a love of mine as literature, and the temptation to try to become a professional actress occurred to me more than once. But the atmosphere of those years and my situation as a young bourgeois girl were not very conducive to that dream. I abandoned it without regret, since literature still appealed to me more than anything. I read many classic works, including plays, poetry, and prose, and devoured with great relish almost all of the novels of the Generation of '98 that my father had in his library. And also those of a Portuguese writer who is not well known but whom I adore: Eça de Queiroz.

In the summer of 1946 I was awarded a scholarship to the Portuguese University of Coimbra, and for the first time I traveled abroad. What's more, I went alone, which was exciting, since at that time it was not customary for a young woman to travel unaccompanied. Portugal, perhaps because of its linguistic ties with Galicia, is a country that has always fascinated me, and I am strongly attracted to its customs and its literature. I spent two months in Coimbra, and also got to know Oporto and Lisbon. During this period I decided to do my doctoral dissertation on the Galician-Portuguese songbooks of the thirteenth century, and I began to take notes for this project.

In 1948 I received my degree in Romance philology, and that same year I was given another scholarship, this time for summer school at the University of Cannes. That interlude was unforgettable. During those courses at Cannes I came into contact with many French authors whom I had not read: Sartre, Camus, Saint-Exupéry, Gide, Proust, et cetera; I became much more fluent in French and, above all, at the age of twenty-two, I got my first real taste of freedom. I danced in *boîtes* ("nightclubs"), I took part in "flower battles,"[3] I played roulette. I interacted with students from other countries, with an open mind; I went to bed whenever I felt like it; and I decided that I did not want to continue living in Salamanca. Never before had the idea of leaving my family and my city been so crystal clear in my mind.

When I returned to Salamanca, I told my parents that I wanted to go to Madrid to work and to prepare my doctorate; that Salamanca had become an environment that was too familiar and too restricting, that it bored me.

From November of 1948 until the spring of 1949 I lived alone in Madrid. My grandmother had recently died, and some of the furniture from the Calle Mayor house had been moved to a small apartment that my father bought in Madrid. My grandmother's elderly maids, Paula and Marcelina, who were like part of the family, lived there. I stayed with them during that time, but I came and went whenever I pleased, and I brought home many friends. In Madrid I renewed my friendship with my old schoolmate Ignacio Aldecoa. He introduced me to many people whom he knew, and they began to form my group: Medardo Fraile, Alfonso Sastre, Jesús Fernández Santos, and Rafael Sánchez Ferlosio, among others. None of them was a very good student or dreamed of becoming a professor; all carried the virus of literature in their blood and started to contribute to Madrid magazines such as *La hora*, *La estafeta literaria*, *Clavileño*, *Alférez*, *El español*, and *Alcalá*. Once involved with these friends, I began to lose interest in graduate school. Progress on my doctoral dissertation, which I had begun on the Galician-Portuguese songbooks and which gradually started to bore me, slowed down considerably. Also contributing to my boredom was the fact that the old professor whom I had chosen to direct my dissertation, don Armando Cotarelo, was an apathetic man who never encouraged me and whom I saw only twice. I worked alone, with no incentive and like a lost soul in the library of the Consejo de Investigaciones Científicas ("Council for Scientific Investigation"). I began to write stories and articles and to see them published in some of the magazines mentioned. I went often to cafés, to the theater, to taverns, and for strolls with my new friends, much less university-oriented than I, much more bohemian, all of them very good writers. I also met poets, painters, actresses, and journalists. Madrid seemed to me to be a fascinating city. I had already decided that I wanted to live there forever.

To earn some money, I worked during the week preparing note cards for a dictionary that was being compiled by the Royal Spanish Academy. They would give me books with certain words underlined, and my job consisted of putting the word on the upper part of the note card, underlined and in capital letters, and beneath it a quotation indicating its context and the reference for the book in which the phrase appeared. They paid me fifteen *céntimos* (cents) per card, but since I worked very quickly, I could earn a bit of money. With the first payment I collected, I bought myself a green velvet dress.

Every morning I went to the university, because I was registered in courses that were required for the doctorate. I was unable to take exams in any of them, however, because at the end of the semester, in May, I caught typhus and developed an extremely high fever. Penicillin had not yet arrived in Spain, and typhus was a very serious illness. My mother came to take care of me, and when I did not improve, she had me moved to Salamanca in an ambulance, on the advice of my uncle Vicente, who was our family doctor. I spent nearly forty days in bed, at death's door, and I was delirious for much of the time. That summer, after I recovered, I began to write a book entitled *El libro de la fiebre* ("The Book of Fever"). There, in a poetic and surrealistic format, I tried to recapture the ephemeral images of my delirium. I was very enthusiastic about the book, and it seemed very lovely to me. But Rafael Sánchez Ferlosio, to whom I showed it a few months later when I saw him again in Madrid, told me that it wasn't any good, that it had turned out to be vague and chaotic. So I had only a few excerpts from it published, in *La hora* ("The Hour"), if I remember correctly.

That same summer of 1949, my father decided to ask for a transfer to Madrid. In the fall we left our house on the Plaza de los Bandos for good. We moved, and by the beginning of 1950 the whole family was living in Madrid, in an apartment at 35 Alcalá Street, where my parents lived until their death in 1978 and where my sister Ana María, who never married, still lives.

During that first stage of my life in Madrid with my family, I taught classes in history, grammar, and literature at a girls' high school. I was popular with the girls; but since my classes were far from conventional and I also looked very young, they had no respect for me whatsoever. They made a lot of commotion in class, and the principal ended up firing me. Then I worked as a clerk in my father's office in the mornings. He had his office on the second floor of the building, and our residence was on the fourth. It wasn't a job that I liked very much, but it gave me some money while waiting for better times.

In January of 1950 I became engaged to Rafael Sánchez Ferlosio. He was two years younger than I and a poor student, but an excellent writer. He dedicated his first book to me, *Industrias y andanzas de Alfanhuí* (*Adventures of the Ingenious Alfanhuí*), and soon afterward he went to fulfill his military service in Morocco.[4] We wrote to each other frequently, and for me it was the first time in my life that I was so in love and so influenced by anyone. I had completely abandoned my doctoral thesis, just as I had stopped planning to compete for an academic position. My experience with those girls from the school on Martínez Campos Street had revealed to me that I had little talent for teaching.

On 14 October 1953 I married Rafael Sánchez Ferlosio, who had finished his military service but not his degree. With Sastre and Aldecoa, he had just founded the *Revista española* ("Spanish Review"). Economically it was a disaster, but copies of the journal are now much sought after by scholars, because all of us prose writers of the so-called generation of the 1950s collaborated on it. On the advice of Rafael and Aldecoa I abandoned the lyrical tone of my early works and became more rigorous and demanding in my writing. My story "La chica de abajo" ("The Girl from Downstairs"), which they liked a lot, is undoubtedly my first creditable narrative, and in it there are already many of the elements and themes that I later developed more fully. Despite the fact that he had found a modest job as secretary to an engineer, Rafael and I intended to earn a living from our literary efforts.

After we got married, we spent several months in Rome, at the home of Rafael's maternal grandparents, on the Piazza de Santa Maria sopra Minerva, where he was born. We later returned to that house on many other occasions. Rafael's grandparents were delightful people, and we developed a strong mutual affection. His grandmother Ida taught me to cook, since I didn't know how, and she spent her spare time talking with me. We also traveled to Naples, Florence, and Venice. Italy became a part of me; moreover, I came in contact with the contemporary literature of the country, which influenced me greatly, especially the work of Pavese and Svevo. We were also in Paris.

From the time I got married, I have lived in Madrid, in a seventh-floor apartment at 43 Doctor Esquerdo Street, which my father gave us and which has a large terrace. (I described it in great detail in my last novel, *The Back Room*, during the conversation with the man dressed in black who visited me one night.)

We never had a maid. We shared the domestic chores and worked completely independently of each another. We maintained the same independence in everything, neither of us interfering in the friendships or idiosyncrasies of the other, while continually welcoming good friends. He wrote mainly at night, and I also became quite nocturnal and was not bound to any schedule. Neither of us liked excessive luxury or formal meals; what united us most was our pleasure in talking and our sense of humor, although he is more critical than I, more maladjusted and less sociable.

In the spring of 1954 I received the Café Gijón Prize for my short novel *El balneario* ("The Spa"). As with the novels I wrote subsequently, Rafael did not read it until it was finished. I did not want to be influenced by his criticism, which often discouraged me. I preferred that he deliver his criticism when the book was already in press.

In October of that same year, 1954, our first child, Miguel, was born. He died of meningitis in May of the following year, when Rafael had just finished writing *El Jarama* (*The River: El Jarama*). This was the first time in my life that I experienced how the ground can fall out from under you suddenly, when you least expect it, and I understood viscerally what I had always known in a more or less abstract way: the precarious, vulnerable, ephemeral nature of happiness. The death of my first child taught me to never again give much importance to minor irritations; it was my first step toward maturity, and I wanted to have another child more than I had ever wanted anything in this world.

On 22 May 1956, my daughter Marta was born. I have not had any more children.

In 1957 I finished my first long novel, *Entre visillos* (*Behind the Curtains*), and I sent it to the Nadal Prize Committee, without telling anyone, using the pseudonym Sofía Veloso (the name of my maternal grandmother). Rafael had won the prize two years before, with *El Jarama*, and I didn't want the fact that I was his wife to influence the jury in any way. I won the Nadal Prize on 6 January 1958. I heard the news on the radio, when I was home alone with my daughter asleep in her cradle.

Since it is not my intention here to repeat my list of publications, which the reader will find covered in the text by Joan Lipman Brown that follows, I will limit myself to saying that the Nadal Prize helped publish my books, since at the time it was the most important prize awarded in Spain, and it reaffirmed my goal of continuing to write forever. Aside from that, it represented significant economic relief, because the novel sold very well.

In the following years I fulfilled my domestic, maternal, and literary roles concurrently, with a new surge of interest in scholarship. I began to concentrate on the Spanish eighteenth century, since there were huge gaps in my knowledge of that period. I would do my research at the library of the Ateneo ("Atheneum") of Madrid, which closes at one in the morning. I usually went after eight in the evening, after putting my daughter to bed, and quite often, when the bell rang to announce the closing of the Ateneo, I was the only reader left in the room. In the course of this belated mission as an autodidact, my interest was aroused by a very contradictory character, pursued by the Inquisition, about whom no one had done a serious study: don Melchor de Macanaz. To follow his trail I abandoned my literary works, I buried myself in archives, I made trips to Simancas and Paris, and after seven years of tenacious investigation, I had gathered sufficient information for a biography, which appeared in 1970. As I was sorting through the documents in those archives, I also had my curiosity awakened by the love and courtship customs of the eighteenth century; after finishing with old Macanaz, I continued to research this topic. Those investigations culminated in a second work, *Usos amorosos del siglo XVIII en España* (*Love Customs in Eighteenth-Century Spain*). Before publishing it, I thought it might serve me as a doctoral dissertation in order to complete, albeit much later, that brilliant university career I had begun in Salamanca, which had been cut short when I came to Madrid. I didn't plan to devote myself to university teaching, but I have always liked to finish what I start. So that is how in 1972, already turning gray, I defended my dissertation at the University of Madrid. On the committee were my old professors Rafael Lapesa and Alonso Zamora Vicente, the latter as dissertation director. They awarded me the Extraordinary Prize, and there was no doubt that my case was indeed quite extraordinary for being so unexpected.

And here ends—at least for now—this hiatus of almost ten years during which I was dedicated to research, mainly because I realized one thing: that archives are very absorbing, and that once you get involved in them unconditionally, you will be trapped for life by the imperceptible poison they secrete. And I was eager to return to fiction, which I had abandoned since the publication of *Ritmo lento* ("A Slower Rhythm") in 1962.

Since the fall of 1970 I have lived alone with my daughter Marta, in the same apartment on Doctor Esquerdo that I shared with Rafael for seventeen years. Our separation was amicable, and we continue to see each other often. He comes here whenever he likes. I am very fond of this home, and it has never occurred to me to move to another; there is no place where I feel as comfortable as I do here. My daughter is currently finishing her studies in English philology, and she already does translations and teaches classes at a school, where they seem to respect her more than those girls respected me long ago. My daughter and I are good friends; we laugh a lot together and tell each other everything.

Except for one eight-month period in 1973, when I worked at the Salvat Publishing House, I have never held a job that involved a fixed schedule, and it can be said that I have lived exclusively by the pen, as was my wish. I have done critical editions, translations, prefaces, articles, screenplays, adaptations of classics, and radio scripts, and I have even sung Galician songs in a theater. But even at the cost of living more modestly, I have always avoided any employment that might enslave me and steal time from reading, writing, and another favorite passion: the cultivation of friendship. For me friends are the most important thing in the world, the most gratifying and consoling, and they require a special kind of tact and sensitivity so as not to lose them. I think that the secret lies in not tyrannizing them or demanding more than they are able to give you, however and whenever they can; in respecting their free will; in being tolerant of their faults; and in not trying to monopolize them, possess them, or exert any kind of influence over them. This is the only way not to lose them, to have them always reappear like a miracle, unexpectedly, because one truly possesses only what is not subjected to the rules of obligation or possession, what is born free. I am not afraid of being alone; I have become accustomed to it, and I tolerate it better than most of the people I know. But I am always ready to break my solitude when a friend comes to perfume it with conversation and company. Talking with people of the most diverse backgrounds and ages is something that delights me, and listening as much as or more than speaking. It represents an inexhaustible source of learning and renewal. For a bit of good conversation I would drop everything.

Since 1974 I have been involved in a very ambitious treatise where I try to analyze the motives of conversation, and the differences between spoken and written narration. I think that if one could always communicate with one's peers in the right way and at the right time, there would be no need to write. Writing is like a substitute used to alleviate the lack of communication that we suffer today. This work, which carries the previously-given title of *El cuento de nunca acabar* ("The Never-Ending Tale"), threatens to be too faithful to its title, because I never manage to finish it, open as it is by its very nature to all types of interruptions.

From October 1976 to May 1980 I have written weekly book reviews for the newspaper *Diario-16*. Doing so has given me a broader view of contemporary Spanish and international literature, bringing me new ideas and viewpoints that enrich "The Never-Ending Tale," at the same time that they interrupt and delay it.

I don't know what else I can say about myself. Perhaps that I am basically good-natured and not a pessimist: even in the darkest moments I try to keep in mind that hope may always be reborn, while there is life. The only truly terrible thing is death.

My father died in October 1978, and my mother in December of the same year. By fifteen days she missed hearing that the National Prize for Literature had been awarded to the novel of mine that she liked best, *The Back Room*. In the spring of the year after her death, 1979, I attended a conference on contemporary Spanish literature held at Yale and discovered the most fascinating city in the world: New York. There was something of a farewell to one world and the discovery of another in that dazzling and unexpected trip, which on one hand assuaged the wound of the recent loss of my parents and on the other hand accentuated it, when I realized that now I could never again write to them to share my impressions. They never stopped encouraging me in my work, or sharing all my joys, or waiting for my letters when I was away.

I write this autobiographical sketch from the empty space that they left in me and dedicate it to their memory, which will be with me for as long as I live. I have tried here to reflect, dimly, some of the light that they so generously gave me, ever since that bright and cold midday of the eighth of December when they leaned over my cradle to look at me. My mother always told me that I also looked at them—that I had my eyes wide open. "Like two black stars," she used to say.

Madrid, June 1980

NOTES

1 The Spanish profession of notary is different from the American position of notary public. In Spain, a notary is a specialized attorney, with some of the responsibilities of a judge. A Spanish *tertulia* is a gathering of people who meet regularly to discuss literature, art, politics, sports, or other topics.

2 *Krausismo* was a German philosophical doctrine formulated by Karl C. F. Krause (1781–1832), a disciple of Kant and colleague of Schelling and Hegel. The Spanish intellectual Julián Sanz del Río brought Krause's ideas to Spain in the late 1850s and attracted a coterie of important thinkers who agreed that a balance must be maintained among reason, science, and religion. The most important legacy of *krausismo* in Spain was its enormous influence on education. Self-teaching, freedom of thought, and tolerance were cornerstones of the educational system endorsed by Spanish proponents of

Krause's doctrine. The Instituto Libre de Enseñanza ("Free Institute of Education") was founded in 1876 by Franciso Giner de los Ríos.

[3]To celebrate local holidays and other events, so-called flower battles were very popular along the Spanish Costa del Sol and the French Côte d'Azure in the 1940s. These battles consisted of open cars full of flowers in which beautiful young women rode, dressed in formal gowns. The women tossed flowers to bystanders as the procession moved through a town. Before this summer, the author had seen flower battles but had never ridden in a car as a participant. (Personal communication from Carmen Martin Gaite, 26 Oct. 1980, New York.)

[4]He served in Tetuán (Tetouan), which from 1913 to 1956 was the capital of the Spanish protectorate in Morocco.

Appendix B: Selected Bibliography of the Works of Carmen Martín Gaite

This list gives first editions, subsequent editions with added content, teaching editions, and recent editions. Unless otherwise indicated, the medium is print.

Fiction

"Las ataduras." In *Las ataduras*. Barcelona: Destino, 1960; pref. Ana María Moix (1978), Madrid: Siruela, 2011, 15–67. The collection *Las ataduras* contains the eponymous novella and six short stories: "Tendrá que volver," "Un alto en el camino," "La tata," "Lo que queda enterrado," "La conciencia tranquila," and "La mujer de cera."

"El balneario." In *El balneario*. Madrid: Afrodisio Aguado, 1955; Madrid: Siruela, 2010, 14–77. The collection *El Balneario* first contained the eponymous novella and three short stories: "Los informes," "Un día de libertad," and "La chica de abajo." In the 1968 edition, "La oficina," "La trastienda de los ojos," "Ya ni me acuerdo," and "Variaciones sobre un tema" were added. In the 1977 edition, "Tarde de tedio" and "Retirada" were added.

Caperucita en Manhattan. Madrid: Siruela, 1990, 2010.

El castillo de las tres murallas. Barcelona: Lumen, 1981; in *Dos cuentos maravillosos* (1993), Madrid: Siruela, 2009, 19–75.

El cuarto de atrás. Barcelona: Destino, 1978; Madrid: Siruela, 2009.

Cuentos completos. Madrid: Alianza, 1978, 2007. Contains *El balneario* and *Las ataduras*.

Cuentos completos y un monólogo. 3rd ed. Barcelona: Anagrama, 1994. Contains *El balneario*, *Las ataduras*, and *A palo seco*.

Dos cuentos maravillosos. Madrid: Siruela, 1993, 2009. Contains *El castillo de las tres murallas* and *El pastel del diablo*.

Dos relatos fantásticos. Barcelona: Lumen, 1986. Contains *El castillo de las tres murallas* and *El pastel del diablo*.

Entre visillos. Barcelona: Destino, 1958; introd. Marina Mayoral, Madrid: Espasa Calpe, 2007; Barcelona: Destino, 2008.

Fragmentos de interior. Barcelona: Destino, 1976, 2001.

Irse de casa. Barcelona: Anagrama, 1998.

Nubosidad variable. Barcelona: Anagrama, 1992, 2007.

El pastel del diablo. Barcelona: Lumen, 1983; in *Dos cuentos maravillosos* (1993), Madrid: Siruela, 2009. 77–156.

Lo raro es vivir. Barcelona: Anagrama, 1996, 2006.

La Reina de las Nieves. Barcelona: Anagrama, 1994, 2008.

Retahílas. Barcelona: Destino, 1974, 2003; ed. Montserrat Escarpín Gual, Barcelona: Crítica, 2003; Madrid: Siruela, 2009.

Ritmo lento. Barcelona: Seix Barral, 1963; Barcelona: Destino, 1975 (with epilogue restored); introd. José-Carlos Mainer, Barcelona: Destino, 2007; Madrid: Siruela, 2009.

Todos los cuentos. Barcelona: Destino, 1994, 2005. Contains *El balneario* and *Las ataduras*.

Nonfiction

Agua pasada: Artículos, prólogos y discursos. Barcelona: Anagrama, 1993.

La búsqueda de interlocutor y otras búsquedas. Madrid: Nostromo, 1973; Barcelona: Anagrama, 2000.

El conde de Guadalhorce, su época y su labor. Madrid: Colegio de Ingenieros de Caminos, Canales, y Puertos, 1977; Madrid: Turner, 1983; Madrid: Tabla Rasa, 2003.

El cuento de nunca acabar: Apuntes sobre la narración, el amor y la mentira. Madrid: Trieste, 1983; Madrid: Siruela, 2009.

Desde la ventana: Enfoque femenino de la literatura española. Madrid: Espasa-Calpe, 1987, 1999.

"De su ventana a la mía." *Madres e hijas*. Ed. Laura Freixas. 1996. Barcelona: Anagrama, 2006. 39–44.

Esperando el porvenir: Homenaje a Ignacio Aldecoa. 1994. Madrid: Siruela, 2006; Madrid: Punto de Lectura, 2007.

Macanaz, otro paciente de la Inquisición, 2nd ed., Madrid: Taurus, 1975; Barcelona: Destino, 1982. Rpt. as *El proceso de Macanaz: Historia de un empapelamiento* (1970), Barcelona: Anagrama, 1988.

Usos amorosos de la postguerra española. Barcelona: Anagrama, 1987, 2007.

Usos amorosos del dieciocho en España. Madrid: Siglo XXI de España, 1972; Barcelona: Anagrama, 1988.

Poetry

A rachas. Madrid: Hiperión, 1979, 1986.

Después de todo: Poesía a rachas. Ed. Jesús Munárriz. Madrid: Hiperión, 1993, 2001.

Screenplays

Celia. Episodes by Carmen Martín Gaite and José Luis Borau; adapt. *Celia*, by Elena Fortún; dir. José Luis Borau; perf. Ana Duato, Cristina Cruz, and Pedro Díez del Corral; RTVE, 1992. Television <http://www.rtve.es/television/celia/>.

Emilia, parada y fonda. By Carmen Martín Gaite and Juan Tébar. Adapt. "Un alto en el camino," by Carmen Martín Gaite; dir. Angelino Fons; perf. Ana Belén, Francisco Rabal, María Luisa San José, and Juan Diego; Cámara P.C., 1976. Film.

Teresa de Jesús. Episodes by Carmen Martín Gaite and Victor García de la Concha; dir. Josefina Molina; perf. Concha Velasco, Francisco Rabal, and Héctor Alterio; RTVE, 1983. Television.

Stage Plays

A palo seco. In *Cuentos completos y un monólogo,* 311–44.

La hermana pequeña. Barcelona: Anagrama, 1999, 2001.

Textbook

Brown, Joan L., and Carmen Martín Gaite. *Conversaciones creadoras: Mastering Spanish Conversation*, Boston: Heath, 1994; 3rd ed., Boston: Houghton, 2006. Print and audio CDs.

Posthumously Published Works

"La charca." In *Novelas I*, 2009, 1105–83.

Cuadernos de todo. Ed. Maria Vittoria Calvi, pref. Rafael Chirbes. Barcelona: Círculo de Lectores, 2002; Barcelona: Debate, 2002; Barcelona: De Bolsillo. 2003.

El libro de la fiebre. Ed. Maria Vittoria Calvi. Madrid: Cátedra, 2007.

Narrativa breve, poesía y teatro. Ed. José Teruel, pref. Carmen Valcárcel, Barcelona: Círculo de Lectores, 2010. Vol. 3 of *Obras completas*.

Novelas I: 1955–1978. Ed. José Teruel, pref. José-Carlos Mainer. Barcelona: Círculo de Lectores, 2008. Vol. 1 of *Obras completas*.

Novelas II: 1979–2000. Ed. José Teruel, pref. Elide Pitarello. Barcelona: Círculo de Lectores, 2009. Vol. 2 of *Obras completas*.

Los parentescos. Pref. Belén Gopegui. Barcelona: Anagrama, 2001; Barcelona: Anagrama, 2003.

Pido la palabra. Pref. José Luis Borau. Barcelona: Anagrama, 2002.

Poemas. Barcelona: Círculo de Lectores, 2001. Print and audio CD.

Tirando del hilo: Artículos, 1949–2000. Ed. José Teruel. Madrid: Siruela, 2006; Madrid: Punto de Lectura, 2007.

Visión de Nueva York. Barcelona: Círculo de Lectores, 2005.

Martín Gaite, Carmen, and Juan Benet. *Correspondencia.* Ed. José Teruel. Barcelona: Galaxia Gutenberg; Círculo de Lectores, 2011.

English Translations

Fiction

The Back Room. Trans. Helen R. Lane. New York: Columbia UP, 1983; San Francisco: City Lights, 2000. Trans. of *El cuarto de atrás*.

Behind the Curtains. Trans. Frances M. López-Morillas. New York: Columbia UP, 1990. Trans. of *Entre visillos*.

The Farewell Angel. Trans. Margaret Jull Costa. London: Harvill, 1999. Trans. of *La Reina de las Nieves*.

Living's the Strange Thing. Trans. Anne McLean. London: Harvill, 2004. Trans. of *Lo raro es vivir.*

Variable Cloud. Trans. Margaret Jull Costa. London: Harvill, 1995. Trans. of *Nubosidad variable*.

Nonfiction

Courtship Customs in Postwar Spain. Trans. Margaret E. W. Jones. Lewisburg: Bucknell UP, 2004. Trans. of *Usos amorosos de la postguerra española*.

Love Customs in Eighteenth-Century Spain. Trans. Maria G. Tomsich. Berkeley: U of California P, 1991. Trans. of *Usos amorosos del dieciocho en España*.

"The Virtues of Reading." Trans. Marcia L. Welles. *PMLA* 104.3 (1989) 348–53.

NOTES ON CONTRIBUTORS

Josefa Álvarez is associate professor of Spanish at Le Moyne College. She has published articles on classical motifs, the female lyrical voice and expressions of desire in the poetry of Aurora Luque. She has written a book entitled "Fabricación de las islas: Aurora Luque: Poesía y metapoesía" and a book entitled "Tradición clásica en la poesía de Aurora Luque: Figuras, formas, ideas."

Frieda H. Blackwell is professor of Spanish and associate dean for humanities in the College of Arts and Sciences of Baylor University. She is the author of *The Game of Literature: Demythification and Parody in Novels of Gonzalo Torrente Ballester* (1985) and the coauthor, with Paul E. Larson, of *Guía básica a la crítica literaria y al trabajo de investigación* (2007).

Joan L. Brown is Elias Ahuja Professor of Spanish at the University of Delaware. She is the author of *Secrets from the Back Room: The Fiction of Carmen Martín Gaite* (1987) and *Confronting Our Canons: Spanish and Latin American Studies in the Twenty-First Century* (2010). She is the editor of *Women Writers of Contemporary Spain: Exiles in the Homeland* (1991). With Carmen Martín Gaite, she wrote the textbook *Conversaciones creadoras: Mastering Spanish Conversation* (1994).

Isabel Estrada is assistant professor of Spanish at City College, City University of New York. In her essays she has analyzed works by the writers Rosalía de Castro, Juan Benet, and Pedro Maestre and by the filmmakers José Luis Guerín and José Luis Garci. She is the author of *El documental cinematográfico y televisivo contemporáneo: Memoria, sujeto y formación de la identidad democrática española*.

Carlos Feal is professor emeritus of Spanish at the State University of New York, Buffalo. He is the author of books on Pedro Salinas, Federico García Lorca, Miguel de Unamuno, the Don Juan myth, and ekphrasis (with Rosemary G. Feal), as well as articles on Rosalía de Castro, Benito Pérez Galdós, Emilia Pardo Bazán, Ramón del Valle-Inclán, Carmen Laforet, Luis Martín-Santos, Carmen Martín Gaite, and others. He is also the author of a novel, *Vidas y muertes mías* (2010), and a collection of short stories, *Yo, profesor, me confieso* (2012).

María Fernández Babineaux Lamarque is associate professor and director of the Spanish graduate program at Texas A&M University, Commerce. She has written on Jorge Luis Borges, Mario Vargas Llosa, José Saramago, Clarice Lispector, Cristina Peri Rossi, Carmen Boullosa, Patrícia Galvão, Ana María Matute, Antonio Robles, and Carmen Laforet. She is completing two manuscripts, on censored children's literature in Spain and on dystopias by Latin American Boom writers.

Ofelia Ferrán is associate professor in the Department of Spanish and Portuguese Studies at the University of Minnesota, Twin Cities. She is the author of *Working through Memory: Writing and Remembrance in Contemporary Spanish Narrative* (2007) and the coeditor, with Kathleen M. Glenn, of *Women's Narrative and Film in Twentieth-Century Spain: A World of Difference(s)* (2002).

Soledad Fox is associate professor of Spanish and comparative literature at Williams College. She is the author of *Flaubert and Don Quixote: The Influence of Cervantes on* Madame Bovary (2009) and *Constancia de la Mora in War and Exile: International Voice of the Spanish Republic* (2007). She is currently working on a book about Jorge Semprún.

Emily C. Francomano is associate professor in the Department of Spanish and Portuguese at Georgetown University. She is the author of *Wisdom and Her Lovers in Medieval and Early Modern Hispanic Literature* (2008), the editor and translator of *Three Spanish Querelle Texts:* Grisel and Mirabella, The Slander against Women, *and* The Defense of Ladies against Slanderers (2013), and is writing a book entitled "Prisons of Love: Translation and the Matter of Romance in the Sixteenth Century."

Jacqueline Gowen-Tolcott teaches French and Spanish at Friends' Central School in Wynnewood, Pennsylvania. She has led student groups to Mexico, France, and Spain. Since her childhood in Havana, Cuba, she has explored different languages and cultures, with a special interest in literature and history.

María Luisa Guardiola is professor of Spanish at Swarthmore College. She is the author of *La temática de García Gutiérrez: Índice y estudio: La mujer* (1993) and the editor of *Pepita Jiménez*, by Juan Valera (2001), and *El trovador*, by Antonio García Gutiérrez (2006). She has worked on Clementina Arderiu, Benito Pérez Galdós, Emilia Pardo Bazán, Caterina Albert, Carme Riera, and Carmen Martín Gaite.

Jessamy Harvey is lecturer in Iberian and Latin American studies in Birkbeck College of the University of London. She is finishing a book on sanctity, Catholicism, and girlhood in twentieth-century Spain.

David K. Herzberger is distinguished professor and chair of the Department of Hispanic Studies at the University of California, Riverside. He is the author of *Narrating the Past: Fiction and Historiography in Postwar Spain* (1995) and of books on Juan Benet, Jesús Fernández Santos, and Javier Marías.

Roberta Johnson is professor emerita of Spanish at the University of Kansas. She is the author of *Carmen Laforet* (1981), *El ser y la palabra en Gabriel Miró* (1985), *Crossfire: Philosophy and the Novel in Spain, 1900–1930* (1993), *Las bibliotecas de Azorín* (1996), and *Gender and Nation in the Spanish Modernist Novel* (2003) and coeditor of *Antología del pensamiento feminista español, 1726–2011* (2012).

Vilma Navarro-Daniels is associate professor of Spanish at Washington State University. She is the author of essays on Carmen Martín Gaite's novels *Irse de casa* and *Lo raro es vivir* and on Paloma Pedrero, Concha Romero, Antonio Muñoz Molina, Daniel Calparsoro, Manuel Martínez Mediero, Ignacio Martínez de Pisón, and Pedro Almodóvar.

Patricia O'Byrne is lecturer in Hispanic studies and comparative literature in the School of Applied Language and Intercultural Studies of Dublin City University. She is the coeditor, with Gabrielle Carty and Niamh Thornton, of *Transcultural Encounters amongst Women: Redrawing Boundaries in Hispanic and Lusophone Art, Literature and Film* (2010). She is writing a book entitled "Postwar Spanish Women Novelists and the Recuperation of Historical Memory."

Janet Pérez is Paul Whitfield Horn Professor of Romance languages and Blaise Qualia Chair of Spanish at Texas Tech University. She is the author of *Camilo José Cela Revisited: The Later Works* (2000), *Homenaje a Francisco Ayala en su centenario* (2006), and *El exilio español del 39: Las mujeres* (2011) and has edited volumes on Spanish literature by women, exile literature, and the Spanish Civil War in literature.

Randolph D. Pope is commonwealth professor of Spanish and comparative literature at the University of Virginia. He is the author of *Novela de emergencia: España, 1939–1954* (1984) and *Understanding Juan Goytisolo* (1995) and the coeditor, with Christine Henseler, of *Generation X Rocks: Contemporary Peninsular Fiction, Film, and Rock Culture* (2007). He is researching the unusual case of an international bestseller that also garnered critical esteem.

Dale J. Pratt is professor of Spanish and comparative literature at Brigham Young University. He is the author of *Signs of Science: Literature, Science, and Spanish Modernity since 1868* (2002) and *Sueños, Recuerdos, Memoria: La metaficción en las novelas de Joaquín-Armando Chacón* (1994).

Lissette Rolón Collazo is professor in the Comparative Literature Program at the University of Puerto Rico at Mayagüez. She is the author of *Figuraciones: Mujeres en Carmen Martín Gaite, revistas feministas y ¡Hola!* (2002) and *Historias que cuentan . . . : El motín contra Esquilache en Madrid y las mujeres dieciochescas según voces del XVIII, XIX y XX*. (2009).

José Teruel is professor of Spanish literature at the Universidad Autónoma de Madrid. He is the author of *Otro marco teórico para el medio siglo: La poesía de Miguel Fernández* (2000), *La joven poesía española del medio siglo* (2001) and *Los años americanos de Luis Cernuda, 1947–1963* (2012). He is the editor of *Cinco lecturas de Luis Cernuda en su centenario* (2002) and many of the posthumously published works of Carmen Martín Gaite.

SURVEY PARTICIPANTS

Josefa Álvarez, *Le Moyne College*
Samuel Amago, *University of Notre Dame*
Catherine G. Bellver, *University of Nevada, Las Vegas*
Frieda H. Blackwell, *Baylor University*
María Elena Bravo-Guerreira, *Dominican University*
Joan L. Brown, *University of Delaware*
Debra Castillo, *Cornell University*
Isabel Estrada, *City College, City University of New York*
Carlos Feal, *State University of New York, Buffalo*
María Fernández Babineaux Lamarque, *Texas A&M University, Commerce*
Ofelia Ferrán, *University of Minnesota, Twin Cities*
Soledad Fox, *Williams College*
Emily C. Francomano, *Georgetown University*
David T. Gies, *University of Virginia*
Francisca González-Arias, *University of Massachusetts, Lowell*
Jacqueline Gowen-Tolcott, *Friends' Central School, PA*
Margaret R. Greer, *Duke University*
María Luisa Guardiola, *Swarthmore College*
Jessamy Harvey, *University of London, Birkbeck College*
David K. Herzberger, *University of California, Riverside*
Roberta Johnson, *University of Kansas*
Carol Maier, *Kent State University*
Adelaida Martínez, *University of Nebraska, Lincoln*
Kathleen McNerney, *West Virginia University, Morgantown*
Vilma Navarro-Daniels, *Washington State University, Pullman*
Patricia O'Bryne, *Dublin City University*
Yolanda Pascual Solé, *University of Birmingham*
Janet Pérez, *Texas Tech University*
Randolph D. Pope, *University of Virginia*
Dale J. Pratt, *Brigham Young University, UT*
Lissette Rolón Collazo, *University of Puerto Rico, Mayagüez*
José Teruel, *Universidad Autónoma de Madrid*
María Alejandra Zanetta, *University of Akron*

WORKS CITED

Abbott, H. Porter. *The Cambridge Introduction to Narrative*. Cambridge: Cambridge UP, 2002. Print.

Alborch, Carmen. *Solas: Gozos y sombras de una manera de vivir*. Madrid: Temas de Hoy, 1999. Print.

Allende, Isabel. *Cuentos de Eva Luna*. Barcelona: Debolsillo, 2010. Print.

———. *The Stories of Eva Luna*. Trans. Margaret Sayers Peden. London: Penguin, 2011. Print.

Álvarez, María Edmée, ed. *Cuentos de Perrault*. By Charles Perrault. México: Porrúa, 1974. Print.

Andersen, Hans Christian. "The Snow Queen." *Fairytalescollection.com*. Fairytales collection.com, n.d. Web. 8 July 2012.

Andreu, Alicia G. "La Sección Femenina de la Falange en la obra de Carmen Martín Gaite: La popularidad de las novelas rosa en la posguerra española." *Revista de estudios hispánicos* 36.1 (2002): 145–57. Print.

Arenal, Concepción. *La emancipación de la mujer en España*. Ed. Mauro Armiño. Madrid: Biblioteca Júcar, 1974. Print.

Ariès, Philippe. *Centuries of Childhood: A Social History of Family Life*. Trans. Robert Baldick. London: Cape, 1962. Print.

Auerbach, Nina. Introduction. *Old Maids to Radical Spinsters: Unmarried Women in the Twentieth-Century Novel*. By Laura L. Doan. Urbana: U of Illinois P, 1991. ix–xv. Print.

Aznárez, M. "La rebeldía de una mujer modosa." *El país semanal* 225 (1981): 11–14. Print.

Baker, Martin. *Comics: Ideology, Power, and the Critics*. Manchester: Manchester UP, 1989. Print.

Bal, Mieke. *Teoría de la narrativa: Una introducción a la narratología*. Trans. Javier Franco. Madrid: Cátedra, 1990. Print.

Balfour, Sebastian. "Spain from 1931 to the Present." Carr, *Spain: A History* 243–82.

Barthes, Roland. Introduction. Barthes et al. 9–44.

———. *The Pleasure of the Text*. Trans. Richard Miller. New York: Hill, 1975. Print.

———. *S/Z*. Trans. Richard Miller. New York: Hill, 1974. Print.

Barthes, Roland, et al. *Análisis estructural del relato*. Trans. Beatriz Dorriots. Buenos Aires: Tiempo Contemporáneo, 1970. Print.

Bean, John C. *Engaging Ideas: The Professor's Guide to Integrating Writing, Critical Thinking, and Active Learning in the Classroom*. San Francisco: Jossey-Bass, 1996. Print.

Bécquer, Gustavo Adolfo. *Leyendas*. Ed. Pascual Izquierdo. Madrid: Cátedra, 2003. Print.

Bellver, Catherine G. *Absence and Presence: Spanish Women Poets of the Twenties and Thirties*. Lewisburg: Bucknell UP, 2001. Print.

———. "*El cuarto de atrás* and the Role of Writing." *Continental, Latin-American, and Francophone Women Writers*. Ed. Ginette Adamson and Eunice Myers. Vol. 3. Lanham: UP of Amer., 1997. 5–87. Print.

———. "Gendered Spaces: Boundaries and Border Crossings in *Entre visillos*." Glenn and Rolón Collazo 33–50.

Bergmann, Emilie L. "Narrative Theory in the Mother Tongue: Carmen Martín Gaite's *Desde la ventana* and *El cuento de nunca acabar*." *Spanish Women Writers and the Essay: Gender, Politics, and the Self*. Ed. Kathleen M. Glenn and Mercedes Mazquiarán de Rodríguez. Columbia: U of Missouri P, 1998. 172–97. Print.

Blanes Noguera, Pepa. "Elena Fortún: Celiadicción." *Hibris* 4.20 (2004): 4–17. Print.

Bombal, María Luisa. *"New Islands" and Other Stories*. Trans. Richard Cunningham and Lucía Cunningham. New York: Farrar, 2005. Print.

———. *La última niebla* [and] *El árbol* [and] *Las islas nuevas* [and] *Lo secreto: Textos completos*. Santiago: Andrés Bello, 1982. Print.

Booth, Wayne C. *The Rhetoric of Fiction*. Chicago: U of Chicago P, 1983. Print.

Borderies-Guereña, Josette. "Niños y niñas en familia." *Historia de la infancia en la España contemporánea, 1834–1936*. Ed. José María Borrás Llop. Madrid: Ministerio de Trabajo y Asuntos Sociales, 1996. 21–66. Print.

Boring, Phyllis Zatlin. "Carmen Martín Gaite, Feminist Author." *Revista de estudios hispánicos* 11 (1977): 323–38. Print.

Bottigheimer, Ruth B., ed. *Fairy Tales and Society*. Philadelphia: U of Pennsylvania P, 1986. Print.

Bremond, Claude. "La lógica de los posibles narrativos." Barthes et al. 87–110.

Brown, Joan Lipman. "Carmen Martín Gaite: Reaffirming the Pact between Reader and Writer." *Women Writers of Contemporary Spain: Exiles in the Homeland*. Ed. Brown. Newark: U of Delaware P, 1991. 72–92. Print.

———. "A Fantastic Memoir: Technique and History in *El cuarto de atrás*." *Anales de la literatura española contemporánea (ALEC)* 6 (1981): 13–20. Print.

———. "The Nonconformist Character as Social Critic in the Novels of Carmen Martín Gaite." *Romance Quarterly* 28.2 (1981): 165–76. Print.

———. *Nonconformity in the Fiction of Carmen Martín Gaite*. Diss. U of Pennsylvania, 1976. Ann Arbor: UMI, 1976. Print.

———. "One Autobiography, Twice Told: Martín Gaite's *Entre visillos* and *El cuarto de atrás*." *Hispanic Journal* 7.2 (1986): 37–47. Print.

———. *Secrets from the Back Room: The Fiction of Carmen Martín Gaite*. University: Romance Monographs, 1987. Print.

———. "Teaching the Expanding Canon: A Socio-cultural Approach to Hispanic Literature by Women." *Hispania* 74.4 (1991): 1133–37. Print.

———."*Tiempo de silencio* and *Ritmo lento*: Pioneers of the New Social Novel in Spain." *Hispanic Review* 50.1 (1982): 61–73. Print.

Brown, Joan Lipman, and Carmen Martín Gaite. *Conversaciones creadoras: Mastering Spanish Conversation*. 1994. 3rd ed. Boston: Houghton, 2006. Print.

Brown, Joan Lipman, and Elaine M. Smith. "*El cuarto de atrás*: Metafiction and the Actualization of Literary Theory." *Hispanófila* 3.90 (1987): 63–70. Print.

Burton, Benjamin, Emmet J. Hughes, and Walter Cronkite. *War in Spain*. 1958. McGraw-Hill Text Films, 1960. Videocassette.

Bush, Andrew. "Dwelling on Two Stories (Carmen Martín Gaite, María Zambrano)." *Revista de estudios hispánicos* 36.1 (2002): 159–89. Print.

Calle Mayor. Dir. Juan Antonio Bardem. Suevia Films, 1956. Film.

Calvi, Maria Vittoria. "El autobiografismo dialógico de Carmen Martín Gaite." *Turia* 83 (2007): 223–35. Print.

Calvo Serer, Rafael. "Una nueva generación española." *Arbor* 8.24 (1947): 333–48. Print.

Campbell, Neil. *American Youth Cultures*. Edinburgh: Edinburgh UP, 2004. Print.

Cantarino, Vicente. *Civilización y cultura de España*. Upper Saddle River: Prentice, 1999. Print.

Carbayo-Abengózar, Mercedes. *Buscando un lugar entre mujeres: Buceo en la España de Carmen Martín Gaite*. Málaga: U de Málaga, 1998. Print.

Carmen Martín Gaite: In Search of Conversation. By Carmen Martín Gaite, Immaculada de la Fuente, Alicia Redondo Goicoechea, and Fernando Valls. Princeton: Films for the Humanities and Sciences, 2003. DVD.

Carr, Raymond, ed. *Spain: A History*. Oxford: Oxford UP, 2001. Print.

———. *Spain, 1808–1975*. Oxford: Oxford UP, 1982. Print.

"Cartapacio: Carmen Martín Gaite." *Turia: Revista cultural* 83 (2007): 189–306. Print.

Castellanos, Rosario. *A Rosario Castellanos Reader: An Anthology of Her Poetry, Short Fiction, Essays, and Drama*. Ed. Maureen Ahern. Trans. Ahern et al. Austin: U of Texas P, 1988. Print.

Castellet, José María. "Tiempo de destrucción para la literatura española." *Literatura, ideología y política*. Barcelona: Anagrama, 1976. 135–56. Print.

Castillo, Debra A. "Never-Ending Story: Carmen Martín Gaite's *The Back Room*." *PMLA* 102.5 (1987): 814–28. Print.

Castro, Rosalía de. *El caballero de las botas azules*. Buenos Aires: Emecé, 1942. Print.

Caughie, John. *Television Drama: Realism, Modernism, and British Culture*. Oxford: Oxford UP, 2000. Print.

Cela, Camilo José. *La familia de Pascual Duarte*. Barcelona: Destino, 1942. Print.

———. *The Family of Pascual Duarte*. Trans. Anthony Kerrigan. Normal: Dalkey Archive, 2004. Print.

Censor 27. Report on *Entre visillos*, numbered 183-58, in box 11.605. State Archives in Alcalá de Henares, Madrid. TS.

Cercas, Javier. *Soldados de Salamina*. 2001. Barcelona: Maxi Tusquets, 2007. Print.

———. *Soldiers of Salamis*. Trans. Anne McLean. London: Bloomsbury, 2004. Print.

Cervantes Saavedra, Miguel de. *Don Quijote de la Mancha*. Ed. Martín de Riquer. Barcelona: Planeta, 1980. Print.

———. *Don Quijote de la Mancha*. Barcelona: Juventud, 1955. Print.

———. *Don Quixote*. Trans. Edith Grossman. New York: Ecco, 2003. Print.

———. "El retablo de las maravillas." *Entremeses*. Ed. Eugenio Asensio. Madrid: Castalia, 1989. 169–82. Print.

Chacón, Dulce. *La voz dormida*. Barcelona: Planeta, 2003. Print.

Chukovsky, Kornei. *The Art of Translation: Kornei Chukovsky's* A High Art. Trans. and ed. Lauren G. Leighton. Knoxville: U of Tennessee P, 1984. Print.

Cibreiro, Estrella. "Transgrediendo la realidad histórica y literaria: El discurso fantástico en *El cuarto de atrás*." *Anales de la literatura española contemporánea (ALEC)* 20.1–2 (1995): 29–46. Print.

Cixous, Hélène. "The Laugh of the Medusa." Trans. Keith Cohen and Paula Cohen. Marks and Courtivron 245–64.

———. "Sorties." Trans. Keith Cohen and Paula Cohen. Marks and Courtivron 90–98.

Collins, Marsha S. "Inscribing the Space of Female Identity in Carmen Martín Gaite's *Entre visillos*." *Symposium* 51.2 (1997): 66–78. Print.

Cortázar, Julio. "La noche boca arriba." *Final del juego*. Mexico City: Punto de lectura, 2008. 169–79. Print.

Cruz-Cámara, Nuria. "'Chicas raras' en dos novelas de Carmen Martín Gaite y Carmen Laforet." *Hispanófila* 139 (2003): 97–110. Print.

———. *El laberinto intertextual de Carmen Martín Gaite: Un estudio de sus novelas de las noventa.* Newark: Juan de la Cuesta, 2008. Print.

———. "La re-creación del romanticismo en *La Reina de las Nieves* de Carmen Martín Gaite." *Symposium* 57.2 (2003): 81–92. Print.

Debicki, Andrew P. *Spanish Poetry of the Twentieth Century: Modernity and Beyond.* Lexington: UP of Kentucky, 1994. Print.

Díaz, Elías. *Notas para una historia del pensamiento español actual, 1939–1973*. Madrid: Cuadernos para el diálogo, 1974. Print.

Dorao, Marisol. *Los mil sueños de Elena Fortún*. Cádiz: U de Cádiz, 1999. Print.

Durán, Manuel. "*El cuarto de atrás*: Imaginación, fantasía, misterio: Todorov y algo más." Servodidio and Welles 129–37.

Duras, Marguerite. *Four Novels.* Trans. Richard Seaver. New York: Grove Weidenfeld, 1990. Print.

———. *Moderato cantabile*. Paris: Éditions de Minuit, 1958. Print.

Dvorak, Trisha. "Writing in the Foreign Language." *Listening, Reading, Writing: Analysis and Application.* Ed. Barbara H. Wing. Middlebury: Northeast Conf. on the Teaching of Foreign Langs., 1986. 145–67. Print.

El Saffar, Ruth. "Carmen Martín Gaite and *El castillo de las tres murallas*." *Letras Femeninas* 8.2 (1982): 46–53. Print.

———. "Liberation and the Labyrinth: A Study of the Works of Carmen Martín Gaite." Servodidio and Welles 185–96.

Escartín Gual, Montserrat. "Noticia de Carmen Martín Gaite y *Retahílas*." Martín Gaite, *Retahílas* [2003] 169–232.

Feal, Carlos. "Hacia la estructura de *Fragmentos de interior*." Servodidio and Welles 93–105.

Felman, Shoshana. *What Does a Woman Want? Reading and Sexual Difference*. Baltimore: Johns Hopkins UP, 1993. Print.

Fernández Cubas, Cristina. "Mi hermana Elba." *Mi hermana Elba y los altillos de Brumal*. Barcelona: Tusquets, 1988. 53–81. Print.

Ferré, Rosario. *La casa de la laguna*. 1997. New York: Vintage, 2000. Print.

———. *The House on the Lagoon*. New York: Plume, 1996. Print.

———. *Papeles de Pandora*. 1976. New York: Vintage, 2000. Print.

———. *The Youngest Doll*. Lincoln: U of Nebraska P, 1991. Print.

Flynn, Elizabeth A., and Patrocinio P. Schweickart. Introduction. *Gender and Reading: Essays on Readers, Texts, and Contexts*. Ed. Flynn and Schweickart. Baltimore: Johns Hopkins UP, 1986. 9–30. Print.

Folguera, Pilar. *El feminismo en España: Dos siglos de historia*. Madrid: Iglesias, 1988. Print.

Fortún, Elena. *Celia en la revolución*. Madrid: Aguilar, 1987. Print.

———. *Celia lo que dice*. Madrid: Alianza, 2001. Print.

Foucault, Michel. *Ethics: Subjectivity and Truth*. Ed. Paul Rabinow. New York: New, 1994. Print.

The Fourth Annual AP Report to the Nation. College Board, 13 Feb. 2008. Web. 19 Nov. 2012.

France, Alan. *Understanding Youth in Late Modernity*. Maidenhead: Open UP, 2007. Print.

Franco, Marie. "Elena Fortún par Martín Gaite." *Regards sur les espagnoles créatrices (XVIIIe–XXe siècle)*. Ed. Françoise Étienvre. Paris: Sorbonne Nouvelle, 2006. 221–37. Print.

Freixas, Laura. *Literatura y mujeres: Escritoras, público y crítica en la España actual*. Barcelona: Destino, 2000. Print.

Freud, Sigmund. "Femininity." *New Introductory Lectures on Psycho-analysis*. New York: Norton, 1989. 139–67. Print.

———. *The Uncanny*. Trans. David McLintock. London: Penguin, 2003. Print.

Friedrich, Caspar David. *Wanderer above the Sea of Fog*. 1818. *Web Gallery of Art*. Web Gallery of Art, n.d. Web. 8 July 2012.

Gagliardi, Tiffany D. "Determined, Detached, and Drowning: The Use of Rhetoric of Enclosure in Carmen Martín Gaite's *Entre visillos*." *Letras peninsulares* 16.3 (2003): 431–43. Print.

Galvarriato de Alonso, Eulalia. *Cinco sombras*. Barcelona: Destino, 1947. Print.

García Hortelano, Juan. *Nuevas amistades*. Barcelona: B, 2000. Print.

García Lorca, Federico. *Poeta en Nueva York*. Madrid: Cátedra, 1987. Print.

García Morales, Adelaida. *The South* [and] *Bene*. Trans. Thomas G. Deveny. Lincoln: U of Nebraska P, 1999. Print.

———. *El sur (seguido de) Bene*. Barcelona: Anagrama, 1993. Print.

Garro, Elena. *Recollections of Things to Come*. Trans. Ruth L. C. Simms. Austin: U of Texas P, 1969. Print.

———. *Los recuerdos del porvenir*. 1963. Madrid: 451, 2011. Print.

"Gender." *A Feminist Dictionary*. Ed. Cheris Kramarae and Paula A. Treichler. London: Pandora, 1985. 173–74. Print.

Genette, Gérard. *Figuras III*. Trans. Nora Rosenfeld and Maria Cristina Mata. Córdoba: Nagelkop, 1970. Print.

———. *Figures III*. Paris: Seuil, 1972. Print.

———. *Narrative Discourse: An Essay in Method*. Trans. Jane E. Lewin. Ithaca: Cornell UP, 1980. Print.

Gies, David T., ed. *The Cambridge Companion to Modern Spanish Culture*. Cambridge: Cambridge UP, 1999. Print.

———, ed. *The Cambridge History of Spanish Literature*. Cambridge: Cambridge UP, 2004. Print.

Gil de Biedma, Jaime. "Carta de España (o todo era Nochevieja en nuestra literatura al comenzar 1965)." *El pie de la letra: Ensayos, 1955–1979*. Barcelona: Crítica, 1980. 200–06. Print.

———. "Domingo." *Las personas del verbo*. Barcelona: Galaxia Gutenberg–Círculo de Lectores, 2006. 93. Print.

Gilligan, Carol. "In a Different Voice: Woman's Conception of Self and of Morality." *The Future of Difference*. Ed. Hester Eisenstein and Alice Jardine. New Brunswick: Rutgers UP, 1985. 274–317. Print.

Ginzburg, Natalia. *Family Sayings*. Trans. D. M. Low. New York: Arcade, 1989. Print.

———. *Lessico famigliare*. 1963. Torino: Einaudi, 2010. Print.

Gittins, Dianne. "The Historical Construction of Childhood." *An Introduction to Childhood Studies*. Ed. Mary Jane Kehily. Maidenhead: Open UP, 2004. 25–39. Print.

Glenn, Kathleen M. "Collage, Textile, and Palimpsest: Carmen Martín Gaite's *Nubosidad variable*." *Romance Languages Annual* 5 (1993): 408–13. Print.

———. "*El cuarto de atrás*: Literature as *Juego* and the Self-Reflexive Text." Servodidio and Welles 149–59.

———. "Martín Gaite, Todorov, and the Fantastic." *The Scope of the Fantastic: Theory, Technique, Major Authors*. Ed. Robert A. Collins and Howard D. Pearce. Westport: Greenwood, 1985. 165–72. Print.

Glenn, Kathleen M., and Lissette Rolón Collazo, eds. *Carmen Martín Gaite: Cuento de nunca acabar / Never-Ending Story*. Boulder: Soc. of Spanish and Spanish-Amer. Studies, 2003. Print.

González, Ángel. "Palabra muerta, realidad perdida." *Sin esperanza, con convencimiento*. Barcelona: Colliure, 1961. 108–09. Print.

Goytisolo, Juan. *El furgón de cola*. 1967. 3rd ed. Barcelona: Seix-Barral, 2001. Print.

———. "Literatura y eutanasia." *El furgón de cola*. 2nd ed. Barcelona: Seix-Barral, 1976. 75–94. Print.

———. *Señas de identidad*. 1966. Madrid: Alianza, 1999. Print.

Gracia, Jordi, and Francisco Rico, eds. *Historia y crítica de la literatura española: Los nuevos nombres, 1975–2000 primer suplemento*. Barcelona: Crítica, 2000. Print.

Gracia, Jordi, and Domingo Ródenas. *Derrota y restitución de la modernidad, 1939–2010*. Madrid: Crítica, 2011. Print. Vol. 7 of *Historia de la literatura española*.

Graham, Helen. "Gender and the State: Women in the 1940s." Graham and Labanyi 183–95.

Graham, Helen, and Jo Labanyi, eds. *Spanish Cultural Studies: An Introduction: The Struggle for Modernity*. Oxford: Oxford UP, 1995. Print.

Greimas, Algirdas Julien. *Semántica estructural: Investigación metodológica*. Trans. Alfredo de la Fuente. Madrid: Gredos, 1971. Print.

Grossman, Edith. *Why Translation Matters*. New Haven: Yale UP, 2010. Print.

La guerra filmada. Gobierno de España, Ministerio de Cultura / Filmoteca Española. 2006, television; 2009, DVD.

"El hada en el sotabanco." *Celia*. RTVE, 4 Jan. 1993. Television.

Hadot, Pierre. *What Is Ancient Philosophy?* Trans. Michael Chase. Cambridge: Harvard UP, 2002. Print.

Harper, Sandra, ed. *Puntos de vista: Narrativa moderna española*. Lexington: Heath, 1993. Print.

Heffernan, James A. W. "Ekphrasis and Representation." *New Literary History* 22.2 (1991): 297–316. Print.

Herman, David, Manfred Jahn, and Ryan Marie-Laure, eds. *Routledge Encyclopedia of Narrative Theory*. London: Routledge, 2005. Print.

Herzberger, David K. *Narrating the Past: Fiction and Historiography in Postwar Spain*. Durham: Duke UP, 1995. Print.

———. "Split Referentiality and the Making of Character in Recent Spanish Metafiction." *MLN* 103.2 (1988): 419–35. Print.

Honeyman, Susan. *Elusive Childhood: Impossible Representations in Modern Fiction*. Columbus: Ohio State UP, 2005. Print.

Hooper, John. *The New Spaniards*. 2nd ed. London: Penguin, 2006. Print.

Humm, Maggie. *A Reader's Guide to Contemporary Feminist Literary Criticism*. New York: Harvester Wheatsheaf, 1994. Print.

Hutcheon, Linda. *Narcissistic Narrative: The Metafictional Paradox*. New York: Methuen, 1984. Print.

Irigaray, Luce. *Speculum of the Other Woman*. Trans. Gillian G. Gill. Ithaca: Cornell UP, 1985. Print.

———. *This Sex Which Is Not One*. Trans. Catherine Porter with Carolyn Burke. Ithaca: Cornell UP, 1985. Print.

Iser, Wolfgang. *The Implied Reader: Patterns of Communication in Prose Fiction from Bunyan to Beckett*. Baltimore: Johns Hopkins UP, 1974. Print.

Jahn, Manfred. *Narratology: A Guide to the Theory of Narrative*. English Dept., U of Cologne, 28 May 2005. Web. 15 Nov. 2012. Vers. 1.8.

Jiménez, Juan Ramón. *Antología poética*. Ed. Vicente Gaos. Madrid: Cátedra, 1982. Print.

Jiménez, Mercedes. *Carmen Martín Gaite y la narración: Teoría y práctica*. New Brunswick: SLUSA, 1989. Print.

Jones, Ann Rosalind. "Writing the Body: Toward an Understanding of *l'Écriture Féminine*." *Feminisms: An Anthology of Literary Theory and Criticism*. Ed. Robyn R. Warhol and Diane Price Herndl. 2nd ed. New Brunswick: Rutgers UP, 1997. 370–83. Print.

Joyce, James. *Ulysses*. London: Bodley Head, 1937. Print.

Jurado Morales, José. *Del testimonio al intimismo: Los cuentos de Carmen Martín Gaite*. Cádiz: U de Cádiz, 2001. Print.

———. "La mirada ajena: Medio siglo de bibliografía sobre la obra de Carmen Martín Gaite." *Anales de la literatura española contemporánea* 29.1 (2004): 135–65. Print.

———. *La trayectoria narrativa de Carmen Martín Gaite, 1925–2000.* Madrid: Gredos, 2003. Print.

Kaplan, Janet A. *Remedios Varo: Unexpected Journeys*. New York: Abbeville, 2000. Print.

Kermode, Frank. *The Sense of an Ending: Studies in the Theory of Fiction*. New York: Oxford UP, 1967. Print.

Kidd, Kenneth. "Psychoanalysis and Children's Literature: The Case for Complementarity." *The Lion and the Unicorn* 28.1 (2004): 109–30. Print.

Kindt, Tom, and Hans Harald Müller. *The Implied Author: Concept and Controversy*. Berlin: de Gruyter, 2006. Print.

———. *The Implied Author: Explication and Use of a Controversial Concept*. Interdisciplinary Center for Narratology, U Hamburg, 10 Aug. 2008. Web. 15 May 2011.

Kolbenschlag, Madona. *Adiós Bella Durmiente: Crítica de los mitos femeninos*. Barcelona: Kairós, 1994. Print.

Kristeva, Julia. *The Kristeva Reader*. Ed. Toril Moi. New York: Columbia UP, 1986. Print.

———. *Revolution in Poetic Language*. Trans. Margaret Waller. New York: Columbia UP, 1984. Print.

Kronik, John W. "A Splice of Life: Carmen Martín Gaite's *Entre visillos*." Servodidio and Welles 49–60.

La Belle, Jenijoy. *Herself Beheld: The Literature of the Looking Glass*. Ithaca: Cornell UP, 1988. Print.

Labanyi, Jo. *Myth and History in the Contemporary Spanish Novel*. Cambridge: Cambridge UP, 1989. Print.

———. "Resemanticizing Feminine Surrender: Cross-Gender Identifications in the Writings of Spanish Female Fascist Activists." *Women's Narrative and Film in Twentieth-Century Spain*. Ed. Ofelia Ferrán and Kathleen Glenn. New York: Routledge, 2002. 75–92. Print.

Lacan, Jacques. "The Mirror Stage as Formative of the Function of the I as Revealed in Psychoanalytic Experience." *Écrits: A Selection*. Trans. Alan Sheridan. New York: Norton, 1977. 1–7. Print.

Laffey, Lee-Ann. "Frente al espejo: Escritura epistolar y creación de un nuevo 'yo' en *Nubosidad variable*." *Cincinnati Romance Review* 15 (1996): 90–96. Print.

Laforet, Carmen. *Nada*. Barcelona: Destino, 1945. Print.

———. *Nada: A Novel*. Trans. Edith Grossman. New York: Modern Lib., 2008. Print.

Lanser, Susan. "Toward a Feminist Narratology." *Style* 20.3 (1986): 341–63. Print.

Lawless, Cecilia Burke. "*Retahílas* and the Loose Threads of Home, Sweet Home." *Revista de estudios hispánicos* 25.3 (1991): 73–101. Print.

Lesnik-Oberstein, Karin. *Children's Literature: Criticism and the Fictional Child*. Oxford: Oxford UP, 1994. Print.

Levine, Steven Z. "Seascapes of the Sublime: Vernet, Monet, and the Oceanic Feeling." *New Literary History* 16 (1985): 377–400. Print.

Lope de Vega, Félix. *El caballero de Olmedo*. Ed. Francisco Rico. Madrid: Cátedra, 1989. Print.

Lowe, Lisa. "Decolonization, Displacement, Disidentification: Asian American 'Novels' and the Question of History." *Cultural Institutions of the Novel*. Ed. Deidre Lynch and William B. Warner. Durham: Duke UP, 1996. 96–128. Print.

Mainer, José-Carlos. *La escritura desatada: El mundo de las novelas*. Madrid: Temas de Hoy, 2001. Print.

———. Introduction. Martín Gaite, *Ritmo lento* [2007] 10–58.

———. "La novela de un chico raro." Preface. *Ritmo lento*. By Carmen Martín Gaite. 3rd ed. Barcelona: Destino, 1993. 9–27. Print.

———. "Prólogo: Las primeras novelas de Carmen Martín Gaite." Martín Gaite, *Obras completas* 1: 55–89.

Manchón, Rosa M., and Pieter de Haan. "Editorial: Writing in Foreign Language Contexts: An Introduction." *Journal of Second Language Writing* 17 (2008): 1–6. Print.

Manuel, Don Juan. "Exemplo XI: Lo que conteşçió a un deán de Santiago con don Yllán, el grand maestro de Toledo." *El conde Lucanor*. Ed. Alfonso I. Sotelo. Madrid: Cátedra, 2007. 117–23. Print.

Marcus, Roxanne B. "Ritual and Repression in Carmen Martín Gaite's *Entre visillos*." *Studies in Honor of Gustavo Correa*. Ed. Charles B. Faulhaber, Richard P. Kinkade, and T. A. Perry. Potomac: Scripta Humanistica, 1986. 137–49. Print.

Marks, Elaine, and Isabelle de Courtivron, eds. *New French Feminisms: An Anthology*. New York: Schocken, 1980. Print.

Martinell Gifre, Emma, ed. *Al encuentro de Carmen Martín Gaite: Homenajes y bibliografía*. Barcelona: Departamento de Filología Hispánica, U of Barcelona, 1996. Print.

———, ed. *Cuéntame*. Madrid: Espasa Calpe, 1999. Print.

———, ed. *Espéculo: Página de Carmen Martín Gaite*. Madrid: U Complutense de Madrid, 1998–2003. Web. 31 Oct. 2011.

———. Introduction. Martín Gaite, *Hilo* 13–26.

Martínez Cachero, José María. *La novela española entre 1936 y 1980: Historia de una aventura*. Madrid: Castalia, 1985. Print.

Martín Gaite, Carmen. *Agua pasada: Artículos, prólogos y discursos*. Barcelona: Anagrama, 1993. Print.

———. "Los amores malditos." Martín Gaite, *Pido* 312–24.

———. *A palo seco. Cuentos completos y un monólogo*. 3rd ed. Barcelona: Anagrama, 1994. 311–44. Print.

———. *A rachas*. 1976. 2nd ed. 1979. 3rd ed. Madrid: Hiperión, 1986. Print.

———. "Las ataduras." *Abriendo puertas: Antología de literatura en español*. Vol. 1. Evanston: McDougal Littell, 2003. 75–133. Print.

———. *Las ataduras*. Barcelona: Destino, 1960. Print.

———. "Las ataduras." Harper 42–87.

———. "Las ataduras." Martín Gaite, *Cuentos* 91–138.

———. "An Autobiographical Sketch." Trans. Joan Lipman Brown. Brown, *Secrets* 20–34.

———. *The Back Room*. Trans. Helen R. Lane. 1983. San Francisco: City Lights, 2000. Print.

———. "El balneario." *Todos los cuentos: El balneario y Las ataduras.* 2nd ed. Barcelona: Destino, 2004. 15–81. Print.

———. *Behind the Curtains*. Trans. Frances M. López-Morillas. New York: Columbia UP, 1990. Print.

———. "Un bosquejo autobiográfico." Martín Gaite, *Agua* 11–25. Brown, *Secrets* 193–206.

———. "Buscando el modo." Martín Gaite, *Desde la ventana* 41–62.

———. *La búsqueda de interlocutor*. Barcelona: Anagrama, 2000. Print.

———. "La búsqueda de interlocutor." Martín Gaite, *Búsqueda* [2000] 23–32.

———. *La búsqueda de interlocutor y otras búsquedas*. Madrid: Nostromo, 1973. Barcelona: Destino, 1982. Print.

———. *Caperucita en Manhattan*. Madrid: Siruela, 1990. Print.

———. "Carmen Martín Gaite: Contemplar la vida con una pluma en la mano." Interview by Juan Cantavella. *Semblanzas entrevistas: Carmen Martín Gaite, Narciso Yepes, Manuel Gutiérrez Mellado*. Ed. Cantavella. Madrid: PPC, 1995. 12–90. Print.

———. *El castillo de las tres murallas*. Barcelona: Lumen, 1981. Print.

———. "La chica de abajo." Martinell, *Cuéntame* 61–87.

———. "La chica rara." Martín Gaite, *Desde la ventana* 101–22.

———. *El conde de Guadalhorce, su época y su labor.* Madrid: Colegio de Ingenieros de Caminos, Canales, y Puertos, 1977. Print.

———. "Conversación con Carmen Martín Gaite." Interview by Héctor Medina. *Anales de la literatura española contemporánea* (*ALEC*) 8 (1983): 183–94. Print.

———. "Conversación con Carmen Martín Gaite." Interview by Alicia Ramos. *Hispanic Journal* 1.2 (1980): 117–24. Print.

———. "Conversación con Carmen Martín Gaite en Nueva York, 1980." Interview by Marie-Lise Gazarian Gautier. *Ínsula* 9 Feb. 1981: 1, 10–11. Print.

———. *Courtship Customs in Postwar Spain.* Trans. Margaret E. W. Jones. Lewisburg: Bucknell UP, 2004. Print.

———. "El crecimiento de Celia." Martín Gaite, *Tirando* [2007] 525–35.

———. *Cuadernos de todo.* Ed. Maria Vittoria Calvi. Madrid: Debate, 2002. Print.

———. *El cuarto de atrás.* Barcelona: Destino, 1978. Print.

———. *El cuarto de atrás.* Madrid: Siruela, 2009.

———. *El cuento de nunca acabar: Apuntes sobre la narración, el amor y la mentira*. Madrid: Trieste, 1983. Print.

———. *Cuentos completos.* 1978. Madrid: Alianza, 2009. Print.

———. "De madame Bovary a Marilyn Monroe." Martín Gaite, *Búsqueda* [2000] 103–12.

———, *Desde la ventana: Enfoque femenino de la literatura española*. 1987. Madrid: Espasa Calpe, 1992. Print.

———. *Después de todo: Poesía a rachas.* Ed. Jesús Munárriz. Madrid: Hiperión, 1993. Print.

———. *Dos cuentos maravillosos*. Madrid: Siruela, 1992. Print.

———. *Dos relatos fantásticos*. Barcelona: Lumen, 1986. Print.

———. *Entre visillos*. Barcelona: Destino, 1958. Print.

———. *Entre visillos*. Ed. Marina Mayoral. Barcelona: Destino, 1997. Print.

———. *Entre visillos*. Introd. Marina Mayoral. Barcelona: Espasa Calpe, 2007. Print.

———. *Entre visillos*. Barcelona: Destino, 2008. Print.

———. "Entrevista con Carmen Martín Gaite." Interview by Celia Fernández. *Anales de la novela de posguerra* 4 (1979): 165–72. Print.

———. "Entrevista con Carmen Martín Gaite." Interview by Emma Martinell. *Espéculo: Revista de estudios literarios*. 1998. U Complutense de Madrid, n.d. Web. 9 Oct. 2012.

———. *Esperando el porvenir: Homenaje a Ignacio Aldecoa*. Madrid: Siruela, 1994. Print.

———. *The Farewell Angel*. Trans. Margaret Jull Costa. London: Harvill, 1999. Print. Trans. of *La Reina de las Nieves*.

———. *Fragmentos de interior*. Barcelona: Destino, 1976. Print.

———. *La hermana pequeña*. Barcelona: Anagrama, 1999. Print.

———. *Hilo a la cometa: La visión, la memoria y el sueño*. Ed. Emma Martinell. Madrid: Espasa Calpe, 1995. Print.

———. "Los incentivos de la ventana." Martín Gaite, *Desde la ventana* 129–41.

———. "La influencia de la publicidad en las mujeres." Martín Gaite, *Búsqueda* [2000] 89–95.

———. Interview. By José María Conget and Raquel Chang-Rodríguez. *Charlando con Cervantes*. CUNY TV, New York, 18 Mar. 1996. Television.

———. Interview. By Joaquín Soler Serrano. *A Fondo*. Editrama: Videoteca de la memoria literaria, 1981. Film.

———. *Irse de casa*. Barcelona: Anagrama, 1998. Print.

———. *El libro de la fiebre*. Ed. Maria Vittoria Calvi. Madrid: Cátedra, 2007. Print.

———. *Living's the Strange Thing*. Trans. Anne McLean. London: Harvill, 2004. Print.

———. *Love Customs in Eighteenth-Century Spain*. Trans. Maria G. Tomsich. Berkeley: U of California P, 1991. Print.

———. "Los malos espejos." Martín Gaite, *Búsqueda* [2000] 15–22.

———. "La mujer en la literatura." Martín Gaite, *Pido* 325–41.

———. "Las mujeres liberadas." Martín Gaite, *Búsqueda* [2000] 96–102.

———. *Narrativa breve, poesía y teatro*. Ed. José Teruel. Barcelona: Galaxia Gutenberg; Círculo de Lectores, 2010. Print. Vol. 3 of *Obras completas*.

———. *Novelas I, 1955–1978*. Ed. José Teruel. Barcelona: Galaxia Gutenberg; Círculo de Lectores, 2008. Print. Vol. 1 of *Obras completas*.

———. *Novelas II, 1979–2000*. Ed. José Teruel. Barcelona: Galaxia Gutenberg; Círculo de Lectores, 2009. Print. Vol. 2 of *Obras completas*.

———. *Nubosidad variable*. Barcelona: Anagrama, 1992. Print.

———. *Obras completas*. 3 vols. Ed. José Teruel. Barcelona: Galaxia Gutenberg; Círculo de Lectores, 2008–10. Print.

———. *Los parentescos*. Barcelona: Anagrama, 2001. Print.

———. *El pastel del diablo*. Barcelona: Lumen, 1985. Print.

———. Personal interview. By Joan L. Brown. Madrid, 6 Aug. 1978.

———. "Personalidad y libertad." Martín Gaite, *Busqueda* [2000] 85–88.

———. "Pesquisa tardía sobre Elena Fortún." Foreword. Fortún, *Celia lo que dice* 7–37.

———. *Pido la palabra*. Barcelona: Anagrama, 2002. Print.

———. *Poemas*. Madrid: Plaza y Janés; Círculo de Lectores, 2001. Print. Audio CD.

———. *El proceso de Macanaz: Historia de un empapelamiento*. Madrid: Moneda y Crédito, 1970. Print.

———. *Lo raro es vivir*. Barcelona: Anagrama, 1996. Print.

———. *La Reina de las Nieves*. Barcelona: Anagrama, 1994. Print.

———. *Retahílas*. 5th ed. Ed. Montserrat Escartín Gual. Barcelona: Crítica, 2003. Print.

———. *Retahílas*. Madrid: Siruela, 2009. Print.

———. *Ritmo lento*. Ed. José-Carlos Mainer. Barcelona: Destino, 1996. Print.

———. *Ritmo lento*. Barcelona: Destino, 2007. Print.

———. "Salamanca." *Esta es mi tierra*. Narr. Carmen Martín Gaite. Dir. Manuel Serrano. Televisión Española. 13 Apr. 1983. Television. RadioTelevisión Española, 1985. Film.

———. *Tirando del hilo: Artículos, 1949–2000*. Ed. José Teruel. Madrid: Siruela, 2006. Madrid: Punto de Lectura, 2007. Print.

———. "La trastienda de los ojos." *Cien años de cuentos, 1898–1998: Antología del cuento español en castellano*. Ed. José María Merino. Madrid: Alfaguara, 1998. 278–83. Print.

———. *Usos amorosos de la postguerra española*. Barcelona: Anagrama, 1987. Print.

———. *Usos amorosos del dieciocho en España*. Madrid: Siglo Veintiuno de España, 1972. Print.

———. *Variable Cloud*. Trans. Margaret Jull Costa. London: Harvill, 1995. Print.

———. "The Virtues of Reading." Trans. Marcia L. Welles. *PMLA* 104.3 (1989): 348–53. Print.

———. *Visión de Nueva York*. Madrid: Círculo de Lectores; Siruela, 2005. Print.

Martín-Santos, Luis. "Noticia del coloquio sobre realismo y realidad en la literatura contemporánea." 1963. *Guías de lectura: Tiempo de silencio*. Ed. Juan Luis Suárez Granda. Madrid: Alhambra, 1986. 141–42. Print.

———. *Tiempo de silencio*. Barcelona: Destino, 1962. Print.

———. *Time of Silence*. Trans. George Leeson. New York: Columbia UP, 1989. Print.

Matute, Ana María. *Primera memoria*. Barcelona: Destino, 1960. Print.

———. *School of the Sun*. Trans. Elaine Kerrigan. New York: Columbia UP, 1989. Print.

———. "A Wounded Generation." Trans. A. Gordon Ferguson. *Nation* 29 Nov. 1965: 420–21. Print.

Mayo, C. M. Flash Fiction. The Writer's Center, Bethesda. 5 Oct. 2008. Workshop.

MLA Ad Hoc Committee on Foreign Languages. "Foreign Languages and Higher Education: New Structures for a Changed World." *Profession* (2007): 234–45. Print.

Moi, Toril. *Sexual/Textual Politics: Feminist Literary Theory.* 2nd ed. New York: Routledge, 2001. Print.

Montero, Rosa. *The Delta Function = La función Delta.* Trans. Kari A. Easton and Yolanda Molina Gavilán. Lincoln: U of Nebraska P, 1991. Print.

———. *La función Delta.* 1981. Madrid: Punto de Lectura, 2009. Print.

Moreiro Prieto, Julián, ed. *Antología de Carmen Martín Gaite: Traer a cuento.* Junta de Castilla y León: Leonesas, 2002. Print.

Munárriz, Jesús. "Nota editorial." Martín Gaite, *Después de todo* 12.

Murray, Donald M. "Write before Writing." *College Composition and Communication* 29.4 (1978): 375–81. Print.

Nash, Mary. "Un/contested Identities: Motherhood, Sex Reform, and the Modernization of Gender Identity in Early-Twentieth-Century Spain." *Constructing Spanish Womanhood: Female Identity in Modern Spain.* Ed. Victoria Lorée Enders and Pamela Radcliffe. New York: State U of New York P, 1999. 25–50. Print.

Navajas, Gonzalo. "El diálogo y el yo en *Retahílas* de Carmen Martín Gaite." *Hispanic Review* 53.1 (1985): 25–39. Print.

Neuschäfer, Hans-Jörg. *Adiós a la España eterna: La dialéctica de la censura: Novela, teatro y cine bajo el franquismo.* Barcelona: Anthropos, 1994. Print.

Núñez Puente, Sonia. *Una historia propia: Historia de las mujeres en la España del siglo XX.* Madrid: Pliegos, 2004. Print.

O'Leary, Catherine, and Alison Ribeiro de Menezes. *A Companion to Carmen Martín Gaite.* Woodbridge: Tamesis, 2008. Print.

Onega, Susana, and José Ángel García Landa, eds. *Narratology: An Introduction.* London: Longman, 1996. Print.

Ordóñez, Elizabeth. "The Decoding and Encoding of Sex Roles in Carmen Martín Gaite's *Retahílas.*" *Kentucky Romance Quarterly* 27 (1980): 237–44. Print.

———. "Reading, Telling, and the Text of Carmen Martín Gaite's *El cuarto de atrás.*" Servodidio and Welles 173–84.

Oropesa, Salvador. "*Nubosidad variable* de Carmen Martín Gaite: Una alternativa ética a la cultura del pelotazo." *Letras peninsulares* 8.1 (1995): 55–72. Print.

Palacio Atard, Vicente. "Menéndez y Pelayo, historiador actual." *Arbor* 14.47 (1949): 254–59. Print.

Palley, Julian. "Dreams in Two Novels of Carmen Martín Gaite." Servodidio and Welles 107–16.

Pardo Bazán, Emilia. *La mujer española.* Ed. Leda Schiavo. Madrid: Nacional, 1981. Print.

———. "La santa de Karnar." *Un destripador de antaño y otros cuentos.* Madrid: Alianza, 2003. 98–112. Print.

Pasamar Alzuria, Gonzalo. *Historiografía e ideología en la postguerra española: La ruptura de la tradición liberal.* Zaragoza: U de Zaragoza, 1991. Print.

Payne, Stanley G. *Spain's First Democracy: The Second Republic, 1931–1936.* Madison: U of Wisconsin P, 1993. Print.

Pérez, Janet. "Carmen Martín Gaite: The Gender Trap, the Single Woman, and the Search for Feminine Autonomy." Glenn and Rolón Collazo 169–82.

———. "*Nubosidad variable*: Carmen Martín Gaite and Women's Words." *Inti: Revista de literatura hispánica* 40–41 (1994): 301–15. Print.

———. "Portraits of the *Femme Seule* by Laforet, Matute, Soriano, Martín Gaite, Quiroga and Medio." *Feminine Concerns in Contemporary Spanish Fiction by Women*. Ed. Roberto Manteiga and Carolyn Galerstein. Potomac: Scripta Humanistica, 1988. 54–77. Print.

———. "Presencia de la 'Quest Romance' en las últimas obras de Carmen Martín Gaite." *Escribir mujer: Narradoras españolas hoy*. Ed. Cristóbal Cuevas García. Málaga: Congreso de Literatura Española Contemporánea, 2000. 89–111. Print.

———. "Structural, Thematic, and Symbolic Mirrors in *El cuarto de atrás* and *Nubosidad variable* of Carmen Martín Gaite." *South Central Review* 12.1 (1995): 47–63. Print.

Pérez Embid, Florentino. "Ante la nueva actualidad del 'Problema de España.'" *Arbor* 14.45–46 (1949): 149–60. Print.

Pérez-Reverte, Arturo. *The Painter of Battles*. Trans. Margaret Sayers Peden. New York: Random, 2009. Print.

———. *El pintor de batallas*. 2006. Madrid: Punto de Lectura, 2007. Print.

Perrault, Charles. "Little Thumb." *The Tales of Mother Goose*. Trans. Charles Welsh. New York: Heath, 1901. 29–44. Print.

Persin, Margaret. "Carmen Martín Gaite's *A rachas:* Dreams of the Past and Memories of the Future, Text(ure)s Woven of Many-Colored Threads." *Monographic Review* 6 (1990): 93–104. Print.

———. *Getting the Picture: The Ekphrastic Principle in Twentieth-Century Spanish Poetry*. Lewisburg: Bucknell UP, 1997. Print.

———. *Poesía como proceso: Poesía española de los años 50 y 60*. Trans. Catherine Attelé. Madrid: Turanzas, 1986. Print.

Pittarello, Elide. "Las últimas novelas de Carmen Martín Gaite." Martín Gaite, *Obras completas* 2: 9–45.

Pompeia, Núria. *Mujercitas*. Barcelona: Kairós, 1977. Print.

Poniatowska, Elena. *Dear Diego*. Trans. Nathaniel Eli Gardner. Oxford: Aris, 2012. Print.

———. *Querido Diego, te abraza Quiela*. México: Era, 1978. Print.

Preston, Paul. *Franco: A Biography*. New York: Harper, 1994. Print.

———. *La Guerra Civil española: Reacción, revolución y venganza*. Trans. Francisco Rodríguez de Lecea, Maria Borràs, and Jordi Beltrán. Barcelona: Random, 2006. Print. Trans. of *Spanish Civil War*.

———. *The Spanish Civil War: Reaction, Revolution, and Revenge*. Rev. ed. New York: Norton, 2006. Print.

Preston, Paul, and Ann L. Mackenzie, eds. *The Republic Besieged: Civil War in Spain, 1936–1939*. Edinburgh: Edinburgh UP, 1996. Print.

La prima Angélica. Dir. Carlos Saura. *Saura Essential*. Manga Films, 2009. DVD.

Prince, Gerald. *Dictionary of Narratology*. Lincoln: U of Nebraska P, 1987. Print.

Propp, Vladimir. *Morphology of the Folktale*. Austin: U of Texas P, 1990. Print.

Prout, Alan, and Allison James. "A New Paradigm for the Sociology of Childhood? Provenance, Promise and Problems." *Constructing and Reconstructing Childhood: Contemporary Issues in the Sociological Study of Childhood*. Ed. James and Prout. London: Falmer, 1990. 7–31. Print.

Puente Samaniego, Pilar de la. *La narrativa breve de Carmen Martín Gaite*. Salamanca: Plaza Universitaria, 1994. Print.

Real Academia Española. *Diccionario de la lengua española*. 22nd ed. 2 vols. Madrid: Espasa, 2001. Print.

Rebecca. Dir. Alfred Hitchcock. 1940. MGM, 2008. DVD.

Ricoeur, Paul. *Time and Narrative*. Trans. Kathleen McLauglin Blamey and David Pellauer. 3 vols. Chicago: U of Chicago P, 1984–88. Print.

Riera, Carmen. "Te entrego, amor, la mar, como una ofrenda." *Palabra de mujer: Bajo el signo de una memoria impenitente*. Trans. Riera. 4th ed. Barcelona: Laia, 1987. 9–32. Print.

Rimmon-Kenan, Shlomith. *Narrative Fiction: Contemporary Poetics*. London: Methuen, 1983. Print.

Rodoreda, Mercè. *La Calle de las Camelias.* Planeta: Barcelona, 1970. Print.

———. *Camellia Street.* Trans. David H. Rosenthal. Saint Paul: Graywolf, 1993. Print.

———. *La Plaza del Diamante*. Trans. Enrique Sordo. Barcelona: Edhasa, 2009. Print. Trans. of *La Plaça del Diamant.*

———. *The Time of the Doves*. Trans. David H. Rosenthal. Saint Paul: Graywolf, 1986. Print. Trans. of *La Plaça del Diamant.*

Rodríguez, Rodney T., comp. *Momentos cumbres de las literaturas hispánicas: Introducción al análisis literario*. Upper Saddle River: Pearson, 2003. Print.

Rolón Collazo, Lissette. "Diálogo creativo: La ensayística de Carmen Martín Gaite." *Torre de Papel* 4.1 (1994): 63–84. Print.

———. *Figuraciones: Mujeres en Carmen Martín Gaite, revistas feministas y "¡Hola!"* Madrid: Iberoamericana; Frankfurt am Main: Vervuert, 2002. Print.

"Romance del Infante Arnaldos." *Flor nueva de romances viejos*. Ed. Ramón Menéndez Pidal. Madrid: Espasa-Calpe, 1984. 203. Print.

Rose, Jacqueline S. "The Case of Peter Pan: The Impossibility of Children's Fiction." *The Children's Culture Reader*. Ed. Henry Jenkins. New York: New York UP, 1998. 58–66. Print.

Ruiz Franco, Rosario. *¿Eternas menores? Las mujeres en el franquismo*. Madrid: Biblioteca Nueva, 2007. Print.

Sánchez Ferlosio, Rafael. "La forja de un plumífero." *Archipiélago* 31 (1997): 71–89. Print.

———. *El Jarama*. Barcelona: Destino, 1955. Print.

Sanz Villanueva, Santos. *Historia de la novela social española, 1942–1975*. Madrid: Alhambra, 1980. Print.

Scanlon, Geraldine. *La polémica feminista en la España contemporánea, 1868–1974*. Madrid: Akal, 1986. Print.

Seneca. *Epistles 66–92*. Trans. Richard M. Gummere. Cambridge: Harvard UP, 2001. Print. Loeb Classical Lib. 76.

Servodidio, Mirella d'Ambrosio, and Marcia L. Welles, eds. *From Fiction to Metafiction: Essays in Honor of Carmen Martín Gaite*. Lincoln: Soc. of Spanish and Spanish-Amer. Studies, 1983. Print.

"Shantung." *Merriam-Webster's Collegiate Dictionary*. 11th ed. 2003. Print.

Shyamalan, M. Knight, dir. *The Sixth Sense*. Hollywood, 1999. Film.

———, dir. *Unbreakable*. Touchstone, 2000. Film.

Sieburth, Stephanie. "The Conversation I Never Had with Carmen Martín Gaite." *Revista de estudios hispánicos* 36.1 (2002): 227–39. Print.

Slevin, James F. *Introducing English: Essays in the Intellectual Work of Composition*. Pittsburgh: U of Pittsburgh P, 2001. Print.

Smith, Frank, ed. and prod. *Voces de España: La historia del siglo XX español / Voices of Spain: The History of Spain in the Twentieth Century*. Nashville: Champs-Elysées, 2004. Print. CD.

Smith, Paul Julian. *Television in Spain: From Franco to Almodóvar*. Woodbridge: Tamesis, 2006. Print.

Sobejano, Gonzalo. "Carmen Martín Gaite." *Historia y crítica de la literatura española: Época contemporánea, 1939–1975: Primer suplemento*. Ed. Francisco Rico and Santos Sanz Villanueva. Barcelona: Crítica, 1999. 523–26. Print.

———. *Novela española de nuestro tiempo: En busca del pueblo perdido*. Madrid: Prensa Española, 1970. Print.

Soliño, María Elena. *Women and Children First: Spanish Women Writers and the Fairy Tale Tradition*. Potomac: Scripta Humanistica, 2002. Print.

Sopeña Monsalve, Andrés. *El florido pensil: Memoria de la escuela nacional católica*. Barcelona: Grupo Grijalbo; Mondadori, 1994. Print.

The Spanish Civil War. Films for the Humanities and Sciences, 1993. Film.

Spires, Robert C. *Beyond the Metafictional Mode: Directions in the Modern Spanish Novel*. Lexington: UP of Kentucky, 1984. Print.

———. "Embodied History: *Usos amorosos de la postguerra española* and *La Codorniz*." Glenn and Rolón Collazo 141–68.

———. "Intertextuality in *El cuarto de atrás*." Servodidio and Welles 139–48.

Stone, Kay F. "Feminist Approaches to the Interpretation of Fairy Tales." Bottigheimer 229–36.

Sullivan, Constance A. "The Boundary-Crossing Essays of Carmen Martín Gaite." *The Politics of the Essay: Feminist Perspectives*. Ed. Ruth-Ellen Boetcher Joeres and Elizabeth Mittman. Bloomington: Indiana UP, 1993. 41–56. Print.

Talbot, Lynn K. "Female Archetypes in Carmen Martín Gaite's *Entre visillos*." *Anales de la literatura española (ALEC)* 12.1–2 (1987): 79–94. Print.

Talbot, Toby. "Two Spanish Fantasies." *New York Times* 11 Dec. 1983: 11+. Print.

Teruel, José, ed. *El legado de Carmen Martín Gaite*. *Ínsula* Jan.–Feb. 2011: 1–48. Print.

———. "Nombres y tramos para una vida en 'obras.'" Martín Gaite, *Novelas I* 9–54.

———. "Nota a esta edición." Martín Gaite, *Obras completas* 3: 45–53.

Todorov, Tzvetan. *The Fantastic: A Structural Approach to a Literary Genre*. Trans. Richard Howard. Ithaca: Cornell UP, 1975. Print.

———. "Structural Analysis." Trans. Arnold Weinstein. *Novel: A Forum on Fiction* 3.1 (1969): 70–76. Print.

Triana-Toribio, Núria. *Spanish National Cinema*. London: Routledge, 2003. Print.

Tristana. Dir. Luis Buñuel. Public Media, 1970. Videocassette.

Tsuchiya, Akiko. "Women and Fiction in Post-Franco Spain." Turner and López de Martínez 212–30.

Turner, Harriet S., and Adelaida López de Martínez, eds. *The Cambridge Companion to the Spanish Novel: From 1600 to the Present*. Cambridge: Cambridge UP, 2003. Print.

Tusón, Vicente. *La poesía española de nuestro tiempo*. Madrid: Anaya, 1990. Print.

Tusquets, Esther. *El mismo mar de todos los veranos*. Ed. Santos Sanz Villanueva. Madrid: Castalia, 1997. Print.

———. *The Same Sea as Every Summer*. Trans. Margaret E. W. Jones. Lincoln: U of Nebraska P, 1990. Print.

Ugalde, Sharon Keefe. *En voz alta: Las poetas de las generaciones de los 50 y los 70: Antología*. Madrid: Hiperión, 2007. Print.

Unamuno, Miguel de. *Niebla*. Ed. Mario J. Valdés. Madrid: Cátedra, 1982. Print.

———. *La novela de Don Sandalio, jugador de ajedrez*. Ed. Manuel García Blanco. Madrid: Escelicer, 1966. Print. Vol. 2 of *Obras completas*.

Valdés, Guadalupe, Paz Haro, and María Paz Echevarriarza. "The Development of Writing Abilities in a Foreign Language: Contributions toward a General Theory of L2 Writing." *Modern Language Journal* 76.3 (1992): 333–52. Print.

Valente, José Ángel. "Ramblas de julio, 1964." *Poesía y prosa*. Ed. Andrés Sánchez Robayna. Barcelona: Galaxia Gutenberg; Círculo de Lectores, 2006. 202–04. Print. Vol. 1 of *Obras completas*.

———. "Tendencia y estilo." *Ínsula* Nov. 1961: 6. Print.

Valis, Noël, ed. *Teaching Representations of the Spanish Civil War*. New York: MLA, 2007. Print.

Valls Montés, Rafael. *La interpretación de la historia de España y sus orígenes ideológicos en el bachillerato franquista, 1938–1953*. Valencia: U de Valencia, 1984. Print.

Vilarós, Teresa M. *El mono del desencanto: Una crítica cultural de la transición española, 1973–1993*. Madrid: Siglo Veintiuno, 1998. Print.

Villán, Javier. "Carmen Martín Gaite, habitando el tiempo." *Estafeta literaria* 549 (1974): 21–23. Print.

Villarini, Ángel R. *Manual para la enseñanza de destrezas de pensamiento*. San Juan: Proyecto de Educación Liberal Liberadora, 1991. Print.

Waugh, Patricia. *Metafiction: The Theory and Practice of Self-Conscious Fiction*. London: Methuen, 1984. Print.

———. "What Is Metafiction and Why Are They Saying Such Awful Things about It?" Waugh, *Metafiction* 1–19.

Weil, Kari. "French Feminism's *Écriture Féminine*." *The Cambridge Companion to*

Feminist Literary Theory. Ed. Ellen Rooney. New York: Cambridge UP, 2006. 153–71. Print.

White, Hayden V. *The Content of the Form: Narrative Discourse and Historical Representation*. Baltimore: Johns Hopkins UP, 1987. Print.

Wilson, Caroline. "Carmen Martín Gaite: La autoridad femenina y el partir de sí." *Duoda* 14 (1998): 73–82. Print.

Wolf, Christa. Cassandra*: A Novel and Four Essays*. Trans. Jan Van Heurck. New York: Farrar, 2000. Print.

———. *Kassandra: Erzählung*. 1984. Berlin: Suhrkamp, 2011. Print.

Wright, Elizabeth, ed. *Feminism and Psychoanalysis: A Critical Dictionary*. Oxford: Blackwell, 1992. Print.

Ynduráin, Domingo, and Francisco Rico, eds. *Historia y crítica de la literatura española: Época contemporánea, 1939–1980*. Barcelona: Crítica, 1980. Print.

Zayas y Sotomayor, María de. "La fuerza del amor." *Novelas amorosas y ejemplares*. Ed. Julián Olivares. Madrid: Cátedra, 2000. 345–70. Print.

Ziolkowski, Jan M. "A Fairy Tale from before Fairy Tales: Egbert of Liège's 'De puella a lupellis seruata' and the Medieval Background of 'Little Red Riding Hood.'" *Speculum* 67.3 (1992): 549–75. Print.

Zipes, Jack. *Don't Bet on the Prince: Contemporary Feminist Fairy Tales in North America and England*. New York: Routledge, 1989. Print.

———. "The Potential of Liberating Fairy Tales for Children." *New Literary History* (1982): 309–25. Print.

———. *The Trials and Tribulations of* Little Red Riding Hood*: Versions of the Tale in Sociocultural Context*. 2nd ed. New York: Routledge, 1993. Print.

Zomeño, Fuencisla. "La constitución del texto femenino en *Nubosidad variable* de Carmen Martín Gaite." *Letras peninsulares* 8.1 (1995): 73–87. Print.

INDEX

Modern Language Association of America

Approaches to Teaching World Literature

To purchase MLA publications, visit www.mla.org/bookstore.

Achebe's Things Fall Apart. Ed. Bernth Lindfors. 1991.

Arthurian Tradition. Ed. Maureen Fries and Jeanie Watson. 1992.

Atwood's The Handmaid's Tale *and Other Works*. Ed. Sharon R. Wilson, Thomas B. Friedman, and Shannon Hengen. 1996.

Austen's Emma. Ed. Marcia McClintock Folsom. 2004.

Austen's Mansfield Park. Ed. Marcia McClintock Folsom and John Wiltshire. 2014.

Austen's Pride and Prejudice. Ed. Marcia McClintock Folsom. 1993.

Balzac's Old Goriot. Ed. Michal Peled Ginsburg. 2000.

Baudelaire's Flowers of Evil. Ed. Laurence M. Porter. 2000.

Beckett's Waiting for Godot. Ed. June Schlueter and Enoch Brater. 1991.

Behn's Oroonoko. Ed. Cynthia Richards and Mary Ann O'Donnell. 2014.

Beowulf. Ed. Jess B. Bessinger, Jr., and Robert F. Yeager. 1984.

Blake's Songs of Innocence and of Experience. Ed. Robert F. Gleckner and Mark L. Greenberg. 1989.

Boccaccio's Decameron. Ed. James H. McGregor. 2000.

British Women Poets of the Romantic Period. Ed. Stephen C. Behrendt and Harriet Kramer Linkin. 1997.

Charlotte Brontë's Jane Eyre. Ed. Diane Long Hoeveler and Beth Lau. 1993.

Emily Brontë's Wuthering Heights. Ed. Sue Lonoff and Terri A. Hasseler. 2006.

Byron's Poetry. Ed. Frederick W. Shilstone. 1991.

Works of Italo Calvino. Ed. Franco Ricci. 2013.

Camus's The Plague. Ed. Steven G. Kellman. 1985.

Cather's My Ántonia. Ed. Susan J. Rosowski. 1989.

Cervantes' Don Quixote. First edition. Ed. Richard Bjornson. 1984.

Cervantes's Don Quixote. Second edition. Ed. James A. Parr and Lisa Vollendorf. 2015.

Chaucer's Canterbury Tales. First edition. Ed. Joseph Gibaldi. 1980.

Chaucer's Canterbury Tales. Second edition. Ed. Peter W. Travis and Frank Grady. 2014.

Chaucer's Troilus and Criseyde *and the Shorter Poems*. Ed. Tison Pugh and Angela Jane Weisl. 2006.

Works of Anton Chekhov. Ed. Michael C. Finke and Michael Holquist. 2015.

Chopin's The Awakening. Ed. Bernard Koloski. 1988.

Coetzee's Disgrace *and Other Works.* Ed. Laura Wright, Jane Poyner, and Elleke Boehmer. 2014.

Coleridge's Poetry and Prose. Ed. Richard E. Matlak. 1991.

Collodi's Pinocchio *and Its Adaptations.* Ed. Michael Sherberg. 2006.

Conrad's "Heart of Darkness" and "The Secret Sharer." Ed. Hunt Hawkins and Brian W. Shaffer. 2002.

Dante's Divine Comedy. Ed. Carole Slade. 1982.

Defoe's Robinson Crusoe. Ed. Maximillian E. Novak and Carl Fisher. 2005.

DeLillo's White Noise. Ed. Tim Engles and John N. Duvall. 2006.

Dickens's Bleak House. Ed. John O. Jordan and Gordon Bigelow. 2009.
Dickens's David Copperfield. Ed. Richard J. Dunn. 1984.
Dickinson's Poetry. Ed. Robin Riley Fast and Christine Mack Gordon. 1989.
Narrative of the Life of Frederick Douglass. Ed. James C. Hall. 1999.
Works of John Dryden. Ed. Jayne Lewis and Lisa Zunshine. 2013.
Duras's Ourika. Ed. Mary Ellen Birkett and Christopher Rivers. 2009.
Early Modern Spanish Drama. Ed. Laura R. Bass and Margaret R. Greer. 2006.
Eliot's Middlemarch. Ed. Kathleen Blake. 1990.
Eliot's Poetry and Plays. Ed. Jewel Spears Brooker. 1988.
Shorter Elizabethan Poetry. Ed. Patrick Cheney and Anne Lake Prescott. 2000.
Ellison's Invisible Man. Ed. Susan Resneck Parr and Pancho Savery. 1989.
English Renaissance Drama. Ed. Karen Bamford and Alexander Leggatt. 2002.
Works of Louise Erdrich. Ed. Gregg Sarris, Connie A. Jacobs, and James R. Giles. 2004.
Dramas of Euripides. Ed. Robin Mitchell-Boyask. 2002.
Faulkner's As I Lay Dying. Ed. Patrick O'Donnell and Lynda Zwinger. 2011.
Faulkner's The Sound and the Fury. Ed. Stephen Hahn and Arthur F. Kinney. 1996.
Novels of Henry Fielding. Ed. Jennifer Preston Wilson and Elizabeth Kraft. 2015.
Fitzgerald's The Great Gatsby. Ed. Jackson R. Bryer and Nancy P. VanArsdale. 2009.
Flaubert's Madame Bovary. Ed. Laurence M. Porter and Eugene F. Gray. 1995.
García Márquez's One Hundred Years of Solitude. Ed. María Elena de Valdés and Mario J. Valdés. 1990.
Gilman's "The Yellow Wall-Paper" and Herland. Ed. Denise D. Knight and Cynthia J. Davis. 2003.
Goethe's Faust. Ed. Douglas J. McMillan. 1987.
Gothic Fiction: The British and American Traditions. Ed. Diane Long Hoeveler and Tamar Heller. 2003.
Poetry of John Gower. Ed. R. F. Yeager and Brian W. Gastle. 2011.
Grass's The Tin Drum. Ed. Monika Shafi. 2008.
H.D.'s Poetry and Prose. Ed. Annette Debo and Lara Vetter. 2011.
Hebrew Bible as Literature in Translation. Ed. Barry N. Olshen and Yael S. Feldman. 1989.
Homer's Iliad *and* Odyssey. Ed. Kostas Myrsiades. 1987.
Hurston's Their Eyes Were Watching God *and Other Works*. Ed. John Lowe. 2009.
Ibsen's A Doll House. Ed. Yvonne Shafer. 1985.
Henry James's Daisy Miller *and* The Turn of the Screw. Ed. Kimberly C. Reed and Peter G. Beidler. 2005.
Works of Samuel Johnson. Ed. David R. Anderson and Gwin J. Kolb. 1993.
Joyce's Ulysses. Ed. Kathleen McCormick and Erwin R. Steinberg. 1993.
Works of Sor Juana Inés de la Cruz. Ed. Emilie L. Bergmann and Stacey Schlau. 2007.
Kafka's Short Fiction. Ed. Richard T. Gray. 1995.
Keats's Poetry. Ed. Walter H. Evert and Jack W. Rhodes. 1991.
Kingston's The Woman Warrior. Ed. Shirley Geok-lin Lim. 1991.
Lafayette's The Princess of Clèves. Ed. Faith E. Beasley and Katharine Ann Jensen. 1998.
Writings of Bartolomé de Las Casas. Ed. Santa Arias and Eyda M. Merediz. 2008.

Works of D. H. Lawrence. Ed. M. Elizabeth Sargent and Garry Watson. 2001.
Lazarillo de Tormes *and the Picaresque Tradition*. Ed. Anne J. Cruz. 2009.
Lessing's The Golden Notebook. Ed. Carey Kaplan and Ellen Cronan Rose. 1989.
Works of Primo Levi. Ed. Nicholas Patruno and Roberta Ricci. 2014.
Works of Jack London. Ed. Kenneth K. Brandt and Jeanne Campbell Reesman. 2015.
Works of Naguib Mahfouz. Ed. Waïl S. Hassan and Susan Muaddi Darraj. 2011.
Mann's Death in Venice *and Other Short Fiction*. Ed. Jeffrey B. Berlin. 1992.
Marguerite de Navarre's Heptameron. Ed. Colette H. Winn. 2007.
Works of Carmen Martín Gaite. Ed. Joan L. Brown. 2013.
Medieval English Drama. Ed. Richard K. Emmerson. 1990.
Melville's Moby-Dick. Ed. Martin Bickman. 1985.
Metaphysical Poets. Ed. Sidney Gottlieb. 1990.
Miller's Death of a Salesman. Ed. Matthew C. Roudané. 1995.
Milton's Paradise Lost. First edition. Ed. Galbraith M. Crump. 1986.
Milton's Paradise Lost. Second edition. Ed. Peter C. Herman. 2012.
Milton's Shorter Poetry and Prose. Ed. Peter C. Herman. 2007.
Molière's Tartuffe *and Other Plays*. Ed. James F. Gaines and Michael S. Koppisch. 1995.
Momaday's The Way to Rainy Mountain. Ed. Kenneth M. Roemer. 1988.
Montaigne's Essays. Ed. Patrick Henry. 1994.
Novels of Toni Morrison. Ed. Nellie Y. McKay and Kathryn Earle. 1997.
Murasaki Shikibu's The Tale of Genji. Ed. Edward Kamens. 1993.
Nabokov's Lolita. Ed. Zoran Kuzmanovich and Galya Diment. 2008.
Works of Ngũgĩ wa Thiong'o. Ed. Oliver Lovesey. 2012.
Works of Tim O'Brien. Ed. Alex Vernon and Catherine Calloway. 2010.
Works of Ovid and the Ovidian Tradition. Ed. Barbara Weiden Boyd and Cora Fox. 2010.
Petrarch's Canzoniere *and the Petrarchan Tradition*. Ed. Christopher Kleinhenz and Andrea Dini. 2014.
Poe's Prose and Poetry. Ed. Jeffrey Andrew Weinstock and Tony Magistrale. 2008.
Pope's Poetry. Ed. Wallace Jackson and R. Paul Yoder. 1993.
Proust's Fiction and Criticism. Ed. Elyane Dezon-Jones and Inge Crosman Wimmers. 2003.
Puig's Kiss of the Spider Woman. Ed. Daniel Balderston and Francine Masiello. 2007.
Pynchon's The Crying of Lot 49 *and Other Works*. Ed. Thomas H. Schaub. 2008.
Works of François Rabelais. Ed. Todd W. Reeser and Floyd Gray. 2011.
Novels of Samuel Richardson. Ed. Lisa Zunshine and Jocelyn Harris. 2006.
Rousseau's Confessions *and* Reveries of the Solitary Walker. Ed. John C. O'Neal and Ourida Mostefai. 2003.
Sand's Indiana. Ed. David A. Powell and Pratima Prasad. 2015.
Scott's Waverley Novels. Ed. Evan Gottlieb and Ian Duncan. 2009.
Shakespeare's Hamlet. Ed. Bernice W. Kliman. 2001.
Shakespeare's King Lear. Ed. Robert H. Ray. 1986.
Shakespeare's Othello. Ed. Peter Erickson and Maurice Hunt. 2005.
Shakespeare's Romeo and Juliet. Ed. Maurice Hunt. 2000.

Shakespeare's The Taming of the Shrew. Ed. Margaret Dupuis and Grace Tiffany. 2013.

Shakespeare's The Tempest *and Other Late Romances.* Ed. Maurice Hunt. 1992.

Shelley's Frankenstein. Ed. Stephen C. Behrendt. 1990.

Shelley's Poetry. Ed. Spencer Hall. 1990.

Sir Gawain and the Green Knight. Ed. Miriam Youngerman Miller and Jane Chance. 1986.

Song of Roland. Ed. William W. Kibler and Leslie Zarker Morgan. 2006.

Spenser's Faerie Queene. Ed. David Lee Miller and Alexander Dunlop. 1994.

Stendhal's The Red and the Black. Ed. Dean de la Motte and Stirling Haig. 1999.

Sterne's Tristram Shandy. Ed. Melvyn New. 1989.

Works of Robert Louis Stevenson. Ed. Caroline McCracken-Flesher. 2013.

The Story of the Stone (Dream of the Red Chamber). Ed. Andrew Schonebaum and Tina Lu. 2012.

Stowe's Uncle Tom's Cabin. Ed. Elizabeth Ammons and Susan Belasco. 2000.

Swift's Gulliver's Travels. Ed. Edward J. Rielly. 1988.

Teresa of Ávila and the Spanish Mystics. Ed. Alison Weber. 2009.

Thoreau's Walden *and Other Works*. Ed. Richard J. Schneider. 1996.

Tolkien's The Lord of the Rings *and Other Works*. Ed. Leslie A. Donovan. 2015.

Tolstoy's Anna Karenina. Ed. Liza Knapp and Amy Mandelker. 2003.

Vergil's Aeneid. Ed. William S. Anderson and Lorina N. Quartarone. 2002.

Voltaire's Candide. Ed. Renée Waldinger. 1987.

Whitman's Leaves of Grass. Ed. Donald D. Kummings. 1990.

Wiesel's Night. Ed. Alan Rosen. 2007.

Plays of August Wilson. Ed. Sandra G. Shannon and Sandra L. Richards. 2016.

Works of Oscar Wilde. Ed. Philip E. Smith II. 2008.

Woolf's Mrs. Dalloway. Ed. Eileen Barrett and Ruth O. Saxton. 2009.

Woolf's To the Lighthouse. Ed. Beth Rigel Daugherty and Mary Beth Pringle. 2001.

Wordsworth's Poetry. Ed. Spencer Hall, with Jonathan Ramsey. 1986.

Wright's Native Son. Ed. James A. Miller. 1997.